Fundamentals of Engineering Economics

By Kal Renganathan Sharma
Prairie View A&M University

cognella
San Diego, CA

First published in the United States of America in 2011 by Cognella, a division of University Readers, Inc.

15 14 13 12 11 1 2 3 4 5

Printed in the United States of America

ISBN: 978-1-60927-826-7

cognella™

www.cognella.com 800.200.3908

Contents

Dedication

This book is dedicated to my eldest son R. Hari Subrahmanyan Sharma (alias Ramkishan) who turned nine on Aug-13-2010.

About the Author

Kal Renganathan Sharma serves as Adjunct Professor of Chemical Engineering at the Roy G. Perry College of Engineering at Prairie View A & M University, Prairie View, TX. He instructs CHEG 2003 Economic Analysis and Technical Applications. He received his B.Tech. from Indian Institute of Technology, Chennai, India, in 1985, MS and Ph.D degrees in 1987 and 1990 from West Virginia University, Morgantown, WV, all three degrees in chemical engineering. He received the once in a school time prize from nursery to higher secondary school for the Best All Round Student of the Penultimate year from the Rev. Brothers of St. Gabriel at RSK Higher Secondary School, Trichy, India. He has held a number of high level academic positions in India and USA.

Dr. Sharma, KR, is the author of 10 books, 4 Book-Chapters, 19 journal articles, 503 conference papers and 108 other presentations. He has instructed over 2500 students in 83 semesterwise courses in India and USA over the past 15 years.

Honors received include Honorary Fellowship, Australian Institute of High Energetic Materials, Melbourne, Australia, 2010, Fellow, Indian Chemical Society, Kolkata, India, 2007, Who's Who in America, 2009-2010, Marquis Who's Who, Upper Saddle River, NJ, International Biographical Center, Cambridge, UK, 2007, member, New York Academy of Sciences, New York, NY, 1996, Phi Kappa Phi, 1990, Sigma Xi, 1995, cash award, SASTRA University, Thanjavur, India, 2005, cash award, Monsanto, Indian Orchad, MA, 1990, Who's Who in Plastics and Polymers, CRC Press, Baco Raton, FL, 2000. He is a naturalized citizen of USA.

Preface

The economy has changed rapidly. Both the nation's economy and the world economy has undergone changes since the Word War II. The end of cold war has given impetus to rise of globalization. China and India are now invited to attend G20 meetings. Engineering education imparts a variety of skills to the student. Skills from economics can be synergistically applied. The engineering economy is a field of endeavor that explains different methods to evaluate alternates available to the business owner. Engineering Economy is the study of the feasibility and evaluation of the cost of possible solutions to engineering problems. When benefits outweigh costs the alternate becomes a acceptable one. The lowest cost among alternates can be selected by using different methods discussed in detail in the textbook. This is calculated at a certain interest rate over a certain prescribed period of time.

The inverse problem of determining the interest rate, i, given the F, A and N is explained in detail in this work. The binomial series expansion of $(1+i)^N$ is used to obtain mathematical expressions. N can be estimated given the future amount, F, uniform series of payments, A and interest rate i by obtaining the logarithms where necessary.

The fundamental principles, concepts and methods of engineering economy are provided. Current trends and issues are reflected in the worked examples and end of chapter exercises. Alnernates are drawn from case studies. These include the Keystone pipeline project, CW of World Trade Center, six different methods to prepare bioethanol, biodiesel plant in Taiwan, micro power plant, combined cycle power plant, meglumine antimonoate drug from supercritical extraction, on-shore oil well, solar hats, stirling dish solar power plant, photovoltaic panel solar power plant, liquefaction plants, copper chlorine thermochemical cycle for hydrogen, energy efficient windows, contiuous mass polymerization process to manufacture ABS, renovation of Macy's department store, heap leaching and agitation leaching of gold, rechargeable batteries for electric car, PEVs and HEV, hybrid electric vehicles, four different cooling tower designs, oil refinery, economics of life insurance, social security, printing press vs. e-book, anti-allergic cream, sequestration by dimethyl carbonate formation, micro-filtration, SWRO, sea water reverse osmosis plant, catalytic process to manufacture CNTs, carbon nanotubes, hexane extraction of rice bran oil, municipal garbage collection truck, activated carbon from bamboo, poly-propylene gas manufacture, custom foam fabricator, car rental, coffee house, frozen yoghurt parlor, short path distillation, olive oil business, bonds from private sector, Chevy volt, public internet, gas sales and convenience store, condominiums at Galveston beach, outpatient drug treatment center, overseas travel ticket, snack factory. Break-even points in flower shop, soda beverage, cars, quandratic price-demand relations for tomatoes, peaches, inelastic supply of common salt, dualistic relations of price and demand, Le-Chatellier-Samuelson principle are discussed in detail. G20 nations and GDP estimates by PPP, purchasing power parity and the changing world order in economies is touched upon. Life-cycle costs of aviation lighting, LED, photocopier, HVAC systems are discussed. Depreciation, taxes, replacement analysis are discussed.

Unique Features

Optimization concepts are discussed in detail. Brainstorming can be used to develop alternates for a given problem.

- The five methods of analysis, PW, FW, AW, IRR and ERR can be used to evaluate the alternates. Evaluation of alternates can be used to invest in the more profitable process, selection of the lower cost alternate, quantitate the savings accrued from implementation of a process improvement and assessment of environmental impact of chemical processes. Alternates can be mutually exclusive, independent projects and screening by other criteria.
- When the PWs of both alternates are within 20% of each other the projects can be adjudged as too close to call within the sensitivity of the estimates of the capital and operating expenses and expected revenues.
- Rudiments of household finance are discussed.
- The capitalization worth factors and sinking fund factors are calculated and presented as annuity tables as well as in graphical form.
- In addition to P/A, F/A, A/F, A/P, F/P, P/F closed form analytical expressions to calculate the interest rate, i and pay period, N has been developed.
- Benefit/Cost Ratio of public sector projects are discussed

Chapter 1.0

Overview of Engineering Economy

Main Topics Discussed in this Chapter

- Definitions of Engineering, Economy
- Alternates and Rules of Brainstorming
- Economic Merits of Alternates
- Deviation Analysis, Decision Analysis
- Action Plan
- Principles of Engineering Economy
- Steps of Problem Solving

1.1 What Is Engineering, What Is Economy, and What Is Engineering Economy?

Technological advances in machines, materials, computers, structures, and electronics have changed the job description of the engineer rapidly. Economic merits of the different alternatives available to the solution of a given problem can be evaluated in a systematic manner. The dollars-and-cents side of decision making is discussed in detail in this book. According to an estimate in 2005, there are about 240 million vehicles on the road in the United States. The economy fueled by the automotive sector is large.

Engineering is defined by ABET (Accreditation for Engineering and Technology) as the profession in which the knowledge gained in physics, chemistry, life sciences, and mathematics is applied to make products in large scale that increase the prosperity of man. This must be achieved with a judicious choice of materials, at the lowest cost in a manner that is benign to the environment, and that keeps all the stakeholders safe. Examples of engineering achievements can be seen in the top engineering inventions of the 20th century. According to the National Academy of Engineering, the top 20 engineering achievements of the 20th century are listed in Table 1.0 (1).

Economy consists of the sum total of all income from goods produced and services offered in a state or nation. It deals with the interactions between people and wealth. The size of the United States' economy can be measured using parameters such as GDP (Gross Domestic Product) GNP (Gross National Product) is different from GDP with respect to inclusion of income earned abroad. GDP sticks to within the domicile of the nation. The sizes of the economies of 20 nations that meet regularly as G20 are listed in Table 2.0. The 19 nations, other than the European Union, are listed according to the sizes of their economies. The numbers in Table 2.0 were developed by the prices laid down by the IMF, the International Monetary Fund, for the year 2008.

Table 1.0 Top 20 Engineering Achievements of the 20th Century

#	Feat	#	Feat
1	Electrification	11	Highways
2	Automobile	12	Spacecraft
3	Airplane	13	Internet
4	Water Supply and Distribution	14	Imaging
5	Electronics	15	Household Appliances
6	Radio and Television	16	Health Technologies
7	Agricultural Mechanization	17	Petroleum and Petrochemical Technologies
8	Computers	18	Laser and Fiber Optics
9	Telephone	19	Nuclear Technologies
10	Air Conditioning and Refrigeration	20	High Performance Materials

Table 2.0 GDP of G20 Nations (Purchasing Power Parity or PPP)

#	Nation	GDP (in Billions of US$) PPP	#	Nation	GDP (in Billions of US$) PPP
1	United States	14,256	11	Mexico	1466
2	China	7903	12	South Korea	1364
3	Japan	4159	13	Canada	1281
4	India	3526	14	Indonesia	962
5	Germany	2806	15	Turkey	880
6	United Kingdom	2139	16	Australia	851
7	Italy	2118	17	Argentina	584
8	Russia	2110	18	South Africa	493
9	France	2108	19	Saudi Arabia	370
10	Brazil	2013	20	European Union+	14,793

The combined GDP of 19 nations listed in Table 2.0 is about 51 trillion US dollars. This is a significant portion of the *world economy*.

Currency exchange rates used to be based upon the wealth of nations as measured by the amount of gold each nation possessed. The wealth of a nation is not the same as the nation's economy. The calculation of the size of economy varies among one method to another. The PPP method used to calculate the size of the G20 economies listed in Table 2.0 is called the *Purchasing Power Parity* method. This idea can be traced back to the School of Salamanca in the 16th century. The concept stems from the development of exchange rates between two countries based on long-term considerations of relative price levels between the two countries. Identical goods are expected to have the same price and cannot vary with markets. According to Wikipedia (2), more haircuts can be purchased in Thanjavur, India, for 1 US dollar than in San Francisco, California. The PPP method provides for cost-of-living differences between different regions in the world. In 2003, 1 US$ was equivalent to 1.8 yuan (Chinese) using PPP method. The nominal exchange rate is 1 US$ exchanged at 7.6 yuan (Chinese). Based on PPP, China is the world's second largest economy and India is the world's fourth largest economy. India recently added 100 million cellular phones. It has the second largest sugar production by the sugarcane industry. The cement and paper industries are large in India. The population of both China and India are more than 1 billion each. When the economic activities of *all people* are taken into account, the sizes of their economies go through a sudden jump in value! According to Mahatma Gandhi, India consisted of 300,000 villages during the freedom struggle from Great Britain. According to the 2001 India census, 74% of Indians live in 638,365 different villages. The middle-class wallet in India is bulging. The world's least expensive car was launched recently in India: Tata Nano can be picked up for Rs. 1 lakh (nominally about 2105 US$). The discussions of G20 and a PPP method of calculation are illustrative of the need to be better informed about the evaluation methods of economic alternatives offered by engineering solutions. The *basis* used for the calculations is important.

Engineering Economy is the study of the feasibility and evaluation of the cost of possible solutions to engineering problems. When benefits outweigh costs, the alternate becomes an *acceptable* one. The lowest cost among alternates can be selected by using different methods discussed in detail in the textbook. This is calculated at a certain interest rate over a certain prescribed period of time. Here are some alternates that can be resolved into one selected for implementation by using one of the methods explained in later chapters:

(i) The inclusion of ER fluids (electro rheological fluids) as automatic transmission fluids by Chrysler Corp. is going to increase the mpg of the new line called Dodge Cognizance by 15%. It extends the life of the transmission by 20,000 miles. How much can the company afford to spend in order to implement this invention?

(ii) You are hired by a leading credit card company, Ford Chase Bank. One of their directors, Julie Hollas, wants you to perform a small calculation for her. A customer wants to charge a Japanese robot to his credit card. The price of the robot, including sales tax, is $850.50. How many years will it take to pay off the credit card balance if the monthly payment is $16.70 and the annualized credit card interest rate is 23%?

(iii) Gasoline prices have skyrocketed in the nation. The national average price per gallon of gasoline has risen to $4. The president is considering increasing off-shore drilling to get more oil. Each oil rig would cost $10 million. It would require 70,000 oil rigs to deliver 0.5 billion gallons of gas for automobiles every week. The utility costs run to $120,000 per year. The situation is expected to continue for the next four years. Calculate the IRR for this investment. The MARR can be taken as 8.0%.

(iv) Calculate the monthly payment on a 2007 Toyota Corolla costing $12,999. Another $1000 was needed to obtain the title, license plate, and taxes. After cash down of $1500, the number of pay periods was 72 months. The interest rate per annum is 7%. A $2500 one-time charge for power train warranty up to 100,000 miles was levied up front.

(v) Alice Jones operates a flower shop in downtown Houston. It costs her $5 per day to pay the rent, $1 per day for the water used to preserve the freshness of the flowers, and $2.5 per day for air conditioning the flowers per day. The cost to pluck and bring the flowers from the garden in rural Texas to Houston city runs her a quarter per flower. The price-demand relation for the flowers takes the form of:

$$p = 0.65 - 0.001D$$

Calculate the break-even points. Construct the total revenue and total cost as a function of demand, D in the attached graph paper. What is the demand at maximum profit to Alice?

(vi) K. R. Sridhar, CEO of Bloom Box, was featured on CBS's *60 Minutes*. Bloom Box makes *micro power plants* using SOFC, solid oxide fuel cell technology. A bloom box can be purchased for $3000. It consists of miniaturized fuel cells made of silica. The cost of electricity to power up a new home would be 8.0 cents per kWh. Should the existing utility company charge 12.5 cents per kWh, calculate the number of years it would take for a bloom box to be a good investment for new homeowner Jack Tripper. Jack Tripper is the head of a family of 6 members with 4 children. Use the present worth method to evaluate the single project of micro power plants for individual homes. Assume that 600 kWh of electricity is consumed every month at the Tripper residence. (i=10%).

(vii) You are hired by Cowboy Investments upon graduation. They are developing a new investment plan for customers named "U-Pay-Now & I-Pay-Later." The deal is that the client pays $500 every month to Cowboy Investments. After a said period in a number of years, Cowboy Investments will have the client cease payments and begin to receive $500 every month forever. At 10% annualized interest rate (the historic performance of Dow Jones), how many years would you recommend be the said period?

(viii) Furniture-to-Stay offers you the following deal: A sofa, loveseat, and chair are available for $1250. A mattress is built in with the sofa, which can be pulled out when you have guests over. This is at an additional cost of $200. The delivery charge is $100 and a 3-year warranty for stain resistance is available for $200. For the first 3 years there is no interest rate charged (i.e., "No Interest 'Til 2012").

For the following three years, an annualized interest rate of 12% is charged. Calculate the monthly payment over 6 years.

(ix) Sam Malone is considering whether to invest in solar panels. This homeowner has gathered the following information for his town:

(a) Average cost of residential energy is 12 cents per kWh
(b) Government subsidy runs to 60% of investment by homeowner
(c) Each square foot of panel produces 18 kWh every year and the cost of installation per square foot of solar panel is $99.

Sam has 385 sq. ft. of roof space. What is the break-even point in years for the installation of solar panels? Assume an interest rate of 5% per year.

(x) Should overnight delivery courier mail be conducted using airplanes flown by pilots or personal rapid transit systems without onboard operators?
(xi) Should assembly lines for putting together desktop computers be filled with workers or by automated robots?
(xii) Should college computer labs be serviced using a hotline or by a manned computer help desk?

Example 1.0 Start of Technocrats of Texas

A team of alumni and faculty from a leading university in Texas conceived a business plan to develop a consulting service on how to assess, prevent, and remediate the damage caused by oil spills such as the recent one by BP America in Houston. One hundred professionals and technicians are going to join the venture. A new building is obtained at lease in Hempstead, Texas. How would you develop the alternates for setting up the utilities, such as electrification of the building?

Alternate A: To sign up with companies such as Reliant Energy under one of their plans.

Alternate B: To install solar panels and generate all the electricity needs of the enterprise.

Alternate C: To buy enough fuel cells and install a micro power plant to meet all the electricity needs of the enterprise.

1.2 Seven Principles of Engineering Economy

The foundation of the discipline of Engineering Economy can be seen in terms of seven principles (3). These seven principles are:

1.0 Make a List of Alternates: Plan A, Plan B, etc.
2.0 What Is Different among the Alternates?
3.0 Be Clear on What You Want.
4.0 Develop Common Performance Measures.
5.0 Meet <u>ALL</u> Relevant Criteria.
6.0 Weigh the Risk Against the Projected Rewards.
7.0 Check the Results of Action Plan and Revise Plan If/When Necessary.

The decision has to come from the alternates developed. The alternates can be developed using a *brainstorming session*. The more creative and resourceful the team members are, the better the selection of alternates available for a go/no-go decision would be. The problem can be reformulated and restated to ease the flow of alternates. An open mind is recommended during the development of alternates. The method may not be used to justify a certain course of action. Four rules of brainstorming were dictated by Osborn (4). These are as follows:

(a) Negative feedback can become overly critical and stifle creative juices and alternates from flowing.
(b) Poet-like free flow of ideas is welcome.
(c) Quantity breeds quality.
(d) Improvement can be aimed. Combinations can work out.

The basic steps of brainstorming include:

(a) Preliminary Discussion: Problem is stated and participants get warmed up. This acts as a prelude to the main session.
(b) Brainstorming Main Session: An unrelated problem is first brainstormed. Then the assigned problem is brainstormed. Ideas are allowed to flow and are recorded objectively.
(c) The ideas are evaluated for possible flowering into alternates.

In Principle 2, deviation analysis is used and the focus is on the differences. The future outcomes from the alternates are set as higher priority. Based on differences among alternates, a future course of action is selected. Goal setting is extremely important as emphasized in Principle 3. A common unit of measure (such as dollars and cents) totals costs or total profits that can be generated from the alternate considered is captured in Principle 4. All relevant criteria as mentioned in Principle 5 are important. For instance, retail giant Wal-Mart posts low prices for its customers. However, the company had to pay several million dollars as compensation for discrimination based on the skin color of an African American woman. She was apprehended for forging her money order. Later, she was cleared of any wrongdoing. The Civil Rights Act of 1964, signed into law by President Lyndon B. Johnson, must be followed in all activities of the enterprise. The risks assumed in a potential venture must be identified and understood. The payoff or the reward-to-risk ratio can be considered before taking a decision. One can follow the *Plan-Do-Check*. The results from implementation of the plan can be checked against goals identified. If needed, the plan can be revised.

1.3 Summary

Engineering is defined by ABET (Accreditation for Engineering and Technology) as the profession in which the knowledge gained in physics, chemistry, life sciences, and mathematics is applied to make products in large scale that increase the prosperity of man. This must be achieved with a judicious choice of materials, at the lowest cost in a manner that is benign to the environment, and that keeps all the stakeholders safe. *Economy* consists of the sum total of all income from goods produced and services offered in a state or nation. It deals with the interactions between people and wealth. *Engineering Economy* is the study of the feasibility and evaluation of the cost of possible solutions to engineering problems. When benefits outweigh costs, the alternate becomes an *acceptable* one. The lowest cost among alternates can be selected by using different methods discussed in detail in the textbook.

Examples of alternates are given such as electro rheological fluids for automatic transmission fluid, a pay-off period for a Japanese robot using a credit card, off-shore drilling, monthly car payment, flower shop, micro power plant, pay-now-cash-in-later schemes, deferred interest, solar panels, overnight mail delivery, use of robots in assembly lines in place of labor, college computer lab help desk, etc. The GDP of nations is discussed. The top engineering achievements of the 20th century are listed.

The seven principles of engineering economy are: (i) develop alternates; (ii) differences among alternates; (iii) what do you want?; (iv) develop common performance measures; (v) meet all relevant criteria; (vi) weigh the risks against the projected rewards; (vii) check the results of action plan and revise the plan if necessary. Brainstorming sessions can be used to develop alternates. The four rules of brainstorming are not to give negative feedback; encourage poet-like free flow of ideas; quantity breeds quality; and improvements and combinations are good. The main steps of brainstorming include: (i) preliminary session; (ii) brainstorming session; (iii) evaluation of ideas and development of alternates.

1.4 References

1. G. Constable and B. Somerville, *A Century of Innovation: Twenty Engineering Achievements That Transformed Our Lives*. The National Academies Press (2003), Washington, DC.
2. http://en.wikepedia.org/wiki/Purchasing_power-parity.
3. W. G. Sullivan, E. M. Wicks, and C. P. Koelling, *Engineering Economy*, 14th Edition. Pearson Prentice Hall (2009), Upper Saddle River, NJ.
4. A. F. Osborn, *Applied Imagination*, 3rd Edition. Charles Scribner's Sons (1963), New York, NY.
5. *Houston Chronicle*, Sunday, June 6th 2010, D2 of Business Section.

1.5 Exercises

1.0 What are the differences between GDP and GNP ?
2.0 What is the connection between a nation's GDP and its wealth?
3.0 Based on PPP (Purchasing Power Parity), China and India moved up in the rankings based on the size of a nation's GDP, while Australia moved down. Why is this?
4.0 What is engineering, what is economy, and what is engineering economy?
5.0 What are the rules of brainstorming?
6.0 Which of the principles of engineering economy is required by law?
7.0 What does the "Plan-Do-Check" cycle mean?
8.0 Why should risks be weighed against rewards?
9.0 What is the importance of a common unit of measure?
10.0 Why should a consistent viewpoint be maintained when comparing alternates?

Problems

11.0 Rahall Gandhi has purchased a new home in Fairfield, Texas. The price of the 1776 sq. ft. home is $131,000. Develop the alternates for Mr. Gandhi to buy homeowner's insurance for hazards such as floods, fire, hurricane, windstorm, etc. (Hint: consider deductibles).

12.0 After starring in a summer blockbuster film, actress Julia Roberts explores purchasing a mansion near Houston. She is willing to sign a mortgage amount up to $1.5 million. Action Mortgage gives out 15-year loans over $417,000 at 5.6255% fixed rate. Develop the alternates for Julia to apply for the mortgage. Consideration may be given to an ARM (adjustable rate mortgage), fixed-rate 30-year mortgage, fixed-rate 15-year mortgage, or FHA (federal housing loan). Some of the lenders and rates offered are shown in Table 3.0 (5).

Table 3.0 Mortgage Interest Rate List

#	Lender	15-yr loans over $417,000	30-yr loans over $417,000
1	Action Mortgage	5.125%	5.625%
2	Allegiance Financial Services	5.375%	6.125%
3	Home Loan Specialists	5.0%	5.75%
4	Mortgage Associates	6.25%	6.75%
5	Residential Finance	6.75%	7.0%
6	Texas Mortgage Link	7.0%	7.375%

13.0 About five years ago the rides at AstroWorld were dismantled and the 104 acres housing the amusement park were left barren. Fort Worth Investment Partnership has purchased the property recently. The undisclosed purchase price can be estimated at $100 million. The old AstroWorld property sits across Loop 610 from Reliant Park and near a light-rail stop. Develop alternates for use of this land. Choose from real estate development, hotel development, amusement park, horse racing track, etc.

14.0 Develop alternates for the following scenario: Enterprise Products Partners and Duncan Energy partners have announced that Acadian Gas has entered into an additional long-term contract with a shipper to transport natural gas on Acadian's Haynesville Extension pipeline, now under construction. It increases total capacity commitments by 200 million cu. ft. per day. Work on the 270-mile Haynesville Extension is expected to be finished in the 3rd quarter of 2011.

15.0 You have been awarded a contract to provide design and early engineering services for development of the Araromi Refinery project in Nigeria. You shall provide services for a 160,000 barrel-per-day Greenfield refinery and marine facility that will produce motor gasoline, automotive gas oil, and kerosene and jet fuel. What are the alternates in order to deliver the same amount of fuel in terms of calorific value?

16.0 Richard Stock arrived in the United States from Great Britain in order to purse graduate studies in chemical engineering. He wanted to apply for a credit card. Select two or three from the following that would be suitable alternates for Richard. Discuss which of the seven principles of engineering economy can be used in the selection.

(1) A credit card is offered by the local credit union. The interest rate is at the prime lending rate. The credit line is low at $1000.
(2) Chase Bank offers a credit line of $12,000, but the interest rate is 24%.
(3) Macy's department store offers a credit line of $10,000 at an interest rate of 20%, but you have to shop at Macy's stores. It is not valid in other locations.
(4) Chevron Oil Co. offers a credit card that offers a credit line of $2800 at an interest rate of 10%.
(5) The local bank offers personal loans up to $5000 with collateral of your automobile.

17.0 Mary Corleone is ready to go to college. The Eduserv provides student loans at low interest rates. Mary's friend is willing to pay for her tuition and living expenses. Wells Fargo Bank is willing to give papa Michael Corleone a home equity loan at little over the prime rate to pay for his daughter's college education. Develop the alternates available to Mary to obtain the financial resources needed to pay for college tuition.

18.0 Upon graduation you have been hired by Consolidation Coal Co. The coal contains 3% sulfur-containing compounds. When coal-fired steam boilers are used to raise steam, which is then used to turn turbines that are used to raise electricity, the sulfur can cause SO_2 emissions that can pollute the atmosphere. One way to keep the environment clean is to remove the sulfur from the coal fuel before usage. Another method would be to scrub the gases from the boiler plant using calcium oxide lining. CaO would react with SO_2 to form $CaSO_4$. The exit gases would be devoid of sulfur dioxide. Pyropower has developed a fluidized bed combustor (FBC) that mixes the coal and CaO and then the combustion process takes place. The SO_2 and other SO_x gases are captured *in situ* in the FBC. Develop the alternates for clean coal technologies. Which of the seven principles was used in the analysis?

19.0 Anita Murthy wanted to visit with Ann Tataglia in Boston. Anita has to travel from Morgantown, West Virginia. She called up the Hertz car rental company, who would allow her to rent a new car for a week. Anita will pay for the gas, and there are no caps on the driving mileage. A Greyhound bus can take her from Morgantown to Pittsburgh. She can also fly Continental Airlines from Pittsburgh to Boston. From Logan Airport, Anita can hail a taxicab to Ann's place. Her friend's friend can drive her in his car to Boston. Develop the alternates for Anita to travel to Ann Tataglia's in Boston.

Victor Whiting was planning on having six guests over at his new home in Cypress, Texas.

20.0 He can purchase Pillsbury flour and a recipe book from Wal-Mart and bake his own bread in a bread maker. The Pepperidge Farm truck delivers fresh loaves Mondays and Thursdays. What are the alternates for making bread available for Mr. Whiting's guests?

11.0 George Tataseo bought a new car that can run on different fuels. He knows a gas pump that supplies fuel at the following prices:

Gasoline	\$2.49 per gallon
Diesel	\$2.00 per gallon
Ethanol-Gasoline Blend, E20	\$1.75 per gallon

If George's Dodge Colt gave him 30 mpg, how much money can be saved by using E20 instead of gasoline or diesel when driving 28,600 miles?

Chapter 2.0

Fixed and Variable Costs

Learning Objectives

- Delineate Direct and Indirect Costs
- Familiarity with Cash Cost, Book Cost, Sunk Cost, and Opportunity Cost
- Fixed, Variable, and Incremental Costs
- Life Cycle of Enterprise
- Total Cost, Total Revenue, and Profit
- Break-Even Analysis
- Second Break-Even Point—What Does This Mean?

2.1 One-Time and Recurring Costs

An eminent expert in the field of business administration defines the ABCs of the MBA program as: (i) Accounting; (ii) Finance; and (iii) Economics. Executives tending to do well with limited resources usually thank accountants for where they derived their critical information. Sound accounting practices need a good understanding of costing principles. The types of costs can be delineated based on the frequency of their occurrence. For instance, *fixed costs* are usually one-time occurrences. *Variable costs* occur more frequently, usually once every billing period. *Incremental costs* are those that are incurred proportionally to the number of goods produced. Instances of fixed costs, variable costs, and incremental costs can be seen in Example 2.1.

In the Garlic Bread Nibbler snack factory as discussed below in Example 2.1, the following are examples of fixed costs:

- Property Tax
- Equipment Cost of Kneader
- Equipment Cost of Mixer
- Equipment Cost of Chopper
- Equipment Cost of Roaster
- Equipment Cost of Coloring Bowl
- Insurance Fees
- Interest on Borrowed Capital
- General Management & Administration Salaries.

Examples of variable costs are:

- Utility Costs: Gas Heating, Telephone Wires, Electric Utilities, Air Conditioning
- Labor Benefits.

Examples of incremental costs:

- Wheat Flour
- Maize Flour
- Butter
- Salt.

The planned costs per unit of output, anticipated labor hours, materials, and overhead categories are called *standard costs. Direct costs* can be measured and attributed to a specific activity or output. *Indirect costs* cannot be attributed to a single activity. Secretarial staff in an office building is an example of overhead costs. In addition to the above discussion, the following costs are also explained:

Cash Cost:	Transactions that involve payment of cash.
Book Cost:	This is a noncash cost such as depreciation on machinery, etc.
Sunk Cost:	Cost that has occurred in the past and has no relevance to estimates of future costs and revenues. It is a nonrefundable cash outlay. Examples of sunk cost are money spent on a passport or an earnest money deposit on a new home purchase.
Opportunity Cost:	Incurred because of the use of limited resources. For example, consider a recent graduate from a BS program at an Ivy League institution. When he signs up for graduate school, the salary he may have made from joining the work force is foregone. The difference in the salary in work force and the stipend received during graduate studies, say for five years, is called the opportunity cost.
Investment Cost:	The capital required in the acquisition phase is called investment cost.
O & M Cost:	Operation and Maintenance cost. This can be incurred by hiring people, purchasing machines, materials, information, and energy.
Working Capital:	These are funds required for the day-to-day operation of the enterprise.
Salvage Value:	The trade-in value of equipment after its full use is called salvage value.

A state of perfect competition is said to exist when there is more than one supplier of a product in demand. Some goods are *necessities* and some are *luxuries*. A necessity is a good that is vital to the function of the enterprise. For example, cash supply for the snack factory to pay its employees their wages is a necessity. Luxury is an item that is in surplus of need. For example, any guest in a five-star hotel is asked to pay a luxury tax. Staying in a five-star hotel is taxable as it is a surplus of need. Luxury is an item that is not needed for the survival of the enterprise. A fur coat is an example of luxury.

2.2 The Life Cycle Of An Enterprise

A life cycle exists for every business enterprise. The life cycle of an enterprise consists of the following stages:

(i) Identification of Need

(ii) Conceptual Preliminary Design
(iii) Bench Unit Trial or Prototype Testing
(iv) Detailed Design
(v) Production or Construction
(vi) Operation
(vii) Maintenance
(viii) Customer Use
(ix) Retirement and Disposal
(x) Recycling.

The cost associated with each step during the life cycle of an enterprise can be categorized according to the step in the cycle.

2.3 Total Revenue, Total Cost, and Profitable Region

The total cost incurred during the operation of an enterprise can be written as follows:

$$C_T = C_F + D\,C_V \tag{2.1}$$

where CV is the variable cost, D is the demand in number of units, and CF is the fixed cost. The price of the product usually falls with increase in demand in a linear manner.

$$p = a - bD \tag{2.2}$$

where p is the price and D is the demand in number of units; a is the price and zero demand and b is the rate of fall of price with increase in demand. It has been found that price is determined by supply and demand of goods in a market with perfect competition. The price changes by either falling or rising to equalize the goods produced and goods consumed. The price moves in such a fashion that some *equilibrium* is maintained. Other factors that may affect demand and supply—such as income of customers, price of raw materials that went into the manufacture of the product—do not figure into the price determination directly. Supply is usually driven by marginal cost. Additional output is determined by marginal cost.

The *law of demand* (*ceteris paribus*) states that the customers will be ready to buy more goods as the price decreases [1]. Eq. (2.2) is congruent with the law of demand. It is also consistent with the *elasticity* of supply and demand. Elasticity of demand is measured by the change in demand in response to a change in price. Elasticity of supply is measured by the change in supply in response to a change in price. If the quantity of demand changes considerably with changes in unit price, the price-demand curve is said to be *elastic*. If the change in quantity was small, then the price-demand curve is said to be *inelastic*. Income elasticity of demand is not considered here. These are the changes that come about in supply and demand in response to change in income levels of the customers. There can be other factors that are not considered, such as cross elasticity of demand.

The total revenue generated by the business—TR—can be calculated as

$$TR = pD \tag{2.3}$$

$$TR = D(a - bD) \tag{2.4}$$

The total revenue reaches a maximum at a certain demand, D". This can be calculated as follows:

$$\frac{dTR}{dD} = 0$$

$$a = 2bD''$$

$$D'' = \frac{2b}{a}$$

The break-even point is one where the total revenue, TR, exceeds total cost, CT. This happens when

$$TR = C_T \tag{2.5}$$

Combining Eq. (2.1), Eq. (2.4), and Eq. (2.5):

$$0 = bD^2 + D(C_V - a) + C_F \tag{2.6}$$

From Eq. (2.6), it can be realized that there can be *more than one* break-even point. The number of break-even points that will occur during a given enterprise depends on the order of the algebraic equation given by Eq. (2.6). For the price-demand relation given by Eq. (2.2), it can be seen from Eq. (2.6) that two break-even points can be expected. For enterprises where the price falls with demand in a nonlinear manner, more than two break-even points can be expected. The break-even points occur at D' which can be calculated as

$$D' = \frac{(a - C_V) \pm \sqrt{(a - C_V)^2 - 4bC_F}}{2b} \tag{2.7}$$

The first break-even point occurs when the revenue from the sale of goods produced exceeds the costs incurred. The second break-even point occurs when there is overproduction. From the second break-even point forward, it is *counterproductive* to increase further the demand, D. Here the costs rise at a steady rate and the revenue reaches maxima and begins to fall with further increases in demand. At some point a *loss* is incurred due to excess production. The region in the revenue-demand graph where total revenue exceeds total cost is called a *profitable* region.

Example 2.1 ***Garlic Bread Nibbler Snack Factory***

A team of professors and alumni got together to form a venture to make the Garlic Bread Nibbler Snack Factory. The raw materials procured were wheat, maize and corn flour, butter, and salt. The unit operations used in the preparation were kneader, mixer, baking oven, chopper, roaster, coloring, and packaging. The fixed costs that include leasing the building and land, insurance, taxes, and franchise fees to Snyder's of Hanover Pretzel Makers can be estimated at 1 million US$. The variable costs, including electric utilities, air conditioning, gas heating, telephone wires, etc. run the enterprise roughly 2 US$ per bag of snacks. The price-demand relation can be given by a *linear* relation such as

$$p = a - bD \tag{2.8}$$

When p is the price per bag and D is the number of bags of Nibblers produced, a and b can be given as $10 and 5* 10-6 ($/bag). Find the two break-even points. Sketch the total revenue and total cost as a function of demand.

Total Revenue, $TR = pD = aD - bD^2$ (2.9)

Total Cost, $C_T = C_F + C_V D$ (2.10)

CF = 1 million US$ (2.11)

C_V = 2 US$ per bag (2.12)

The total revenue and total cost as a function of bags of Nibbler produced is shown in Figure 2.1. At optimal production, the rate is about 114 bags per hour, assuming that the factory operates 24 hours, 7 days a week, and 52 weeks in a given calendar year. At this point, the revenue is a maximum. This can be seen in Figure 2.1 at 1 million bags produced in a year. The same can be obtained by the use of calculus as follows:

$$\frac{d(TR)}{dD} = 0 = a - 2bD \tag{2.13}$$

At maximum revenue,

$$D_{TR} = \frac{a}{2b} = \frac{10}{10 * 10^{-6}} = 10^6\, bags \tag{2.14}$$

The profit generated can be calculated as

Table 2.1 Total Revenue, Total Cost for Garlic Bread Nibbler Snack Factory

# Bags	Price, p (per bag $)	TR, Total Revenue (Thousands of US$)	C_T, Total Cost (Thousands of US$)
0	10	0	1000
100,000	9.5	950	1200
200,000	9	1800	1400
300,000	8.5	2550	1600
400,000	8	3200	1800
500,000	7.5	3750	2000
600,000	7	4200	2200
700,000	6.5	4550	2400
800,000	6	4800	2600
900,000	5.5	4950	2800
1,000,000	5	5000	3000
1,100,000	4.5	4950	3200
1,200,000	4	4800	3400
1,300,000	3.5	4550	3600
1,400,000	3	4200	3800
1,500,000	2.5	3750	4000
1,600,000	2	3200	4200
1,700,000	1.5	2550	4400
1,800,000	1	1800	4600
1,900,000	0.5	950	4800
2,000,000	0	0	5000

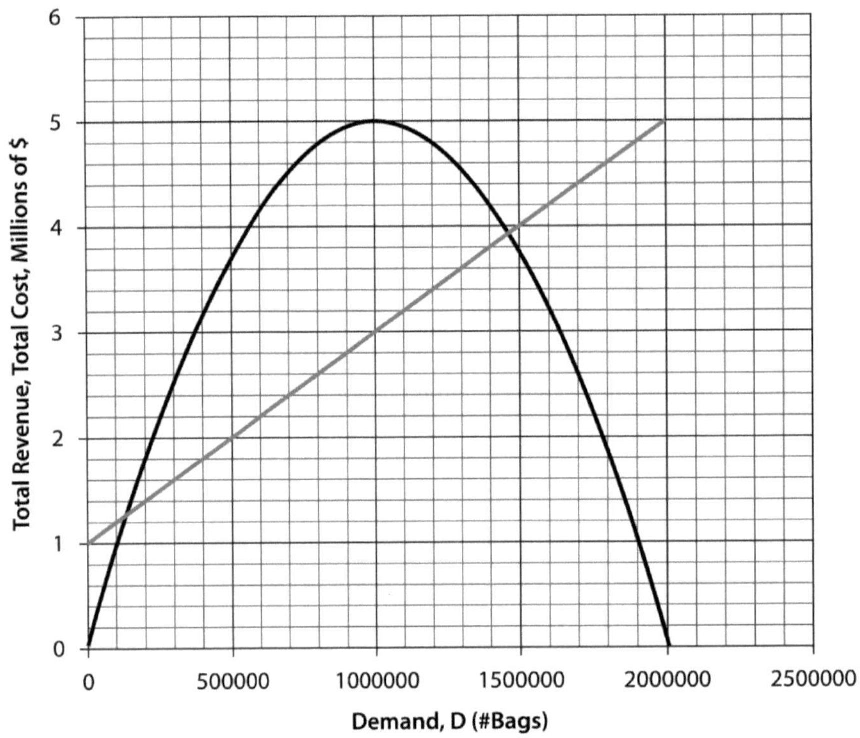

Figure 2.1 Total Revenue and Total Cost vs. Demand for Garlic Bread Nibbler Snack Factory

$$\text{Profit} = P = TR - C_T = aD - bD^2 - C_F - DCv = -bD^2 + D(a\text{-}Cv)\text{-}CF \tag{2.15}$$

For maximum profit,

$$\frac{dP}{dD} = 0 = -2bD + (a - C_v) \tag{2.16}$$

At maximum profit, the demand would be calculated as:

$$D_P = \frac{(a - C_v)}{2b} = \frac{(10 - 2)}{2 * 5 * 10^{-6}} = 800{,}000 bags \tag{2.17}$$

800,000 bags checks out in the graphical solution or by generation of columns using a Microsoft Excel spreadsheet on a desktop computer.

The break-even points are when the total revenue equals the total cost. The first break-even point is when, for additional units produced, the total revenue exceeds the total cost incurred. The second break-even point indicates a point of overproduction to a point of being counterproductive. Here, for additional units produced, the total revenue falls below the total cost.

$$TR = C_T \tag{2.18}$$

$$aD - bD^2 = C_F + DC_V \tag{2.19}$$

The break-even points can be obtained by the solution of the following quadratic equation:

$$bD^2 - D(a - C_V) + C_F = 0 \tag{2.20}$$

The first BEV (break-even) point occurs at a demand of 136,000–137,000 bags of Nibbler bags per year. The second BEV point occurs between 1,460,000 and 1,470,000 Nibbler bags per year. Further production of Nibbler bags would be counterproductive for revenue. The reason for the occurrence of the second break-even point is because the price falls inversely with the demand. When prices are low, the total revenue generated is not sufficient to exceed total cost. Total cost increases with demand in a linear manner.

2.4 Giffen and Veblen Goods

Not all goods obey the law of demand. Examples of *Veblen goods* are diamonds, luxury cars, fur coats, etc. These are status symbols. Families with higher incomes tend to buy them to show their higher status in society. The price of these goods rises with increase in demand. *Giffen goods* experience an increase in demand as the price rises. This does not obey the law of demand. During a potato famine, the price rises. Rather than less demand, poor families buy more potatoes to show their status.

An *elasticity of supply* can be defined as follows:

$$E_{sup} = \frac{\Delta S}{\Delta p} \tag{2.21}$$

Elasticity of supply as defined by Eq. (2.21) denotes the change in supply that can be expected for a small change in price. *E*sup in most cases is positive, as stated by the law of supply. The supply curve is *concave curvature* facing upward. The elasticity of supply for a considered good depends on factors such as availability of raw materials, length and complexity of production, time to respond, excess capacity, inventories, etc. The elasticity for gasoline is reported as 1.61 and that of cotton as 0.3. One of the assumptions of the law of demand is that the supply and demand are independent of each other.

An *elasticity of demand* can be defined in a similar manner to Eq. (2.21) as

$$E_{dem} = \frac{\Delta D}{\Delta p} \tag{2.22}$$

Elasticity of demand as defined by Eq. (2.22) denotes the change in demand that can be expected for a small change in price. *Edem* in most cases is *negative* as stated by the law of demand. Price changes come about to equalize the product of price and demand. As demand increases, price decreases and vice versa. The demand y curve is *concave curvature* facing upward.

Example 2.2 Japanese Robots

The price-demand relation for a certain Japanese robot is given by

$$p = a - bD + cD^2 \tag{2.23}$$

How many break-even points do you expect? What is the demand at

(i) Maximum revenue?
(ii) Maximum profit?
(iii) Break-even point(s)?

Total Revenue, TR = pD = $aD - bD^2 + cD^3$ (2.24)

The maximum revenue occurs at a demand that can be calculated as follows:

$$\frac{d(TR)}{dD} = 0 = a - 2bD + 3cD^2 \quad (2.25)$$

The extremas occur at

$$D' = \frac{2b \pm \sqrt{4b^2 - 12ac}}{6c} \quad (2.26)$$

For maxima, the second derivative of the TR (total revenue function) has to be negative, and evaluated at the extremum values of demand. The second derivative of TR is seen to be

$$\frac{d^4(TR)}{dD^2} = -2b + 6cD \quad (2.27)$$

This depends on the actual values of a, b, and c.

The cost function remains the same as

$$C_T = C_F + DC_V \quad (2.28)$$

The total profit can be calculated as:

$$\text{Total Profit} = (a\text{-}C_V)D - bD^2 + cD^3 - CF$$

The demand at maximum profit can be estimated as follows:

$$\frac{dP}{dD} = 0 = 3cD^2 - 2bD + (a - C_V) \quad (2.29)$$

The maxima have to be confirmed by ensuring the second derivative of the profit function is positive evaluated at one of the extremum demand values. The second derivative of the profit function is given by

$$\frac{d^2P}{dD^2} = 6cD - 2b \quad (2.30)$$

The break-even points can be estimated when the total revenue and total cost are equal to each other.

$$(a\text{-}C_V)D - bD^2 + cD^3 - C_F = 0 \quad (2.31)$$

There are three break-even points that can be expected. These are obtained by the solution to the above cubic equation. The solution to cubic equations can be solved by two methods:

(i) Vieta's Substitution to Depressed Cubic Equation
(ii) and Numerical Solution.

Example 2.3 Lawn Mowers from China

The price-demand relation for lawn mowers made by a Chinese manufacturer can be given by the following relation:

$$p = 80 - 0.19D + 10^{-4}(D^2) \tag{2.32}$$

This is shown in Figure 2.2.

The fixed cost to produce the lawn mowers, including taxes, license fees, and insurance is about \$2000. The variable cost that includes electric, gas, and water utilities can be taken as \$10 per lawn mower.

$$\text{Total Revenue, TR} = pD = aD - bD^2 + cD^3 = 80D - 0.19D^2 + 1E\text{-}4D^2 \tag{2.33}$$

The maximum revenue occurs at a demand that can be calculated as follows:

$$\frac{d(TR)}{dD} = 0 = a - 2bD + 3cD^2 \tag{2.34}$$

The extremas occur at

$$D' = \frac{2b \pm \sqrt{4b^2 - 12ac}}{6c} = \frac{+0.38 \pm 0.22}{0.0006} = 266.67 \;\&\; 1000 \tag{2.35}$$

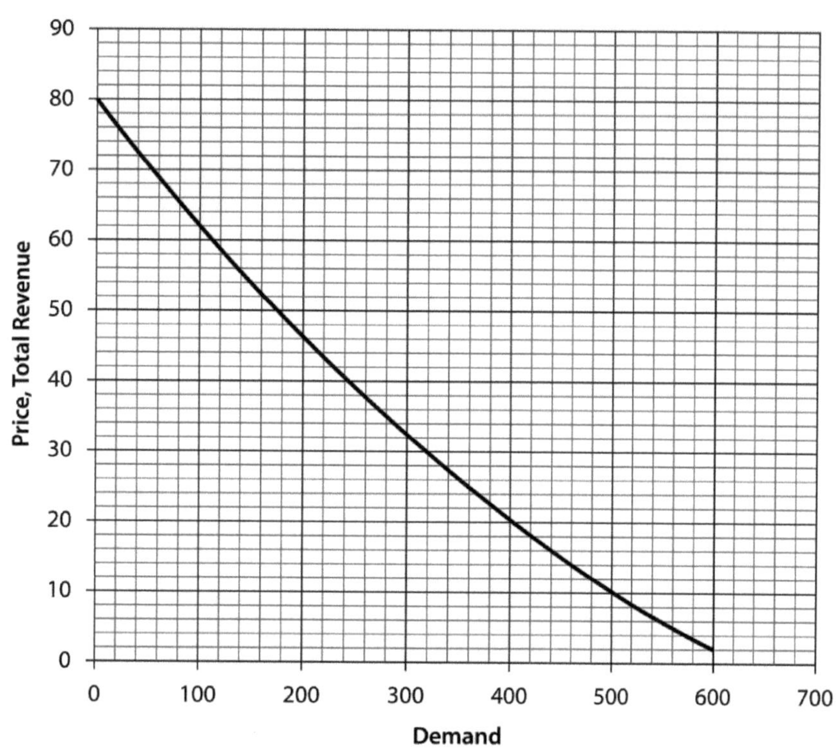

Figure 2.2 Price-Demand Curve for Chinese Lawn Mowers in Example 2.3

For maxima, the second derivative of the TR, total revenue function, has to be negative, evaluated at the extremum values of demand. The second derivative of TR would be seen to be

$$\frac{d^2(TR)}{dD^2} = -2b + 6cD \qquad (2.36)$$

Eq. (2.36) evaluated at the two roots for demand that causes an extremum value in the TR, total revenue function, are as follows:

$$D' = 266.67, \text{ Eq. } (2.36) = -0.160002 \qquad (2.37)$$

$$D' \text{ at } 1000, \text{ Eq. } (2.36) = 0.22 \qquad (2.38)$$

Thus the extremum of TR function at D' = 1000 corresponds to a minima. The other demand, D' = 266.7, corresponds to a maxima. The TR, total revenue function, is plotted using Microsoft Excel spreadsheets and shown in Figure 2.3. The maxima can be confirmed from the figure corresponding to a demand, D' = 266.7.

The cost function remains the same as

$$C_T = C_F + DC_V \qquad (2.39)$$

The total profit can be calculated as

$$\text{Total Profit} = (a-C_V)D - bD^2 + cD^3 - C_F$$

The demand at maximum profit can be estimated as follows:

$$\frac{dP}{dD} = 0 = 3cD^2 - 2bD + (a - C_V) \qquad (2.40)$$

The maxima have to be confirmed by ensuring the second derivative of the profit function is positive evaluated at one of the extremum demand values. The second derivative of the profit function is given by

$$\frac{d^2P}{dD^2} = 6cD - 2b \qquad (2.41)$$

The break-even points can be estimated when the total revenue and total cost are equal to each other.

$$(a-C_V)D - bD^2 + cD^3 - C_F = 0 \qquad (2.42)$$

The demand corresponding to maximum profit can be obtained by inspecting the table generated by an MS Excel spreadsheet. This can be seen to come about at a demand of about 225 lawn mowers. The demand, price, total cost, total revenue, and profit for 0–600 lawn mowers is shown in Table 2.2. The two break-even points can be seen from Table 2.2 to occur at 35 and 450 units.

A third break-even point can be expected, according to Eq. (2.42). In order to search for the third break-even point, the TR function was calculated for demands greater than 600 and plotted using an MS Excel spreadsheet and shown in Figure 2.4. A *third break-even point* can be seen at a demand corresponding to about 1420 units, and can be identified from Figure 2.4. This is subject to the applicability of the law of demand given by Eq. (2.32). For demand units greater than 629 lawn mowers, it can be seen from Eq. (2.32) that a "negative" price is associated with the lawn mowers. What is going on in the market is not clear in this regime. The Chinese manufacturer has to pay money to have customers haul away their product. This is also not that uncommon given the cash-down and free promotional offers, etc. advertised time and again on TV commercials. The price comes back again to positive territory for demand greater than 1270 lawn mowers. Maybe at this point the advertisement program and customer reports have worked in favor of the Chinese manufacturer. From this point onward the price increases (!), with increase in further demand. Thus the profits increase with further increase in demand after the third break-even point. It does not decline into a nonprofitable region like in the Garlic Nibbler Snack Factory in Example 2.1. Then again, in that example, the price-demand relation was linear. It obeys the law of demand and price falls with increase in demand.

The break-even points, the demand at which the TR (total revenue) reaches a maximum value, the demand at maximum profit needs to be calculated for every enterprise. The methodology is explained in the above sections. Much depends on the price-demand relation. If it is linear, then enterprise fortunes will conform to behavior as explained in Example 2.1. If the price-demand relation follows a quadratic or quadrilinear relation, the enterprise fortunes will behave in a fashion as explained in Example 2.3.

2.5 Dualistic Relations

Before the dawn of the industrial revolution and scientific progress, nations were affected by periodic famines. The marriage rate was inversely proportional to the price of bread. Floods, droughts, hurricanes, tsunamis, earthquakes, volcano eruptions, and other natural disasters resulted in the deaths of millions of the populace.

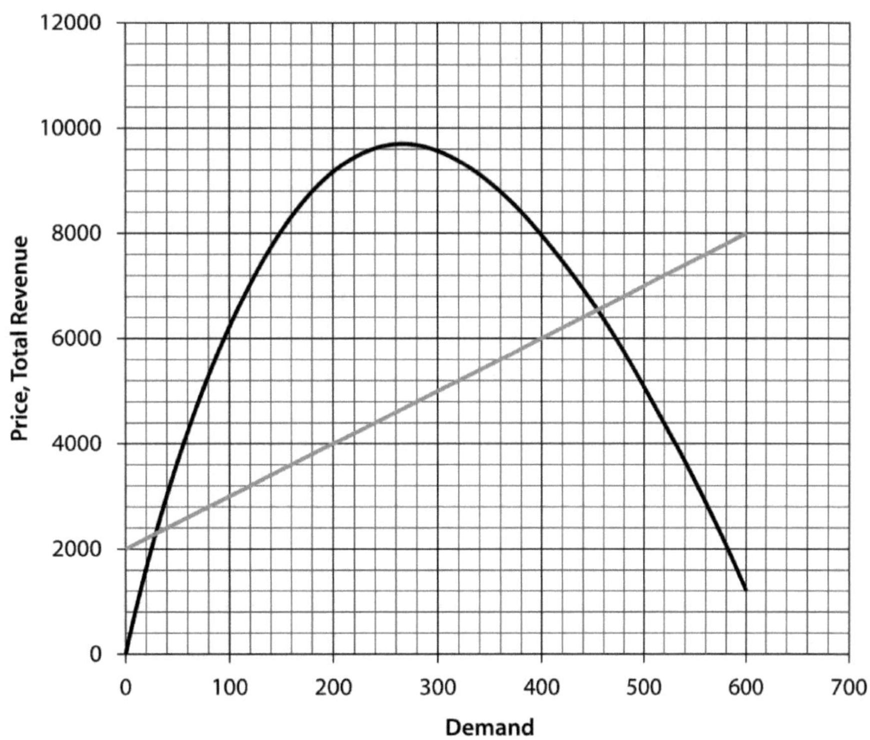

Figure 2-3 Maximum Total Revenue, Break-Even Points for Chinese Lawn Mowers in Example 2.3

Table 2.2 Total Revenue and Profit for Chinese Lawn Mowers

Law of Demand

		Demand	Price	Total Revenue	Total Cost	Profit
a	80	D	p	TR	C_T	P
b	0.19	0	80	0	2000	-2000
c	0.0001	20	76.24	1524.8	2200	-675.2
		40	72.56	2902.4	2400	502.4
C_v	10	60	68.96	4137.6	2600	1537.6
C_F	2000	80	65.44	5235.2	2800	2435.2
		100	62	6200	3000	3200
		120	58.64	7036.8	3200	3836.8
		140	55.36	7750.4	3400	4350.4
		160	52.16	8345.6	3600	4745.6
		180	49.04	8827.2	3800	5027.2
		200	46	9200	4000	5200
		220	43.04	9468.8	4200	5268.8
		240	40.16	9638.4	4400	5238.4
		260	37.36	9713.6	4600	5113.6
		280	34.64	9699.2	4800	4899.2
		300	32	9600	5000	4600
		320	29.44	9420.8	5200	4220.8
		340	26.96	9166.4	5400	3766.4
		360	24.56	8841.6	5600	3241.6
		380	22.24	8451.2	5800	2651.2
		400	20	8000	6000	2000
		420	17.84	7492.8	6200	1292.8
		440	15.76	6934.4	6400	534.4
		460	13.76	6329.6	6600	-270.4
		480	11.84	5683.2	6800	-1116.8
		500	10	5000	7000	-2000
		520	8.24	4284.8	7200	-2915.2
		540	6.56	3542.4	7400	-3857.6
		560	4.96	2777.6	7600	-4822.4
		580	3.44	1995.2	7800	-5804.8
		600	2	1200	8000	-6800

Natural disasters were known; not much was done about them. The 21st millennium is a period of abundant supply of goods and services. The boom-and-bust cycles of economies sometimes leads to periods of depression. Present-day marriage and divorce rates rise and fall as a function of job opportunities rather than the cost of bread. Famine due to crop failure is averted by trade and the exchange of food supplies from other parts of the globe. The economic policy of the government is to foster economic progress, minimize damage from the bust cycles of the economy, and improve and maintain high standards of living.

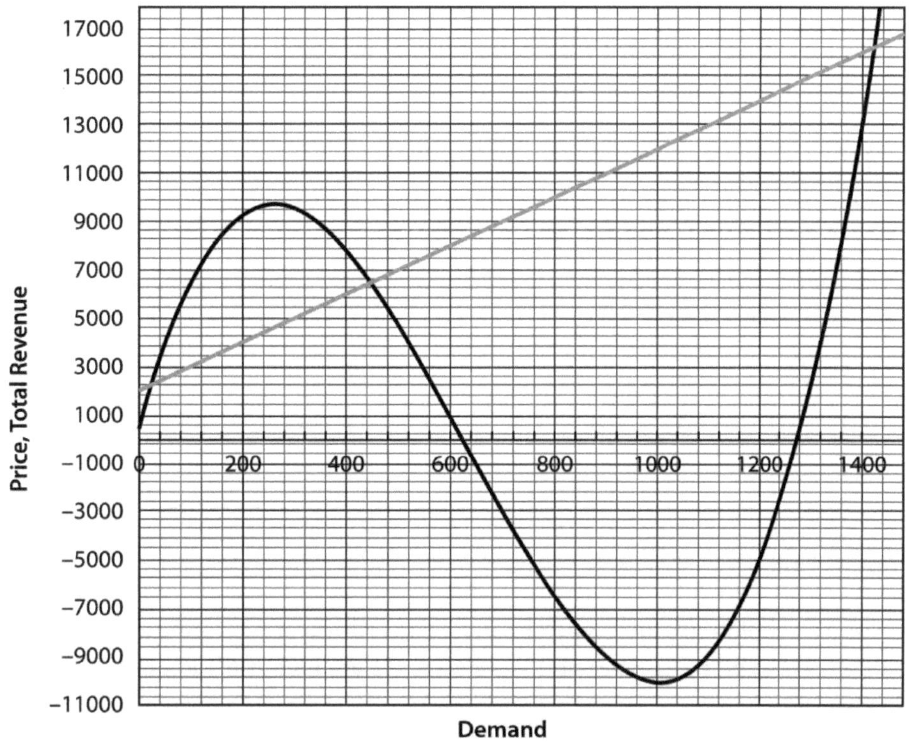

Figure 2.4 Third Break-Even Point for Manufacture of Chinese Lawn Mowers in Example 2.3

Paul Samuelson [2] presented the first lesson in economics: Things are often not what they seem. For instance, if all farmers work hard and a bumper crop is realized, the total farm income falls! In his Nobel lecture in 1970, Samuelson drew an analogy from optics and thermodynamics to economics. He considered a profit-maximizing firm that sells its output along a demand curve, in which price received is a nonincreasing function of the amount sold. Furthermore, suppose that the output can be generated from 2, 3, or 99 different inputs. He assumed that the production function relating outputs to inputs is smooth and concave. These time and age neural networks can be designed based on this example. Storing the 99 inputs and outputs on the computer is an interesting problem in data management and storage. It is difficult to find 99 independent surfaces. Knowledge of a single parent surface is sufficient to calculate exact information about 99 children. Observed demand curves are solutions to the maximum-profit problem.

Simple regularity conditions of calculus can be used to show that the demand curves are inverse functions of a family of partial derivatives of the TR (total revenue function). When smooth and *strongly concave*, the parent TR function has as its children 99 x 99 matrix of second partial derivatives. This matrix is symmetric and negative definite. Some algebraic manipulation can be used to show that these functions can be uniquely inverted to form a new family of children with the same properties—99 such children must have a parent function. The parent function may have been formed in a Pygmalion fashion.

$$\text{Max}\ (\text{TR}(v1, v2,\ldots\ldots,v99)) - \sum_{1}^{99} p_k v_k = \text{TR}(v1^*, v2^*,\ldots.,v99^*) - \sum_{1}^{99} p_k v_k \tag{2.43}$$

The TR function can be written in terms of a Hessian matrix. The necessary conditions of maxima can be derived as

$$\frac{\partial TR}{\partial v_i} = p_i \tag{2.44}$$

The Hessian matrix is negative definite. Eq. (2.44) contains necessary and sufficient conditions for maxima. A Hotelling-Roy dual function can be written as

$$v_i^* = \frac{\partial H}{\partial p_i} \qquad (i = 1,\ldots 99) \tag{2.45}$$

Samuelson showed that it follows that

$$\sum \Delta v_i^2 \neq \sum \Delta p_i^2 \neq 0 \tag{2.46}$$

He arrived at the inequality

$$\Delta p_1 \Delta v_1 + \Delta p_2 \Delta v_2 + \ldots + \Delta p_{99} \Delta v_{99} < 0 \tag{2.47}$$

Samuelson went on to combine common-sense and advanced mathematics and revisited the Giffen goods. When the price of potatoes sold to Irish peasants was raised, the amount of potatoes purchased was less. This is consistent with Eq. (2.47), or $\frac{\partial v_i}{\partial p_i} < 0$. This relation is analogous to the Le Chatelier principle: when pressure on a balloon is increased, the volume of the balloon decreases. The pressure volume path taken by an ideal gas is less steep for an isothermal process and a steeper change for an adiabatic process. Or,

$$\left(\frac{\partial v}{\partial p}\right)_T \leq \left(\frac{\partial v}{\partial p}\right)_S \leq 0 \tag{2.48}$$

The rate of change of volume with respect to pressure at constant temperature is less than the rate of change of volume with respect to pressure at constant entropy for an ideal gas. This relation can be used as an analogy in economics. By analogy, wage rate and labor have a *dualistic relation.* For example, as the number of laborers available increases, the wage rate decreases. As the number of laborers is low, or should there be a shortage of labor, the wage rate is bound to increase. The land rent and acres of land also can be seen to have a dualistic relation. The more land available, the lower the rent. Thus land in Australia or rural Texas is available at lower rent and the scarce availability of land in New York City can be used to collect larger rent. These dualistic relations are shown in Figure 2.4.

Two paths are taken in Figure 2.4. The first path is raising price p1 of the first input labor, while holding constant the second input quantity such as land or insurance. The rise in price lowers the labor availability as indicated by the negative slope of the pv diagram. In the second example, the price p1 is increased by the same amount holding the v2, p2 constant. In order to maximize profit, less of v1 will be purchased. This is indicated by the negative slope of the heavy curve in Figure 2.4. These observations are captured in the *Le Chatelier-Samuelson principle.* The heavy curve of long-term correction with other quantities constant must be less steep or *more elastic* compared with the light curve that is used to capture demand relation when the other input is held constant. Thus, quantitatively

$$\left(\frac{\partial v_1}{\partial p_1}\right)_{p_2} \leq \left(\frac{\partial v_1}{\partial p_1}\right)_{v_2} \leq 0 \tag{2.49}$$

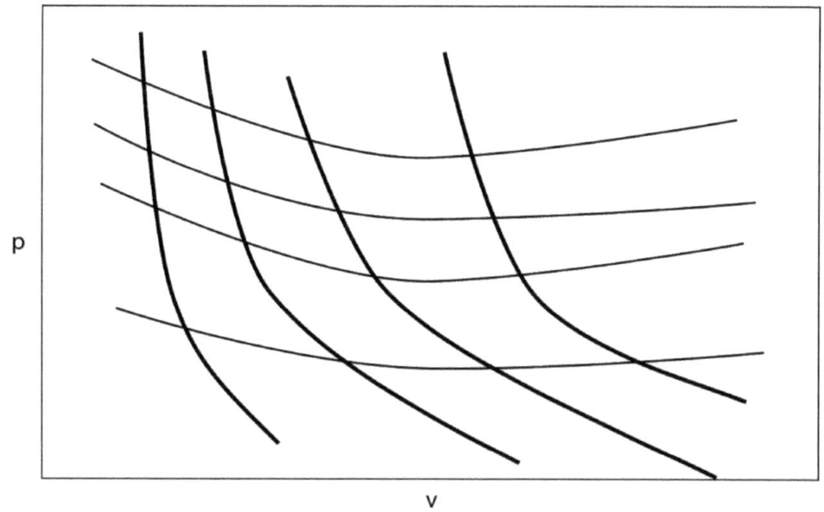

Figure 2.4 Dualistic Relations of Price and Its Variables Such as Demand

Thus,

$$\frac{\partial D}{\partial p} \leq 0 \tag{2.50}$$

where D is demand and p is price of a unit as discussed in the previous sections. When the price-demand relation is

$$p = a - bD \tag{2.51}$$

$$\frac{\partial D}{\partial p} = -\frac{1}{b} \leq 0 \tag{2.52}$$

a and b are usually constants and positive. Hence the Le Chatelier-Samuelson principle can be verified for the price-demand relation discussed in Section 2.3.

The two inputs shown in Eq. (2.49) can be independent of each other. Samuelson [2] notes that the Le Chatelier-Samuelson inequalities will remain good whether the two inputs are complements of each other (such as pumps and insecticides), or they are substitutes (such as organic and inorganic fertilizers). The Le Chatelier-Samuelson principle has several applications in economy, and is consistent with the theory of production and the general theory of constrained rationing.

2.6 Summary

Fixed costs are usually one-time occurrences. *Variable costs* occur more frequently, usually once every billing period. *Incremental costs* are those costs that are incurred proportionally to the number of goods produced. The planned costs per unit of output, anticipated labor hours, materials, and overhead categories are called *standard costs*. *Direct costs* can be measured and attributed to a specific activity or output. *Indirect* costs cannot be attributed to a single activity. Secretarial staff in an office building is an example of overhead costs. Cash cost, book cost, sunk cost, opportunity cost, investment cost, salvage value, and O & M costs are defined. A state of perfect competition is said to exist when there is more than one supplier of a product in demand. Some goods are *necessities* and some are *luxuries.*

The different stages during the life cycle of an enterprise are discussed. The total costs incurred during the operation of a business enterprise can be expressed in terms of the fixed costs, variable costs, and demand, D (Eq. (2.1). The price, p, is assumed to vary inversely with demand, D, and given by Eq. (2.2). The *law of demand* (*ceteris paribus*) states that customers will be ready to buy more goods as the price decreases [1]. Elastic and inelastic price-demand curves are distinguished from each other. The TR, total revenue, generated by the business enterprise is expressed as a product of price and demand and given by Eq. (2-3). The location where the TR reaches a maxima is found to be at demand D" = 2b/a, where a and b are the constants in Eq. (2.2) used to express the price vs. demand relation. The break-even points are determined when the TR equals the total cost. There are two break-even points. The first break-even point occurs when the revenue from the sale of goods produced exceeds the costs incurred. The second break-even point occurs when there is overproduction. From the second break-even point forward, it is *counterproductive* to increase further the demand, D.

Worked examples on the Garlic Nibbler Snack Factory, Japanese robots, and Chinese lawn mowers are discussed. Not all goods obey the law of demand. Examples of Veblen goods are diamonds, fur coats, etc. The price of Veblen goods increases with an increase in demand. Elasticity of supply and elasticity of demand are defined. When the price of Giffen goods increases, the demand also increases and does not fall.

2.7 References

[1] P. A. Samuelson, *Economics: An Introductory Analysis.* McGraw-Hill (1948), New York, NY.

[2] P. A. Samuelson, "Maximum Principles in Analytical Economics," Nobel Prize Lecture (1970), http://nobel.se, Stockholm, Sweden.

2.8 Exercises

Review Questions

1.0 What are the differences between *cash cost* and *sunk cost*?

2.0 How is *standard cost* different from *incremental cost*?

3.0 When does a state of *perfect competition* occur?

4.0 What is the significance of two or more break-even points?

5.0 Are demand at maximum profit and demand at maximum revenue equal to each other? Why ?

Problems

1.0 *Flower Shop*

Alice Jones operates a flower shop in downtown Houston. It costs her \$5 per day to pay the rent, \$1 per day for the water used for preserving the freshness of the flowers, and \$2.5 per day for air conditioning the flowers. The cost to pluck and bring the flowers from the garden in rural Texas to Houston runs her a quarter per flower. The price-demand relation for the flowers takes the form of

$$p = 0.65 - 0.001D$$

Calculate the break-even points. Construct the total revenue and total cost as a function of demand, D in a graph paper. What is the demand at maximum profit to Alice?

2.0 *Gypsy Cola*

Gypsy Cola, Inc. opened a soda can plant in Cancun, Mexico. The price-demand relation was given by

$$p = 0.5 - 10^{-5} D$$

where p is given as cents per can, and D is the number of soda pop cans. The cost of aluminum and transportation to the site of the plant runs 5 cents per can per day. The coloring cost runs 0.5 cents per can per day. The cost of sugar is 4 cents per can per day and water cost is 1 cent per can per day. Further utility costs to operate the belt conveyor and other equipment in the factory run $25 per day. How many aluminum cans per day must be produced for i) maximum revenue; ii) maximum profit? (Use graph paper if needed.)

3.0 *Ashwatama Motor Corporation*

Ashwatama Motor Corp. is looking into globalizing its auto market in the midsize van arena. The fixed costs of insurance, taxes, land, depreciation of manufacturing plants with assembly lines, and other infrastructure runs about $100 billion. The variable costs of utilities, labor, operations and maintenance, and materials and supplies are the better part of $10,000 per unit of vehicle produced. The price-demand relation globally for midsize vans was found to be as follows:

$$p = 500{,}000 - 0.2D$$

where D is the demand and p is the price in $. What are the two BEVs (break-even points)? When is maximum profit realized? What is the production in millions of vehicles when the TR (total revenue) reaches a maxima?

4.0 *Bali Overseas Travel*

Bali Overseas Travel is considering direct service from Kochi, India, to Houston, Texas, via Singapore. The fixed costs that include the depreciation of the aircraft, insurance, and taxes amount to approximately $1 million per day. The variable costs, including wages, fuel, and utilities run close to $900 per passenger per day. The ticket price varies with demand as follows:

$$p = 8375 - 4D$$

where p is the price of a one-way ticket and D is the number of passengers boarding the flight. Find the two BEVs (break-even points). At what point is the maximum profit realized? At what number of passengers per day is the TR (total revenue) function a maxima? Is the price-demand relation for overseas flight elastic ?

5.0 *Vysar Tomatoes*

Vysar Tomatoes is a new venture that grows tomatoes on farms and trucks them to the supermarket every week. The fixed costs, including farm land lease, taxes, insurance, and depreciation on agricultural, storage, and hauling equipment amount to $250,000. The variable costs of fuel, fertilizer, pesticides, and wages are about $500 per pound of tomatoes produced. The price varies with demand with a high elasticity in a quadratic manner as follows:

$$p = 6000 - 5D + 10^{-3}D^2$$

where p is the price in \$ per pound of tomatoes, and D is demand in pounds of tomatoes per week delivered at the supermarket. Find the two BEVs (break-even points). What is the significance of the second break-even point? What is the demand at maximum profit? What is the demand at maximum TR (total revenue)? Why are the two demands different from each other?

6.0 *Hanuman Salt*

Hanuman Salt processes common salt from the sea and delivers it to the supermarket chain every week. The variable costs of utilities of the evaporator, wages, and operations and management run \$150,000 per million pounds of salt delivered every week. The fixed costs of depreciation of the multiple-effect evaporator, crystallizer, and other equipment, insurance, and taxes amount to about \$1 million per million pounds of salt delivered per week. The price varies with demand in an inelastic manner as follows:

$$p = 0.5 - 0.01\ D$$

where p is the price per million pounds of salt and D is the demand in millions of pounds of common salt. Confirm that there are two BEVs (break-even points). What is the demand at: (a) maximum profit; (b) maximum revenue? What is the significance of the point in the TR vs. D curve when it reaches the x axis or zero revenue point?

7.0 *Vibeeshana Peaches*

Vibeeshana Peaches is a new venture that grows peaches in orchards and delivers them by truck to the supermarket chain every week. The fixed costs that include farm land lease, taxes, insurance, depreciation on robotic pluckers, storage, and hauling equipment amount to \$500,000. The variable costs of fuel, fertilizer, pesticides, and wages are about \$250,000 per million pounds of peaches delivered per week. The price varies with demand as follows:

$$p = 0.6 - 0.015D$$

where p is the price of million \$ per million pound of peaches, and D is demand in million pounds of tomatoes per week delivered at the supermarket. Find the two BEVs. What is the significance of the second break-even point? What is the demand at maximum profit? What is the demand at maximum TR? Why are the two demands different from each other? What is the significance of the second BEV occurring close to the maximum in TR (total revenue) function?

8.0 *Markendaya Sedans*

Markendaya Sedans is looking into starting a new plant in South Carolina to manufacture four-door sedans with 4-cylinder engines and front-wheel drive. The fixed costs of insurance, taxes, land, and depreciation of manufacturing plants with assembly lines and other infrastructure run about \$50 billion. The variable costs of utilities, labor, operational and maintenance, materials, and supplies run the better part of \$20,000 per unit of vehicle produced. The price-demand relation globally for midsize vans was found to be as follows:

$$p = 500{,}000 - 0.8D$$

where D is the demand and p is the price in $. What are the two BEVs? When is maximum profit realized? What is the production in millions of vehicles when the TR reaches a maxima ?

9.0 *Parasurama Overseas Travel*

Parasurama Overseas Travel is considering direct service from Moscow, Russia, to Houston, Texas. The fixed costs that include the depreciation of the aircraft, insurance, and taxes amount to approximately $2 million per day. The variable costs, including wages, fuel, and utilities run close to $1500 per passenger per day. The ticket price varies with demand as follows:

$$p = 9{,}200 - 4D$$

where p is the price of a round-trip ticket and D is the number of passengers boarding the flight. Find the two BEVs (break-even points). At what point is the maximum profit realized? At what number of passengers per day is the TR (total revenue) function a maxima? Is the price-demand relation for overseas flight elastic?

10.0 *Coast-to-Coast Car Trip*

A group of Japanese tourists plans to drive a minivan from Disney World Resorts in Orlando, Florida, to Disneyland Resorts in Anaheim, California. The distance is about 2179 miles on the road, according to the AAA's (American Automobile Association) TripTik maps. The minivan has a fuel efficiency of 21 mpg when driving at an average speed of 50 mph, including rest times. The fuel costs and rest area costs such as beverage, motel, and food can be added. The total cost of the trip, C_T, can be seen to vary as follows:

$$C_T = C_V + C_F = \phi L_{trip} pG + 8\left(\frac{L_{trip}}{S}\right)$$

where Ltrip is the length of the trip, S is the average speed of the minivan, and pG is the price per gallon of gas at the pump. The 8 is the amount in dollars that is spent per hour on motel, food, and snacks per hour of the trip. The f is a constant of proportionality, depending on how well the minivan is driven in order to obtain more fuel efficiency.

$$\phi = c_1 S$$

where c_1 is the constant of proportionality. Estimate the *optimal speed*, S at which the total cost, C_T, is minimum.

Chapter 3.0

Time Is Money

Main Topics Discussed in This Chapter

- Simple and Compound Interest
- Future Worth of Series of Uniform Payments, A
- Present Worth of Series of Uniform Payments, A
- Inverse Problem of Finding i
- Inverse Problem of Finding N
- Gradient Series
- Variable Interest Rate
- Deferred Payments

3.1 Simple and Compound Interest

Capital is often needed for starting new business enterprises. Capital can be dollar currency or other assets such as stocks, bonds, and money market accounts owned in the form of a diversified portfolio. The worth of money can be calculated to the nearest dollar and cent. This chapter is devoted to calculations of the cost of money. It is built on the fundamental notion of interest charge on capital.

The simple interest, I on a principal P, can be calculated as follows at a given interest rate i and pay period N:

$$I = P\,i\,N \tag{3.1}$$

where I is the simple interest amount, P the principal amount, i the interest rate expressed as a fraction, and N is the pay period. Over the same pay period, the compound interest and amount owed can be calculated as follows. At the end of the first pay period, the future amount, F, or amount owed is given by

$$F = P + iP = P(1+i) \tag{3.2}$$

At the end of the second pay period, the future amount is given by

$$F = P(1+i) + iP(1+i) = (1+i)(P+iP) = P(1+i)^2 \tag{3.3}$$

In a similar manner, at the end of pay period N the future amount is given by

$$F = P(1+i)^N \tag{3.4}$$

The principal, P, is multiplied with the algebraic expression given by Eq. (3.4), in order to obtain the future amount F. This algebraic expression is called a *single payment compound factor*. Eq. (3.4) can be read from Figure 3.1 for interest rates, i ranging from 0 to 30% and pay period, N, ranging from 2 through 12. The single payment compound factor, P/F, given by Eq. (3.4) can be read from Figure 3.2 for interest rates i ranging from 0 to 30% and pay period, N, ranging from 15 through 100. The P/F axis is in logarithmic scale to accommodate the larger P/F values associated with larger pay period N at larger interest rates, i.

Eq. (3.4) may be rearranged to given P given F, i and N as

$$P = \frac{F}{(1+i)^N} \tag{3.5}$$

The future amount, F, is multiplied with the algebraic expression given by Eq. (3.5), in order to obtain the present amount P . This algebraic expression is called a *single payment present worth factor*.

The pay period N can be calculated given the F, P, and i as follows:

$$N = \frac{\log\left(\frac{F}{P}\right)}{\log(1+i)} \tag{3.6}$$

The interest rate i can be calculated given F, P, and N as follows:

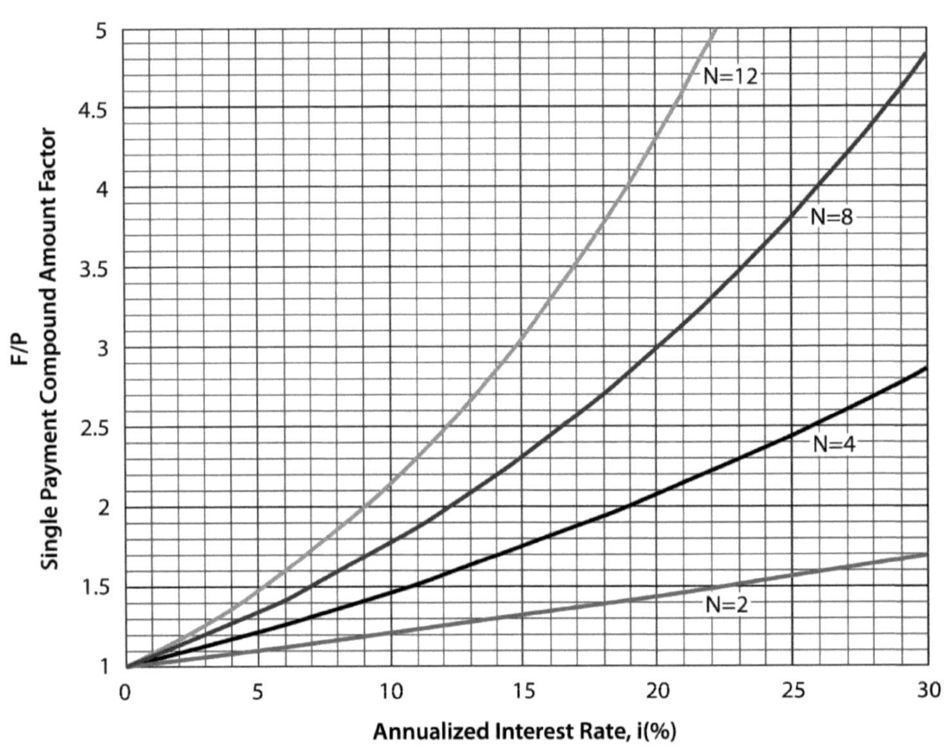

Figure 3.1 Single Payment Compound Amount Factor, F/P for 0 ≤ i ≤ 30% and 2 ≤ N ≤ 12

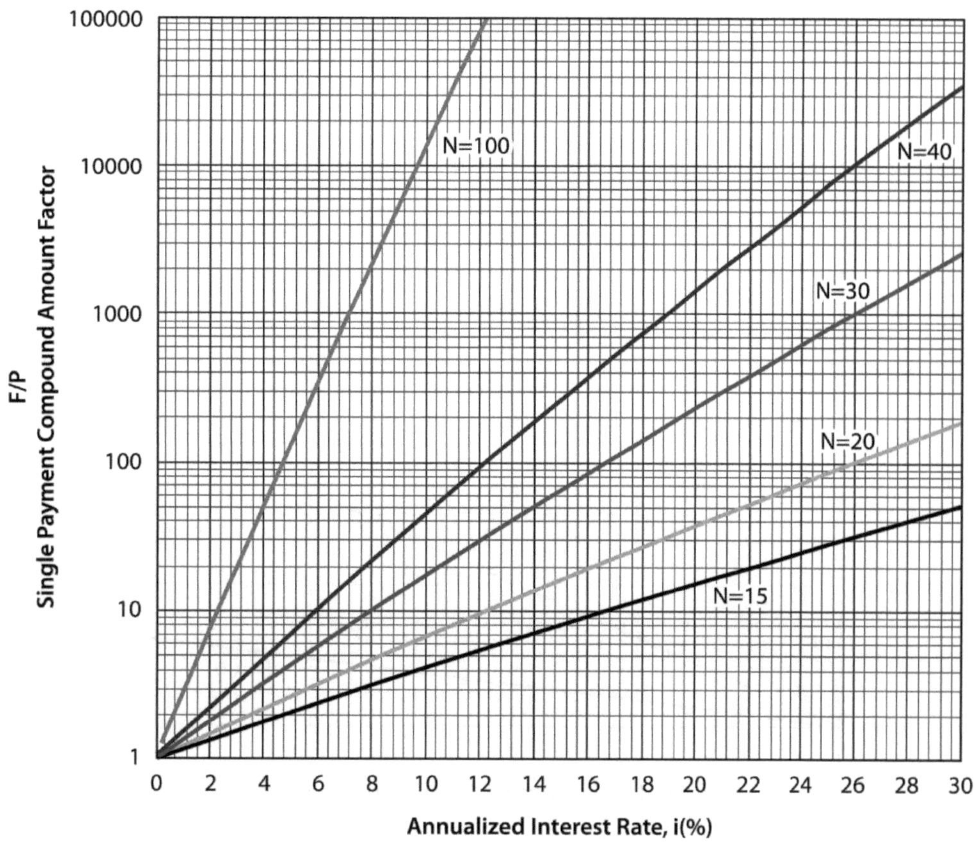

Figure 3.2 Single Payment Compound Amount Factor, P/F for Interest Rate 0 ≤ i ≤ 30% and Pay Period 15 ≤ N ≤ 100

$$i = \left(\frac{F}{P}\right)^{\frac{1}{N}} - 1 \tag{3.7}$$

Eq. (3.7) is shown in an easily readable chart in Figure 3.3. The interest rates can be read from Figure 3.3 when F/P, the single payment compound factor and pay period N, are known. Different lines in the figure are for different pay periods N ranging from 2 through 100 years.

The compound interest can be calculated by subtracting P from the future amount given by Eq. (3.4).

$$I = P((1+i)^N - 1) \tag{3.8}$$

Example 3.1 Compound Interest Calculated on an Everyday Basis

Your local bank branch recently announced a new savings plan with an interest rate of 0.0274% compounded daily. What is the interest payment on $52,000 at the end of one year?

$$F = P(1+i')^N = 50{,}000^*(1.000274)^{365} = \$55258.34 \tag{3.9}$$

From Eq. (3.8), the interest payment, I = $55,258.34-$50,000 = $5,258.34.

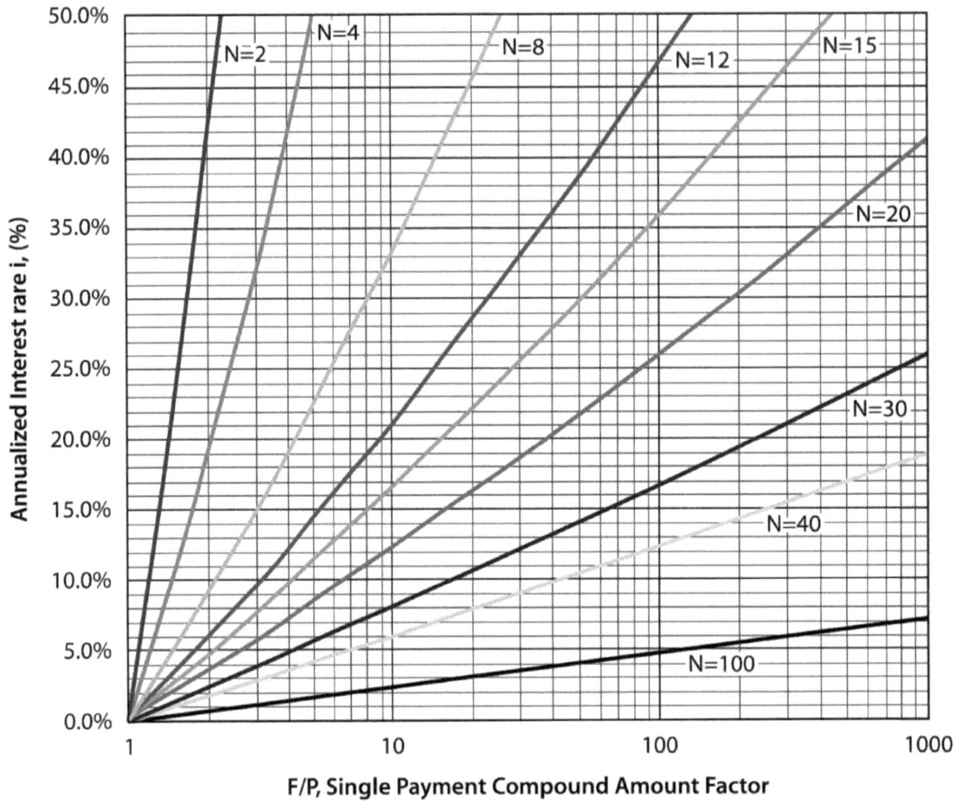

Figure 3.3 Interest Rate, i (%) vs. Single Payment Compound Amount Factor for Different Pay Periods, N

The history of mankind has seen the *uses* and *abuses* of compound interest. The farmers in India were persecuted by the feudal lords, or *Zamindars*, for late payment or nonpayment of loans. This was called bonded labor. Here the sons inherited the debts of their fathers and had to work them off. Over time, the compound interest ballooned in payment until the laborers could not repay the debt. Upon India's declaration of independence from the British Empire, the first prime minister, Jawaharlal Nehru, along with another prime minister who smiled on farmers, Mrs. Indira Gandhi, used to forgive the debts of farmers. The two political heads abolished bonded labor.

Bonded labor is an arrangement by which a person pays off his loan with direct labor in lieu of currency over a long period, sometimes even lifetimes. The term *debt slavery* is reserved for arrangements where the value of the work done is significantly greater than the original sum of money borrowed.

Peons are laborers who are bound in servitude until their debts are paid in full. Employers are allowed to extend credit to laborers to buy goods and services from employer-owned stores at exorbitant prices. This was used in the South after the Civil War. Poor African American and Caucasian farmers were called *sharecroppers*. They were given credit to purchase seed, fertilizer, and oxen from the landlord and made payments to him via a share of the crops.

3.1.2 Effective Interest Rate

Effective interest rate is the interest rate that gets compounded on an annual basis. Not all applications of interest rate are charged on an annual basis. Other applications need interest rate compounded on different bases, such as

(i) Daily

(ii) Weekly
(iii) Monthly
(iv) Quarterly
(v) Semiannual.

The interest rate compounded on any pay period is called the nominal interest rate. Federal laws such as the *truth-in-lending* law passed in Congress in 1969 require a statement regarding the APR (annual percentage rate) being charged on promissory notes and contracts involving monetary transactions. Compounding is not included.

An *effective interest rate,* i can be defined as a function of the nominal interest rate as follows [1]:

$$i = \left(1 + \frac{i'}{P}\right)^{P} - 1 \qquad (3.10)$$

where i' is the *nominal interest rate* and P is the number of compounding periods per year. This is the interest earned on the principal on one year. Effective interest rates are expressed on an annual basis. For example, the effective interest rate for a nominal rate of 12% compounded on a monthly basis would be

$$i = \left(1 + \frac{0.12}{12}\right)^{12} - 1 = 0.12683 \qquad (3.11)$$

A number of banks post their interest on savings accounts on a monthly basis and credit card companies calculate the interest charges due on the unpaid balance on a daily basis. A summary of effective interest rate i and nominal rate i' for different compounding periods is calculated using Eq. (3.10) and summarized below in Table 3.1.

3.2 Uniform Series of Payments

Cash Flow Diagrams are illustrations that show all the monetary transactions during the time of an enterprise. They can be used to calculate the equivalence of a series of uniform payments in terms of its present worth, P, or in terms of its future worth, F. For example, consider the uniform payments A made as shown in Figure 3.4:

Table 3.1 Effective Interest Rate i, as a Function of Nominal Interest Rate i'

		Nominal Rates							
	P	28%	24%	21%	18%	15%	12%	9%	6%
Daily	365	32.30%	27.11%	23.36%	19.72%	16.18%	12.75%	9.42%	6.18%
Weekly	52	32.21%	27.05%	23.32%	19.68%	16.16%	12.73%	9.41%	6.18%
Monthly	12	31.89%	26.82%	23.14%	19.56%	16.08%	12.68%	9.38%	6.17%
Quarterly	4	31.08%	26.25%	22.71%	19.25%	15.87%	12.55%	9.31%	6.14%
Semiannual	2	29.96%	25.44%	22.10%	18.81%	15.56%	12.36%	9.20%	6.09%
Annual	1	28.00%	24.00%	21.00%	18.00%	15.00%	12.00%	9.00%	6.00%

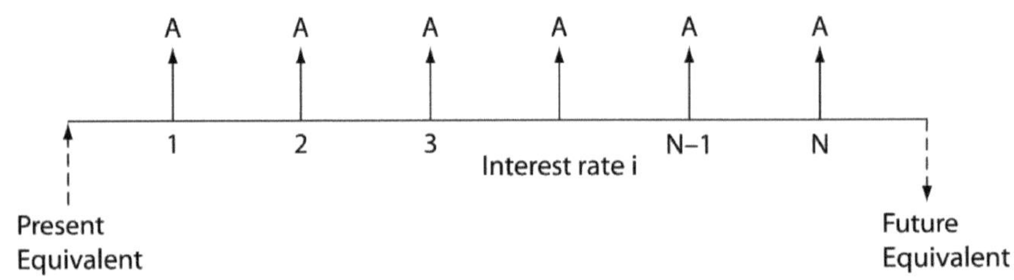

Figure 3.4 Cash Flow Diagram for Uniform Series of Payments A

3.2.1 GIVEN A, i, and N FIND F

The equivalence of the uniform series of payments A for a said period N at a fixed interest rate i as shown in Figure 3.1 can be established. The future equivalent worth of the uniform series of payments can be estimated as follows:The payment A at time period 1 will grow after N years on account of compound interest using Eq. (3.4) to $A(1+i)^N$. In a similar manner, the payment A at time period 2 will grow on account of compound interest accrued to $A(1+i)^{N-1}$ at the end of the pay period. Thus, the future equivalent worth of the uniform series of payments A can be given by

$$F = A(1+i)^N + A(1+i)^{N-1} + A(1+i)^{N-2} + \ldots + \ldots A(1+i) + A \tag{3.12}$$

Eq. (3.12) can be seen to be a geometric series. This can be summed up by multiplying Eq. (3.12) by the ratio of the series, (1+i) as follows:

$$F(1+i) = A(1+i)^N + A(1+i)^N + A(1+i)^{N-1} + \ldots + A(1+i)^2 + A(1+i) \tag{3.13}$$

Subtracting Eq. (3.12) from Eq. (3.13), it can be seen that all but the term A in Eq. (3.10) and $A(1+i)^N$ in Eq. (3.13) gets canceled, and

$$F(1+i-1) = A(1+i)^N - A \tag{3.14}$$

Or

$$F = \frac{A\left((1+i)^N - 1\right)}{i} \tag{3.15}$$

The uniform series payment A needs to be multiplied with the algebraic expression given by Eq. (3.13) in order to obtain the future worth, F. This algebraic expression is called the *uniform series compound amount factor.* Given the future amount F, interest rate I, and pay period N, the uniform series payment A can be calculated by rearranging Eq. (3.15) as

$$A = \frac{iF}{(1+i)^N - 1} \tag{3.16}$$

The future equivalent worth, F, needs to be multiplied with the algebraic expression given by Eq. (3.16) in order to obtain the uniform series payment A. This algebraic expression is called a *sinking fund factor.* The sinking fund factor given by Eq. (3.16) is shown in Figure 3.5 for values of interest rates, i (%) ranging from 0 to 30% and pay period N, ranging from 12 to 100. The sinking fund factor, A/F, given by Eq. (3.16) is shown as charts in Figure 3.6 for values of interest rates i(%) ranging from 0 to 30% and pay period N ranging from 2 to 8. It can be seen from Figures 3.5 and 3.6 that the nature of the function A/F vs. interest rate changes about N =10. The power ponentiated expression $(1+i)^N$ after N = 10 changes in a steeper manner. The curvature of the sinking fund factor vs. interest rate changes more rapidly at higher pay period values of N.

Example 3.2 Doubling Time of Investment

An investor deposits \$1000 every month into his mutual fund with a savvy investment banker. The money was invested into stocks of companies that were marked as aggressively growing in the coming years. In how many pay periods would the future worth of the investments double in value?

In order for the Future worth, F, to double in value after pay period N,

F = 2 NA (NA would be the value of the fund if the interest rate was 0%)

Using Eq. (3.13)

$$F/A = 2N = \frac{F}{A} = 2N = \frac{\left((1+i)^N - 1\right)}{i} \tag{3.17}$$

Expressing $(1+i)^N$ as a binomial series such as $1 + Ni + N(N-1)i^2/2!$ at a truncation error of the order of magnitude of $O(i^3/3!)$, the above expression can be seen to be:

$$i = \frac{2}{(N-1)} \tag{3.18}$$

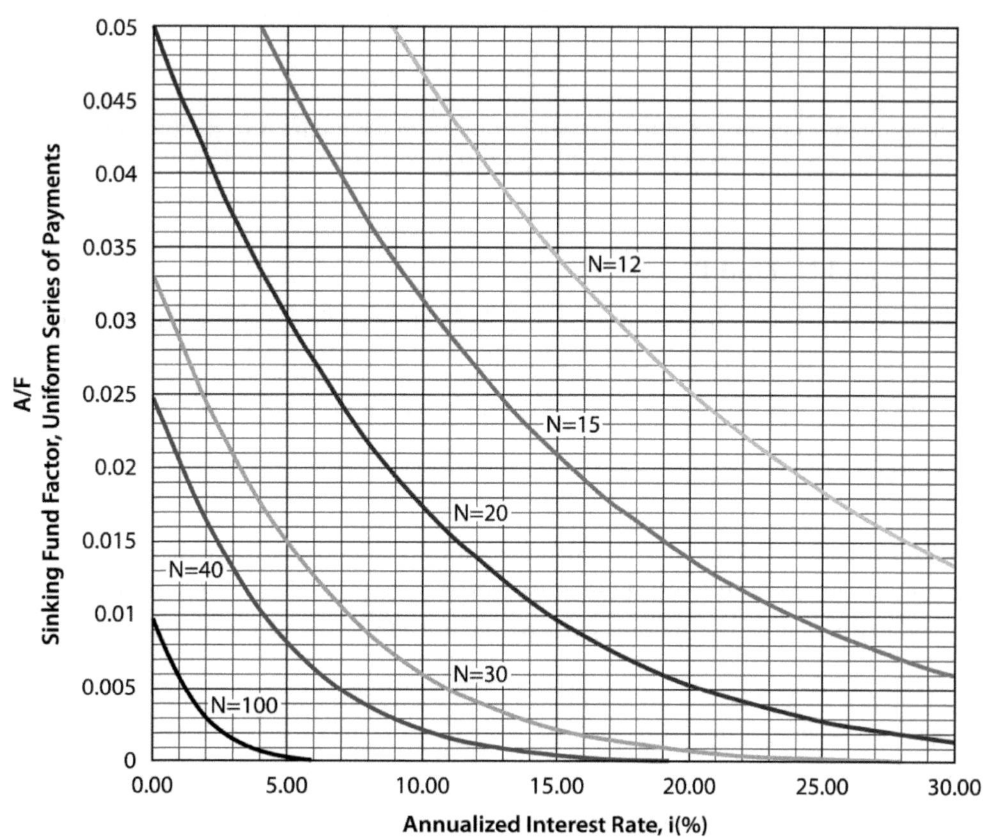

Figure 3.5 Sinking Fund Factor, A/F for Interest Rates, 0 ≤ i ≤ 30% and Pay Period 12 ≤ N ≤ 100

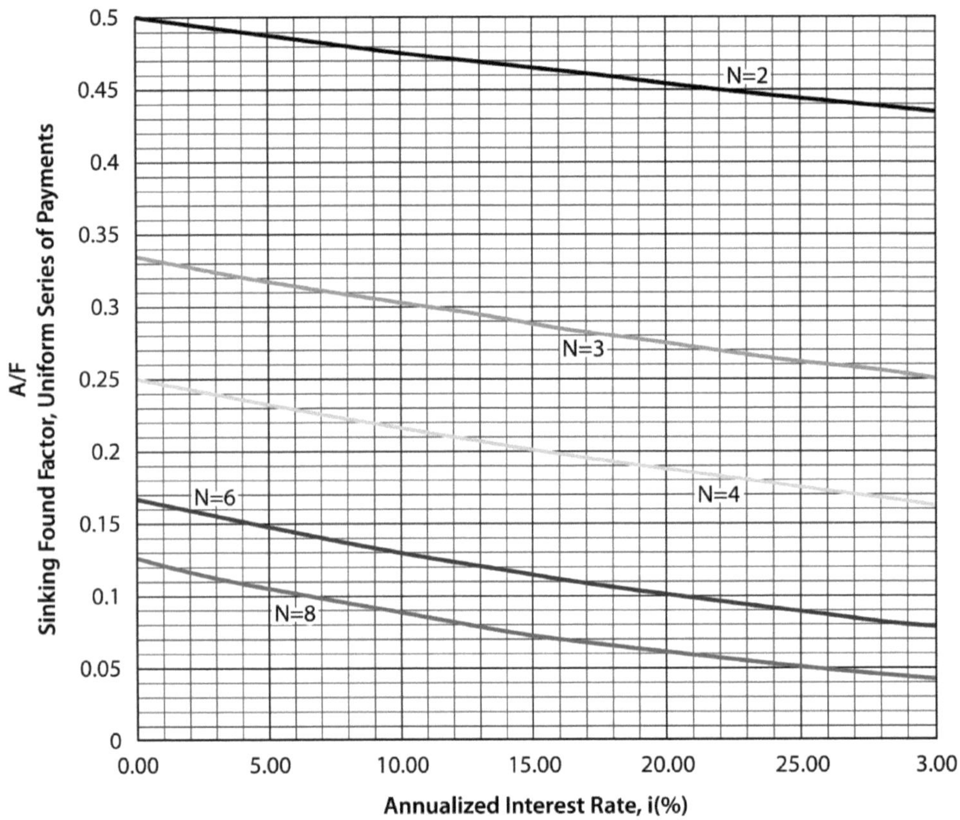

Figure 3.6 Sinking Fund Factor, A/F for Interest Rates 0 ≤ i ≤ 30% and Pay Periods, 2 ≤ N ≤ 8

The annualized interest rate i needed for the series of uniform payments A to double in value on account of compound interest paid—i.e., F = 2AN is shown in Table 3.2.

3.2.2 Given A, I, and N, Find P

The present worth, P, of the uniform series of payments, A, for the cash flow diagram shown in Figure 3.1 can be calculated by combining Eq.(3.15) and Eq. (3.4) to yield

$$P = \frac{A\left((1+i)^N - 1\right)}{i(1+i)^N} \tag{3.19}$$

The algebraic expression given by Eq. (3.10) that the uniform series payment, A, needs to be multiplied with in order to obtain present worth, P, is called the *uniform series present worth factor*. Given the present amount P, interest rate I, and pay period N, the uniform series payment A can be calculated by rearranging Eq. (3.19) as

$$A = \frac{i(1+i)^N P}{(1+i)^N - 1} \tag{3.20}$$

The present worth P needs to be multiplied with the algebraic expression given by Eq. (3.20) in order to obtain the uniform series payment A. This algebraic expression is called a *capital recovery factor*. The capital recovery factor A/P for interest rates 0 ≤ i ≤ 30% for pay periods 0 ≤ N ≤ ∞ is shown as easily usable charts in

Table 3.2 Interest Rate vs. Doubling Time of Investment(s)

End of Year #	Interest Rate Annualized, i
2	24%
3	12%
4	8%
5	6%
6	4.8%
7	4%
8	3.4%
9	3%
10	2.67%
11	2.4%
12	2.18%
13	2%
14	1.85%
15	1.71%

Figure 3.8. It can be seen from the figure even for N = 12 the capital recovery factor is only 4% from the values at perpetual payment for N is ¥, infinity for higher values of interest rate.

Perpetual payment plan is one when the pay period N becomes infinity. The limit when N tends to infinity in Eq. (3.20) can be calculated as

$$A = \underset{N \to \infty}{Lt} \frac{iP}{1 - \frac{1}{(1+i)^N}} = iP \tag{3.21}$$

In Appendix A annuity tables are provided to read F/P, P/F, F/A, A/F, P/A, and A/P values for various values of interest rates ranging from 1/8% to 30% and pay periods N ranging from 1 to 100. In addition to the annuity tables for the uniform series of payments A, annuity tables for uniform gradient series of payments G are also provided in Appendix A.

Example 3.3 Perpetual Payment and Father's Day Prize

The general manager of a factory that makes oil-fired steam boilers wants to establish a prize in a high school that caters to the children of the employees of the boiler plant factory. The prize is forever and for the best all-around student in the penultimate year of schooling. It is awarded as a once-in-a-school-time prize, from nursery school to graduating high school. Calculate the present amount that needs to be paid at an annualized interest rate of 10% for the prize amount to be $150 during Father's Day celebrations. Father's Day occurs once a year on June 21st, when daytime hours and nighttime hours are equal to each other.

$$\text{From Eq. (3.17)}, \; P = \frac{A}{i} = \frac{150}{0.1} = 1500 \tag{3.22}$$

Example 3.4 0% Interest Rate

Calculate the present worth of a series of uniform payments of $300 per month for 72 months. This is for leasing a car from the car dealer near you. The interest rate has dropped to near zero, such that the effective interest rate i can be considered with little error to be zero.

Use of Eq. (3.19) for this example may seem like P would be infinity! This is because i is zero. On careful examination of Eq. (3.19), it can be seen that when i becomes zero, Eq. (3.19) takes on the $\frac{0}{0}$ indeterminate form. The present worth can be re-derived from Figure 3.1 when interest rate is 0. When interest rate is 0, there is no interest charged or compound interest levied. Therefore,

$$P = A + A + A + \ldots\ldots + A = AN \tag{3.23}$$

Thus, when i=0, Eq. (3.19) is not applicable to calculate P. But it can be seen to be equal to AN, where N is the pay period and A is the uniform series payment. This is the *asymptotic limit* of the principal amount when the interest rate i tends to 0%. The federal fund rates are 0.0% recently in the year 2010. During years when there is *deflation* instead of inflation, this may be more applicable.

Example 3.5 Nest Egg of Alice Smith

Alice Smith signed up with her company's 401(k) retirement savings plan. She pays $330 per month. Her employer matches dollar for dollar and pays as much per month into her retirement savings account. She is 26 years old. When she retires at 65, she hopes to obtain two lump-sum distributions. She can expect a return of 10% compounded annually as interest for her plan. Calculate the future equivalent amount of Alice Smith's retirement savings plan.

Eq. (3.15) can be used to calculate F.
A = 2*$330 = $660
N = 39 years
i = 10%

$$F = \frac{A\left((1+i)^N - 1\right)}{i} = \frac{660((1.1)^{39} - 1)}{0.1} = \$264{,}956 \tag{3.24}$$

Example 3.6 Diversified Portfolio

Darlene Shuster was the sole beneficiary of a life insurance benefit payment of $200,000 when her husband died. She invested the face amount as follows:

Stocks	$50,000
Bonds	$50,000
Money Market	$100,000.

The Dow Jones Industrial Average has performed at an average of 10% growth in value every year for the past 100 years, including the Great Depression and the market corrections of 1987 and 2007. The bond funds' yield is about 6% per year. The money market rates are 2.5% for the years 2010–2015; 5.0% for the years 2015–2020; and 8% for the years 2020–2030. After 20 years, what would the future worth of Ms. Shuster's inheritance be?

By Eq. (3.4), the investment in stocks would grow to = $(F_s/50{,}000,\ 10\%,\ 20)$
$= 50{,}000(1+0.1)^{20}$ (3.25)
$= \$336{,}375$

By Eq. (3.4), the investment in bonds would grow to = $(F_B/50{,}000,\ 6\%,\ 20)$
$= 50{,}000(1+.06)^{20}$ (3.26)
$= \$160{,}357$

From the derivation of Eq. (3.4) from Eq. (3.3), it can be seen that the money market funds would grow to

$$100{,}000(1+0.025)^5(1+0.05)^5(1+0.08)^{10} = \$311{,}748 \quad (3.27)$$

Adding the results from Eqs. (3.20–3.22), the future worth of Darlene's investment portfolio would be

$$336{,}375 + 160{,}357 + 311{,}748 = \$808{,}480$$

Example 3.7 George Tataseo's Royalty Payments and Investment

George Tataseo writes books. He receives royalty payments ranging from 8%–15% of the cover price of every book sold in the market. The twice-yearly payment is roughly about \$8000. The expenses incurred every month during the preparation of the book are about \$400. George invests the balance completely into a stock-based mutual fund. The return is about 9.5% on an annualized basis. After 10 years, what would the future worth of George's investments be?

Effective interest rate for six months for return on stock fund = 9.5%/2 = 4.75% (3.28)

Number of six-month periods in 10 years = 10* 2 = 20
Future Worth = (F/8000, 4.75%, 20) – (F/400,9.5/12,120) (3.29)

$$= 8000 * \frac{(1.0475)^{20} - 1}{0.0475} - 400 * \frac{(1.0475)^{120} - 1}{0.0475}$$

$= 8000*32.2056-400*12.4027$ (3.30)
$=\$252{,}684$

3.2.3 Given F, I, and A, Find N

Current books on the subject refer to numerical solutions or trial-and-error methods for obtaining the pay period N given the future equivalent worth F, interest rate i, and uniform series payment A. Here, a closed-form analytical solution is obtained to calculate the pay period N. Eq. (3.15) can be rearranged as follows:

$$\frac{iF}{A}+1=(1+i)^{N} \tag{3.31}$$

$$N=\frac{\log\left(\frac{iF}{A}+1\right)}{\log(1+i)}$$

Eq. (3.31) is shown in Figure 3.7 as an easily readable chart. The pay period N needed to achieve a certain investment goal F using a uniform series of payments A for various interest rates ranging from 1% ≤ i ≤ 30% can be read from Figure 3.6. Both the axes are logarithmic. This scale captures the functionality of N with respect to F/A and i as shown in Eq. (3.31).

3.2.4 GIVEN P, I, and A, FIND N

Current books on the subject refer to numerical solutions or trial-and-error methods for obtaining the pay period N given the present equivalent worth P, interest rate i, and uniform series payment A. Here, a closed-form analytical solution is obtained to calculate the pay period N. Eq. (3.19) can be rearranged as follows:

$$1-\frac{iP}{A}=\frac{1}{(1+i)^{N}} \tag{3.32}$$

$$N=\frac{\log\left(\frac{A}{A-iP}\right)}{\log(1+i)}$$

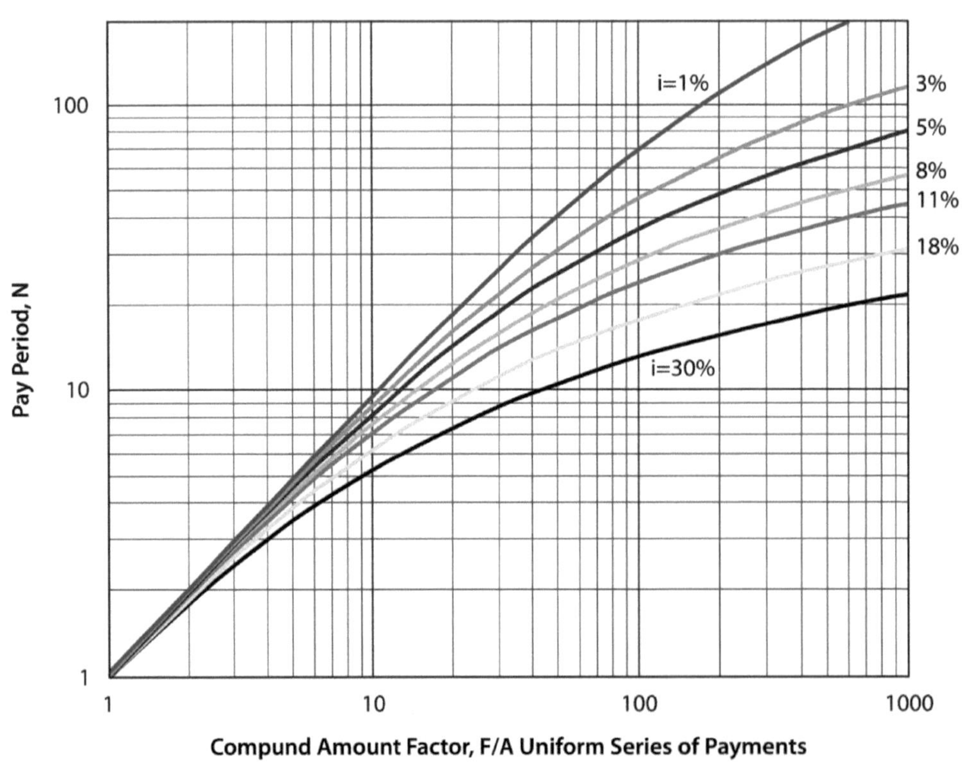

Figure 3.7 Pay Period N vs. Compound Amount Factor, F/A for Interest Rates 1% ≤ i ≤ 30%

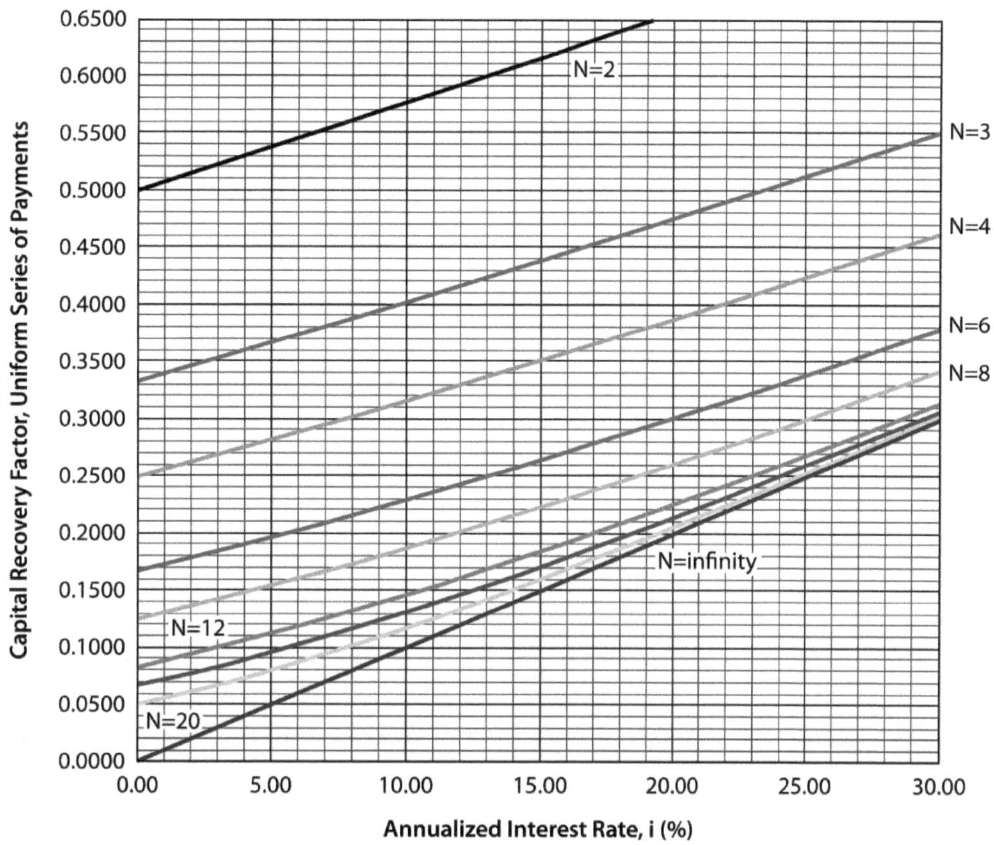

Figure 3.8 Capital Recovery Factor, A/P for Interest Rates $1 \le i \le 30\%$ and Pay Period $2 \le N \le \infty$

3.2.5 GIVEN F, A, and N, FIND i

Current books on the subject refer to numerical solutions or trial-and-error methods for obtaining the interest rate i, given the pay period N and given the future equivalent worth F, and uniform series payment A. Here, a closed-form analytical expression is obtained to calculate the interest rate i. It can be noted that the i in the $(1+i)^N$ is a small number. Given 1 is present, the expression is better suited for expansion in the form of a binomial infinite series as follows:

$$(1+i)^N = 1 + Ni + \frac{N(N-1)i^2}{2!} + \ldots\ldots \tag{3.33}$$

The terms with i^3 and higher order terms are neglected. The truncation error involved is of the order of magnitude of $O(i^3/3!)$

Combining Eq. (3.33) and Eq. (3.15)

$$\frac{iF}{A} = Ni + \frac{N(N-1)i^2}{2!} \tag{3.34}$$

$$or, i = \frac{2}{(N-1)}\left(\frac{F}{AN} - 1\right)$$

3.2.6 GIVEN P, A, and N, FIND i

Numerical solutions or trial-and-error methods are needed for obtaining the interest rate i, given the pay period N, and given the present equivalent worth P, and uniform series payment A. Here, a closed-form analytical expression is obtained to calculate the interest rate i. It can be noted that the i in the $(1+i)^N$ is a small number. Given 1 is present, the expression is better suited for expansion in the form of a binomial infinite series as follows:

$$(1+i)^N = 1 + Ni + \frac{N(N-1)i^2}{2!} + \ldots\ldots\ldots \tag{3.35}$$

The terms with i^3 and higher order terms are neglected. The truncation error involved is of the order of magnitude of $O(i^3/3!)$.

Combining Eq. (3.24) and Eq. (3.15)

$$\frac{P}{AN} = \frac{2+(N-1)i}{2+2i+N(N-1)i^2} \tag{3.36}$$

$$\frac{P(N-1)}{A}i^2 + i\left(\frac{2P}{AN} - (N-1)\right) + \frac{2P}{AN} - 2 = 0$$

The interest rate i can be calculated by solution of the quadratic equation arrived at in Eq. (3.25). Thus,

$$ai^2 + bi + c = 0 \tag{3.37}$$

where,

$$a = \frac{P(N-1)}{A}; b = \frac{2P}{AN} + 1 - N$$

$$c = \frac{2P}{AN} - 2$$

Example 3.8 U-Pay-Now & I-Pay-Later

You are hired by Cowboy Investments upon graduation. They are developing a new investment plan called "U-Pay-Now & I-Pay-Later" for customers. The deal is that the client pays \$500 every month to Cowboy Investments. After a said period in a certain number of years, Cowboy Investments will have the client cease payments; the client then receives \$500 every month forever. At a 10% annualized interest rate (the historic performance of Dow Jones), how many years would you recommend the said period be?

Let the said period of investments = N years (Figure 3.9)

(F/A,I,N) = (F/6000,10%,N)

$$F = A\left(\frac{(1+i)^N - 1}{i}\right)$$

The future worth after N years is invested until perpetuity

(P/A, 10%, ∞)

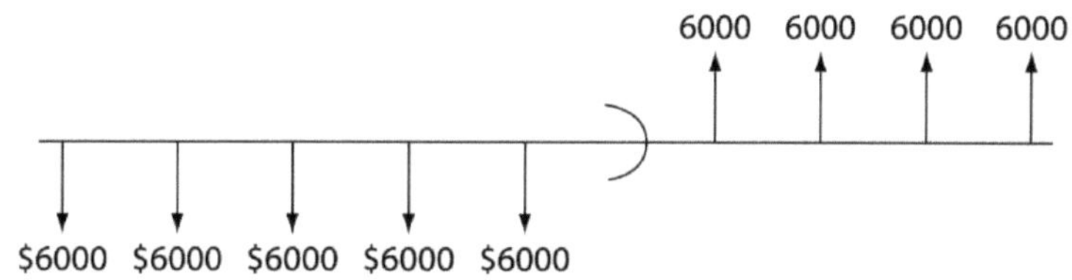

Figure 3.9 Cash Flow Diagram for "U-Pay-Now & I-Pay-Later"

$$\frac{P}{A} = \frac{(1+i)^N - 1}{i(1+i)^N}$$

$$\underset{N\to\infty}{Lt}\left(\frac{iP}{A}\right) = 1 - \frac{1}{(1+i)^N} = 1$$

$$P = \frac{A}{i} \tag{3.38}$$

It can be seen that from the "U-Pay-Now & I-Pay-Later" plan

$$F = A\left(\frac{(1+i)^N - 1}{i}\right) = P = \frac{A}{i}$$

$$(1+i)^N = 2 \tag{3.39}$$

$$N = \frac{\ln(2)}{\ln(1.1)} = 7.3 years$$

Example 3.9 When does a Micro-Power Plant become a more attractive investment?

K. R. Sridhar, CEO of Bloom Box, was featured on CBS's *60 Minutes.* Bloom Box makes micro power plants using SOFC, solid oxide fuel cell technology. A bloom box can be purchased for $3000. It consists of miniaturized fuel cells made of silica. The cost of electricity to power up a new home would be 8.0 cents per kWh. Should the existing utility company charge 12.5 cents per kWh, calculate the number of years it would take for a bloom box to be a good investment for new homeowner Jack Tripper. Jack heads a family of six members with four children. Assume that 600 kWh of electricity is consumed every month at the Tripper residence. (i=10%).

At the point when a Bloom Box will become lower cost compared with existing utility company rates, i.e., after N years

$$\$3000 + 600*.08*12(P/A,10\%,N) = 600*0.125*12(P/A,10\%,N) \tag{3.40}$$

$$\$3000 = \$324\left(\frac{1.1^N - 1}{0.1(1.1)^N}\right)$$
$$0.9259 = 1 - \frac{1}{1.1^N}$$
$$\frac{1}{1.1^N} = 0.07407$$
$$N = \frac{\ln(13.5)}{\ln(1.1)} = 27.3 years \tag{3.41}$$

3.3 Uniform Gradient Series of Payments

Under certain circumstances, the receipts and expenses of an enterprise are projected to change by a uniform amount each period. A portion of the periodic payment *multiplies* each pay period. These sequences of cash flows are called uniform gradient series of cash flows.

The present equivalent worth of the uniform gradient series of cash payments shown in Figure 3.10 can be calculated as follows:

$$P = \frac{G}{(1+i)} + \frac{G(2)}{(1+i)^2} + \frac{G(3)}{(1+i)^3} + \ldots + \frac{G(N-1)}{(1+i)^{N-1}} + \frac{G(N)}{(1+i)^N} \tag{3.42}$$

$$P = G\sum_{n=1}^{N} \frac{n}{(1+i)^n} \tag{3.43}$$

Multiply Eq.(3.42) on both sides by $(1+i)^N$

$$P(1+i)^N = G(1+i)^{N-1} + 2G(1+i)^{N-2} + 3G(1+i)^{N-3} + \ldots\ldots\ldots + (N-1)G(1+i) + NG \tag{3.44}$$

The right-hand side, RHS of Eq. (3.44), can be split as follows:

$$RHS = G\left[(1+i)^{N-1} + (1+i)^{N-2} + (1+i)^{N-3} + (1+i) + 1\right] + G\left[(1+i)^{N-2} + (1+i)^{N-3} + \ldots (1+i)) + 1\right]$$
$$+ G\left[(1+i)^{N-3} + \ldots\ldots + (1+i) + 1\right] + \ldots\ldots\ldots\ldots G \tag{3.45}$$

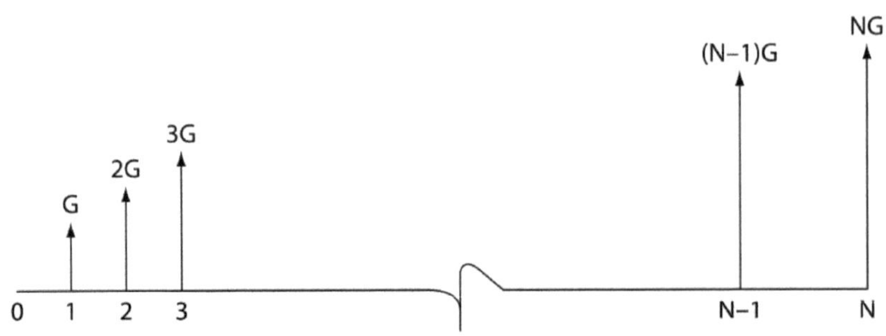

Figure 3.10 Cash Flow Diagram of Uniform Gradient Series of Payments

Each of the terms within the square brackets in Eq. (3.45) is a geometric series and can be summed up as

$$RHS = G\frac{(1+i)^N - 1}{i} + G\frac{(1+i)^{N-1} - 1}{i} + G\frac{(1+i)^{N-2} - 1}{i} + G\frac{(1+i)^{N-3} - 1}{i} + ... + G\frac{(1+i) - 1}{i} \tag{3.46}$$

Combining Eq. (3.46) and Eq. (3.44) and simplifying

$$iP(1+i)^N = G\left(\frac{(1+i)^{N+1} - 1}{i} - N\right) \tag{3.47}$$

Thus, P/G can be seen to be

$$P = \frac{G}{i(1+i)^N}\left(\frac{(1+i)^{N+1} - 1}{i} - N\right) \tag{3.48}$$

A *gradient to uniform series conversion factor* can also be defined by combining Eq. (3.48) and that for A/P, Eq. (3.20). Thus,

$$A = \frac{G}{(1+i)^N - 1}\left(\frac{(1+i)^{N+1} - 1}{i} - N\right) \tag{3.49}$$

The future worth of the uniform gradient series of payments can be calculated by combining Eq. (3.48) and Eq. (3.4). Thus,

$$F = \frac{G}{i}\left(\frac{(1+i)^{N+1} - 1}{i} - N\right) \tag{3.50}$$

3.4 Continuous Compounding

As discussed in Section 3.1.2, compounding periods may vary from daily, weekly, monthly, quarterly, semiannually, yearly, etc. All these are discrete compounding periods. The interest gets calculated after discrete periods of time. Eq. (3.10) gives the relation between the nominal interest rate per compounding period and the effective interest rate per year.

$$i = \left(1 + \frac{i'}{P}\right)^P - 1 \tag{3.51}$$

Let P/i' = m, Eq. (3.51) then becomes

$$i = \left(1 + \frac{1}{m}\right)^{mi'} - 1 \tag{3.52}$$

When the compounding period is changed from discrete to continuous, m in Eq. (3.52) becomes ∞, infinity. Further,

$$\underset{m\to\infty}{Lt}\left(1+\frac{1}{m}\right)^{m} = 1^{m} + m(1)^{m-1}\frac{1}{m} + \frac{m(m-1)}{2!m^{2}}1^{m-2} + \frac{m(m-1)(m-2)}{3!m^{3}}1^{m-3} + \ldots$$

$$= \underset{m\to\infty}{Lt}\ 1+1+\frac{1}{2!}(1-\frac{1}{m})+\frac{1}{3!}(1-\frac{1}{m})^{2}+\ldots\ldots = 1+1+\frac{1}{2!}+\frac{1}{3!}+\ldots\ldots \tag{3.53}$$

By Taylor series expansion, e^x evaluated at x = 1 can be seen to be

$$e^{1} = 1+1+\frac{1^{2}}{2!}+\frac{1^{3}}{3!}+\ldots = 2.71828182845905 \tag{3.54}$$

Comparing Eq. (3.53) and Eq. (3.54)

$$\underset{m\to\infty}{Lt}\left(1+\frac{1}{m}\right)^{\infty} = e \tag{3.55}$$

Combining Eq. (3.52) and Eq. (3.55)

$$i = e^{i'} - 1 \tag{3.56}$$

The effective interest rate for *continuous compounding* is given by Eq. (3.56).

3.4.1 F/P, F/A, P/A, A/F, AND A/P FOR CONTINUOUS COMPOUNDING

The corresponding formulae for F/P, F/A, and P/A with continuous compounding that were presented for discrete compounding earlier are given side by side in Table 3.3.

Table 3.3 Factors Used to Calculate Discrete and Continuous Compound Interest

To Find	Given	Discrete Factor by Which to Multiply	Compounding Factor Name	Factor Functional Symbol	Continuous Factor by Which to Multiply	Compounding Functional Symbol
F	P	$(1+i)^N$	Single Payment Compound Amount	(F/P,i'%,N)	$e^{i'N}$	(F/P,i%,N)
F	A	$\frac{(1+i)^N-1}{i}$	Uniform Series Compound Amount	(F/A,i%,N)	$\frac{e^{i'N}-1}{e^{i'}-1}$	(F/A,i'%,N)
P	A	$\frac{(1+i)^N-1}{i(1+i)^N}$	Uniform Series Present Worth	(P/A,i%,N)	$\frac{e^{i'N}-1}{e^{i'N}\left(e^{i'}-1\right)}$	(P/A,i'%,N)
A	F	$\frac{i}{(1+i)^N-1}$	Sinking Fund	(A/F,i%,N)	$\frac{e^{i'}-1}{e^{i'N}-1}$	(A/F,i'%,N)
A	P	$\frac{i(1+i)^N}{(1+i)^N-1}$	Capital Recovery	(A/P,i%,N)	$\frac{e^{i'N}\left(e^{i'}-1\right)}{e^{i'N}-1}$	(A/P,i'%,N)

Example 3.10 Continuous Compounding

Show the effect of continuous compounding by comparing the future worth of the nest egg of Alice Smith as discussed in Example 3.4. Sketch the future worth of Alice Smith's nest egg as a function of number of years N. Use the same interest rate for discrete as well as continuous compounding.

$$\text{Discrete Compounding: } F_D = \$660^*(F/A,10\%,N) = \frac{(1+i)^N - 1}{i} = \frac{1.1^N - 1}{0.1} \tag{3.57}$$

The interest rate used is 10%, which is the average performance of the Dow Jones over the past 100 years.
Continuous Compounding:
The nominal interest rate i' is taken as 10%.

$$\text{Continuous Compounding: } F_C = \$660^*(F/A,i'\%,N) = \frac{e^{i'N} - 1}{e^{i'} - 1} = \frac{e^{0.1N} - 1}{e^{0.1} - 1} \tag{3.58}$$

Eq. (3.58) and Eq. (3.57) were calculated in an MS Excel spreadsheet and plotted in Figure 3.3. It can be seen from Figure 3.11 that the effect of continuous compounding is only seen after 25 years!

3.4.2 GIVEN F, A, AND i', FIND N DURING CONTINUOUS COMPOUNDING

Current books on the subject refer to numerical solutions or trial-and error-methods for obtaining the pay period N given the future equivalent worth F, interest rate for continuous compounding, i'% per year and uniform

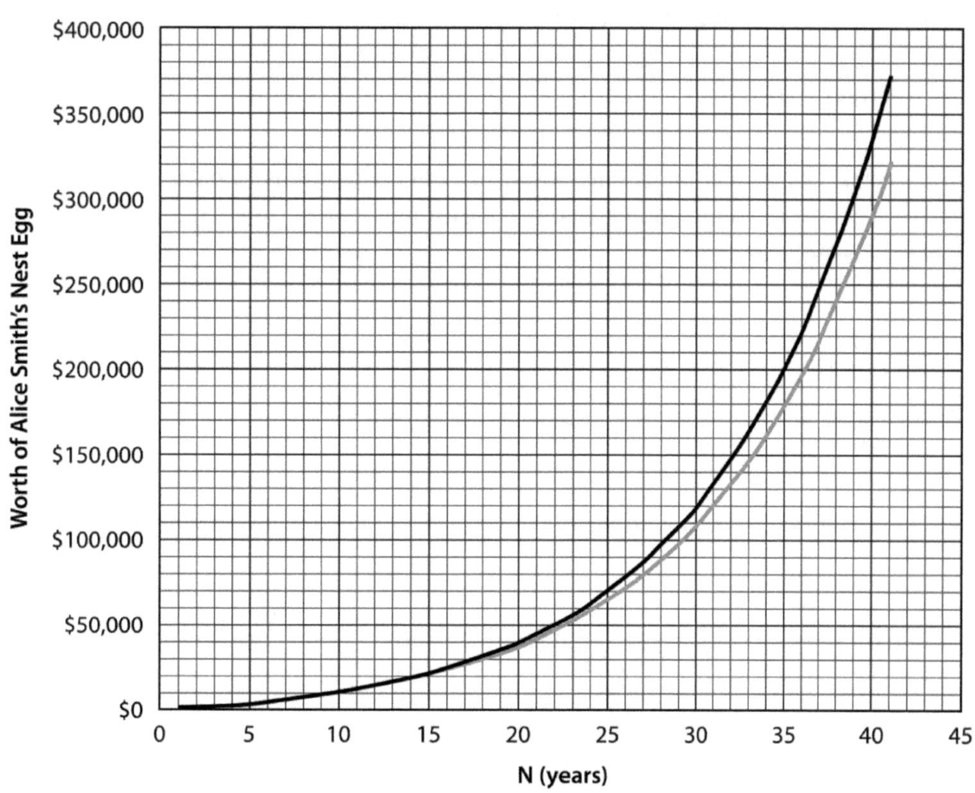

Figure 3.11 Worth of Alice Smith's Nest Egg (F/A) for Continuous & Discrete Compounding

series payment A. Here, a closed-form analytical solution is obtained to calculate the pay period N. The factor for obtaining F/A for continuous compounding given in Table 3.3 can be seen to be

$$F/A = \frac{e^{i'N} - 1}{e^{i'} - 1} \tag{3.59}$$

Rearranging Eq. (3.50)

$$\left(e^{i'} - 1\right)\frac{F}{A} + 1 = e^{i'N} \tag{3.60}$$

Obtaining the natural logarithms on either sides of Eq. (3.51), the period N can be calculated as

$$N = \frac{1}{i'}\ln\left(1 + \frac{F(e^{i'} - 1)}{A}\right) \tag{3.61}$$

Example 3.11 Time Taken to Achieve Investment Goal

Adam Jackson met with his financial planner and came up with his financial goal of making 1 million dollars. He was willing to deposit $1050 every month with the financial planner, who was going to invest Mr. Jackson's monies into stocks, bonds, money market, and gold. The financial planner projected a return of a nominal rate of 12% compounded on a monthly basis. How many years will it take for

(i) Adam to achieve his financial goal using discrete compounding
(ii) Adam to achieve his financial goal using continuous compounding?

$$F/A = 10^6/1000 = 1000 \tag{3.62}$$

The effective interest rate for a nominal interest rate of 12% per month is 12.68% (3.63)

By Eq. (3.31) for discrete compounding (natural logarithms may be used) the time taken to attain the investment goal may be estimated as

$$N = \frac{\log\left(\frac{iF}{A} + 1\right)}{\log(1+i)} = \frac{\ln(0.1268 * 1000 + 1)}{\ln(1.1268)} = 40.63 years \tag{3.64}$$

By Eq. (3.61) for continuous compounding, the time taken to attain the investment goal may be estimated as

$$N = \frac{1}{i'}\ln\left(1 + \frac{F(e^{i'} - 1)}{A}\right) = \frac{1}{0.1268}\ln\left(1 + 1000 * (e^{0.1268} - 1)\right) = 38.75 years \tag{3.65}$$

The time taken to achieve the investment goal of Adam Jackson changes only by about 1.88 years, even when continuous compounding is considered.

Example 3.12 Biodiesel Production from Waste Cooking Oil

The study of alternate fuel sources to gasoline and coal is of national importance, given the supply-and-demand characteristics of fuels that are used extensively. Biodiesel is derived from vegetable oil or animal fats. It is recommended for use as a substitute for petroleum-based diesel because it is renewable and biodegradable. The common method of preparation of biodiesel is the transesterification of triacylglycerols in vegetable oil or animal fat with an alcohol such as methanol in the presence of an alkali or acid catalyst. The products are FAME (fatty acid methyl esters) and are called biodiesel. Glycerin is formed as a byproduct. Sodium hydroxide or potassium hydroxide is used as an alkali catalyst. A recent study [2] evaluated the economic feasibility of a plant producing approximately 22 million pounds per year of biodiesel. Tallow was transesterified with methanol in the presence of an alkali catalyst. A second plant is based on canola seed used as the raw material. A by-product of credit can be awarded for glycerin produced from seed crushing. A summary of the capital investment, process cost, and revenue accrued of the three different plants is shown in Table 3.4. The capital cost can be assumed to be paid off over a 30-year period at an interest charge of 6% per year.

Which process is the most profitable?

It is assumed that the capital cost is amortized at an interest rate of 6% per year for 30 years.

Plant I

(A/P, 6%, 30) from Table A-10, the capital recovery factor can be seen to be 0.072649

Profit = 2*22 – 12*(A/P, 6%,30) – 34 + 6 = 15.128 million

Revenue – capital recovery – cost of production + by-product credit = profit (3.66)

Plant II

(A/P, 6%, 30) from Table A-10, the capital recovery factor can be seen to be 0.072649

Profit = 4*1.7 – 1*(A/P, 6%,30) – 5.95 + 0.9 = 1.68 million

Revenue – capital recovery – cost of production + by-product credit = profit (3.67)

Plant III

(A/P, 6%, 30) from Table A-10 the capital recovery factor can be seen to be 0.072649

Profit = 3*2.2 – 3.12*(A/P, 6%,30) – 3.4 + 1.2 = 4.17 million

Revenue – capital recovery – cost of production + by-product credit = profit (3.68)

Thus, Plant I is the most profitable, followed by Plant III and then Plant II.

Table 3.4 Economic Evaluations for Biodiesel Production Plants

	Plant I Alkali-Catalyzed Continuous Process	Plant II Alkali-Catalyzed Batch Process	Plant III Alkali-Catalyzed Continuous Process
Plant Capacity	22 million pounds per year	1.7 million pounds per year	2.2 million pounds per year
Raw Material Used	Beef Tallow	Canola Oilseed	Animal Fats
Total Capital Cost	$12 million	$1 million	$3.12 million
Total Manufacturing Cost	$34 million	$5.95 million	$3.4 million
Glycerin Credit	$6 million	$0.9 million	$1.2 million
Price	$2/lb	$4/lb	$3/lb

Example 3.13 Credit Card Debt of U.S. Households

A recent survey shows there are about 114 million households in the United States. The average credit card debt carried per household is \$15,519. There are about 576.4 million credit cards in circulation. At an average credit card interest rate of 21% per year, what would the debt be if not paid back in another 10 years?

P = 576.4*15,519 = \$8.9451516 trillion (3.69)
(F/P,21%,10) = 6.73 (From Table A-21) (3.70)
F = 6.73*8.9451516 = \$60.2 trillion (3.71)

Example 3.14 Time Taken to Pay Off Credit Card Debt

In Example 3.11, how many years will it take for U.S. households to pay off their current household debts at a rate of 21% per year? Assume that the monthly payment per credit card is \$300 per month.

P/A = 15,519/3600 = 4.3108 (3.72)
From Table A-21, N can be seen to be $12 < N < 14$ (3.73)

Another way to calculate the number of years to pay off the debt is by applying Eq. (3.32)

$$N = \frac{\log\left(\frac{A}{A-iP}\right)}{\log(1+i)} = \frac{\ln\left(\frac{3600}{3600-3259}\right)}{\ln(1.21)} = 12.36\,years \tag{3.74}$$

Example 3.14 Deferred Annuity

Katy Gerstner, a widow, was planning for her son Joe's college education. What principal amount should Katy set aside now to allow for annual withdrawals of \$4500 each on Joe's 18th, 19th, 20th, and 21st birthdays? The interest rate is taken at 11% per year.

Four withdrawals are to be made of \$4500 each on Joe's 18th, 19th, 20th, and 21st birthdays, as shown in Figure 3.12. The present equivalent worth of this annuity on Joe's 17th birthday is P_{17}.

P_{17} = \$4500(P_{17}/A,11%,4)
(P_{17}/A, 11%, 4) from Table A-15 can be seen to be 3.1024 (3.75)
P_{17} = \$4500*3.1024 = \$13,961

The present equivalent worth of P_{17} can be calculated from a single payment compound factor as follows:

$P = P_{17}(1+i)^{-17}$ (3.76)

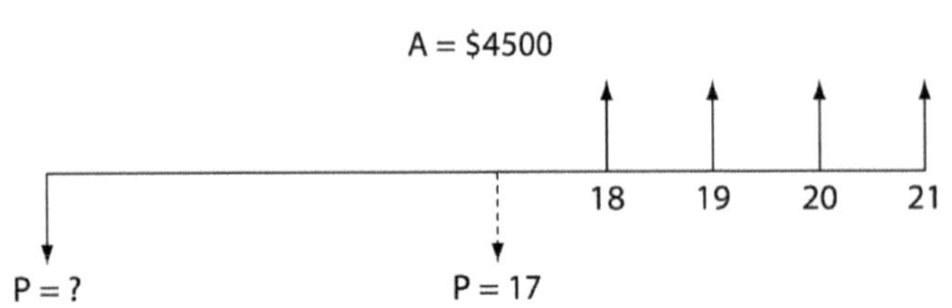

Figure 3.12 Deferred Annuity Payments for Joe Gerstner's College Education

(P/F, 11%, 17) from Table A-15 can be seen to be 0.170557 by interpolating between N= 16 and N = 18

$$P = P_{17}*0.170557 = \$13,961*0.170557 = \$2381.15 \tag{3.77}$$

3.5 Summary

Expressions to calculate simple interest and compound interest given the principal, P, interest rate i%, and pay period N are provided. The single payment compound amount factor, F/P, as a function of an annualized interest rate, i, is plotted in Figures 3.1 and 3.2 for different pay periods. The characteristics of the curve change for N > 12. Expressions for pay period N and interest rate i% in terms of the F and P are given in Eq. (3.6) and Eq. (3.7). The interest rate vs. F/P for different N is shown in Figure 3.3. *Nominal interest rates* get compounded on a different basis other than annual. The relation between nominal interest rate and *effective interest rate* is summarized in Table 3.1.

Cash Flow Diagrams are illustrations that show all the monetary transactions during the time of an enterprise. They can be used to calculate the equivalence of a series of uniform payments in terms of its present worth, P, or in terms of its future worth, F. The sum of a geometric series is used to develop an expression for F/A in terms of interest rate, i%, and pay period N for a uniform series of constant payments, A. F/A is called the *uniform series compound amount factor*. A/F is the *sinking fund factor*. Sinking fund factor is plotted vs. effective interest rate for different pay periods in Figures 3.5 and 3.6. In Appendix A, annuity tables are provided to read F/P, P/F, F/A, A/F, P/A, and A/P values for various values of interest rates ranging from 1/8% to 30%, and pay periods N ranging from 1 to 100. In addition to the annuity tables for the uniform series of payments A, annuity tables for uniform gradient series of payments G are also provided in Appendix A. Expressions for *uniform series present worth factor* are also developed. When N becomes infinity, perpetual payment schemes can be developed. Expressions for *capital recovery factor*, A/P are provided. Cash flow diagrams with a uniform gradient series of payments are discussed. Closed-form analytical expressions for P/G, F/G, and A/G are developed.

The inverse problem of finding N given F, A, and i% or P, A and i% is discussed. Closed-form analytical expressions for N are developed using logarithms. Graphical methods and interpolation in annuity tables may also be used. The inverse problem of finding interest rate i% given F, A, and N or P, A, and N are discussed. In addition to the use of annuity tables, graphical methods, a closed-form analytical expression is developed. This is achieved via the use of binomial expansion of $(1+i)^N$. As many terms in the infinite series as needed for desirable accuracy can be taken.

Worked examples on doubling time of investment, nominal interest rate, perpetual payment for college days prize, 0% interest rate, nest egg estimates, diversification of portfolio, royalty payment and investment, payment and reimbursement schemes, micro power plant, biodiesel production from waste cooking oil, credit card debt for all U.S. households, deferred annuity, time taken to pay off credit card debt, are provided. Exercises on monthly car payments, number of years taken to pay off the credit card debt, IRR of off-shore drilling, deferred interest rate charges, federal government debt, a Versailles-type home, variable interest rate, deferred payments, payment amount of a uniform series of payments, 0% interest, perpetual payment, design of a social security system for a town, and hydrogen from biomass are developed.

Continuous compounding methods, as opposed to discrete compounding methods, are also developed. The corresponding formulae for F/P, F/A, and P/A with continuous compounding that were presented for discrete compounding earlier are given side by side in Table 3.3. Appendix B provides the annuity tables for continuous compounding.

3.6 References

[1] W. G. Sullivan, E. M. Wicks, and C. P. Koelling, *Engineering Economy*, 14th Edition. Pearson Prentice Hall (2009), Upper Saddle River, NJ.

[2] Y. Zhang, M. A. Dube, D. D. McLean, and M. Kates, "Biodiesel Production from Waste Cooking Oil: Economic Assessment and Sensitivity Analysis," *Bioresource Technology*, Vol. 90, 3 (2003), 229–240.

[3] P. L. Spath, J. M. Lane, M. K. Mann, and W. A. Amos, "Update of Hydrogen from Biomass-Determination of the Delivered Cost of Hydrogen," Milestone Report for U.S. Department of Energy's Hydrogen Program (2001), NREL Laboratory, Golden, CO.

3.7 Exercises

1.0 *Simple Interest*

Calculate the simple interest on a loan of \$4000 at a rate of 8% per year for a period of four years.

2.0 *Compound Interest, Yearly*

What is the future worth of a principal amount of \$2000 after six years at an effective interest rate of 7%?

3.0 *Compound Interest, Weekly*

Your local bank branch recently announced a new savings plan with an interest rate of 0.16% compounded weekly. What is the interest payment on \$52,000 at the end of one year?

4.0 *Effective Interest Rate*

(i) What is the effective interest rate forNominal rate of 15% compounded daily

(ii) Nominal rate of 18% compounded quarterly

(iii) Nominal rate of 21% compounded monthly?

5.0 *Nominal Interest Rate*

Show that given the effective interest rate per year, the nominal rate for a said compounding period can be calculated as

$$i' = P(\,1+i)^{1/P} - 1)$$

where P is the number of compounding periods in a year.

6.0 Use the expression developed in Exercise 4.0 and calculate the nominal compounding rate on a weekly basis for

(i) An effective rate of 24.99%

(ii) A nominal rate of 10% on a daily basis.

7.0 *Monthly Car Payment*

Calculate the monthly payment on a 2007 Toyota Corolla that cost \$12,999. Another \$1000 was needed to obtain the title, license plate, and taxes. After a cash down of \$1500, the number of pay periods was 72 months. The interest rate per annum is 7%. A \$2500 one-time charge for power train warranty up to 100,000 miles was levied up front.

8.0 *Number of Years to Pay Off the Credit Card Debt*

You are hired by a leading credit card company, Ford Chase Bank. One of their directors, Julie Hollas, wants you to perform a small calculation for her. A customer wants to charge a Japanese robot to his credit card. The price of the robot, including sales tax, is $850.50. How many years will it take to pay off the credit card balance if the monthly payment is $16.7 and the annualized credit card interest rate is 23%?

9.0 *IRR of Off-Shore Drilling*

Gasoline prices have skyrocketed in the nation. The national average price per gallon of gasoline has risen to $4.00. The president is considering increasing off-shore drilling to get more oil. Each oil rig would cost $1 million. It would require 70,000 oil rigs to deliver 0.5 billion gallons of gas for automobiles every week. The utility costs run $120,000 per year. The situation is expected to continue for the next four years. Calculate the IRR for this investment. The MARR can be taken as 8.0%.

10.0 *Deferred Interest Charges*

Furniture-to-Stay offers you the following deal: a sofa, loveseat, and chair are available for $1250. The sofa has a built-in mattress that can be pulled out when you have guests over. This has an additional cost of $200. The delivery charge is $100 and a three-year warranty for stain resistance is available for $200. For the first three years, there is no interest rate charged, i.e., "No Interest 'Til 2012." For the following three years, an annualized interest rate of 12% is charged. Calculate the monthly payment over six years. Show the cash flow diagram using a neat schematic.

11.0 *Akshaya Bowl*

For their customers, Cowboy Investments are developing a new investment plan named "U-Pay-Now & I-Pay-Later." The deal is that the client pays $100 every month to Cowboy Investments. After a said period in a number of years, Cowboy Investments will have the client cease payments and begin to receive $1000 every month forever. At an effective interest rate of 12%, how many years would you recommend the said period be?

12.0 *Federal Government Debt*

The U.S. government owed about 2.6 trillion dollars in 1988. By 2008 this debt had increased to 9.6 trillion dollars. The federal government makes out interest on debt payments every year through interest on bonds issued, etc. What is the compounded percentage increase in federal debt over a period of 20 years?

13.0 *Versailles—Largest Home for Sale in the United States*

David Siegel, a timeshare tycoon, started work on a 90,000-sq.-ft. mansion called "Versailles" in Windermere, Florida. It has 23 bathrooms, 13 bedrooms, 10 kitchens, a 20-car garage with additional space for two limousines, three pools, a bowling alley, indoor roller rink, two-story movie theater, video arcade, fitness center, baseball fields, and two tennis courts. Siegel charges $75 million. The building can be finished upon carpeting, tiling, and interior wall construction for an additional $25 million. Calculate a 100-year monthly mortgage payment at an interest rate of 3.25% on the purchase of Versailles.

14.0 *Variable Interest Rate*

Recalculate the monthly mortgage payment for Versailles in problem 8.0 with the interest rate changing once every five years. The interest rate table is projected as follows for the next 100 years:

#	Years	Interest Rate i
1	2010–2015	3.255
2	2015–2020	4.0
3	2020–2025	5.0
4	2025–2030	6.0
5	2030–2035	6.5
6	2035–2040	7.0
7	2040–2045	4.5
8	2045–2050	4.0
9	2050–2055	5.0
10	2055–2060	5.5
11	2060–2065	5.75
12	2065–2070	6.0
13	2070–2075	8.0
14	2075–2080	10.0
15	2080–2085	12.0
16	2085–2090	16.0
17	2090–2095	20.0
18	2095–2100	18.0
19	2100–2105	16.0
20	2105–2110	14.0

15.0 *Deferred Payments*

Annette Kulifay went to medical school. She purchased a new car when she was in her third year of medical school. The car dealer allowed her to defer payments for 24 months. Annette makes 48 monthly payments thereafter. If the original promissory note was for $29,000 and interest rate is ¼% per month on the unpaid balance, how much will Annette's payments be ?

16.0 *Present Amount of a Series of Uniform Payments*

Calculate the present worth of a uniform series of payments of $1052 every month for 30 years at an interest rate of ¼% per month.

17.0 *Perpetual Payment*

A distinguished alumnus wants to give an endowment to his alma mater. The monies are to be used to issue a prize every year to pay the tuition fees for the student with the best character content. How much is present equivalent worth of a perpetual annual prize in the amount of $8000? A savvy investor has been found who guarantees payment of interest at an annual rate of 11%.

18.0 *0% Interest*

Retail giant Sears has a promotional offering to clear their inventory of Japanese robots. What would the monthly payment be for a robot that can move objects to the attic of a house during hurricane season? The price tag on the robot is $800. The customer can take six years to repay the amount.

19.0 *Nest Egg of Alice Smith*

In Example 3.4, Alice Smith signed up with her company's 401(k) retirement savings plan. Her employer matches dollar for dollar and pays as much per month into her retirement savings account. She is 26 years old. When she retires at 65 she hopes to obtain two lump-sum distributions in the amount of $250,000 each. She can expect a return of 10% compounded annually as interest for her plan. Calculate the monthly contribution Alice must make to achieve her retirement goals.

20.0 *Diversified Portfolio*

In Example 3.5, Darlene Shuster was the sole beneficiary of a life insurance benefit payment of $200,000 when her husband died. She invested the face amount as follows:

Gold Coins	$50,000
Stocks	$50,000
Bonds	$50,000
Money Market	$50,000.

The stock fund manager projects a rate of return of 11% per year. The bond funds' yield is about 8% per year. The money market rates are 3.5% for the years 2010–2015; 5.0% for the years 2015–2020; and 7.0% for the years 2020–2030. After 20 years, what would be the future worth of Ms. Shuster's inheritance? Gold coins appreciate in value at about 25% per year.

21.0 *George Tataseo's Royalty Payments and Investment*

In Example 3.6, George Tataseo writes books. He receives royalty payments ranging from 8%–15% of the cover price of every book sold in the market. The once-per-quarter payment is roughly about $5000. The expenses incurred every month during the preparation of the book are about $180. He invests the balance completely into gold coins. The return on gold coins is about 24.5% on an annualized basis. After 10 years, what would be the future worth of George's investments?

22.0 *U-Pay-Now & I-Pay-Later*

In Example 3.7, you are hired by Cowboy Investments upon graduation. They are developing a new investment plan called "U-Pay-Now & I-Pay-Later" for customers. The deal is that the client pays $1000 every month to Cowboy Investments. After a said period in a number of years, Cowboy Investments will have the client cease payments and the client will begin to receive $750 every month forever. At an 11% annualized interest rate (the historic performance of Dow Jones), how many years would you recommend the said period be?

23.0 In the new investment plan of Example 3.7, "U-Pay-Now & I-Pay-Later," consider the following goal of another client. The client is willing to wait for 15 years before receiving payments. She would like to receive $1200 per month from the plan. How much should she invest every month for the first 10 years at an annualized return of 11%?

24.0 *Social Security for an Independent Kancheepuram*

Per the 2001 census, Kancheepuram in India has a population of about 150,000 people; 60% of its population are in the workforce. The average age of a Kancheepuram resident is 40. The sages of Kanchi want to develop a social security system for all residents of Kancheepuram who have been in the workforce for a said period of time. The retirement age at Kancheepuram is 58. The average age of mortality is 70 years. For a monthly payment of Rs. 2000, what should be the monthly social security tax payment levied to the workforce? A rate of return on investments of 11% is guaranteed by investors who are also devotees of the Kanchi Mutt.

25.0 *Micro Power Plant*

In Example 3.8, the micro power plant of K. R. Sridhar, CEO of Bloom Box, was discussed. Bloom Box makes micro power plants using SOFC, solid oxide fuel cell technology. A Bloom Box can be purchased, say, for $2500. It consists of miniaturized fuel cells made of silica. The cost of electricity to power up a new home would be 8.0 cents per kWh. Should the existing utility company charge 13.0 cents per kWh, calculate the number of years it would take for Bloom Box to be a good investment for new homeowner Jack Tripper. Jack heads a family of six members with four children. Assume that 600 kWh of electricity is consumed every month at the Tripper residence. (i=10%).

26.0 *Deferred Annuity*

In Example 3.14, Katy Gerstner's deferred annuity was discussed. What should the interest rate be for the following goal: annual withdrawals of $8000 each on Joe's 18th, 19th, 20th, and 21st birthdays are to be made. The principal amount Katy has set aside is $5000.

27.0 *Hydrogen from Biomass by Batelle/FERCO Low-Pressure Process*

An alternative to fossil fuels is hydrogen. Hydrogen is manufactured from renewable resources such as sunlight, wind, and biomass and is more environmentally friendly. The Batelle/FERCO low-pressure process involves gasification of the biomass followed by steam reforming of the syngas produced. Hydrogen is produced by a water-gas shift reaction of syngas. Pressure swing adsorption is used to separate the hydrogen from the raw materials and by-products. This process is used at the existing McNeil small power plant in Burlington, Vermont [3]. The capital cost for a 22,737 kg/day plant can be taken as $53.8 million. The biomass feed rate is 314 Mg/day. At a selling price of $14.19 per GJ, what is the profit made using the process? The investors of the capital investment require a uniform series of payments over a 30-year period at a 3.25% annualized interest rate. The biomass feedstock cost can be taken as $16.50/dry Mg for the small plant. The calorific value of hydrogen is 141.8 MJ/kg. The plant can be assumed to be operating at 80% capacity utilization during the year. The utility costs can be taken as $5/kg of feedstock processed.

Chapter 4.0

Five Methods for Evaluation of Capital Project

Learning Objectives

- Present Worth Analysis
- Future Worth Analysis
- Annual Worth Analysis
- Internal Rate of Return, IRR
- External Rate of Return, ERR
- Payback Period

4.1 Overvew

The *profitability* of projects can be evaluated in terms of dollars and cents. In this chapter, five different methods are presented that can be used to determine the worthiness of undertaking an enterprise or project. The time taken for recovery of investment can also be calculated. The five different methods are:

(i) Present Worth, PW;
(ii) Future Worth, FW;
(iii) Annual Worth, AW;
(iv) Internal Rate of Return, IRR;
(v) External Rate of Return, ERR.

In addition to these five methods, the *payback period* is a method to estimate the time period over which the monies invested can be recovered. This is not recommended as a primary decision rule. Hence, it is not listed in the five methods mentioned above. The above methods can be used to make decisions based on dollars and cents.

A MARR, minimum acceptable rate of return, can be specified. In order to be selected as a project, a return from the business enterprise has to be established that exceeds a minimum specified level. This minimum level can be called a MARR. A number of factors can go into the determination of a MARR. These include, but are not limited to:

a) Amount of Monies;
b) Source of Monies;

c) Cost of Monies;
d) Number of Feasible Projects;
e) Purpose of Feasible Projects;
f) Risk of Investment Opportunities;
g) Organizational Ethos.

The cost of monies can be calculated using the methods discussed in Chapter 3.0.

4.2 Present Worth Analysis (PW)

The PW, present worth of a project, can be calculated by the equivalence of all cash inflows (such as receipts) and all cash outflows (such as expenses) to the current time at an interest rate that is a MARR. When the calculated PW is positive, the project is acceptable for further pursuits. The period of time, N, can be obtained suitably from the cash flow diagram. The factors considered during PW analysis are as follows:

(i) Purchase Price of Equipment Needed;
(ii) Estimated Useful Life;
(iii) Operational and Maintenance Costs;
(iv) Energy and Other Utility Costs;
(v) Salvage Value;
(vi) Revenue Accrued;
(vii) Interest Rate, i (%).

The effect of *inflation* and *deflation* on raw materials and energy costs can be taken into account as well, using inflation factors. This will be illustrated in Worked Example 4.4. The inflation factor gives the rate at which the prices go up every year. This information can be obtained from the Bureau of Labor Statistics. Consumer Price Indices are reported and available readily via Internet in the public literature.

When N becomes infinity, PW of such projects can also be called CW, the *capitalized worth* of the projects. The CW method is popular when endowments are established and public projects with indefinite lives are pursued.

Example 4.1 Hydrogen from Fast Pyrolysis and Steam Re-Forming [1]

Hydrogen is seriously considered as an alternative fuel in the transportation sector. In one process, the biomass is pyrolyzed and then steam re-formed to yield hydrogen. Biomass is dried and then converted to oil by very quick exposure to heated particles in a fluidized bed. The char and gases produced are combusted to supply heat to the reactor. The product oils are cooled and condensed. Bio-oil is then shipped by truck from the plant location(s) to the hydrogen production facility. By shipping the bio-oil, which has a higher energy density than the biomass, transportation costs are reduced. On arrival, the bio-oil is fractionated using water extraction into carbohydrate fraction and lignin fractions. The carbohydrate fraction is steam re-formed and the hydrogen that is formed is separated using PSA, pressure swing adsorption. Consider a plant that produces 75,790 kg/day of hydrogen by the pyrolysis process. The biomass feed rate is about 1806 Mg/day. Capital investment fixed costs are \$59.4 million. The selling price of hydrogen is \$10/GJ. The storage and transportation cost of hydrogen through railroad is \$0.94/GJ. The calorific value of hydrogen is 142 MJ/kg. At a MARR of 11%, calculate the PW of the project. The plant has operated for five years. The biomass feedstock cost was \$16.5/Mg. The plant operated at 80% time during the year. The costs of utility and wages of laborers can be lumped into 15c/kg of hydrogen produced.

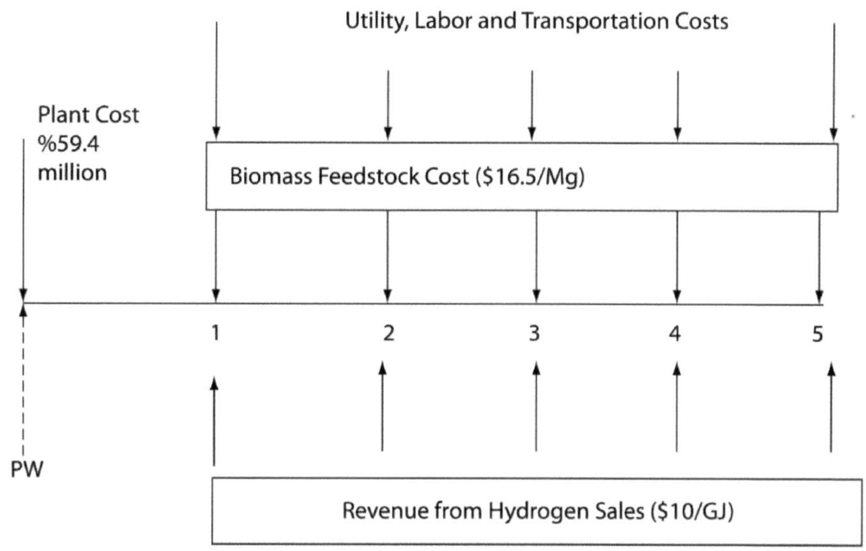

Figure 4.1 Cash Flow Diagram for Revenue and Costs for Hydrogen Production from Pyrolysis and Steam Re-Forming

PW = -$59.4 million (capital cost)
−16.5*1806*365*0.8 (P/A,11%,5) (raw material cost)
– 365*0.8*75,790*142/1000*0.94 (P/A,11%,5) (transportation cost)
– 0.15*75790*365*0.8/10^6(P/A, 11%,5) (utility and wages)
+ 10*75,790*365*0.8*142/1000(P/A,11%,5) (revenue from sales of hydrogen) (4.1)

(P/A,11%,5) = 3.6959 (From Table A-15) (4.2)

PW =- $59.4 million – 3.6959*8.7 – 3.6959*2.9603 – 3.6959*3.31 + 3.6959*31.43
= $1.433405 million = $1,433,405 (4.3)

A present worth of $1.433 million indicates that the project can be selected at 11% MARR. It can be seen that as the interest rate or MARR is increased, at some interest rate the PW will become 0. This interest rate later will be seen to be the IRR, the internal rate of return. For interest rates less than the IRR, the project will be profitable.

Example 4.2 Replacement for the World Trade Center (WTC)

One proposal to replace the World Trade Center (WTC) came from an architect and real estate tycoon named Donald Stone. He proposed another high-rise to replace the WTC, which was destroyed by terrorists on September 11, 2001. In a typical week, 50,000 people are expected to work in these towers and 200,000 visitors are expected to go the top floor to obtain a glimpse of New York City from the 110th floor. The cost of constructing the building is estimated at $5 billion. Assuming a net profit of collecting rent from the occupants is $250 per person per week and a visitor fee of $10, how many years would it take to see a profit? The interest rate can be taken to be 4%.

Rental Fee collected per year = 250*50,000*52/10^6 = $ 650 million (4.4)
Visitor Fee collected per year = 200,000*10*52/10^6 = $104 million (4.5)
A/P = (650+104)/5000 = 0.1508 (4.6)

From Table A-8, (4% annuity table) for A/P = 0.1508, N can be seen to be a little less than eight years. In a little less than eight years, the venture of replacing the WTC will be profitable.

Example 4.3 Capitalized Worth of Stone's Replacement for the WTC

In Example 4.2, calculate the capitalized worth of Stone's proposed replacement for the WTC destroyed by terrorists in the 2001 bombings. The interest rate is 4% and the revenues can be taken as the same in Example 4.2.

$$CW = (P/A,\ 4\%,\ \infty) \tag{4.7}$$

By Eq. (3.19)

$$P = \frac{A\left((1+i)^N - 1\right)}{i(1+i)^N} \tag{4.8}$$

When N°∞, Eq. (4.8) becomes

$$P = \frac{A\left(1 - \dfrac{1}{(1+i)^N}\right)}{i} = \frac{A}{i} \tag{4.9}$$

Thus, CW = ($650+104)/0.04 = $18.850 billion dollars.

Thus, the capitalized worth of the replacement for the WTC proposed by architect Stone would be $18.5 billion dollars.

4.3 Future Worth Analysis (FW)

The FW (future worth) of a project can be calculated by the equivalence of all cash inflows such as receipts and all cash outflows such as expenses to a future time at an interest rate that is a MARR. When the calculated FW is positive, the project is acceptable for further pursuits. The period of time, N, can be obtained suitably from the cash flow diagram.

Example 4.4 University Apartments

A group of university alumni and professors invests $25 million to build 250 new student apartments near a state university. The money is borrowed at the prime rate of 3.25% calculated on a yearly basis. The period of the loan is for 30 years. The variable expenses that include maintenance and operation run the group $3000 per apartment per year. The rental fees collected are about $12000 per apartment per year. The occupancy rate is about 70%. What is the future worth of the enterprise, should the salvage value of the apartments be $5 million at the end of 30 years?

(F/P,3.25%,30) = Interpolated from Table A-8 and Table A-7 for 4% & 3%

= 2.427262 +0.25*(3.243398-2.427262) = 2.6313 (4.10)

(F/A,3.25%,20) = Interpolated from Table A-8 and Table A-7 for 4% & 3%
= 47.575416+0.25(56.084938-47.575516) = 49.7028 (4.11)

F W = -25(F/P, 3.25%, 30) (principal invested)
3000*250*(F/A,3.25%,30) (annual operational expenses)
+12000*250*0.70(F/A,3.25%,30) (rental revenue)
+5 (salvage value) (4.12)

FW = -65.7825-37.2771+104.37588+5 = $6.31628 million. (4.13)

It is profitable to invest in the apartments. The FW of the project would be $6.163 million.

Example 4.5 Present Worth of a Sugar Mill

A business plan was presented to get a sugar mill installed in rural Texas. The cost of raw materials such as sugarcane and utility costs rise every year due to inflation. The revenue from the sale of sugar rises and falls in synchrony with the boom-and-bust cycles of the economy. The EOY (end of year) revenues and costs are shown in Table 4-1.

Table 4-1 EOY Receipts and Costs

Year	Receipts Millions $	Cost Millions $
1	2.3	1.00
2	2.5	1.10
3	2	1.21
4	1.5	1.33
5	2	1.46
6	2.5	1.61
7	3	1.77
8	3.5	1.95
9	4	2.14
10	3.5	2.36
11	3	2.59

The capital cost of the sugar mill, including land and all the necessary equipment, is estimated at $8 million. What is the PW of the sugar business at an interest rate of 3%?

Another table is generated using an MS Excel spreadsheet on a desktop computer. Two more columns are added to Table 4-1. One is the profit, Pr, obtained each year. This is determined by subtracting the costs from the receipts. The contribution of each cell in the next column to the present worth is obtained using the relation for compound interest given by Eq. (3.5)

$$PW_J = \frac{\Pr_J}{(1+i)^J} \qquad (4.14)$$

where $\Pr_J$ is the profit obtained in year J. J varies from 1 to 11 as given in column 1.

Table 4-2 Present Worth Analysis of EOY Cash Flows (Millions $) in Table 4-1

Year	Receipts	Cost	Profit	(P/F,3%,Year)
1	2.3	1.00	1.30	1.262136
2	2.5	1.10	1.40	1.319634
3	2	1.21	0.79	0.722962
4	1.5	1.33	0.17	0.150154
5	2	1.46	0.54	0.462272
6	2.5	1.61	0.89	0.744934
7	3	1.77	1.23	0.998833
8	3.5	1.95	1.55	1.224597
9	4	2.14	1.86	1.422785
10	3.5	2.36	1.14	0.849794
11	3	2.59	0.41	0.293489
			Total	9.451591

PW = -8.0 + SUM(P/F,3%,Year)

=-8.0 + 9.451591 = +1.451591. (4.15)

Thus, the PW of the sugar business is $1 million and 451,591. It is profitable to start the sugar from sugarcane business.

Example 4.6 Invest in Gold or Stock Market

The gold prices and DJIA (Dow Jones Industrial Average) current, 50, and 100 years ago are given in Table 4-3.

Table 4-3 Gold and DJIA Current, 50, and 100 Years Ago

Year	Gold (per ounce)	Stock (DJIA Dow Jones Industrial Average)
1909	$20.67	70
1959	$35.25	600
2009	$1087.50	10,000

Which would be a better investment of $50,000 today in another 30 years, gold or stocks ?
Gold has performed at an annualized rate of

F/P = 1087.5/20.67 = 52.61 (4.16)

For N = 100 the interest rate can be seen from Appendix A as roughly 4%

FW (gold) = 50,000(F/P, 4%, 30) (4.17)

From Table A-8, (F/P, 4%, 30) = 3.243398*50,000 = $162,115
DJIA has performed at an annualized rate of

$$F/P = 10{,}000/70 = 142.86 \quad (4.18)$$

From Appendix A for N = 100, F/P = 142.86 the interest rate can be seen to be 5%

$$\text{From Table A-9 } (F/P,5\%,30) = 4.321942*50{,}000 = \$216{,}097 \quad (4.19)$$

$219,097 is greater than $162,115. Hence, it is better to invest in the U.S. stock market rather than in gold. The 5% is the historic performance of DJIA. notwithstanding the Great Depression and stock market corrections in 1987 and 2007. The gold price has increased at 4% despite the government changes in the early 1970s.

Example 4.7 Electric/Gas Hybrid Vehicle

A hybrid electric/gas car such as the 2010 Toyota Prius costs about $29,000. The achievable fuel economy using the vehicle is 50 miles per gallon. A comparable all-gasoline vehicle such as the 2010 Toyota Corolla costs $21,000, and the fuel economy for the Corolla is 32 miles per gallon. At what price of gasoline is it more attractive to purchase the Toyota Prius? It is estimated that the average passenger travels 15,000 miles per year and the life of an automobile is 100,000 miles. The interest rate may be taken as 11%.

The cash flow diagram for Example 4.7 is shown in Figure 4.2.

Let the price of gasoline per gallon be Z $/gallon. Assume that the lives of both the Toyota Corolla and the Toyota Prius are seven years and the passenger drives either vehicle at 15,000 miles per year.

PW of all payments in order to own the Toyota Prius, PW_{prius}, is;

$$PW_{prius} = -\$29{,}000 - Z*(15{,}000/50)*(P/A,11\%,7) \quad (4.20)$$

From Table A-15

$$(P/A,11\%,7) = ½*(4.2305+5.1461) = 4.6883$$
$$PW_{prius} = -29{,}000 - 1407Z \quad (4.21)$$

PW of all payments in order to own the Toyota Corolla, $PW_{corolla}$ is

$$PW_{corolla} = -\$21{,}000 - Z*(15{,}000/32)*(P/A,11\%,7) \quad (4.22)$$

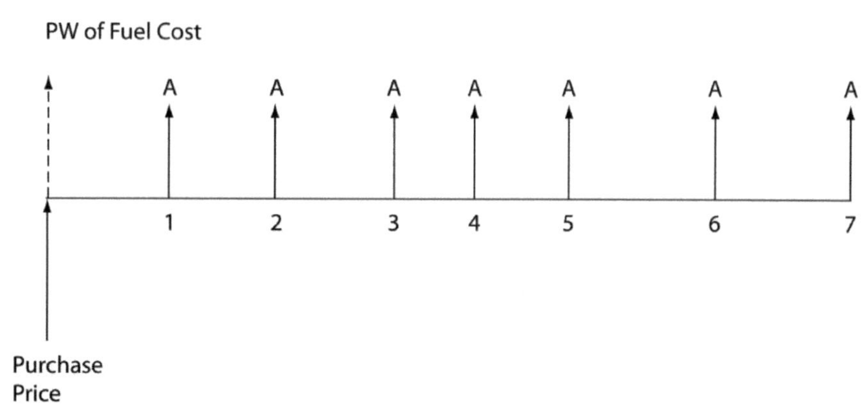

Figure 4.2 Cash Flow Diagram of Fuel Cost for Toyota Prius and Toyota Corolla

From Table A-15

$(P/A, 11\%, 7) = ½*(4.2305+5.1461) = 4.6883$

$$PW_{corolla} = -21{,}000 - 2198Z \tag{4.23}$$

At a certain gasoline price, Z, the PW_{prius} will become equal with that of $PW_{corolla}$. Thus, Eq. (4.23) and Eq. (4.21) can be set equal to each other.

$$-29{,}000 - 1407Z = -21{,}000 - 2198Z \tag{4.24}$$

$$\text{Or, } Z = \frac{(29{,}000 - 21{,}000)}{(2198 - 1407)} = 10.13$$

For gasoline prices greater than $10.13, the Toyota Prius is a lower-cost alternative compared with the Toyota Corolla. For gasoline prices less than $10.13, the Corolla is a better alternative compared to the Prius.

Example 4.8 Effect of Inflation on PW

The inflation rates for the past 10 years (1999–2009) are given below in Table 4-4. This table was prepared using the information provided by the Bureau of Labor Statistics.

Table 4-4 Inflation Rates for 1999–2009

	(%)
Year	Inflation
1999	2.19
2000	3.38
2001	2.83
2002	1.59
2003	2.27
2004	2.68
2005	3.39
2006	3.24
2007	2.85
2008	3.85
2009	-0.34

In 1999 dollars, calculate the PW (present worth) of an ABS (acrylonitrile butadiene styrene) engineering thermoplastic continuous polymerization plant. The capital cost of a new plant in 1999 dollars was $80 million. The selling price of ABS is $4 per pound. The raw materials cost rises every year on account of inflation. The price in year 1998 was $2.8 per pound of ABS sold. The process cost also goes up with inflation on account of increase in utility costs and wages to workers. The process cost can be taken as 30 cents per pound of ABS produced in 1998. The production rate from the two CSTR and falling strand devolatilizer plant is 10,000 lb/hr. The plant can be expected to run about 85% of the time. The selling price of ABS remains flat during the 10-year period. An interest rate of 11% may be assumed.

The inflation rates given in Table 4-4 were used to calculate the materials cost and process cost. This is shown in the column in Table 4-5 under Cost–Materials and Cost–Process. Each row was $(1+f_i)$ times the previous row, where f_i is the inflation rate. Inflation rate was calculated by dividing the values provided under the column (%) inflation by 100. The revenue was calculated at a flat price of $4 per lb. of ABS multiplied with the quantity of ABS produced, i.e., 74.46 million lbs. This was arrived at from the production rate of 10,000 lb/hr multiplied with the operating time of the plant 24*365*0.85, where 0.85 is the utilization factor. The inflation effects on the materials and process costs resulted in loss in the years 2008 and 2009. In other years there was a profit. The profit was obtained by subtracting the total expenses of materials and process from the revenue from sales of ABS. The PW contribution of each cell in the profit column was calculated using the single payment compound amount factor of $\frac{Pr_J}{(1+i)^{Year-1999}}$ where J varied from 0 to 10 and Pr_J was the profit earned in each year. All the PW contributions from 1999 to 2009 were added using the SUM command in MS Excel spreadsheets on a desktop computer. The capital cost of $80 million was also subtracted as a one-time charge. No salvage value was attributed in 2009. The PW of the ABS plant in 1999 dollars was seen to be $157.07 million.

Example 4.9 Life-Cycle Cost Analysis of HVAC Systems

Life-cycle cost analysis has been found to be advantageous over impressions created from one-time sticker-price numbers. A piece of equipment that may appear initially attractive due to its lower cost may "nickel and dime" you in costs during its operation. Maintenance costs may mushroom and repair costs may make another

Table 4-5 Present Worth Analysis with Inflation Effects Accounted For

Effect of Inflation				(%)	Cost	Cost	Revenue	Profit	PW
			Year	Inflation	Materials	Process	Millions $	Million $	Million $
			1999	2.19	2.861	0.3066	297.84	61.95891	$61.96
Product Rate	10000	lb/hr	2000	3.38	2.958	0.3169	297.84	53.98613	$48.64
ABS Price	4	$/lb	2001	2.83	3.042	0.3259	297.84	47.08507	$38.22
Materials	2.8	$/lb	2002	1.59	3.090	0.3311	297.84	43.09806	$31.51
Process Cost	0.3	$/lb	2003	2.27	3.160	0.3386	297.84	37.31542	$24.58
			2004	2.68	3.245	0.3477	297.84	30.33336	$18.00
Production (lbs)	7E+07		2005	3.39	3.355	0.3595	297.84	21.26489	$11.37
	74.46	million lb	2006	3.24	3.464	0.3711	297.84	12.30385	$5.93
i	11	%	2007	2.85	3.562	0.3817	297.84	4.16607	$1.81
			2008	3.85	3.700	0.3964	297.84	-7.14037	($2.79)
			2009	-0.34	3.687	0.3950	297.84	-6.10344	($2.15)
Capital Cost of Plant									($80)
								Total	$157.07

alternative a better prospect. So how do you arrive at which equipment to select? This can be best accomplished by a life-cycle cost analysis. Here all the relevant costs are considered by the use of PW analysis.

Consider the residence of Sharron Stone. A new HVAC (heating, ventilation, and air conditioning) system was installed in her residence. The estimated useful life is 15 years. A novel high-efficiency gas furnace with add-on air conditioner costs $11,183. The energy costs per year are $928 and maintenance cost of $60. The salvage value of the equipment is $60. Use PW analysis and calculate its life-cycle cost. An interest rate for funds can be taken as 5%.

$$\text{Life Cycle Cost of HVAC, } C_L = \$11{,}183 - 60^*(P/F,5\%,15) + (\$928+\$60)^*(P/A,5\%,15) \tag{4.25}$$

From Table A-9,

$(P/F,5\%,15) = ½^*(0.505068+0.458112) = 0.48159$

$(P/A, 5\%, 15) = 1/2^*(9.8986+10.8378) = 10.3682$

Eq. (4.25) becomes

$$C_L = \$11{,}183-\$60^*0.48149+\$988^*10.3682 = \$21{,}397.89 \tag{4.26}$$

The life-cycle costs associated using PW analysis of the HVAC equipment in Stone's residence was found to be $21,398.

Example 4.10 Municipal Garbage Collection Truck

The cost for the truck used for collecting garbage from residences is about $81,450. It can be used to serve 1000 households. A weekly charge per household of $5 can be collected. The gasoline costs run $150 per month. The labor costs for two drivers are $3200 per month. A one-time tax credit of $5000 from the federal government for recycling is given. Is it profitable to run the garbage business at a MARR of 11%. The life of the truck is expected to be eight years.

$$\begin{aligned} PW = & -\$81{,}450 \text{ (purchase price of truck)} \\ & + \$5000 \text{ (tax credit for recycling)} \\ & + 1000^*\$5^*4^*12(P/A,11\%,8) \text{ (revenue from garbage collection fees per year)} \\ & - 3200^*12(P/A,11\%,8) \text{ (salary for two drivers per year)} \\ & - \$150^*12(P/A,11\%,8) \text{ (gasoline cost of truck per year)} \end{aligned} \tag{4.27}$$

$(P/A,11\%,8) = 5.1461$ (from Table A-15)

$$\begin{aligned} PW &= -\$81{,}450+\$5{,}000+\$240{,}000^*(5.1461)-\$36{,}000^*(5.1461)-\$1{,}800^*(5.1461) \\ &= -\$81{,}450 + \$5000 + \$1{,}235{,}064 - \$197{,}610.24 - \$9262.98 = \$951{,}741 \end{aligned} \tag{4.28}$$

It would be profitable to run the garbage business at a MARR of 11%.

Example 4.11 Hexane Extraction of Rice-Bran Oil

Rice-bran lipids can be extracted using hexane solvent from rice bran at a yield of about 26%. Rice is milled to produce the white long-grain rice sold in supermarkets. The outer layers of the rice kernel are removed. These layers include the hull, the germ, and the bran. The bran includes the testa, peripcarp, nucellus, and aleurone layers. Rice bran becomes rancid and has to be discarded in landfills. Parboiled rice bran has higher lipid levels than unstabilized rice bran. Rice-bran oil consists largely of saponifiable compounds. Hexane costs about $1.15

per gallon. It is an excellent solvent for nonpolar lipids. Calculate the PW of a hexane extraction unit. The following information was obtained from the *Journal of the American Oil Chemists' Association* [2] and modified suitably for the PW analysis in Example 4.11.

Table 4-6 Cost Data for Hexane Extraction Plant for Rice-Bran Oil

Description	Hexane Extraction Unit
Capital Investment	\$220,000
Manufacturing Cost	\$5.18 /year/kg of rice bran
Materials Cost	\$0.22/year/kg of rice bran
Labor Cost	\$9.62/hr
Revenue from Rice-Bran Oil	\$8.08/kg
Revenue from Rice Protein	\$4.928/kg
Production Rate	30.96 gal rice-bran oil/day
Useful Life of Equipment	10 years
Operational Hours per Year	8332 hrs
% Protein in Rice Bran	14.6%
Interest Rate, i	3.0%

Annual Labor Cost = 8332h*\$9.62 = \$80,154
Rice Bran Processed = 30.96*3.7854*365/0.26 = 164,525 kg/year
Annual Revenue = 30.96*3.7854*365*\$8.08 = \$345,634 (from rice-bran oil)
+ \$4.928*164525*0.146 = \$118,374 (4.29)

Annual Materials & Labor Cost = 164,525*(5.18+0.22) = \$888,436 (4.30)
(P/A,3%,10) = 8.530203 (From Table A-7)

PW = -\$220,000 + (-888,436 + 345,634+ 118,374 – 80,154) 8.530203 = -\$4.52418 million (4.31)
The hexane extraction of rice-bran oil is not a profitable venture.

4.4 Annual Worth Analysis (AW)

Another method of evaluating a business can be completed by reducing all cash flows, including the capital investment, and salvage value in terms of annualized cash flow at a certain interest rate, i. Thus, the AW (annual worth) of a project may be estimated as follows:

$$AW = R_k - E_k - \text{Capital Recovery Factor} + \text{Sinking Fund Factor} \quad (4.32)$$

Eq. (4.32) is calculated at a certain annualized interest rate i%. The capital recovery factor can be estimated from Eq. (3.20) and looked up in the annuity tables given in Appendix A or read from Figure 3.8. The capital recovery factor (A/P,i%,N) distributes all the capital investments into an annualized equivalent uniform series of payments. In a similar manner, the salvage value can be distributed using the sinking fund factor (A/F,i%,N) over a uniform series of payments.

Example 4.12 Annual Worth (AW) of a Biodiesel Plant in Taiwan [3]

Table 4-7 Cost and Revenue Data for Biodiesel Production in Taiwan

Biodiesel Production in Taiwan				
#	Description	Cost	Quantity	
1	Transesterification Reactor	$335,000		
2	Neutralization Reactor	$25,000		
3	Washing Column	$115,000		
4	FAME Distillation Column	$181,000		
5	Heat Exchangers	$4,000		
6	Pumps	$53,000		
7	Separator, Vacuum Systems	$52,000		
	Production Rate		800,000	kg/year
	Materials			
8	Soybean Oil Feedstock	$6,234,000		
9	Methanol	$196,000		
10	Catalyst and Solvent	$368,000		
	Labor Cost	$564,000		
	Utilities	$124,000		
	Overhead	$431,000		
	Revenue from Biodiesel	$6,845,000		
	Glycerin Credit	$3,038,000		

Biodiesel is produced by transesterification reactions. Triglycerides present in virgin soybean oil are reacted with anhydrous alcohol such as methanol, ethanol, propanal, etc. to form FAME, fatty acid methyl esters, or *biodiesel* and glycerol. The alkali catalyst used was sodium hydroxide, NaOH. It can potentially be used as an alternative fuel to the ones currently in vogue that tend to be culprits of pollution causing global warming, acid rain, greenhouse gas emissions, etc. Biodiesel is an attractive fuel due to the environmental benefits it has to offer. It is prepared from renewable energy resources such as vegetable oil. Using the information provided in Table 4-7, calculate the AW of the biodiesel plant. The plant is expected to last for 20 years. The interest rate for equivalence calculations can be taken as 3%. The main costs in these plants are the raw material costs.

The AW analysis is completed using an MS Excel spreadsheet as shown in Table 4-8. The capital cost is obtained by using the SUM command from cells D4 to D10. These are the costs of reactors, washing column, distillation column, heat exchangers, pumps, and vacuum systems. The capital cost of $765,000 is amortized over a 20-year period by using the capital recovery factor. The capital recovery factor is obtained from Table A-7 in Appendix A for (A/P,3%,20). This was found to be 0.067216. The materials costs include the soybean oil, methanol, catalyst, and solvent. The annual costs are obtained by adding the materials costs, labor costs, utility costs, and overhead costs. The annual revenue is obtained by adding the sales of biodiesel and glycerin. The AW was calculated as shown by plugging the information available into Eq. (4.32). The AW is about $1.915 million. Thus, it is profitable to operate the biodiesel plant as described in Taiwan.

Example 4.13 Debt Consolidation

A debt consolidation company worked out a payment plan for Mr. Dan Wardrop. Calculate the monthly payment at an annualized interest rate of 11%, should the loan be repaid in 26 years. Mr. Wardrop's credit card balances carried are shown in Table 4-9.

Table 4-8 AW Analysis of Biodiesel Plant in Taiwan

#	Description	Cost	Quantity	
1	Transesterification Reactor	$335,000		
2	Neutralization Reactor	$25,000		
3	Washing Column	$115,000		
4	FAME Distillation Column	$181,000		
5	Heat Exchangers	$4,000		
6	Pumps	$53,000		
7	Separator, Vacuum Systems	$52,000		
	Production Rate		800,000	kg/year
	Materials			
8	Soybean Oil Feedstock	$6,234,000		
9	Methanol	$196,000		
10	Catalyst and Solvent	$368,000		
	Labor Cost	$564,000		
	Utilities	$124,000		
	Overhead	$431,000		
	Revenue from Biodiesel	$6,845,000		
	Glycerin Credit	$3,038,000		
	Capital Cost	$765,000		SUM(D4:D10)
	Materials Cost	$6,798,000	per year	SUM(D13:D15)
	Labor, Utility, and Overhead	$1,119,000		SUM(D16:D18)
	Total Revenue	$9,883,000	per year	SUM(D19:D20)
	(A/P,3%,20)	0.067216	(From Table A-7)	0.067216
	Capital Recovery	$51,420.24	per year	D26*D22
	AW	$1,914,579.76		D25-D24-D23-D27

Table 4-9 Credit Card Balances of Mr. Dan Wardrop

#	Credit Card Company	Balance	Annualized Interest Rate (%)
1	Wachovia Platinum Visa	$11,500	19%
2	Sears MasterCard	$3,500	21%
3	Amazon Visa	$2,400	17%
4	Rooms-to-Go Furniture	$5000	15%
5	Macy's Department Store	$2000	25%
6	Gap Apparel	$400	19%
7	JC Penney Retail	$900	21%

$$AW = P/12\ (A/P,11\%,26) \qquad (4.33)$$

(A/P,11%,26) = 0.117813 (Table A-)

P = SUM(all balances in third Column in Table 4-9) = $25,700

$$\text{AW } 1/12\ (3027.70) = \$252.32 \tag{4.34}$$

Example 4.14 Solar Panel

Radio Shack has advertised Sunforce 130 W Solar panels with a Sharp module for $999. Consider purchase of five of these panels for a new home. The monthly utility bill in the new home runs about 750 kWh. The current utility company charges 12 cents for 1 kWh. How many years will it take for the new solar panels to be cost effective if purchased to replace the existing utility? The interest rate is about 11%.

$$\text{Annual Cost of Utilities: } 750*0.12*12 = \$90*12 = \$1008 \tag{4.35}$$

Cost of Solar Panels = 20*$999 = $4995
P/A = 4.9553
From Table A-15, N is about eight years.

It would take eight years for the investment in solar panels to be more attractive compared with the current utility company.

Another method to calculate the pay period is from Eq. (3.32)

$$1-\frac{iP}{A}=\frac{1}{(1+i)^N} \tag{4.36}$$

$$N=\frac{\log\left(\dfrac{A}{A-iP}\right)}{\log(1+i)}=\frac{\log(\dfrac{1008}{1008-0.11*4995})}{\log(1.11)}=7.55 years$$

N is plotted as a function of P/A for interest rate, i = 11% in Figure 4.3. It can be seen in Figure 4.3 that there is an abrupt change in curvature at about P/A = 8.0. The significance of this is that the annualized payment must be above a threshold amount to keep the repayment time within a reasonable timeframe. Should A be lowered any further, the time taken for repayment is large.

4.5 IRR (Internal Rate of Return)

The most widely used method of evaluation of a capital project is the Internal Rate of Return Method, or IRR. Other phrases used for the same method are investor's method, discounted cash flow method, profitability interest, etc. An interest rate is calculated, at which point the PW of the project goes from negative territory to positive territory. This interest rate is called the IRR of the project. In addition, the IRR rate has to be greater than the MARR rate in order for the project to be considered acceptable. The IRR rate is the interest rate at which point the equivalent worth of all cash outflows and equivalent worth of cash inflows are equated to each other. It can be viewed as another *break-even* point. At the IRR

$$\sum_{j=0}^{N} R_j (P/F, i''\%, j) = \sum_{j=0} E_j (P/F, i'\%, j) \tag{4.37}$$

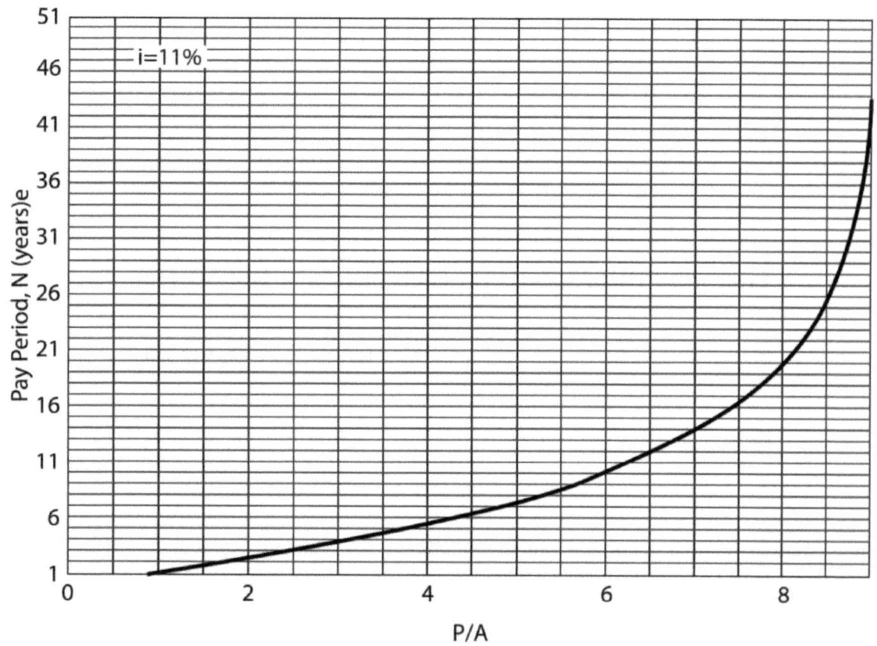

Figure 4.3 Pay Period N for Solar Panels to be Attractive Compared with Current Utility

The IRR can be calculated using graph paper. The PW of the project can be evaluated at various interest rates such as 2%, 4%, 6%, 8%, 10%, 12%, …, etc. The PW is plotted as a function of interest rate. The *x-intercept* or the interest rate at which the PW emerges into the positive territory from negative territory is called the IRR. Software is available to perform the trial-and-error calculations. For example, the MS Excel Spreadsheet has an IRR (range, guess) function call for obtaining the IRR for a set of cash flows.

Although a popular method, some pitfalls of an IRR include the occurrence of multiple values for the IRR. The variation of PW as a function of interest rate, i, is a function of several factors and may vary from project to project. When multiple values of an IRR result, one of the other methods of evaluation of the project such as FW, AW, payback period, etc. can be used instead of the IRR method. An IRR method also assumes that the revenues generated are reinvested back into the business. The ERR method does not assume such a thing.

Example 4.15 Profitability of Liquefaction Plants

The conversion of natural gas to liquid (GTL) fuel using the Fischer-Tropsch process was first developed in 1923. Syngas ($CO + H_2$) was converted into synthetic fuels. At a Society of Petroleum Engineers symposium, a novel method of evaluation of the economics of GTL plants was presented [4]. The capital expenses (CAPEX) are pegged to the production of one barrel of hydrocarbon liquid per day (BLPD). Annual operational expenses (OPEX) are expressed as a certain percentage of CAPEX. It is assumed that the overall thermal efficiency of GTL plants is 60% and the plant operates 330 days per annum. Consider one instance of CAPEX of $40,000/BLPD and OPEX of 7% of CAPEX. Plant is considered to be in existence for eight years. The price of crude oil is $37.65/bbl. Calculate the IRR for the project.

Basis of Production: 1 bbl a day of liquid fuel/oil

Annual Revenue = $37.65*330* 1 = $12,424.5

Capital Expenses = $40,000

Annual Expenses = 0.07*$40,000 = $2800

PW = -$40,000 + $12,424.5*(P/A,i%,8) – 2800*(P/A,i%,8)

The PW for different interest rates was calculated using an MS Excel Spreadsheet on a desktop computer. The P/A values for the interest rates used in the simulation were read from the annuity tables given in Appendix A. The values are given in Table 4-10 below. The PW as a function of interest rate is plotted in Figure 4.4. The IRR can be read from Figure 4.4 as 17.5%. Should the MARR be less than the IRR, the project is considered *profitable.*

Table 4-10 IRR Analysis for GTL Plant at 1 Bbl per Day

N	8		CAPEX	-$40,000
P/A	i (%)	PW	Revenue	$12,424.50
7.325481	2	$30,504.09	OPEX	-$2800
6.732745	4	$24,799.30		
6.2098	6	$19,766.22		
5.7466	8	$15,308.15		
5.3349	10	$11,345.75		
4.9676	12	$7,810.67		
4.4873	15	$3,188.02		
3.9544	19	-$1,940.88		
3.7256	21	-$4,142.96		
3.3289	25	-$7,961.00		
2.9247	30	-$11,851.22		

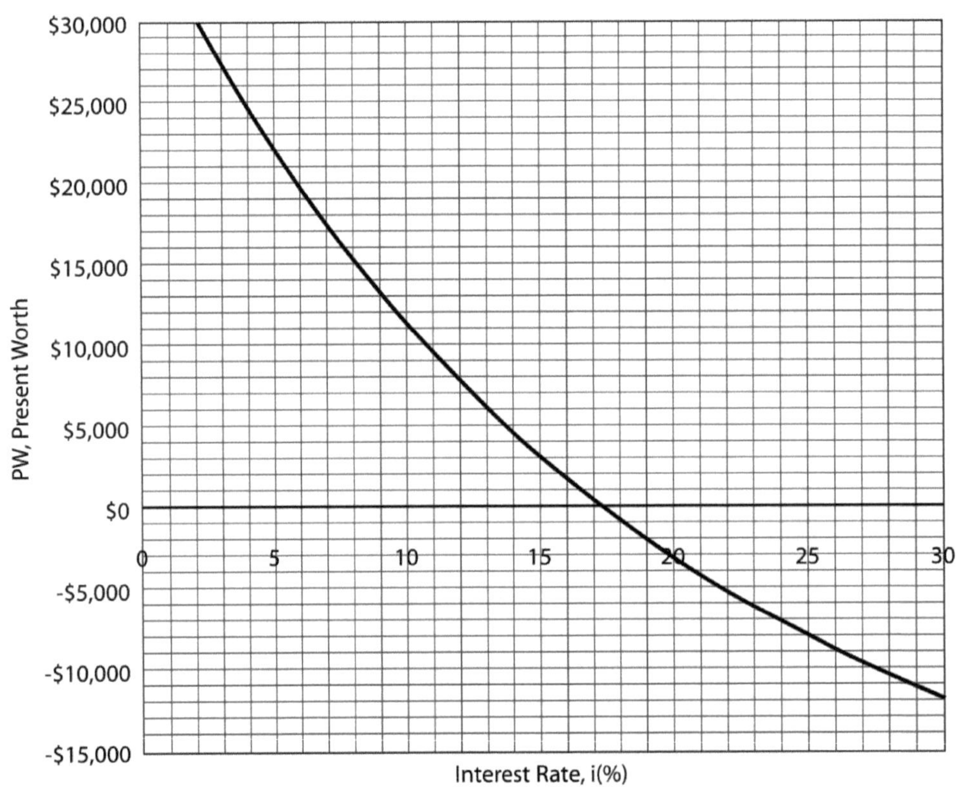

Figure 4.4 IRR Calculations for GTL Plant

Table 4-11 Cost Information for Six Methods

(M = million)

#	Description	Steam Stripping Process	Flash Fermentation	Single Column Distillation	Two Column Distillation	Distillation with Heat Pump	Flash and Vacuum Distillation
1	Capital Equipment Cost	$6.0M	$18.0M	$14M	$6M	$10M	$25M
2	Utility Cost	$5.5M/year	$7.5M/year	$6.5M/year	$3.5M/year	$3.6M/year	$5.5M/year
3	Feedstock Cost	$10.6M	$14M	$39.1M	$41.7M	$7.9M	$25.6M
4	Revenue	$50M	$50M	$50M	$50M	$50M	$50M
5	Plant Life	10 years	10 years	10 years	10 years	10 years	10 years
6	IRR	565%	157%	28%	77%	385%	77%

Example 4.16 Ethanol Production by Fermentation

Bioethanol can be produced by the fermentation of sugars obtained from saccharine biomass such as sugarcane or sugar beets, starchy biomass such as corn, or cellulosic biomass such as agricultural wastes. Bioethanol, which comes from renewable resources, can be used as an alternative to fossil fuel resources such as coal and petroleum. Six different methods have been identified for recovering ethanol from fermentation broth. These methods are:

(i) Steam Stripping and Distillation;
(ii) Flash Fermentation and Distillation;
(iii) Single Column Distillation;
(iv) Two Column Distillation;
(v) Distillation with Heat Pump;
(vi) Flash and Vacuum Distillation.

The ethanol production rate was set at 100 million liters/year in the process simulation study [5]. The cost data for cases where the ethanol concentration in the fermenter was 40 g/l is shown in Table 4-11. At an ethanol price of 50 cents per gallon, calculate the IRR for the six methods.

The IRR in row 6 of Table 4-11 was calculated using an MS Excel spreadsheet on a desktop computer. The PW as a function of interest rate for the six methods of recovery of ethanol from biofeedstock is shown in Figure 4.5.

4.6 ERR (External Rate of Return)

Some of the pitfalls encountered in the IRR method of evaluation of the capital projects are overcome in the ERR method. In the IRR method, the revenues generated are assumed to be reinvested at the IRR. An external interest rate, e, external to the project at which net cash flows required by a project over its life can be borrowed is identified. This is MARR, minimum acceptable rate of return. Identical results are generated from the methods of IRR and ERR when the ERR happens to equal the project's IRR.

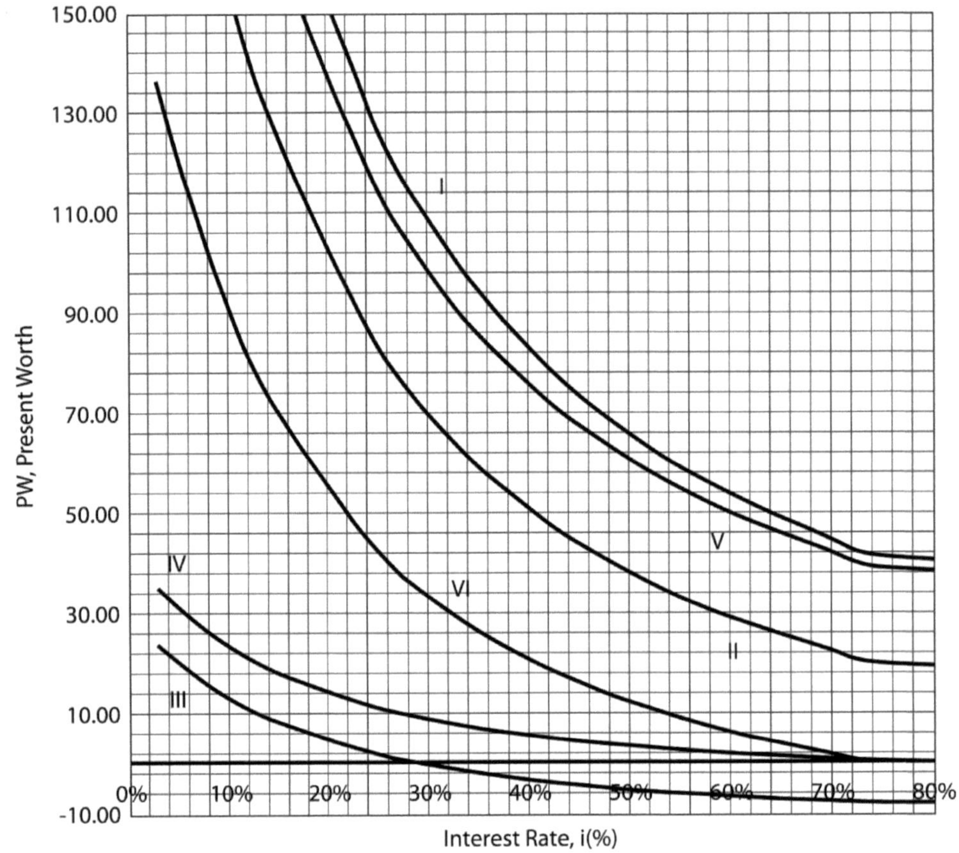

Figure 4.5 IRR Analysis for Six Methods of Recovery of Ethanol from Biomass

During the ERR procedure, all net cash outflows to time 0 at e% per compounding period are discounted. Then all net cash inflows are compounded to period N at e%. The ERR is obtained by establishment of equivalence of the two quantities.

$$\sum_{k=0}^{N} E_k (P/F, \varepsilon\%, k)(F/P, i''\%, N) = \sum_{k=0}^{N} R_k (F/P, \varepsilon\%, N-k)$$

Where R_k = excess of receipts over expensed in period k

E_k – excess of expensed over receipts in period k

N – project period

ε - external reinvestment rate per period

4.7 Payback Period

Payback period is the number of years for the cash inflows to equal the cash outflows. It is a measure of the liquidity. It is a simple method. A number of years for break-even point attainment is obtained. But the cash flows occurring after the payback period q is not available using this method. The project desirability is not clear. The speed at which the investment can be recovered is calculated. It can be used as supplemental information to one of the other five methods discussed earlier in this chapter.

Example 4.17 Copper-Chlorine Thermochemical Cycles for Hydrogen Production

The hybrid copper-chlorine (CuCl) cycle is one promising method of a thermochemical cycle that can be used for hydrogen production with nuclear or solar heat. A CuCl cycle plant producing 125 MT H_2/day required 210 MW of thermal energy and 87.8 MW of electrical energy. The total capital investment for the CuCl plant using Turton et al.'s software package [6] can be estimated at \$131 million. Estimated price of hydrogen is \$5.0/kg. Calculate the payback period at an interest rate of 5%. The cost of electricity can be taken as \$60 per 1000 kWh. Bulk CuCl costs \$7200 per pound and bulk HCl costs \$241/metric ton. A 50% yield can be assumed for the three major reactions that are needed in the process: (i) electrolysis reaction, by which cupric chloride, $CuCl_2$, is produced at the anode and H_2 at the cathode; (ii) hydrolysis of cupric chloride leads to the formation of copper oxychloride; and (iii) molten cuprous chloride is produced from the decomposition reaction. Thermal utility is \$20 per 1000 kWh. Assume 1% loss of HCl and 1 ppm loss of CuCl during the operation of the cycle.

$2CuCl + 2HCl + 4H_2O$ ® $2CuCl_2.2H_2O + H_2$

$2CuCl_2 + H_2O$ ® $CuOCl_2 + 2HCl$

$CuOCl_2$ ® $\frac{1}{2} O_2 + 2CuCl$

Revenues from H_2 Sales per Year = (125)*(100)*(\$5)*365/10^6 = \$22.8125 million

Material Cost–HCl per Year = (125)*(\$241)*(365)*(18.25)*(0.01)/10^6 = \$2.0067 million

Material Cost–CuCl per Year = (125)*(100)*(\$7200*2.2)*(99)*(365)*(10^{-12})= \$7.1547 million

Thermal Energy Cost per Year = (\$20)*(210)*(365)/10^6 = \$1.533 million

Electric Energy Cost per Year = (\$60)*(87.8)*(365)/10^6 = \$1.92282 million

(Revenue–Expenses) per year = \$22.8125 - \$2.0067-\$7.1547-\$1.533-\$1.92282

= \$10.1953 million

Capital Cost = \$131 million

$$\frac{P}{A} = \frac{\$131}{\$10.1952} = 12.8491$$

From Table A-9, N for P/A = 12.8491 1t 5% interest rate can be seen to be 21 years.

4.6 Summary

There are five methods to evaluate a single project. These are: (i) PW (present worth) analysis; (ii) FW (future worth) analysis; (iii) AW (annual worth) analysis; (iv) IRR (internal rate of return) analysis; and (v) ERR (external rate of return) analysis. In addition to these five methods, a *payback period* can be calculated that denotes the time taken over which the monies invested can be recovered back. The MARR is the minimum acceptable rate of return. For a project to be selected, it has to have a rate of return (ROR) greater than that of a MARR.

The PW of a project can be estimated by finding out the equivalence of all the cash inflows (such as receipts) and cash outflows (such as expenses) to the present time at a specified interest rate that is usually greater than the MARR. When PW falls in positive territory, the project is considered to be acceptable. The project study period, N, may be determined after establishing the useful lives of critical equipment used in the execution of the project. The factors considered during PW analysis are capital costs incurred in the purchase of equipment, estimated useful life, variable costs of labor, materials, and utilities, salvage value, revenues accrued from sales of product and the interest rate. Inflation factors may be used to account for the variability in materials costs incurred. When the study period reached infinity, the PW becomes the CW, capitalized worth of the project. Examples of PW analysis were developed using hydrogen production from fast pyrolysis of biomass and steam re-forming, replacement for the World Trade Center (WTC), sugar mill, hybrid gas/electric vehicle, inflation rates seen in the U.S. economy, life-cycle cost analysis of HVAC systems, municipal garbage collection truck, and hexane extraction of rice-bran oil.

The FW of a project can be estimated by finding out the equivalence of all the cash inflows, such as receipts and all the cash outflows, such as expenses to a future time. Worked examples were developed on a university apartment business and investment in gold or stock.

The AW of a project can be estimated by reducing all cash flows including the capital investment, salvage value in terms of annualized cash flows at an interest rate i. Worked examples on AW analysis were implemented from case studies of the manufacture of a biodiesel plant in Taiwan and debt consolidation.

Worked examples on calculation of payback period were created for solar panels for homes and hydrogen from the thermochemical cycle of copper-chlorine.

The IRR is the most widely used method of evaluation of capital projects. The PW of the project is calculated as a function of interest rate i (%). The point in the graph of PW vs. interest rate where the PW goes from positive territory to negative territory is called the IRR. Worked examples on IRR analysis have been constructed for GTL (gas to liquefaction) plants and ethanol production via fermentation by six different methods.

There are some deficiencies in the IRR method of analysis. Results of multiple IRR is one of them. The ERR method is developed to overcome these deficiencies. The revenues generated are not assumed to be reinvested in this method. An external interest rate external to the project at which net cash flows required by a project over its life can be borrowed is used.

End-of-chapter exercises have been developed on the life-cycle costs of HVAC systems, hybrid electric vehicle, PEV (plug-in-electric vehicle), time taken to repay credit card balances, capitalized worth of a vacation condominium in Galveston, Texas, the AW of energy efficient windows, deferred interest charges, profitability of outpatient drug treatment center, PW of a convenience store and gas station complex, AW of public Internet, video and printing services, bonds, profitability of an olive oil business, IRR for the short path distillation method of extraction of paraffin wax, car rental business, payback period of a frozen yogurt parlor, FW of a coffeehouse, turnaround business, PW of an onshore oil well, a custom foam fabricator, polypropylene bag manufacture, activated carbon from bamboo, meglumine antimonite drug manufacture, ABS engineering, thermoplastic manufacture, hydrogen from biomass, use of additional wells in an oil field, long-term parking lot, recycling of plastics using closed-loop granulation, solar hats, savings from using PFR (plug flow reactor) over CSTRs, and the use of gradient series.

4.7 References

[1] P. L. Spath, J. M. Lane, M. K. Mann, and W. A. Amos, "Update of Hydrogen from Biomass-Determination of the Delivered Cost of Hydrogen," Milestone Report for U.S. Department of Energy's Hydrogen Program (2001), NREL Laboratory, Golden, CO.

[2] D. Sparks, R. Hernandez, M. Zappi, D. Blackwell, and T. Fleming, "Extraction of Rice Bran Oil Using Supercritical Carbon Dioxide and Propane, "*Journal of the American Oil Chemists' Society*, Vol. 83, 10 (2006), 885–891.
[3] Y. D. You, J. L. Shie, C. Y. Chang, S. H. Huang, C. Y. Pai, Y. H. Yu, and C. H. Chang, "Economic Cost Analysis of Biodiesel Production: Case in Soybean Oil," *Energy & Fuels*, Vol. 22 (2008), 182–189.
[4] F. T. Al-Saadoon, "Economics of GTL Plants," SPE Hydrocarbon Economics and Evaluation Symposium, April 2005, Dallas, TX.
[5] J. B. Haelssig, A. Y. Tremblay, and J. Thibault, "Technical Economic Considerations for Various Recovery Schemes in Ethanol Production by Fermentation," Ind. Eng. Chem. Res., Vol. 47 (2008), 6185–6191.
[6] R. Turton, R. C. Bailie, W. B. Whiting, and J. A. Shaeiwitz, *Analysis, Synthesis and Design of Chemical Processes*. Prentice Hall (2003), Upper Saddle River, NJ.
[7] K. H. Keith, J. P. Choy, J. P. Barford, and G. McKay, "Production of Activated Carbon from Bamboo Scaffolding Waste—Process Design, Evaluation and Sensitivity Analysis," *Chemical Engineering Journal*, 109 (2005), 147–165.

4.8 Exercises

1) Calculate the life-cycle costs associated with the HVAC equipment installed in Don Cameron's residence. A novel gas furnace with an add-on air conditioner was part of the HVAC package. The information given is as follows:

2) Calculate the life-cycle costs associated with the HVAC equipment installed in Marc St. Onge's residence. A heat pump with auxiliary gas backup was part of the package. The information given is as follows:

3) Hybrid Electric Vehicle

How much more can be paid for a hybrid electric/gas car compared with a Toyota Corolla at the same total cost to the passenger? The fuel economy that can be achieved using the hybrid vehicle is 50 miles per gallon. A comparable all-gasoline car such as a 2010 Toyota Corolla costs $21,000; the fuel economy achieved in the Corolla is 32 miles per gallon. The price of gasoline can be taken as $3.50 per gallon. It is estimated that the average passenger travels 15,000 miles per year and the life of an automobile is 105,000 miles. The interest rate may be taken as 8%.

4) Time Taken to Repay Credit Card Balances

Calculate the time period in years that it would take for Mr. Dan Wardrop to repay his credit cards for the balances at the interest rates shown in Table 4-9 in Example 4.9 for:

Table 4-12 Don Cameron's HVAC System

Category	Cameron's HVAC
Useful Life	15 years
Purchase Price of Equipment	$11,733
Electric and Gas Utilities	$1200 per year
Maintenance Cost	$75 per year
Interest Rate, i (%)	8.0
Salvage Value	$40

(a) Platinum Visa at a monthly payment of $190;
(b) Sears MasterCard at a monthly payment of $65;
(c) Amazon Visa at a monthly payment of $40;
(d) Rooms-to-Go Furniture at a monthly payment of $70;
(e) Macy's Department Store at a monthly payment of $50;
(f) Gap Apparel at a monthly payment of $15;
(g) JC Penney Retail at a monthly payment of $18.

5) Capitalized Worth of a Vacation Condominium in Galveston Beach, Texas

A vacation rental in Galveston, Texas, charges rental fees of $1250 per week. What is the CW (capitalized worth) of a uniform series of such rental payments for the condominium? The interest rate is about 6%.

6) Annual Worth of Energy-Efficient Windows

Window World claims they can install vinyl replacement windows in your new home. These double-hung, premium white windows are expected to be more energy efficient and can result in savings on energy utility bills. The federal government gives a tax credit for $1500. Each window is priced at $189. The number of windows to be installed can be taken as 14. What should the monthly savings in energy be to justify this purchase? The interest rate is 6% and the life of the windows may be taken as 20 years.

7) Variable Interest Rate

Bel Furniture has advertised in the Sunday edition of the *Houston Chronicle* "no down payment, no interest until 2013." Ms. Lori Heffelfinger walks away with a leather sofa at $399.99, an 18-piece mini-theater seating at $1699.99, a five-piece marble-top table with four twisted chairs, a huge 38" x 66" table at $499.99, and a five-piece bedroom set with queen headboard, footboard, rails, and nightstands at $499.99. If Lori is willing to repay Bel Furniture in 11 years, and should the credit interest rate after 2013 be 11%, what is the monthly payment for Lori?

8) Outpatient Drug Treatment Center

A successful outpatient addiction treatment center with methadone maintenance and intensive counseling was established in 2002. Addiction disease is an epidemic. The treatment center has 14 employees, who find working

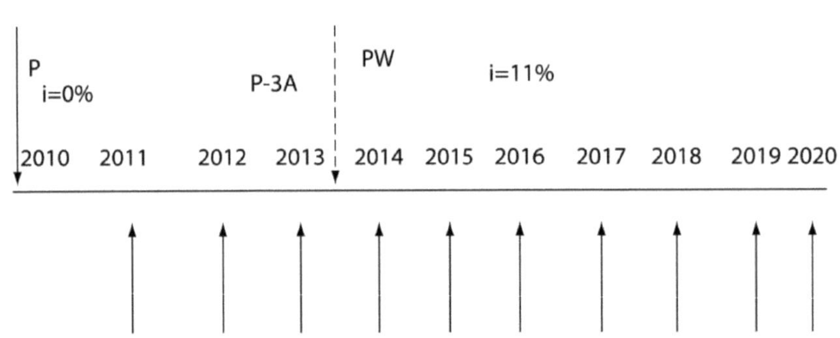

Figure 4.6 Cash Flow Diagram for Furniture Purchase from Bel Furniture with Variable Interest Rates

in the center emotionally rewarding. The asking price of the business is $3.5 million dollars. The net profit generated per year is around $650,000. At an interest rate of 8%, what would be the future worth of the business 10 years from now if the treatment center were purchased today?

9) Gas Station and Convenience Store

A lucrative group of businesses includes a gas station, convenience store, tunnel car wash, and dog wash, as well as the land and improvements. An average of 2 million gallons of gasoline are pumped every year at the gas station. Over 700 transactions per day can be expected at the convenience store at an average transaction of $30. In 2009, 75,000 cars were washed at the conveyorized soft-cloth car wash. The system can wash over 120 cars per hour. The average cost of gasoline per gallon in 2009 was $3.50. What is the present worth of the business? The group of businesses was purchased at $3.59 million. The convenience store complex is expected to be in use for 10 years and the interest rate can be taken as 8%. Each car wash fetched an average of $5 per wash. Expenses are about $40,000 per day.

10) Public Internet, Video Chat, and Printing Services

The service offers public Internet, video chat, and printing services in Houston, Texas. It requires 750 sq. ft. of office space. It has 100 high-traffic locations in the city. The company also licenses its services to locations in New York City, San Francisco, Los Angeles, and Las Vegas. The service is ordered by quick-service restaurants and independent food and beverage purveyors. The company's proprietary software and systems enable the company to deliver a reliable, quality service to its customers with minimal employee resources and overhead. The company's services are managed and supported by three full-time employees. End-user demand for the company's services is primarily driven by demand for printing maps, tickets, and other tourist-related information and by the growing use (by both tourists and full-time residents) of social media such as Facebook and other Web 2.0 services. This service was purchased for $1.4 million dollars. It is expected to be in use for 12 years. The annual revenue is about $1.95 million and expenses run about $1.45 million per year. What is the AW of the business at an interest rate of 3.0%?

11.0 Chevy Volt and Solar Panels

The 2011 Chevrolet Volt was unveiled recently by the CEO of General Motors Corp. It is a plugin electric vehicle (PEV). It has a better *range*. For up to the first 40 miles, the Volt is powered by electric energy stored in its onboard lithium-ion batteries, which are charged by connection to an electrical power outlet. The 16 kWh battery pack can be fully charged by connecting to a residential electrical outlet operated at 12–240 Volt AC. The cost of the vehicle is about $41,000. A $7500 federal tax credit can be expected for purchasing a PEV. The fuel efficiency is 230 mpg of gasoline, plus 25 kWh per 100 miles. A comparable all-gasoline vehicle costs about $23,000 and provides a fuel efficiency of 30 mpg. The car is expected to last for seven years. The average American drives 15,000 miles per year. Further investment in solar panels that can charge the batteries can be made. Calculate how many solar panels can be purchased by the owner of a Chevy Volt for comparable cost between the Chevy Volt and solar panels and the all-gasoline-operated vehicle. The cost of solar panels may be taken as $199 per panel/7 years needed to charge the batteries in the Chevy Volt. The interest rate can be taken as 8%. The gasoline price is estimated at $4 per gallon.

12.0 Bonds Issued by the Private Sector

Busch Beer issued bonds worth $2 million with a 60-year life. The interest rate is 3% per year.

Table 4-14 Expenses and Revenue from Olive Oil Business

#	Expenses	Revenue
1	$400	$2000
2	$410	$2100
3	$420	$2200
4	$431	$2500
5	$420	$2400
6	$433	$2100
7	$446	$2000
8	$460	$2000

The bonds were sold at par value. The closing fees were $2500 and $100,000 for bookkeeping/year. What is the interest rate paid on the monies?

13.0 Olive Oil Business

Andrew Cuomo has convinced you to invest in his olive oil business. This requires an $8000 initial investment. The revenue and expenses expected every year are as follows:

You can sell your share of the business after eight years for $10,000. What is the profitability of the project at a MARR of 13%?

14.0 Short Path Distillation for Paraffin Wax Fractionation

Paraffin wax is present in crude oil reserves and can be produced using the Fischer-Tropsch process. Paraffin wax is widely used in applications such as treatment of paper and cardboard, printing inks, and in the food, cosmetic, and pharmaceutical industries. Prior to application, paraffin wax has to be de-oiled and fractionated and tailored for the given situation. SPD (short path distillation) is used to recover low volatility components from liquid mixtures. It can operate at low pressures and can be used to fractionate waxes. Low-pressure operation obviates high-temperature operation, which would result in degradation of the wax. Krause and Nieuwoudt [5] discuss an SPD process with four stages at a reflux ratio of 1.4. The capital cost is $17.1 million and the energy cost is $10.8/ton of wax. Calculate the IRR for a pay period of eight years. The capacity of the plant is 100,000 tons/year. The price of paraffin wax is $50/ton.

15.0 Frozen Yogurt Parlor

Jack Smith started a self-serve frozen yogurt parlor in Sacramento, California. Five yogurt machines were purchased at $20,000 each. Up to nine flavors are available for customers to select from. Customers serve their own yogurt and toppings. Jack then weighs the yogurt and collects the money. Around 48 customers can be seated in the 1200-sq-ft. outfit. The three-year lease expires in 2013. The number of transactions per day is about 150 at about $5 per transaction. Assume that the parlor is open for about 300 days in the year. Seven employees work for the parlor at an average salary of $20,000. What is the payback period at an interest rate of 8% ? The utility and material costs are lumped into $1.50 per transaction.

16.0 Coffeehouse

Sam Bush started a 2,280-sq.-ft. coffeehouse in New Milford, Connecticut, 15 years ago. All types of coffees are served, including locally roasted blends; 30 different tea selections are also available. Pastries and cookies are freshly baked on the premises. The coffeehouse serves food for breakfast and lunch only. An average of 250–300 customers per day stop in. The menu includes sandwiches, bagels, homemade muffins, cakes, bars, pies, puddings, and biscotti. During the day, soup, sandwiches, wraps, salads, and quiche are served. Wi-Fi is available, and entertainment with live music and other acts on most Friday nights is common. The revenues are about $328,000 per year. The costs are around $248,600 per year. Mr. Bush purchased the building at $160,000 in 1995. At an interest rate of 5%, what is the 2010 worth of the coffeehouse?

17.0 Libra Rental

Robert Byrd purchased six cars at a total cost of $120,000 to start Libra Rental. He charged $30/car/day for renting a car. The annual maintenance charges were about $150 per car per month. Calculate the IRR for the project for a period of six years. The car rental utilization rate is about 70%. The salvage value of the cars is $1800 per car at the end of the six-year period.

18.0 Turnaround

A cement factory held a loss for a three-year period. The EOY (end of year) cash flows were as follows:

The capital expenses to start the cement factory were $30,000. A Harvard MBA graduate was hired to turn around the company's fortunes. He ordered a new kiln at an additional expense of $10,000. This led to a lower cost of production. A marketing program was introduced, boosting sales. The next five-year cash flows are as follows:

At 8% interest rate, what is the change in the PW (present worth) of the cement factory before the restructuring in year 1 and after the restructuring in year 4?

Table 4-15 Cement Factory—Loss

EOY	Expenses	Revenues
1	$10,000	$8,000
2	$9,000	$6,000
3	$10,000	$9,000

Table 4-16 Cash Flows in the Restructured Cement Factory

EOY	Expenses	Revenues
4	$6,000	$9,500
5	$5,500	$10,000
6	$5,000	$10,500
7	$4,500	$11,000
8	$4,000	$11,500

19.0 Onshore Oil Well

The southern and central Great Plains and the southwestern regions of our nation are dotted by onshore wells. With the recent oil spill disaster in an offshore well (BP America, 2010), interest in onshore wells is on the rise. Onshore wells are less expensive than offshore wells, which must be operated in the depths of the oceans and seas. The capital cost of an onshore well is about \$1.1 million. The life of an oil well consists of the planning, drilling, completion, production, and abandonment phases. A well is created by drilling a hole 5–36" in diameter into the earth with a drilling rig that rotates a drill string with a bit attached. As the hole is drilled, sections of steel pipe, slightly smaller in diameter than the borehole, are placed in the hole. Cement may be placed outside the casing and the borehole. Texas Oil Field is asking \$145,000 to purchase their onshore oil business. Eight BOPD (barrels per day of crude oil) can be produced. The price of crude oil per barrel is \$80. The utility costs and labor wages can be lumped into \$10 per barrel of crude oil produced. For the life of the oil well estimated at 15 years at an interest rate of 6%, is it worth the asking price of the business?

20.0 Custom Foam Fabricator

Evaluate the future worth of a custom foam fabricator in Houston, Texas. The service offers custom packaging, architectural columns and crown molding, monument signs, and theatrical scenery. Coatings and stucco supplies are also sold. Automated equipment and skilled employees are used. Builders, contractors, sign-up companies, stucco distributors, churches, and schools are their customers. The outfit is housed on 1.5 acres in two metal shop buildings with an area of 12,575 sq. ft. The average annual expenses are estimated at \$673,000 and annual revenues are calculated at approximately \$750,000. A period of 21 years can be assumed at 5% interest rate.

21.0 Polypropylene Bag Manufacture

Polypropylene woven products such as fabrics and bags are used in packing agriculture products, military heavy-duty, chemical industry, and regular commercial sandbags. A bag manufacturer works out of Houston, Texas. and is a licensed USDA supplier. The customers include well-known companies such as ADM Milling, Cargill, Chevron Phillips, and JacintoPort International/Seaboard. The company serves as a federal contractor that supplies polypropylene products to the USDA (U.S. Department of Agriculture), the Department of Defense, the U.S. Army, FEMA, and other federal, state, and local entities. A twin-screw extruder was purchased at a price of \$5 million, with appropriate extrusion dies for bagging. The unit is housed on 10 acres of land. The land price is about \$7000 per acre in Texas. Two freestanding buildings are used at a built area of 50,507 sq. ft. The cost of the building may be taken as \$6.43 per sq. ft. Assuming an operation of 250 days in the year at a production rate of 10,000 lbs. per hour, calculate the AW (annual worth) of the business. The life of the extruder is about 21 years. The interest rate is about 6%. The price of a finished polypropylene bag is about 7.67 cents per pound. The utility and labor costs can be lumped into 1 cent per pound of finished polypropylene products.

22.0 Gradient Series

Consider a piece of equipment due to start operation in two years. Should it cost \$1000 to operate in the first year and the costs increase \$1000 each year for a six-year period, what is the PW (present worth) of the operating costs? The effective interest rate is 8%.

23.0 Manufacture of Activated Carbon from Bamboo

Bamboo is a tropical plant common in China, Thailand, and Vietnam. Bamboo is available from construction projects as scaffolding waste. A range of carbon chars and activated carbons can be prepared from bamboo waste. The bamboo cane can be carbonized/charred in a furnace at high temperature under anaerobic conditions in order to produce carbon chars. To increase the *profitability*, the plant is integrated with a thermal electric generating boiler plant. The process consists of reacting bamboo with KOH, potassium hydroxide, in a CSTR. The alkali treatment results in char formation. The activated carbon is made in a carbonization furnace at 700°C. KOH is recovered by washing the solid effluent from the furnace with cold water and KOH is recycled back to the CSTR. The volatile generated is converted to water and CO_2 in a combustion chamber. The heat liberated in this step is used to generate steam, using heat exchanger tube bundles. The steam is used to turn turbines and electricity is generated. This can result in revenues that may improve the profitability of the project. Further, by piggybacking onto an existing power plant, the gas clean-up technology—such as the use of a scrubber—stacks are tapped into, rather than building these devices twice over. This does result in cost savings in capital expenses. Calculate the IRR for the integrated plant. The data provided in Table 4-17 is from Keith et al. [7], suitably modified for analysis here. The life of the plant is estimated at 10 years.

24.0 Meglumine Antimonate Drug by Supercritical Extraction

The price of a meglumine antimonite drug is roughly \$2,000 kg^{-1}. According to the World Health Organization (WHO), leishmaniasis is an endemic health problem in 88 countries. It threatens 350 million men, women, and children. It is a parasitic disease transmitted to humans by sandflies. It has a wide range of clinical symptoms: (i) cutaneous; (ii) mucocutaneous; and (iii) visceral. Cutaneous forms of the disease produce skin ulcers on the exposed parts of the body, such as the face, arms, and legs. The disease can produce a large number of lesions—sometimes up to 200—causing serious disability and leaving the patient permanently disfigured. This stigma can be fodder for serious social prejudice. In mucocutaneous forms of leishmaniasis, lesions can lead to partial or total destruction of the mucous membranes of the nose, mouth, and throat cavities and surrounding

Table 4-17 Integrated Plant to Manufacture Activated Carbon from Bamboo

Item	$ Amount	Quantity
Mixer, Dryer, Washing Unit	$30,000	
Carbonization Furnace	$1.3 million	
Combustor, Cyclone	$114,500	
Steam Boiler	$1,033,338	
Scrubber and Flue Gas Processing	$50,000	
Materials and Utility Cost	$200/hr	
Fixed Operating Cost	$3,450/day	
General Expenses	$1,800/day	
Price of Activated Carbon	$1.93/kg	
Product Rate		800 lb/hour
Days of Operation		250 days/year
Electricity Generated	300kW	
Price of Electricity	12.5 cents/kWh	
Other Capital Expenses	$6.0 million	

tissues. Some disabling and degrading forms of leishmaniasis can result in victims becoming outcasts from society. Visceral leishmaniasis is characterized by irregular bouts of fever, substantial weight loss, swelling of the spleen and liver, and anemia. If left untreated, the fatality rate in developing countries can be as high as 100% within two years.

The alkaloids extracted from *Tabernaemontana catharinensis* showed in vitro antileishmanial activity. *T. catharinensis* is a native tree in the southern part of Brazil. These trees have been studied for their biological properties: antitumoral, anti-inflammatory, analgesic, anticancer, antioxidant, and antimycobacterial, trypanocidal, and antileishmanial activities. Since the yields of indole alkaloids obtained by the low-pressure organic solvent extraction are very lo and the organic solvent consumption in the conventional process is very high, then supercritical extraction can be an advantageous process.

Two supercritical extraction columns cost about $2 million. The tree branches from which the alkaloids are extracted cost $83 per ton. A pre-processing cost of communition and drying is $30 per ton. The other relevant information needed to perform an IRR are given below in Table 4-18. Calculate the AW of the business should the capital expenses be recovered over a 20-year period at an interest rate of 8%.

25.0 Effect of Inflation on PW

The inflation rates for the past 10 years (1999–2009) are given in Table 4-4 in Example 4.8. This table was prepared using information provided by the Bureau of Labor Statistics. In 1999 dollars, calculate the PW (present worth) of an ABS (acrylonitrile butadiene styrene) engineering thermoplastic continuous polymerization plant. The capital cost of a new plant in 1999 dollars was $80 million. The selling price of the ABS was $4 per pound for the first five years and $8 per pound for the next five years. The raw materials cost rises every year due to inflation. The price in year 1998 was $2.8 per pound of ABS sold. The process cost also goes up with inflation

Table 4-18 Cost Information for Supercritical Extraction Process for Alkaloids

Price of Drug	$2,000	per kg		
2 Supercritical Extractors	$2,000,000			
T. catharinensis Tree Branches	$83	per ton		
Pre-processing Cost	$30	per ton		
CO_2	$150	per ton	2%	loss
Ethanol	$221	per ton	10%	loss
Labor Cost	$3.00	per hour		
Days of Operation		330	per year	
Utilities	$828,536/year	5280	batches	
Fractionator & Others	$35,000			Product(kg)
Product		1.29	kg/batch	6811.2
alkaloids		44.70%		3044.61
Fractionating Cost	$440.31		per kg	Alkaloid(kg)
Yield	0.80%			
Raw Materials	851400	kg/year		

because of the increase in utility cost and wages to workers. The process cost can be taken as 30 cents per pound of ABS produced in 1998. The production rate from the two CSTR and falling strand devolatilizer plant is 10,000 lb/hr. The plant can be expected to run around 85% of the time. The selling price of ABS remains flat during the 10-year period. An interest rate of 11% may be assumed.

26.0 Hydrogen as an Alternative Fuel

As discussed in Example 4.1, hydrogen is seriously considered as an alternative fuel in the transportation sector. In one process, the biomass is pyrolyzed and then steam re-formed to yield hydrogen. Biomass is dried and then converted to an oil by very quick exposure to heated particles in a fluidized bed. The char and gases produced are combusted to supply heat to the reactor. The product oils are cooled and condensed. Bio-oil is then shipped by truck from the plant location(s) to the hydrogen production facility. By shipping the bio-oil, which has a higher energy density than the biomass, transportation costs are reduced. On arrival, the bio-oil is fractionated using water extraction into carbohydrate fraction and lignin fractions. The carbohydrate fraction is steam re-formed and the hydrogen that is formed is separated using PSA, pressure swing adsorption. Consider a plant that produces 75,790 kg/day of hydrogen by the pyrolysis process. The biomass feed rate is about 1806 Mg/day. Capital investment fixed costs are $79.4 million. The selling price of hydrogen is $10/GJ. The storage and transportation cost of hydrogen by railroad is $0.94/GJ. The calorific value of hydrogen is 142 MJ/kg. At a MARR of 15%, calculate the PW of the project. The plant has operated for five years. The biomass feedstock cost was $16.5/Mg. The plant operated at 85% time during the year. The cost of utility and wages of laborers can be lumped into 15c/kg of hydrogen produced.

27.0 Replacement for the WTC

One proposal to replace the World Trade Center (WTC) came from architect and real estate tycoon Donald Stone, as discussed in Example 4.2. He proposed another high-rise to replace the WTC, which was destroyed by terrorists on September 11, 2001. In a typical week, 70,000 people are expected to work in these towers. Additionally, 200,000 visitors are expected to go the top floor to obtain a glimpse of New York City from the 110th floor. The cost of constructing the building is estimated at $7 billion. Assuming a net profit of collecting rent from the occupants is $275 per person per week and a visitor fee of $15, how many years would it take to see a profit? The interest rate can be taken to be 8%.

28.0 University Apartments

A group of university alumni and professors invests $20 million to build 200 new student apartments near a state university as discussed in Example 4.4. The money is borrowed at a rate of 7.25%, calculated on a yearly basis. The period of the loan is for 30 years. The variable expenses that include maintenance and operation run the group $3500 per apartment per year. The rental fees collected are about $12000 per apartment per year. The occupancy rate is about 70%. What is the present worth of the enterprise, should the salvage value of the apartments be $4 million at the end of 30 years?

29.0 Present Worth of a Sugar Mill

A business plan was presented that would get a sugar mill installed in rural Texas, a mill similar to the one in Example 4.5. The costs of raw materials such as sugarcane and utility costs rise every year due to inflation. The revenue from the sale of sugar rises and falls in synchrony with the boom-and-bust cycles of the economy. The

Table 4-19 EOY Receipts and Costs

Year	Receipts Millions $	Cost Millions $
1	2.3	3.3
2	2.5	3.6
3	2	3.21
4	1.5	1.33
5	2	1.46
6	2.5	1.61
7	3	1.77
8	3.5	1.95
9	4	2.14

EOY (end of year) revenues and costs are shown in Table 4-19. The capital cost of the sugar mill, including land and all the necessary equipment, is estimated at $8 million. What is the PW of the sugar business at an interest rate of 5%?

30.0 Electric/Gas Hybrid Vehicle

A hybrid electric/gas car such as a 2010 Toyota Prius costs about $24,000. The fuel economy for this vehicle is 50 miles per gallon, as discussed in Example 4.7. A comparable all-gasoline vehicle such as a 2010 Toyota Corolla costs $21,000; the fuel economy achieved in the Corolla is 32 miles per gallon. At what price of gasoline is it more attractive to purchase the Toyota Prius? It is estimated that the average passenger travels 15,000 miles per year and the life of an automobile is 100,000 miles. The interest rate may be taken as 8%. The cash flow diagram for Example 4.7 is shown in Figure 4.2.

31.0 Life-Cycle Cost of HVAC Systems

By using life-cycle cost analysis, all the relevant costs are considered (see Example 4.9). This can be accomplished by use of PW analysis. Consider the residence of Sharron Stone. A new HVAC (heating, ventilation, and air conditioning) system was installed in her residence. The estimated useful life is 10 years. A novel high-efficiency gas furnace with add-on air conditioner cost $15,183. The energy costs per year are $900 and maintenance costs $60. The salvage value of the equipment is $80. Use PW analysis and calculate its life-cycle cost. An interest rate for funds can be taken as 8%.

32.0 Municipal Garbage Collection Truck

The cost of the truck used to collect garbage from residences is about $41,450. It can be used to serve 1000 households, as discussed in Example 4.10. A weekly charge per household of $5 can be collected. The gasoline cost runs $150 per month. The labor wage costs for two drivers are $3200 per month. A one-time tax credit of $5000 from the federal government for recycling is given. Is it profitable to run the garbage business at a MARR of 15%? The life of the truck is expected to be six years.

33.0 Hexane Extraction of Rice-Bran Oil (see Example 4.11)

Rice-bran lipids can be extracted using hexane solvents from rice bran at a yield of about 26%. Rice is milled to produce the white long-grain rice sold in supermarkets. The outer layers of the rice kernel are removed. Rice bran becomes rancid and must be discarded in landfills. Parboiled rice bran has higher lipid levels than unstabilized rice bran. Rice-bran oil consists largely of saponifiable compounds. Hexane costs about $1.15 per gallon. It is an excellent solvent for nonpolar lipids. Calculate the PW of a hexane extraction unit. The following information is provided for purposes of analysis:

Table 4-20 Cost Data for a Hexane Extraction Plant for Rice-Bran Oil

Description	Hexane Extraction Unit
Capital Investment	$250,000
Manufacturing Cost	$5.18 /year/kg of rice bran
Materials Cost	$0.22/year/kg of rice bran
Labor Cost	$12.00/hr
Revenue from Rice-Bran Oil	$8.08/kg
Revenue from Rice Protein	$4.928/kg
Production Rate	25.96 gal rice-bran oil/day
Useful Life of Equipment	8 years
Operational Hours per Year	7332 hrs
% Protein in Rice Bran	14.6%
Interest Rate, i	8.0%

34.0 Biodiesel Plant in Taiwan (see Example 4.12)

Table 4-21 Cost and Revenue Data for Biodiesel Production in Taiwan

Biodiesel Production in Taiwan

#	Description	Cost	Quantity	
1	Transesterification Reactor	$300,000		
2	Neutralization Reactor	$25,000		
3	Washing Column	$115,000		
4	FAME Distillation Column	$175,000		
5	Heat Exchangers	$4,000		
6	Pumps	$50,000		
7	Separator, Vacuum Systems	$50,000		
	Production Rate		800,000	kg/year
	Materials			
8	Soybean Oil Feedstock	$6,000,000		
9	Methanol	$200,000		
10	Catalyst and Solvent	$350,000		
	Labor Cost	$550,000		

Utilities	$100,000
Overhead	$400,000
Revenue from Biodiesel	$7,000,000

Biodiesel is produced by transesterification reactions. The alkali catalyst used was sodium hydroxide, NaOH. Biodiesel is an attractive fuel due to its environmental benefits. It is prepared from renewable energy resources such as vegetable oil. Using the information provided in Table 4-21, calculate the PW of the biodiesel plant. The plant is expected to last for 15 years. The interest rate for equivalence calculations can be taken as 8.0%. The primary costs in these plants are the raw material costs.

35.0 Debt Consolidation (see Example 4.13)

A debt consolidation company worked out a payment plan for Mr. Dan Wardrop. Calculate the monthly payment at an annualized interest rate of 12%, should the loan be repaid in 25 years. Dan Wardrop's credit card balances carried are shown in Table 4-22. Once every five years, Dan retires some debt by making available proceeds from his investment in a restaurant with his partner in New York City. This is in the amount of $2500 each.

Table 4-22 Credit Card Balances of Mr. Dan Wardrop

#	Credit Card Company	Balance	Annualized Interest Rate (%)
1	Wachovia Platinum Visa	$21,500	19%
2	Sears MasterCard	$8,500	21%
3	Amazon Visa	$4,400	17%
4	Rooms-to-Go Furniture	$15,000	15%
5	Macy's Department Store	$4000	25%
6	Gap Apparel	$800	19%
7	JC Penney Retail	$100	21%

36.0 Solar Panel (See Example 4.14)

Radio Shack has advertised Sunforce 130 W Solar panels with a Sharp module for $1,999. Consider purchase of three of these panels for a new home. The monthly utility bill in the new home runs about 750 kWh. The current utility company charges 12.5 cents for 1 kWh. For a 15-year study period, calculate the IRR for solar panels to be an attractive investment.

37.0 Profitability of Liquefaction Plants (see Example 4.15)

At a Society of Petroleum Engineers symposium, a novel method of evaluation of the economics of GTL (gas to liquefied) fuel plants was presented [4]. The capital expenses (CAPEX) are pegged to the production of one barrel of hydrocarbon liquid per day (BLPD). Annual operational expenses (OPEX) are expressed as a certain percentage of CAPEX. It is assumed that the overall thermal efficiency of GTL plants is 60%, and the plant operates 300 days per annum. Consider one instance of CAPEX of $30,000/ BLPD and OPEX of 8% of CAPEX. The plant is considered to be in existence for 12 years. The price of crude oil is $67.65/bbl. Calculate the IRR for the project.

38.0 Copper-Chlorine Thermochemical Cycles for Hydrogen Production (see Example 4.17)

The hybrid copper-chlorine (CuCl) cycle is one promising method of thermochemical cycle that can be used for hydrogen production by using nuclear or solar heat. A CuCl cycle plant producing 125 MT H_2/day required 210 MW of thermal energy and 87.8 MW of electrical energy. The total capital investment for the CuCl plant using Turton et al.'s software package [6] can be estimated at $131 million. Estimated price of hydrogen is $7.0/kg. Calculate the payback period at an interest rate of 5%. The cost of electricity can be taken as $60 per 1000 kWh. Bulk CuCl costs $7200 per pound and bulk HCl costs $241/metric ton. A 50% yield can be assumed for the three major reactions that are needed in the process: (i) electrolysis reaction, by which cupric chloride, $CuCl_2$, is produced at the anode and H_2 at the cathode; (ii) hydrolysis of cupric chloride leads to the formation of copper oxychloride; and (iii) molten cuprous chloride is produced from the decomposition reaction. Thermal utility is $20 per 1000 kWh. Assume a 2% loss of HCl and 5 ppm loss of CuCl during the operation of the cycle.

39.0 Shut-in Wells in Oil Field

Leo Oil Field has 14 producing oil wells, 13 shut-in wells, and 5 saltwater disposal wells. The production of oil is 30 BOPD (barrels of oil per day). The oil field utilization factor is 300 days per year of continuous operation. Each oil well costs about $250,000 to drill. About 10 people are employed at an average salary of $25,000 per year. The selling price of a barrel of oil is $80. The utility charges are about half that of the labor cost. Calculate the PW of the Leo Oil Field for a useful life of 36 years at 6% interest. Ten additional infield oil wells are drilled at the same cost of $250,000 per well. Optimization of production from shut-in wells, production wells, and infield wells leads to an increase in production from 30 BOPD to 70 BOPD. The additional wells need two more people. What is the increase in the PW of Leo Oil Field after the expansion?

40.0 Long-Term Parking Lot

Taurus Parking is considering constructing a long-term parking lot near the Houston Bush Intercontinental Airport. They want to pave the 1-acre land with asphalt at a cost of $7.80 per sq. ft. It is estimated that 100 cars can be parked in four rows, allowing for angle parking. Four people will be employed at an annual salary of $15,000 per year. The real estate taxes that need to be paid are $1.20 per sq. ft. per year. The land acquisition cost is $3000 per acre. The parking fee charged per day is $5 per car. It can be assumed that the parking lot would be open 365 days a year. For a study period of 36 years at an interest rate of 6%, what is the PW of the business?

41.0 Recycling of Plastics

Closed-loop granulation was an innovation in the 1980s for recycling and the reuse of industrial scrap plastic. The machine-side granulation process consists of communition, separation, granulation, and conversion steps. The scrap plastic undergoes a communition process. Upon separation, the scrap is fed into a freestanding granulator. The granulate is collected in a bin and fed in measured quantities to the hopper of the conversion machine. Here, the granules from scrap plastic are mixed with virgin polymer granules and then converted into new products. The arrangement in closed-loop granulation is that a combined separator/granulator is fit directly under the product chute of the conversion machine, where products are separated from the scrap. The scrap is granulated and fed automatically back to the hopper of the machine. The type of granulator used is a low-power, open-rotor type, more effective for injection molding scrap compared with scrap from extrusion processing. Since the process is automatic, there is no need for labor costs in the form of employing operators. It has low utility costs and results in product with less contamination. Evaluate a recycling process by calculating the PW of the operation. The closed-loop machine can be purchased for $5000. The useful life of the machine is six years. The weekly production time can be taken as 35 hours of continuous operation and 5 hours of downtime for overhaul and maintenance. The machine throughput is 20 kg/hr. The electric power consumption of the machine is 78.08 kWh per week. The cost of electricity is 12.5 cents per kWh consumed. The scrap plastic can be purchased for $100 per ton. The finished product granules can be sold for $150 per ton. The interest rate is 6%. A $1500 tax credit for recycling from the government can be obtained.

42.0 Higher Throughput

Consider the closed-loop granulation process discussed in Exercise 41.0. The machine is modified for an additional cost of $2500. The throughput can now be increased to 50 kg/hr. All other factors remaining the same, what is the PW of the closed-loop recycling process with the modification?

43.0 Solar Hats

Solar cells can be made from organic materials such PET-ITO (polyethylene terephthalate on indium tin oxide) substrate and silver electrodes. The sunlight-to-electricity conversion efficiency in these devices is lower compared with silicon-based photovoltaic cells. However, organic materials are less expensive. Calculate the cost savings in using a solar hat to power up an FM radio for listening to music during leisure hours. Four hours of leisure time per day can be estimated. The cost of electricity from the existing utility company is 12.5 cents per kWh. The power draw from the radio is 88.9 milliwatts. The organic PV efficiency is 6.5%. The solar hat has a useful life of 15,000 hrs. A module consumes 1334 kWh. The cost to produce one module is 2 cents. The study period is 10 years. The interest rate is 6%.

44.0 Use of PFR, Plug Flow Reactor

You are asked to choose between two processes for a new polystyrene manufacturing plant using a continuous mass polymerization process: (i) The *Latinen* process uses CSTRs (continuous stirred tank reactors) in series at a capital cost of $53 million. The agitators cost another $53 million. The polystyrene production rate is 20,000 lb/hr. The utilization factor is 300 days/year. The plant life is 14 years and interest rate is 6%. The selling price of polystyrene is 84 cents per lb. The raw materials costs are lumped into 0.659 cents per lb. The utilities cost runs around $1.13 million per year. The plant is expected to employ 30 people at an average salary of $50,000 per year. (ii) The PFR process has a lower capital cost and utility cost and employs less people. The cost of the PFR (plug flow reactor) is $18 million. The utility costs are about $1 million per year. The plant is expected to employ 20 people at an average salary of $50,000 per year. Which process is a better choice ?

Chapter 5.0

Comparison of Alternatives and Decision Analysis

Main Topics Discussed in This Chapter

Develop Alternatives by Brainstorming
Study Period—Don't Compare an Apple and an Orange
Useful Lives—Repeatability and Co-terminated Basis
Rate of Return and Project Ranking
EW, Equivalent Worth Method
Optimal EW
Household Finances

5.1 Overview

As discussed in Chapter 1.0, engineering economy is about the development of alternatives for a given problem. Brainstorming may be used to develop alternatives. All the alternatives selected have to be viable. Decision analysis is to rank the alternatives with the most profitable or lowest cost alternative being given the highest rank. Different alternatives can have different cash flow diagrams. The revenues may be different: costs incurred such as materials, labor, and utility may vary and the interest rate and periods may not be the same. The five methods of evaluation of capital projects discussed in Chapter 4.0 shall be used here to select the best possible solution. These are the PW, present worth analysis, FW, future worth analysis, IRR, internal rate of return, AW, annual worth analysis, ERR, external rate of return. A variation of the IRR method is the payback period analysis. Factors are introduced to take inflation into account.

The right questions must be posed: (i) what are the differences among the alternatives; (ii) what is a common unit of measure; (iii) are all the relevant criteria met; (iv) what is the risk-reward ratio; (v) who pays for the capital investments—government or private companies; (vi) what are the local, state, and federal regulations; (vii) is the product for domestic consumption or for export; (viii) what are the exchange rates for the $; (ix) what are the inflation rates and deflation rates; (x) what are the government incentives given; (xii) is the business capital intensive like a nuclear power plant or cash flow intensive such as the gas station and convenience store complex studied in the end of Chapter 4.0 exercises; (xiii) what is the role of assets and liabilities of the enterprise; and (xiv) what is the MARR (%) (minimum acceptable rate of return).

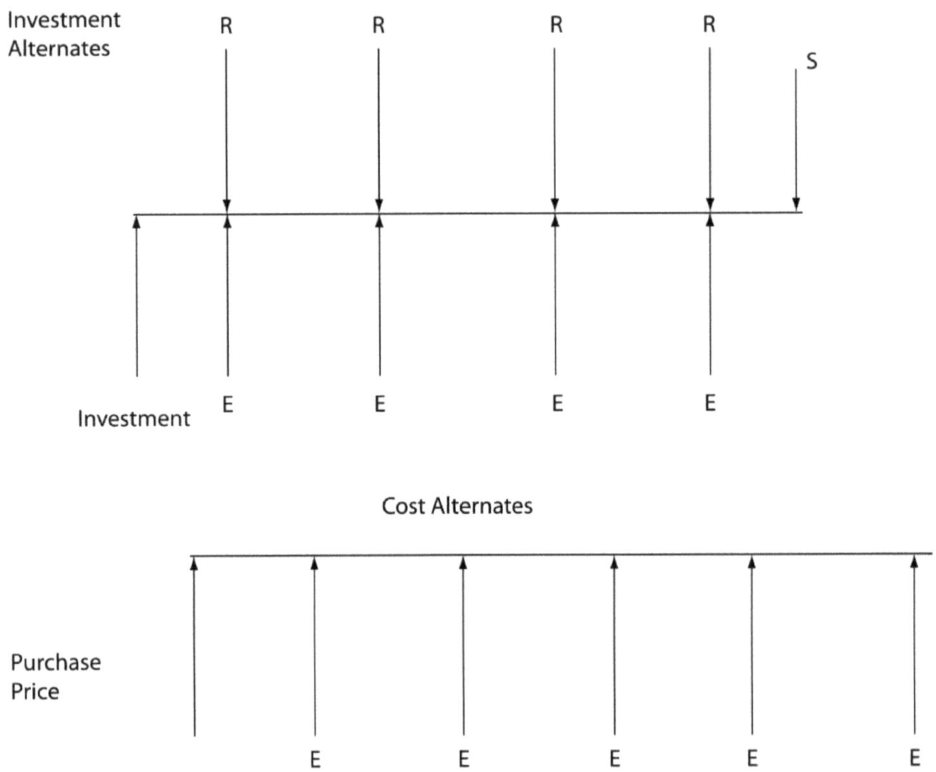

Figure 5-1 Cash Flow Diagrams of Investment and Cost Alternatives

Public sector projects are evaluated slightly differently compared with private sector projects. A benefit-cost analysis will be unveiled at a later chapter. In addition to costs and benefits, the disbenefits are also taken into account in cases of public sector projects.

(i) Comparison of alternatives can be undertaken for the purpose of:
(ii) Invest in the more profitable process—Profit Based;
(iii) The cash flow diagrams have a capital investment and have net cash inflows over the study period as shown in Figure 5.1;
(iv) Select the lower life-cycle cost alternative—Cost Based;
(v) The cash flow diagrams have cash outflows only as shown in Figure 5.1;
(vi) Quantitating the savings accrued from implementation of a process improvement;
(vii) Assessment of environmental impact of different chemical processes—Other Criteria.

Alternatives can be different kinds:

Mutually Exclusive Alternatives: In this category, only one viable alternative can be selected from all the options available. For example, an engineer has to select the right equipment such as CSTR (continuous stirred tank reactor) or PFR (plug flow reactor) in order to accomplish a given process. When one is selected, the other is rejected.

Independent Projects: Here one or more of the available projects may be selected for implementation. The projects can be evaluated using PW, FW, IRR, AW, or ERR methods and rank ordered according to the profitability. For example, a savvy investor with $1 million dollars may put $300,000 in stocks, $200,000 in bonds; $100,000 in FDIC-insured CDs; $100,000 in money market funds; and $300,000 in gold. Here, the different options were rank ordered and monies allocated according to the rank.

Screening by Other Criteria: In some cases, dollars and cents cannot be the sole determining criteria to evaluate alternatives and come to the most profitable decision. All the relevant criteria as discussed in the seven principles in chapter 1.0 have to be met. (Criteria such as all humans are created equally and laborers cannot be discriminated against based on the color of their skin, or national origin, age, gender, etc.) The environmental impact is also rapidly becoming an added criterion for selection of the best possible alternative.

The PW of the identified alternatives are calculated from their respective cash flow diagrams. The project with the highest PW in dollar amount is selected as the best possible alternative. Special cases can be identified when there are two alternatives, A and B, considered.

Case A: PW_A, present worth of Project A is in positive territory and PW_B, present worth of Project B is negative territory. $PW_A > 0$ & $PW_B < 0$. This means that Project A would fetch a profit and Project B would result in a loss when undertaken. In such cases, Project A may be selected.

Case B: Both PW_A and PW_B are in positive territory. Both projects can result in a profit. In such cases, the projects may be *rank ordered*. Sometimes the project with the maximum PW may be selected. $PW_A > 0$ & $PW_B > 0$.

Case C: The dollar value of PW_A and PW_B are within 20% of each other. Such cases may be determined as *too close to call*. This is so because of the uncertainty involved in the estimates of revenues, costs, capital investment and salvage values, interest rates, lives of equipment, inflation rates, etc. In a later chapter, sensitivity analysis and spider plots will be discussed in greater detail.

Any of the five methods such as PW, FW, AW, IRR, and ERR may be used in order to evaluate the alternatives prior to arriving at the decision. In cases of PW, FW, AW, the alternative with the higher dollar value can be selected. In the case of IRR, the project with the higher IRR is not selected. IRR between projects should not be compared. The IRR of a project is compared with MARR. If IRR > MARR, the project is acceptable. The business significance of comparison of IRRs from different projects is low.

Example 5.1 Best Process to Manufacture CNTs (Carbon Nanotubes)

CNTs are one of the four allotropes of carbon: (i) diamond; (ii) graphite; (iii) C_{60} fullerenes; and (iv) CNTs, carbon nanotubes. Graphene sheets of carbon rolled around the needle axis were discovered by Ijima in 1991. The diameter of these tubes is 1–2 nm and length is a few microns. CNTs offer attractive properties ranging from 1 TPa of modulus of elasticity to 2000 w/m/k thermal conductivity, etc. They can be used as a blend substituent to make novel nanocomposites.

There are two processes used to manufacture CNTs. Find out which is more profitable at 12% effective interest rate.

Process A: The HiPCO reactor is used. HiPCO is the high-pressure carbon monoxide process to manufacture CNT using the Boudard reaction [1]. A PFR (plug flow reactor) designed at Rice University in Houston is used at high pressures of 30–50 bar and at temperatures 1273–1473 K. CNTs and CO_2 are produced from CO, carbon monoxide, and iron pent carbonyl catalyst precursor. The conversion was 20%.

Process B: The CoMoCAT reactor is used. CO disproportionation is effected over a mixed cobalt-molybdenum catalyst on silica support in a fluidized bed reactor developed at the University of Oklahoma. The reaction forms

Table 5-1 Two Processes Used to Manufacture CNTs

Item	Process A (Amount)	Process A (Description)	Process B (Amount)	Process B (Description)
Catalyst		Fe		Co-Mo
Reactants		CO & $Fe(CO)_5$		CO
Reactor		Plug Flow Reactor		Fluidized Bed
Temperature		1050°C		950°C
Pressure		450 psia		150 psia
Selectivity		90%		80%
Purification		Oxidation, Filtration		Leaching, Froth Flotation
Product Rate		595 kg/h		595 kg/h
Steam	12.5 cents/kg	2,565 kg/h		2,885 kg/h
Gas	50 cents /kg	486 kg/h		486 kg/h
Electricity	12.5 cents/kWh	1,056 kW		387 kW
Capital Cost of Plant	$4.6 million		$4.4 million	
Price	$38/kg		$25/kg	
Materials Cost	$140 million		$84 million	
Plant Life		10 years		10 years
Operation		330 days/year		330 days/year

CNTs and CO2-at temperatures between 973–1223 K and total pressure ranging from 15–50 psia. The CO selectivity is 80% and conversion about 20%.

The information needed for economic analysis on the processes is given in Table 5-1 from Agboola et al. [2].

Annual Materials Expenses for Process A = $140 million (5.1)

Annual Electricity Expenses for Process A = (1,056)*(24)*(330)*($0.125) = 1.05 million (5.2)

Annual Gas Expenses for Process A = (486)*(24)*(330)*($0.50)/1 E6 = $1.925 million (5.3)

Annual Steam Expenses for Process A = (2,565)*(24)*(330)*($0.125)/1E6 = $2.54 million (5.4)

Annual Sales of CNTs from Process A = (595)*(24)*(330)*($38)/1E6 = $179.1 million (5.5)

Annual Profit (R-E) = ($179.1) – ($140)-SUM(Gas, Steam, Electricity) = $33.562 million (5.6)

Present Worth Factor, (P/A,12%,10) = 5.6502 (5.7)

PW_A = -($4.6) + (R-E)*(P/A,12%,10) = -$4.6 + 5.6502*$33.56185 = $189.63 million (5.8)

Annual Materials Expenses for Process B = $84 million (5.9)

Annual Electricity Expenses for Process B = (387)*(24)*(330)*($0.125)= 0.383 million (5.10)

Annual Gas Expenses for Process B = (486)*(24)*(330)*($0.50) = $1.925 million (5.11)

Annual Steam Expenses - Process B = (2,885)*(24)*(330)*($0.125) = $2.856 million (5.12)

Annual Sales of CNTs from Process B = (595)*(24)*(330)*($25) = $117.81 million (5.13)

Annual Profit (R-E) = ($117.81) – ($84)-SUM(Gas, Steam, Electricity) = $28.646 million (5.14)

Present Worth Factor, (P/A,12%,10) = 5.6502 (5.15)

PW_B = -($4.4) + (R-E)*(P/A,12%,10) = -$4.4 + 5.6502*$28.64616 = $157.4565 million (5.16)

Comparing Eq. (5.8) and Eq. (5.16), Process A has a higher present worth compared with Process B. Hence, Process A is the more profitable route to prepare CNTs.

Example 5.2 Cost Savings by Using Microfiltration Pretreatment During SWRO (Sea Water Reverse Osmosis)

Pretreatment has been used to improve the performance and lower the overall cost of obtaining water using SWRO (sea water reverse osmosis plants). Control of membrane fouling is agreed upon as a problem encountered during the operation of the SWRO plants. The conventional pretreatment method controls and minimizes the plugging potential of the feed water by coagulating, flocculating, and filtering out colloidal and suspended solids and by achievement of reduction in SDI (silt density index) of feed water. MF (microfiltration) pretreatment appears to be an attractive method. Turbidities of water can be lowered less than 0.1 NTU regardless of inflow turbidity level. UF pretreatment results in removal of TC (total coli) from bacteria *Giardia* and *Cryptosporidium.* Viruses are also removed. The novel pretreatment strategy leads to reduction in capital costs, reduction in operating costs

Table 5-2 Economic Data for Evaluation of MF Pretreatment

	Conventional		**Microfiltration**	
Description	$ millions/year	$ (millions)	$ millions/year	$ (millions)
Plant		145.3777		40.64489
Pumps		1.829328		1.829328
Dosing Plant		0.230588		0
Structural		11.89832		11.89832
Subtotal		159.336		54.37253
Electricity	9.648		7.09	
Chemicals	4.662		1.637	
Filters	3.478			
Water Rate		27,276 m^3/day		

due to lower membrane replacement, less chemical consumption, elimination of cartridge filters, less downtime, less maintenance costs, less labor costs, etc. The MF unit is skid mounted and impurities larger than 200 nm are removed using this device. The machine consists of polypropylene filtration modules, circulation pump, associated valves, piping, and instrumentation and control systems.

The data needed to perform comparison of alternatives is given below in Table 5-2 and taken from [3]. The capital expenses such as treatment plants, pumps, etc. are financed over a 30-year period at 5% interest rate.

Cost of Water (Conventional)

Annual Variable Expenses = \$9.648 + \$4.662 + \$3.478 = \$17.788 million (5.17)

Capital Recovery Factor (A/P,5%,30) = 0.065051 (5.18)

Capital Recovery Amount = \$159.336*(0.065051) = \$10.365 (5.19)

Plant operates 330 days in the year

$$\text{Cost of Water} = \frac{(\$17.788 + \$10.365)}{27{,}276 * 330} = \$3.13/m^3 = 0.313c/liter \quad (5.20)$$

Cost of Water (MF Pretreated)

Annual Variable Expenses = \$7.09 + \$1.637 = \$8.727 million (5.21)

Capital Recovery Factor (A/P,5%,30) = 0.065051 (5.22)

Capital Recovery Amount = \$54.37253*(0.065051) = \$3.537 (5.23)

Plant operates 330 days in the year

$$\text{Cost of Water} = \frac{(\$8.727 + \$3.537)}{27{,}276 * 330} = \$1.363/m^3 = 0.1363c/liter \quad (5.24)$$

Comparing Eq. (5.20) and (5.24) the microfiltration pretreatment process modification would lower the cost of producing water by \$1.77/m^3. Hence, the microfiltration pretreatment alternative is preferred over the conventional method of pretreatment.

Example 5.3 Bioethanol from Sugarcane Bagasse

Renewable energy sources are sought the world over in order to provide energy security for our nation and the world. According to a recent Goldman Sachs report, Brazil, Russia, India, and China, BRIC nations, are expected to emerge as the world's largest economies. In Brazil, 387 million tons of sugarcane was produced in 2005/2006. Additionally, 104 million tons of bagasse came from the sugar mills. From a ton of sugarcane, 73 kg of fermentable sugars and 27 kg of dry bagasse can be produced. The composition of bagasse is as follows:

Cellulose	43%
Xylans	25%
Lignin	23%

Hemicellulose is a polymer of xylose and cellulose is a polymer of glucose. The sugarcane bagasse can be burned in boilers to generate electricity. Sugarcane bagasse can be converted to bioethanol and furfural by a dilute acid hydrolysis process. The acid hydrolysis process is a two-stage operation. In the first-stage, hemicellulose is converted into sugar using dilute acid and steam. In the second stage, cellulose is converted to sugar by hydrolysis. Upon hydrolysis, the sugar can be processed in order to produce ethanol, furfural, and other products. Furfural can either be used alone or combined with phenol, acetone, or urea to make solid resins. Such resins are used to make fiberglass, aircraft components, and automotive brakes. It can also be used as a hydrocarbon solvent. Coproduction of ethanol and furfural can make the process more profitable. The acid hydrolysis plant consists of the following equipment:

Pump and Heater;
Reactor to Produce Furfural and Glucose;
Purification and Separation.

After passing through the heater, the feedstock is treated with dilute sulfuric acid solution (0.5 wt%) at high temperature for a short time. Cellulose and pentose are converted to glucose and furfural, respectively. The hydrolyzed stream is then separated using a distillation column. The hydrolyzed material is then neutralized with lime. The upper stream is passed through a condenser leading to the formation of furfural. The unreacted cellulosic residue and lignin from stream can be burned to generate electricity or sold as a by-product. The total capital investment needed for the acid hydrolysis plant is about $4.016 million [4]. The furfural can be sold for $1.91/kg and ethanol can be sold for $1.37/kg. The bagasse suppliers are paid at 18 cents per kg of feedstock. A dilute acid hydrolysis plant can operate at 4000 kg/h of sugarcane bagasse. The utilities and labor costs were estimated and found to be $0.80 per kg of ethanol and $1.11/kg of furfural. The plant utilization factor is 80%. The yield of ethanol is 15% and that of furfural is 7% from the bagasse.

Which would be a better alternative: (i) start a dilute acid hydrolysis plant with an estimated life of 15 years; or (ii) generate electricity from bagasse using a power plant? The cost of the steam boiler and turbine is about $1 million each. The electricity can be sold at 12.5 cents per kWh. The calorific value of bagasse is 8.0 MJ/kg. The power plant thermal efficiency can be taken as 30%. The interest rate is 6%. For purposes of analysis, assume that the power plant life is equal to that of the acid hydrolysis plant and is 15 years. The operating expenses of the power plant are about 4 cents per kWh.

Dilute Acid Hydrolysis Process

Annual Sales of Furfural = (4000)*(24*365*0.8)*(0.07)*($1.91) = $3.748 million (5.25)

Annual Sales of Ethanol = (4000)*(24*365*0.8)*(0.15)*($1.37) = $5.761 million (5.26)

Annual Expenses of Furfural = (4000)*(24*365*0.8)*(0.07)*($1.11) = $2.178 million (5.27)

Annual Expenses of Ethanol = (4000)*(24*365*0.8)*(0.15)*($0.80) = $3.364 million (5.28)

(P/A,6%,15) = 0.5*(9.295+ 10.1059) = 9.723 (from Table A-10)

PW_{acid} = -4.016 +P/A*(R-E) = -4.016+9.723*($3.748+$5.761-$2.178-$3.364) = $34.55 million (5.29)

Power Plant Option

Annual Sales of Electricity = (4000)*(0.3)*(8 E6)*(0.8)*($0.125) = $0.96 million (5.30)
Annual Cost of Power Plant Operation = (4000)*(0.3)*(17 E6)*(0.8)*($0.04) = $0.6528 million

PW_{plant} = -2 + 9.723*($0.96-0.6528) = $0.987 million (5.31)

Comparing Eq. (5.29) and Eq. (5.31), the present worth of the acid hydrolysis plant is at $34.55 million and is greater than the present worth of the power plant at $0.987 million. Hence, it is better to invest in the acid hydrolysis plant compared with the steam power plant.

Example 5.4 Sequestration by Dimethyl Carbonate Formation

Two routes for chemical reuse of CO_2, carbon dioxide, are considered. Interest in sequestration projects is increasing due to the concerns about global warming [5]. Studies have shown that a 10% dimethyl carbonate (DMC) addition to diesel leads to 20% smoke reduction. Both plants operate at 7,200 h/year. CO_2 is available at no cost. Each ton of CO_2 sequestered leads to carbon credits of $19.02. Electric utilities cost 43 cents per kWh. Which is a better alternative at an interest rate of 10% and a plant life of 14 years?

Route A: Production from Ethylene Oxide: Ethylene oxide and CO_2 are allowed to react to form ethylene carbonate. Ethylene carbonate produced is reacted with methanol in a second PFR (plug flow reactor), leading to the production of DMC and ethylene glycol. The capital cost can be taken as $80 million; 36,732 tons/year of CO_2 are sequestered. The energy used in this process is 216 TJ/year. Revenue from the plant is $2500 per ton of CO_2 sequestered.

Route B: Production from Urea: Urea is produced by reacting ammonia and CO_2. DMC is produced by urea methanolysis. The capital cost for this route is given as $100 million; 27,129 tons/year of CO_2 are sequestered. The energy used in this process is 415 TJ/year. The revenue from the plant is $3800 per ton of CO_2 sequestered.

(P/A,10%,15) = 7.3667 (from Table A-14)

Annual Revenue—Route A = (36,732)*(2,500) = $91.83 million (5.32)

Annual Carbon Credit—Route A = (36,732)*($19.02) = $0.698,643 million (5.33)

Annual Energy Expenses—Route A = (216 E12)($0.43)/1000/7200 = $12.94 million (5.34)

PW_A = -$80 + 7.3367*($91.83 + $0.698,643 - $12.94) = $506.292 million (5.35)

Annual Revenue—Route B = (27,129)*(3,800) = $103.09 million (5.36)

Annual Carbon Credit—Route A = (27,129)*($19.02) = $0.515,994 million (5.37)

Annual Energy Expenses—Route A = (414.99 E12)($0.43)/1000/7200 = $24.78 million (5.38)

PW_B = -$100 + 7.3367*($91.83 + $0.698,643 - $12.94) = $480.66 million (5.39)

Comparing Eq. (5.35) and Eq. (5.39), it can be seen that the present worth (PW) of the plant A for sequestration is $506.292 million and the PW of the plant B is $480.66 million. In this case, it is too close to call one better than the other. However, Route A can be ranked higher than Route B, and Route A can be selected as the better alternative.

5.2 Study Period—Don't Compare an Apple and an Orange

When two alternatives are compared, the life of the equipment used by either process may be different from each other. When this happens, comparisons have to be made on a comparable basis. In order to make more meaningful comparisons, the following quantities are defined:

Study Period: The study period is the duration over which the comparisons are drawn. This can be lower, equal to, or greater than the useful life of the equipment used.

Useful Life: The duration over which the equipment is functioning is called the useful life of the equipment.

Repeatability Assumption: This can be used when the useful lives of equipment in Alternative A and Alternative B are different from each other. The study period is selected as the lowest common multiple of the two useful lives. For example, say the decision analysis is to select the best photocopier for the department. Copier A is imported from Japan and has a useful life of nine years. Copier B is from a domestic supplier with a useful life of six years. Then the study period is set at 18 years; 18 is the LCM of (6,9). Two A copiers are allowed to function in series in time, thus lasting 2*9 = 18 years. In a similar manner, three copiers of B are allowed to function one after the next, thus lasting 3*6 = 18 years. The study period of 18 years is now the same for both copiers A and B. The purchase price, annual supplies cost, maintenance cost, utility cost, labor cost, and salvage value obtained at the end of use of the machine can all be accounted for two copiers of A and three copiers of B. In some cases, the quantity may have to be multiplied by the number of copiers—it depends on the given application. Sometimes the LCM may have to be the multiple of the two useful lives. For example, should copier A have a life of five years and copier B have a life of three years, the study period can be selected as LCM(3,5) = 15 years. In this case, five copiers A have to be considered as a basis and three copiers of B have to be considered as a basis. In such cases, projections into the future may cause errors such as changes in interest rates, inflation rates, etc. This method can also be used when the study period tends to infinity or is indefinitely long.

Co-terminated Assumption: The study period is truncated from the useful life of equipment in

one alternative in order to have equal the useful life of the equipment in the second alternative. This can be used when the useful life of alternative A, N_A is greater than useful life of alternative B, N_B_i.e., $N_A > N_B$. The study period can be selected as N_B. All the revenues and expenses for alternative A are then reevaluated for a co-terminated period of N_B. This is feasible because $N_B < N_A$.

Example 5.5 Life-Cycle Cost of Photocopier

The Xerox Work Center can handle up to 200,000 pages per month and has a copy speed of up to 45 pages per minute. Its costs about $2,200 and weighs 80 lbs. The toner cartridge costs about $90 per cartridge. It can be used to print 2000 pages. This machine has a useful life of four years. Toshiba's e-STUDIO 455 can copy

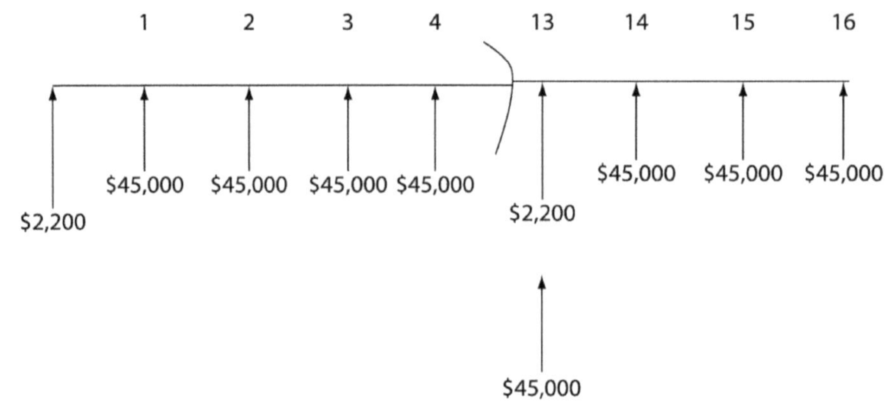

Figure 5.2 Cash Flow Diagram Adjusted for Repeatability Assumption for Xerox Work Center with Useful Life of 4 Years

up to 45 pages per minute and the base unit costs about $10,800. The toner yield is 30,000 pages and cost is $190 each. The useful life of the e-STUDIO 455 is about 16 years. Which copier has the lower life cycle cost: the Xerox Work Center or the Toshiba e-STUDIO? The interest rate is 8.0%. Assume that 1 million pages are copied every year.

The two machines have unequal lives. The repeatability assumption is used. Four Xerox Work Centers are needed for a common study period of 16 years. They are assumed to work one after the other as shown in the cash flow diagram in Figure 5.2. The PW analysis is used in order to calculate the life-cycle cost of the two different photocopiers.

Annual Toner Cost for Xerox Work Center = 1 E6/2000*($90) = $45,000 (5.40)

Annual Toner Cost for Toshiba's e-STUDIO = 1E6/30,000*($190) = $6333.33 (5.41)

(P/A,8%,16) = 8.8514 (From Table A-12) (5.42)

(P/F,8%, 4) = 0.735030 (From Table A-12) (5.43)

(P/F,8%,8) = 0.540269 (From Table A-12) (5.44)

(P/F,8%,12) = 0.397114 (From Table A-12 (5.45)

Life-Cycle Cost of Xerox Work Center = C_X + (P/A,8%,16)*(-$45,000) + (P/F,8%,4)*$C_X$

+ (P/F,8%,8)*C_X + (P/F,8%,12)*C_X (5.46)

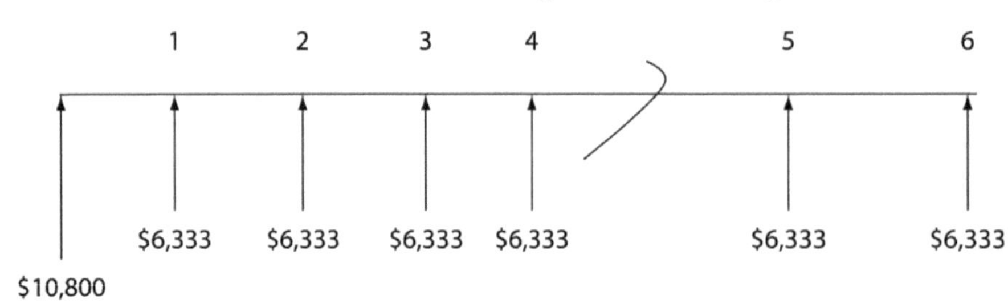

Figure 5.3 Cash Flow Diagram for Toshiba's e-STUDIO with a Useful Life = 16 years

= -$2,200 – (8.8514)($45,000) – 0.735030*($2,200) – 0.540269*($2,200) – 0.397114*($2,200)
= $404,192 (5.47)

The e-STUDIO was purchased at a one-time charge of $10,800. Over 16 years, the toner costs were found to be $6,333.33 every year. The cash flow diagram for expenses for Toshiba's e-STUDIO is shown in Figure 5.3.

Life-Cycle Cost of Toshiba e-STUDIO = -$10,800 – 8.8514*($6333.33) = $66,859 (5.48)

It can be seen that by comparison of Eq. (5.47) and Eq. (5.48), the Toshiba e-STUDIO has the lowest life-cycle cost. This is contrary to the purchase price. The purchase price of the Xerox Work Center is lower at $2,200, compared with Toshiba's $10,800. When taking into account the toner expenses, the Toshiba e-STUDIO turns out to be the lower total cost at $66,859 to that of the Xerox Work Center's $404,192. In both cases, the basis was 1 million copies per year made.

Example 5.6 LED Lighting

Light-emitting diode works on the principle of *electroluminescence*, which is the release of photon energy from electron-hole recombinations within the device. The color of the light depends on the wavelength of the light corresponding to the energy released. LEDs have lower energy consumption and longer lives compared with incandescent lamps. Boeing wants you to calculate the life-cycle cost of LEDs and incandescent lamps for its new aircraft. They need 420 lights at 100 W each. The incandescent lamps have 100 hrs/life and cost $1.36 each. The illumination received is 1680 lumens per bulb. Mercury LED lamps of 400 W cost $32.73 per lamp and can last for 24,000 hours at an illumination of 36,000 lumens [6]. Assume that the Boeing flight is in operation for 200 days in the year. The cost of electricity is 25 cents per kWh. The interest rate is 5%.

(P/A,5%,5) = 4.3295 (5.49)

Number of hours of in-flight service per year = 200*24 = 4800 hrs (5.50)

The LED lamps and incandescent bulbs have unequal lives. The repeatability assumption can be used. The study period is selected as five years.

The number of incandescent bulbs needed for a five-year period = (5)*(4800/100)*420 = 100,800 (5.51)

The cost of purchasing the incandescent bulbs =100,800*($1.36) = $137,88

Annual Electric Utility costs = (100)*(420)*(4800)/1000*($0.25) = $50,400/year (5.52)

Total cost of purchase and operation of incandescent bulbs

= -$137,88 – (4.3295)*($50,400) = $319,007 (5.53)

Number of LED (mercury lamps) needed for a five-year period at the same illumination

= (4800/24,000*420*5)*(1680/36,000) = 19.6 = 20 lamps (5.54)

Cost of purchasing the mercury lamps = 20*($32.73) = $654.60 (5.55)

Annual Electric Utility Costs = (400)*(4)/1000(($0.25) = $0.40 (5.56)

Total cost of purchase and operation of mercury lamps

=-$654.60 - 4.3295*($0.40) = -$656.33 (5.57)

It can be seen that by comparisons of Eq. (5.53) and Eq. (5.57), it is lower in total cost to choose LED mercury lamps as aviation lighting compared with incandescent lamps.

5.3 Equivalent Worth Method

When two alternatives are evaluated and when the critical equipment has unequal lives, other methods of evaluation are considered. One is the *rate of return* method. The rate of return can be calculated as

$$ROR = \frac{(R - E)}{C_I} \quad (5.58)$$

Where R is the revenues generated in a prototypical year, E is the expenses generated in a prototypical year and C_I is the capital investment made less the salvage value received to start the business. The project with the higher rate of return can be selected. The IRRs of two projects should not be compared. The IRR has to be compared with the MARR. IRR comparisons are meaningless because the PW changes with the interest rate depending on the project, particularly the revenue function, cost function changes with the interest rate. Under some conditions, the PW of Project A may be greater than the PW of Project B, although the IRR of Project B may be greater than the IRR of Project A. Under those conditions, Project A has to be selected. Selection is based on the value of PW and not IRR. This is shown in Figure 5.4. As can be seen in Figure 5.4, for interest rates less

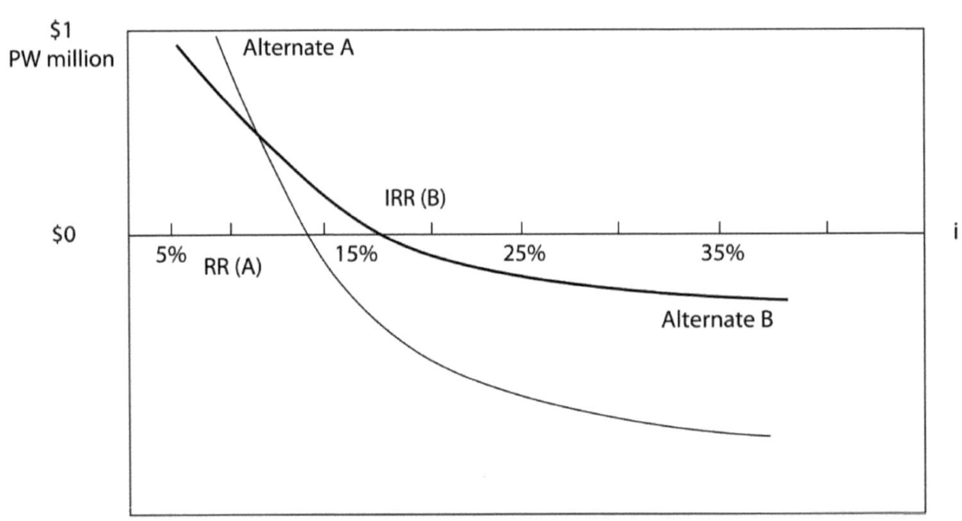

Figure 5.4 Comparison of IRRs Can Lead to Erroneous Conclusions

Table 5-3 Cost and Revenue Information for Pharmaceutical Plant

	Plan A Manual Cartoning	Plan B Automatic Cartoning
Batches	72/year	195/year
Production	959,976 tubes	2,599,936
Capital Cost (Equipment)	———	$900,000
Operating Cost	$1,437,631	$3,847,157
Revenue	$4,001,400	$10,835,500

than 12% $PW_A > PW_B$ and can be selected although the $IRR_B > IRR_A$. Only when the interest rates are high does Project B become more attractive compared with Project A.

AW method analysis may also produce good results. This can be the case when the study period is not equal to useful life.

Example 5.7 Anti-Allergic Cream

A pharmaceutical plant is proposed to manufacture anti-allergic cream. The plant consists of six unit operations: (i) melting; (ii) blending; (iii) filling; (iv) cartoning; and (v) packaging, both shrink wrapping and for shipment. Batches of emulsifying wax and foam stable are independently heated in a jacketed heater. Then emulsifier and ointment are added. Excipient 3 is dissolved in hot deionized water DI and then blended with the other ingredients. The active ingredient is finally added. Cooling procedures are instituted that last for 19 hours. The blended product is filled in tubes of 15 g each. The filling machine can fill 30 tubes per minute. Five sealed boxes per minute are prepared.

In a second method, a new multifunctional blending tank and automatic cartoning machine with line speed of 60 tubes per minute are introduced. The cost is about $900,000. The data needed to evaluate the two alternatives is given in Table 5-3. The interest rate may be taken as 8%. A 20-year life of the modification can be assumed.

The AW method may be used to evaluate the advantages of using automatic cartoning.

The planning horizon is taken as 20 years. The study period is thus the same for Plan A and Plan B.

Plan A—Manual Cartoning

$$AW_A = R_k - E_k = \$4{,}001{,}400 - \$1{,}437{,}631 = \$2{,}563{,}769 \quad (5.59)$$

Plan B—Automatic Cartoning

$$(A/P, 8\%,20) = 0.101852$$

$$AW_B = \$10{,}835{,}500 - \$3{,}847{,}500 - (A/P,8\%,20)*\$900{,}000 = \$6{,}896{,}333 \quad (5.60)$$

It can be seen from comparisons of Eq. (5.59) and (5.60) that Plan B with automatic cartoning has a higher AW compared with Plan A. Plan B with automatic cartoning has been selected.

5.4 Optimization

Often the PW of a business can be *optimized.* There is a trade-off between alternatives with different variable costs and fixed costs. For example, a number of unit operations in chemical processes and the biotechnology industry are operated stagewise and in a continuous manner. Consider a distillation column that can be used to accomplish the given task, for instance the separation of ethyl alcohol from water. The use of an overhead condenser and reflux can improve the performance of the distillation column. At minimum reflux, the number of plates or stages needed to achieve the desired level of purity in the product would be larger. At a larger reflux ratio, the number of stages required to accomplish the given task would be lower. Consider the two alternatives:

Alternative A: Distillation column with lower reflux ratio and larger number of plates needed to achieve the desired level of consistency of alcohol. This route will require a larger capital cost and lower energy or variable cost.

Alternative B: Distillation column with higher reflux ratio and lower number of plates needed to achieve the desired level of consistency of alcohol. This route will require larger energy or variable costs, but should result in lower capital cost.

Which of the two alternatives should be selected? When capital is lower in cost, a low reflux ratio with a higher number of stages can be selected. When energy is cheap, a higher reflux ratio and lower number of stages can be selected. Let the useful life of the distillation column be N years and the interest rate be i(%). The PW for any distillation column can be written as

$$PW = -N_P C'_F - RC'_v * (P/A, i\%, N) \tag{5.61}$$

Where the fixed costs increases linearly with the number of stages and the annual utility costs increase linearly with the reflux ratio needed R. The variable costs will increase with the reflux ratio used. The number of stages and reflux ratio can be related using expressions such as the *Kremser Equation,* which is more applicable when the thermodynamic equilibrium relation between the components separated is linear. The Kremser Equation can be written as

$$N_p = \frac{\ln(Purity)}{\ln\left(\frac{R}{m(R+1)}\right)} \tag{5.62}$$

An optimal PW of the distillation column can be identified when

$$\frac{d(PW)}{dN_p} = 0 \tag{5.63}$$

At the optimal value, the total life-cycle cost of operation of the distillation column in order to achieve a desired level of purity can be *minimized.*

There is increased interest in recent years to perform what is called a *techno-economic analysis.* Here, the technical feasibility of the process and the EW of the process are evaluated together. Ramifications of such analysis can be interesting. For example, there is identified an optimal number of fermenters that would result in a maximum present worth. A battery of fermenters can be used to generate biotechnology products. The batch fill and emptying times are such that the PW of the plant reaches a maximum at a certain number of fermenters.

At a certain number of effects in multiple effect evaporators, the total cost of the process reaches a minimum. The energy cost and additional capital cost as a function of number of effects are calculated. With more effects, more efficiency is reached in the evaporation, and hence the revenue generated from more effects would be greater. It is not clear at what number of effects maximum profit can be generated. The techno-economic analysis can be performed to arrive at a maximum profitable process. This may work out to be three or four. It depends on the additional efficiency that can be generated in the technology used for more effects. It also depends on the interest rates and revenue that can be accrued for better quality.

A number of discussions in the literature are about the golden triangle of *production, quality, and profit*. When quality required goes up, usually production goes down. More care is needed to produce a product with better quality. The product with better quality can be *priced* higher. Usually this results in better revenue. A techno-economic analysis may be conducted and conditions where profitability can be maximized can be identified.

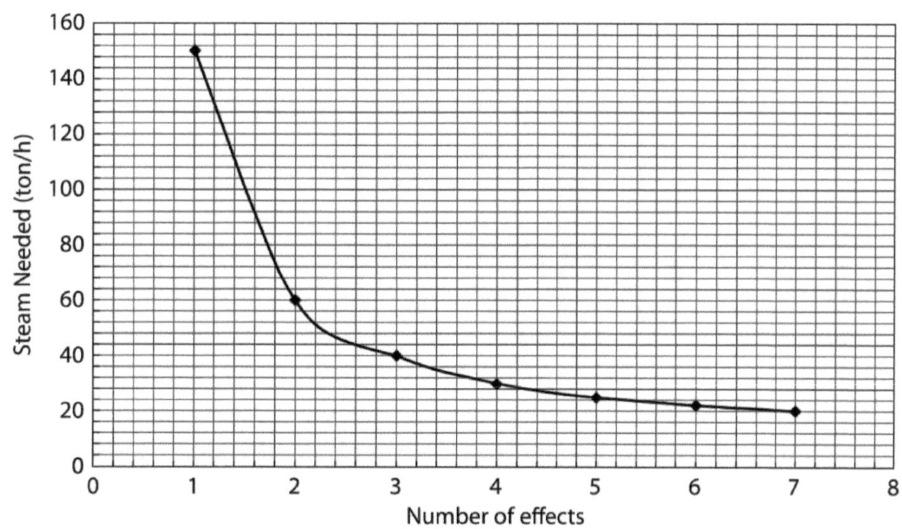

Figure 5.5 Steam Needed as a Function of Number of Effects in a Multiple EffectEvaporator

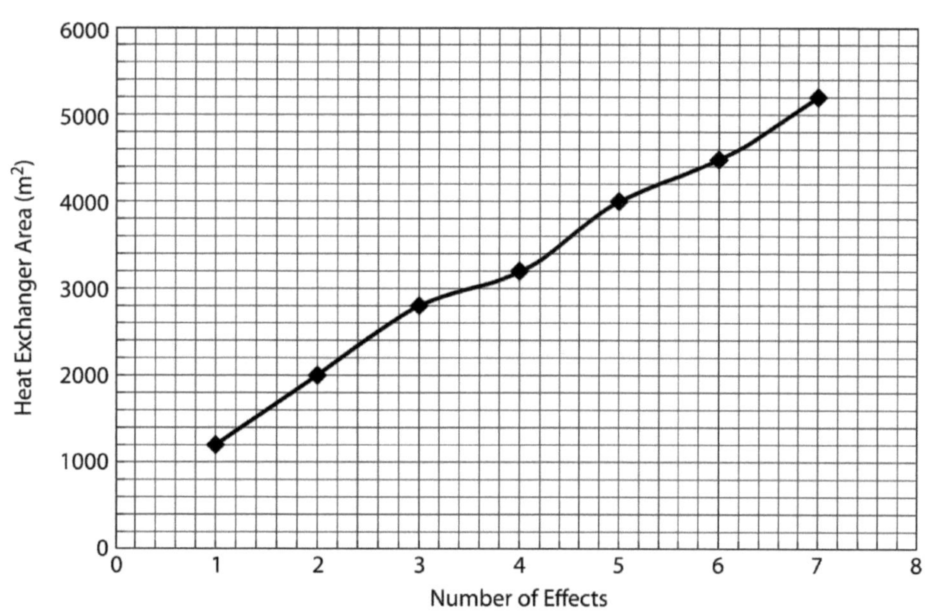

Figure 5.6 Heat Exchanger Area vs. Number of Effects

Table 5-4 Cost and Economic Data for Tomato Paste Factory

Number of Effects, N_E	Capital Cost (Millions, $)	Steam Utilities Cost (Millions, $ per year)	Price $ per kg
1	92	8.1	4
2	108	3.24	4.07
3	115	2.16	4.14
4	122	1.62	4.21
5	129	1.35	4.28
6	136	1.188	4.35
7	143	1.08	4.42

Example 5.8 Optimal Number of Effects in Multiple Effect Evaporator

One of the critical unit operations used to manufacture *tomato paste* is the use of a multiple effect evaporator. With the use of more effects, the capital cost increases linearly and the steam needed decreases in a nonlinear manner. This is shown for a multiple effect evaporator in New Zealand [7] in Figure 5.5 (Steam Flow Rate vs. Number of Effects) and Figure 5.6 (Heat Exchange Area vs. Number of Effects). The cost and economic data to evaluate the multiple effect evaporator needed to concentrate tomato paste is provided in Table 5-4. Calculate the number of effects of the evaporator when the PW of the operation is maximized. The interest rate is 10% and the study period is 13 years. Assume that the plant is operational 225 days per year at 10 tons/h tomato paste production rate.

The quality of the tomato paste from evaporators increases with the number of effects used. Hence, the price of tomato paste from a multiple effect evaporator can be charged higher compared with the product from a single pass evaporator. It can be seen from Figures 5.4 and 5.5 that with more numbers of effects, the capital cost increased but the steam requirement decreased. An *optimal* number of effects can be expected when the PW of the operation is maximized.

The PW of manufacturing tomato paste as a function of number of effects of the evaporator was calculated using an MS Excel spreadsheet using the data given in Table 5-4. The results are shown in Figure 5.7.

It can be seen from Figure 5.7 that the optimal number of effects is about 3 for a maximum PW of the manufacture of tomato paste. The results are shown in Table 5-5.

Table 5-5 PW Analysis for Concentration of Tomato Paste

Number of Effects, N_E	Capital Cost (Millions, $)	Steam Utilities Cost (Millions, $ per year)	Price $ per kg	Revenue (Millions, $)	PW (Millions, $)
1	92	8.1	4	21.6	2.5
2	108	3.24	4.07	21.98	23.2
3	115	2.16	4.14	22.4	26.4
4	122	1.62	4.21	22.7	25.8
5	129	1.35	4.28	23.1	23.3
6	136	1.188	4.35	23.5	20.1
7	143	1.08	4.42	23.9	16.5

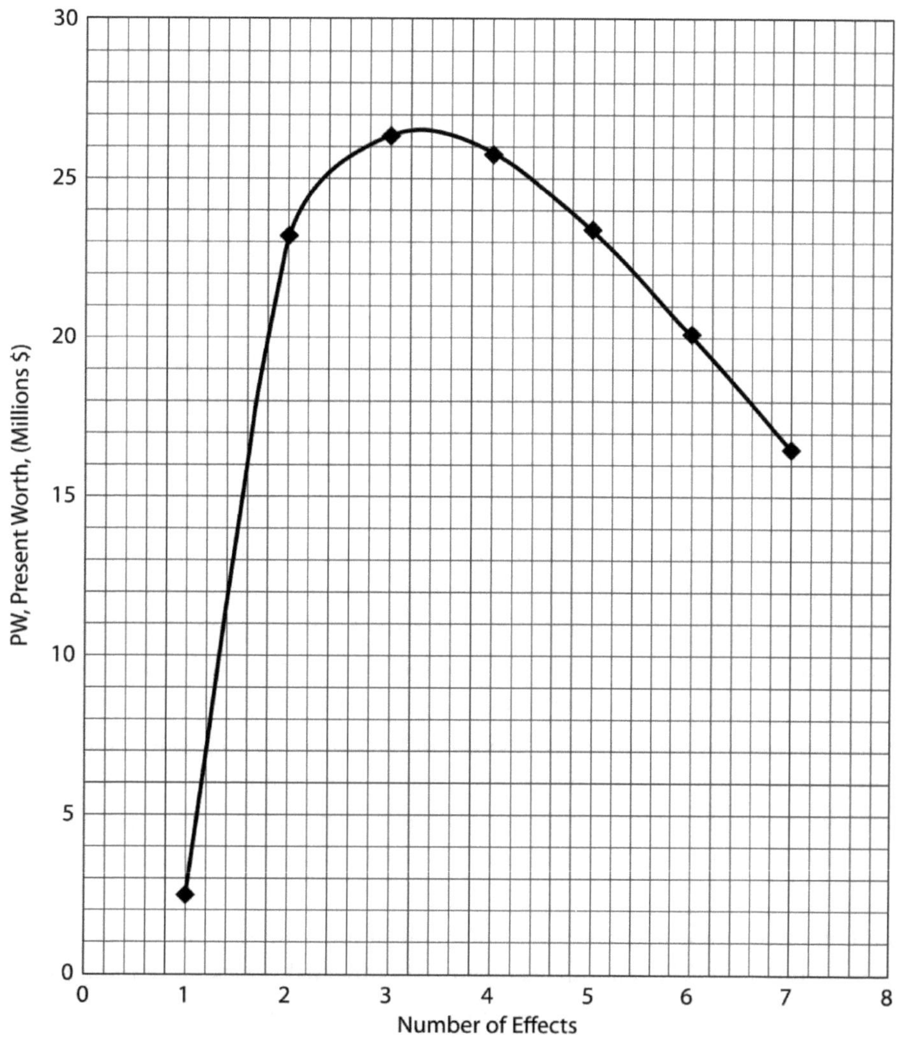

Figure 5.7 PW of the Multiple Effect Evaporator Operation as a Function of Number of Effects

5.5 Household Finances

The head of a household in the 21st century must make a variety of financial decisions. Sometimes the value of money principles and decision analyses explained in the earlier chapters may be applicable to personal finances. The five largest financial decisions that every individual can be expected to make during their earning years are as follows:

Home Ownership and Mortgage;
Car Ownership and Financing;
Insurance and Taxes;
Credit Card Application and Credit Score;
Retirement Planning—Nest Egg.

The time period associated with home mortgages is usually 30 years. New cars are financed over 60 or 72 months. Income tax to the federal government, state government, and city government must be paid every year. Life insurance, health insurance, auto collision and liability insurance, and home owners' or renters' insurance payments are expected once every six months or per quarter. A college graduate starting his career in this day and age would be looking to establish his or her line of credit. Credit card companies loan the principal when one of their customers wants to make a purchase anywhere, anyplace, anytime in the world. In return, the customer pays them every month at an interest rate a lot higher than the prime lending rate to banks and other financial institutions. In the new millennium, social security payments are not sufficient for the elderly after their retirement. Inflation eats into their peace of mind during retirement. IRA, Keogh accounts, and 401(k) savings plan have to be opened and maintained for a secure retirement by middle-class citizens.

The total household wealth in our nation is about $54.2 trillion. According to a recent survey, there are 114 million households in the United States. The number of millionaires has tripled in recent decades.

Home ownership is a means for less-wealthy individuals to attain net worth that will place them in the top quartile of the wealthiest people in America. New homes are built in neighborhoods within commuting distance from major cities. The purchase price of a home ranges from $50,000–$1 million. The purchase price is paid for first by banks that let the individual take out a mortgage. Home mortgages are repaid over a time period of 30 years. As can be seen from the annuity tables in Appendix A, the multipliers for 30 years are not all that different from the multipliers at infinite time. This is a good break for the borrowers and serves as an incentive to purchase mortgages. Banks borrow money from the Federal Bank Reserve at the prime lending rate. Part of these monies is given out as home mortgages at a slightly higher rate compared with the prime rate. The banks operate within the mortgage and prime rates. All their employees' salaries, profits, and building costs come from these two numbers. For example, in 2010 at the time of this writing, the prime rate is 3.25%. The home mortgage rates from leading lenders are about 4.5%. Mortgage rates can be fixed or a mortgage can be an ARM (adjustable rate mortgage). The interest rates over a 30-year period may change. For example, on December 19, 1980, the prime rate was at a record high of 21.5%. During the course of the time period of a 30-year mortgage, a home owner can do what is called *refinancing*. Here the balance of the loan is paid off by the bank in full and a fresh loan is issued at the new refinanced rate.

When the amount owed on the house is close to the value of the house, leading banks would expect payment of a PMI (mortgage insurance). The monthly payment the individual makes every month consists of three or more components: (i) principal and interest; (ii) real estate taxes; and (iii) mortgage insurance. The principal and interest go toward repayment of the loan at the agreed-upon interest rate. The taxes are paid to the state and local governments. They use these monies for several things, including running schools, etc. Often, politicians run and win elections and lower taxes. Some of the leaders feel that government is the problem. Others, equally popular, feel that government can do more. According to them, there is nothing wrong about America that cannot be corrected with what is right about America. The monthly mortgage payment for an individual depends on the price of the home and the individual's income. The three C's of finance are character, capacity, and collateral. The character is the individual's past credit history. Have they issued bounced checks? Have they paid all their bills and credit card payments on time? Capacity is the individual's income. Is he a physician drawing $200,000 in annual salary? Is he a rock star? Collateral is the other assets that the individual has against which the bank can issue the loan. Rules of thumb such as no more than 28% of monthly income can go toward mortgage payment is common in parts of Texas. Some banks in New England require the purchase price to be within two times the borrower's annual salary.

A short sale occurs when the selling price of the house is lower than the amount owed on the house. Foreclosure happens after the individual defaults on mortgage payments and the bank takes possession of the house (and usually sells it). Reverse mortgage is applicable to the elderly who have gained equity on their homes. They can take back their equity in the form of uniform monthly payments as fixed income. This is usually used for expenses incurred during retirement.

Example 5.8 Refinancing of Steve Gandhi

Steve Gandhi purchased a home in New England in 1980 at a mortgage rate of 21% for 30 years. The price of the home was $150,000. In 1992 the mortgage rate fell to 6.5%. He went for refinancing. With closing costs of $3000, by how much did the monthly payment come down for Steve after the refinancing?

(A/P,21%,30) = 0.210692 (from Appendix A)

Monthly Principal and Interest Payment at 21% mortgage rate

= $150,000*0.210692/12 = $2,633.65

In 1992 the balance owed by Steve = X

X =PW($2633.65,21%,18) = (P/A,21%,18)*2,633.65*12 = 4.6079*$2,633.5*12 = $145,627.2

Number of years left in the 30 year mortgage = 30 – 12 = 18 years

(A/P,6.5%,18) = 0.092357 (from Appendix A)

Monthly Payment after Refinancing for Steve = (145,627.2+3000)*0.092357/12 = $1,143.90

Reduction in Monthly Payment of Principal and Interest = $2,633 - $1,143.90 = $1,489.75

Example 5.9 Toyota National Clearance

The 2010 Toyota Corolla can be purchased for $18,890. There is a rebate of $1,500 or 0% financing for 60 months. The finance rate, should the rebate be selected, is 7.0%. Which option has a lower monthly payment, the cash rebate or 0% financing for 60 months? The life of a 4-cylinder-engine car is around 105,000 miles. With an average driving of 15,000 miles per commuter, this can be taken as seven years.

Option A—0% financing for 60 months

Let the annual payment for 7 years be uniform and = X

For the first 5 years the interest rate is 0%

Hence the amount owed at end of year 5 = $18,890 – 5X

For the 6th and 7th year the interest rate = 7.0%

(A/P,7%,2) = 0.553092

X = 0.553092*($18,890 – 5X)

$$X = \frac{0.553092 * \$18{,}890}{(1 + 0.553092 * 5)} = \$2774.67$$

Monthly Payment = X/12 = $231.22

Option B—$1500 Rebate

(A/P,7%,7) = 0.5*(0.20976+0.167468) = 0.188632

Monthly Payment = (A/P,7%,7)*($18,890-$1,500)/12 = $273.36

The option with 0% finance rate for 60 months will result in a lower monthly payment compared with the $1500 cash rebate option.

The wealth of households has to come from savings at some point. Japan, the European Union countries, and China have higher savings rates compared to us. Wealth building can come from saving money and investing in assets such as

Stocks;
Bonds;
Money Market;
CDs;
Gold.

Individuals can purchase shares from companies listed in the NYSE (New York Stock Exchange), NASDAQ (National Association of Securities Dealers Automated Quotations), etc. A broker is needed. Leading brokerage firms such as Quick and Reilly allow clients to trade online and brokerage fees are charged as a percentage of the value of the trade. Often individuals are busy making money and do not have time to follow the stock markets and budget deficits of the federal government on a day-to-day basis. There are investment bankers who are willing to take care of the savings of an individual. They operate through *mutual funds.* The front-end and back-end fees of the mutual fund must be considered prior to the individual investing in mutual funds. These days, the mutual fund units are transferrable. Investment bankers let the principle of *diversification* work for their clients. There is a certain *risk* involved in buying stocks or bonds. Rather than the individual assuming the entire risk, the burden of risk is shared by several mutual fund investors. The investment banker may allocate a certain percentage of the funds to stocks, bonds, and money market accounts. He may trade in foreign markets such as Tokyo, the European Union, Bombay, etc. Examples of mutual funds are given in Table 5-4. The banker may buy more stocks and bonds when the interest rates are *low* and buy more money market funds and gold when interest rates are *high*.

The number of credit cards has increased in the last three decades. There are 576.4 million credit cards with an average balance of $15,519 active today, per a recent survey among U.S. households. There is a website, www.creditcards.com, where comparison shopping of credit cards can be done. There are different types of credit cards. These are

Low-Interest Credit Cards;
Instant Approval Credit Cards;
Balance Transfer Cards;
Cash Back Credit Cards;
Travel and Airline Credit Cards;
Business Credit Cards;
Student Credit Cards;

Table 5-6 Top Mutual Funds (*US News & World Report*)

Name of Mutual Fund	Value of Fund	Last 1-Year Return (August 2010)	Stocks, Bonds, Money Market Mix of Holdings
Invesco van Kampen Equity and Income Fund	$12.07 billion	14.8%	Stocks—68.45% Bonds—15.4%
Yachtman Fund	$2.1 billion	22.5%	Stocks—85.11% Cash—14.5%
FMI Large Cap Fund	$2.7 billion	17.0%	Stocks—88.96% Cash—11.04%
Templeton Global Bond Fund	$34.6 billion	14.0%	Bonds—80.42% Cash—16.68%
Eaton Vance Tax Managed Emerging Markets Fund	$1.8 billion	24.7%	Stocks—92.74% Bonds—0.01% Cash—0.85%
TCW Total Return Bond Fund	$5.0 billion	16.1%	Bonds—94.3% Cash—5.68%
Appleseed Fund	$139.6 million	20.3%	Stocks—71.1% Cash—14.1%
Monetta Young Investor	$6.7 million	26.3%	Stocks—85.1% Cash—14.9%
Marsico Flexible Capital Fund	$61.7 million	33.7%	Stocks—84.9% Bonds—6.9% Cash—8.2%
Boston Trust Small Cap Fund	$156.2 million	24.5%	Stocks—97.6% Cash—2.4%
Tilson Dividend Fund	$16.6 million	25.4%	Stocks—86.5% Cash—9.1%

Prepaid and Debit Cards.

Some of these credit cards can be used at locations all over the world. Many hotels and car rental companies will not transact business with customers without a credit card. Credit cards are used as deposits at several places of business. Some of these cards, such as a Macy's Department Store card, can be used only within the retail chain. An Exxon gasoline card can be used to buy gasoline at Exxon gas stations. Most general-purpose cards are unsecured. The credit line is extended based on credit history. Secured cards are issued after backed up by opening a savings account. Secured cards cater to a market of individuals with challenged credit or little or no credit history. Some universities have a course on *consumer finance*. The average consumer has nine credit cards.

Credit card interest rates can change dramatically over the pay period of a purchase. It can range from 0% limited balance transfer offers to as high as 30%. The prime rate these days is low at 3.25%. The record high prime rate was 21.5% in the last quarter of 1980. The credit card companies are allowed to charge 20% above the prime rate. So should the prime rate reach 21.5% again, the credit card interest rate would be as high as 41.5%. This will increase the minimum monthly payment and the time taken to pay the credit card back. The

APR set for a customer by the credit card issuing bank depends on several factors such as credit score, income, assets, current debt load, credit inquiries, payment history, and economic conditions. The lowest rates are given to customers with positive and proven credit histories.

Banks, credit unions, retailers, and credit card companies are allowed to issue credit cards. Someone who wants to issue a credit card may do so after getting the necessary approvals from state officials. The department that issues the sole proprietorship, partnership, and C corporation can permit people who want to issue credit cards. Visa and MasterCard are companies that help process payments. American Express started like Diners Club as a restaurant card. It used to be that all charges had to be paid at the end of the month when using an American Express card. Discover Card pays some cash back. A small percentage of the purchase amounts are refunded to the customer. Every credit card issued has a signed agreement that has to be followed. The contract is binding. The agreement discloses the credit limit available, APR (annual percentage rate), interest calculation method—such as by daily balance, fixed or variable APR—grace period, fees, etc.

The Credit Card Act of 2009 mandated that credit card bills contain warnings about the consequences of paying only the minimum balance. This act, signed into law by President Obama, limits when issuers of consumer credit cards can increase interest rates and bans billing and payment practices that the Federal Reserve calls "unfair or deceptive."

5.6 Summary

Brainstorming can be used to develop alternatives for a given problem. The five methods of analysis, PW, FW, AW, IRR, and ERR can be used to evaluate the alternatives. Evaluation of alternatives can be used to invest in the more profitable process, selection of the lower cost alternative, quantitate the savings accrued from implementation of a process improvement, and assessment of environmental impact of chemical processes. Alternatives can be mutually exclusive, independent projects, and screening by other criteria.

The PW (present worth) of identified alternatives can be calculated and compared with each other. Three cases are identified. When one PW is greater than zero and the second PW is less than zero, the one greater than zero can be selected over the one that is less than zero. When both PWs are greater than zero, the alternatives are rank ordered. When the PWs of both alternatives are within 20% of each other, the projects can be adjudged as too close to call within the sensitivity of the estimates of the capital and operating expenses and expected revenues.

Worked examples have been developed to select the better process to manufacture CNTs (carbon nanotubes), cost savings by using microfiltration in pretreatment during SWRO (sea water reverse osmosis), evaluation of the process to manufacture bioethanol from sugarcane bagasse, and better routes for sequestration.

When the useful lives of critical equipment are different for different alternatives, two methods for comparison analysis are developed. In the repeatability assumption the study period is selected as a lowest common multiple between the two useful lives. In the co-terminated assumption, the alternative with greater useful life is truncated at the useful life of the second alternative. Expenses and revenues are reevaluated after the truncation. For example, the salvage value can be moved up. Worked examples on comparison on fair basis were discussed on life-cycle costs of copiers with different initial fixed costs and variable costs; life-cycle costs of aviation lighting using LEDs or incandescent bulbs; and evaluation of automatic cartoning vs. manual cartoning in a pharmaceutical plant. The rate of return concept was introduced.

PW can be optimized. This is especially so when there exists a trade-off between variable and incremental capital costs. For example, when tomato paste is manufactured with more effects in a multiple effect evaporator, the energy costs decrease and the capital costs increase. The PW of the plant to manufacture tomato paste reaches a maximum value at an intermediate value of number of effects as the number of effects is increased. There exists a golden triangle of production, quality, and profit. A worked example on optimal number of effects in a multiple effect evaporator was created.

The rudiments of household finances are discussed. These include home mortgage, car ownership and financing, insurance and taxes, credit card application and credit score, and retirement planning and nest eggs. Home mortgages are loans provided for home purchase with a 30-year payback period. During that period, the lender holds the lien on the house. The payback period is nearly infinity. Auto financing is a loan given to the buyer with a six- or seven-year payback period. During that time, the title of the car belongs to the financial service provider. The nest eggs of individuals for retirement can be created with a diversified portfolio of stocks, bonds, money market accounts, and gold. There are many different kinds of credit cards.

End-of-chapter exercises based on case studies were developed. These include evaluation of manufacturing processes for ABS engineering thermoplastic; polystyrene production; snack factory; transcontinental oil pipeline; Stirling dish solar power plant; refinancing scheme; analysis for renting or buying a home; business plan for a software development service; life-cycle costs of a PEV (plug-in electric vehicle); largest solar thermal power plant; and wind energy production in Saudi Arabia. Other examples explored include printing books in hard copy form or e-book form; blow-molding press; life insurance by direct marketing vs. life insurance via the Internet; emissions reduction in an oil refinery; improvements to combined cycle power plants; four different cooling tower designs; rechargeable batteries; and heap leaching and agitation leaching processes for gold recovery.

5.7 References

[1] K. R. Sharma, *Nanostructuring Operations in Nanoscale Science and Engineering*. McGraw-Hill Professional (2010), New York, NY.

[2] A. E. Agboola, R. W. Pike, T. A. Hertwig, and H. H. Lou, "Conceptual Design of Carbon Nanotube Processes," *Clean Techn. Env. Policy*, 9 (2007), 289–311.

[3] S. Ebrahim, S. Bou-Hamed, M. Abdel-Jawad, and N. Burney, "Microfiltration System as a Pretreatment for RO Units: Technical and Economic Assessment," *Desalination*, 109 (1997), 165–175.

[4] B. F. Sarrouh, S. S. Silva, D. T. Santos, and A. Converti, "Technical/Economical Evaluation of Sugarcane Bagasse Hydrolysis for Bioethanol Production," *Chem. Eng. Technology*, Vol. 30, 2 (2007), 270–275.

[5] J. Garcia, M. S. Monteiro, O. de W. F. Araujo, and J. L. de Medeiros, "Sustainability Metrics for Eco-Technologies Assessment, Part II. Life Cycle Analysis," *Clean Techn. Environ. Policy*, Vol. 11 (2009), 459–472.

[6] N. Narendran, J. D. Bullough, N. Maliyagoda, and A. Bierman, "What Is the Useful Life for White Light LEDs " Illuminating Engineering Society, IES Paper #52.

[7] R. Simpson, S. Almonacid, D. Lopez, and A. Abakarov, "Optimum Design and Operating Conditions of Multiple Effect Evaporators: Tomato Paste," *Journal of Food Engineering*, Vol. 89 (2008), 488–497.

[8] T. Tsoutos, V. Gekas, and K. Marketaki, "Technical and Economical Evaluation of Solar Thermal Power Generation," *Renewable Energy*, Vol. 28 (2003), 873–886.

[9] S. Rehman, "Prospects of Wind Farm Development in Saudi Arabia," *Renewable Energy*, Vol. 30 (2005), 447–463.

[10] S. Boonnasa and P. Namprakai, "Sensitivity Analysis for the Capacity Improvement of a Combined Cycle Power Plant (100–600 MW), *Applied Thermal Engineering*, Vol. 28 (2008), 1865–1874.

5.8 Exercises

1.0 Laundry

Sam Malone went through a divorce and is now single. He is considering buying a Kenmore washer and dryer with a total purchase price of $841.08. The electric utility charges run Sam $15/month. If he were to take his clothes to a dry cleaner, each dress shirt and pair of pants would cost him $1 each. The dry cleaners charge $2 per laundry bag of other garments. Each week he needs to wash five dress shirts, five dress pants, and one bag of other garments. At an interest rate of 4.5% for a study period of five years, which is the lower cost alternative: (i) purchase of Kenmore washer and dryer; or (ii) having the laundry done by the dry cleaners?

2.0 Grandma's Hand-Mades

Grandma's Hand-Mades is a business proposal to make peanut balls at a local restaurant, and bag and sell them at local grocery stores. The bags sold, unit price (P) and unit cost (C_v), are shown below in Table 5-7 for a 10-year period. The interest rate for the first five years was 5% and the next five years was 8%.

The capital cost of starting Grandma's Hand-Mades is about $6,500. Business Plan B is to invest $6,500 in a Templeton Fund that returns about $900 per year. Which is a better investment, Grandma's Hand-Mades or a Templeton Fund?

3.0 Globalization of Polystyrene Manufacture

Consider two polystyrene manufacturing plants at two different locations: (i) Lalgudi, India; and (ii) Clarksburg, West Virginia. Calculate the PW of the two plants and select the better alternative. The price of styrene delivered to the plant in Lalgudi is about $0.59 per pound; in Clarksburg, it is $0.66 per pound. The selling price of GP (general purpose) polystyrene is about $0.84 in West Virginia and $0.64 in India. The capital cost of equipment is about $2 million in West Virginia at a production capacity of 11 million pounds per year. The capital cost of equipment for the plant in India is about $1 million at a capacity of 20 million pounds per

Table 5-7 Demand, Price, and Cost for Peanut Balls

Year	Demand	Unit Price	Unit Cost
2011	1000	1.99	0.75
2012	1094.476	2.0497	0.7725
2013	637.889	2.111191	0.795675
2014	514.2253	2.174527	0.819545
2015	837.1806	2.239763	0.844132
2016	1309.831	2.306955	0.869456
2017	1497.625	2.376164	0.895539
2018	1227.904	2.447449	0.922405
2019	748.6497	2.374026	0.894733
2020	500.4856	2.302805	0.867891

year. The plant utilization factor is 80% in Clarksburg and 70% in Lalgudi. The energy and labor costs are 5 cents per pound of PS made in America and 0.5 cents per pound of PS made in India. The interest rate is about 6% in Clarksburg and 11% in Lalgudi. The useful life of the plant in America is 14 years; in India, it is 10 years.

4.0 Manufacturing Location for ABS Plant

Select the better location for the ABS (acrylonitrile butadiene styrene) engineering thermoplastic plant made using continuous mass polymerization technology. The raw materials are PBd (polybutadiene) rubber, styrene monomer, acrylonitrile monomer, ethyl benzene solvent, initiator, anti-oxidant, mineral oil, and other minor additives. A train of three CSTRs in series are used to obtain the grafted two-phase ABS composite product. A twin-screw extruder-cum-devolatilizer is used to recover the unconverted monomers and solvent and recycled back to the reactors. The finished product is in pellet form. It can be sold at $1.03 in Clarksburg. In India, it fetches 81 cents per pound. The monomer costs are 59 cents per pound for styrene in India and 66 cents per pound of styrene in the States, 90 cents per pound of AN, acrylonitrile monomer in India and 80 cents per pound of AN (acrylonitrile) monomer in the United States. The PBd price is 51 cents per pound in India and 70 cents per pound in Clarksburg. The ABS consists of 14% PbS. The copolymer SAN in the ABS graft and matrix is 25 wt % AN. The capital cost of the ABS plant is $40 million in Clarksburg and $10 million in India. The product rate is 28,000 lbs. per hour in both locations. The plant utilization factor is 80% in the USA and 75% in India. The utility and labor costs are 0.5 cents per pound in India and 1 cent per pound in the States. The interest rate is about 6% in America and 11% in India. The useful life of the U.S. plant is 14 years; 10 years in India.

5.0 Keystone XL

A transcontinental pipeline, known as Keystone XL, is proposed that would ferry Canadian crude oil to Texas refineries. The Keystone XL runs from Alberta, Canada, through the states of Montana, South Dakota, Nebraska, Kansas, Oklahoma, and Texas, up to Port Arthur and Houston (in Texas). The length of the 36" pipeline is about 2000 miles. The capacity of the pipeline in 900,000 BPD, barrels per day. The revenue from sales of one barrel of oil is about $75. Given a cost of $66.23 for a 72" stretch of the pipeline, calculate the capital cost to lay the entire pipeline. Include 10 pumps per mile at a cost of $5000 per pump. An estimated 3000 jobs are expected to be created at an average salary of $25,000 per annum. The overhead rate is $1 per $1 of wages. The land lease and taxes run about 30% of the revenue. For a pipeline life of 18 years, calculate the PW of the pipeline at an interest rate of 3.25%. The utility costs to operate the pumps are estimated at $25 million per year.

Consider the alternative of hauling the same amount of crude (900,000 BPD) using trucks. Say 250 barrels can be hauled by one truck at a cost of each truck at $65,000; what would be the capital costs of a fleet of trucks? The annual fuel cost can be estimated at 300 days of operation in a year. The fuel efficiency, or mpg, for a truck is 20 mpg. The wages for truck drivers can be estimated at $30,000 per driver. The number of drivers needed would be 135,000 per year. At a useful life of six years, calculate the PW of the truck freight service. The interest rate is 5%.

Which is a better alternative, the Keystone XL or truck freight service?

6.0 Stirling Dish (SD) Solar Power Plant

Upon graduation you are chartered with the task of selecting between two different plans for generating electricity using Stirling dish technology. There is increased interest in recent years to use solar energy to generate electricity. The Stirling engine is environmentally clean, with zero emissions. Solar-to-electric conversion efficiencies in the range of 30% can be realized using SD (Stirling dish) solar electric generating systems [8]. Individual units range

Table 5-8 Cost and Economic Data for Plans A and B for Stirling Dish Solar Power Plant

	Plan A	Plan B
Capacity	50 MW	50 MW
# SD Units	10,000	2000
Annual Solar Radiation (kWh/m^2)	1.728	1.728
Annual Electricity Generated	7 GWh	7 GWh
Life of Solar Power Plant	30 years	30 years
Interest rate (i)	10%	10%
Sale Price of Electricity	7.3c/kWh	7.3c/kWh
Equipment Costs	$22.4 per unit	$324.45 per unit
Transport Costs	$3.36 per unit	$48.65 per unit
Land Cost	$19,000	$19,000
Earthworks	$22,000	$99,600
Other Costs	$7.46 per unit	$10.8 per unit
Operation & Management Expense	$10,122	$10,122

in capacity between 5–25 kW. Solar power plants become attractive from an economic standpoint when the land cost is low and government incentives are high for generating electricity in a pollution-free manner. Each unit is comprised of a solar concentrator. A power conversion unit is located at the focus of the parabolic dish. It consists of a cavity receiver and a Stirling heat engine with an electric generator or alternator. The concentrator reflects and concentrates solar radiation and delivers it to the receiver. The light is absorbed by the receiver and heat is transferred to a working fluid such as helium or hydrogen. Alternative compression and expansion of the working fluid in a piston arrangement leads to generation of electricity. Parabolic dish concentrators can be used to achieve temperatures greater than 1500°C. A 5 kW unit would require a 5.5 m diameter dish and a 25 kW unit would require a 10 m diameter dish. The cost of the concentrators is 25% of the cost of the SD systems, The cost and economic data for the two Plans, A and B, are given below in Table 5-8. The PW method of analysis is recommended to arrive at the decision.

7.0 Best Process to Manufacture CNTs (Carbon Nanotubes), Example 5.1

As discussed in Example 5.1, there are two processes used to manufacture CNTs. Find out which is more profitable at 5 % effective interest rate:

Process A: The HiPCO reactor is used. HiPCO is the high-pressure carbon monoxide process used in manufacturing CNT using the Boudard reaction [1]. A PFR (plug flow reactor) designed at Rice University in Houston is used at high pressures of 30–50 bar and at temperatures of 1273–1473 K. CNTs and CO_2 are produced from CO, carbon monoxide, and iron pent carbonyl catalyst precursor. The conversion was 20%.

Process B: The CoMoCAT reactor is used. CO disproportionation is effected over a mixed cobalt-molybdenum catalyst on silica support in a fluidized bed reactor developed at the University of Oklahoma. The reaction forms CNTs and CO2-at temperatures between 973–1223 K and total pressure ranging from 15–50 psia. The CO selectivity is 80% and conversion about 20%. The information needed for economic analysis on the processes is given in Table 5-1 from Agboola et al. [2].

Table 5-9 Two Processes to Manufacture CNTs

Item	Process A (Amount)	Process A (Description)	Process B (Amount)	Process B (Description)
Catalyst		Fe		Co-Mo
Reactants		CO & $Fe(CO)_5$		CO
Reactor		Plug Flow Reactor		Fluidized Bed
Temperature		1050°C		950°C
Pressure		450 psia		150 psia
Selectivity		90%		80%
Purification		Oxidation, Filtration		Leaching, Froth Flotation
Product Rate		1000 kg/h		1000 kg/h
Steam	10 cents/kg	5000 kg/h		5,500 kg/h
Gas	40 cents /kg	900 kg/h		900 kg/h
Electricity	0.07 cents/kWh	2 MW		600 kW
Capital Cost of Plant	$8.6 million		$8.4 million	
Price	$42/kg		$20/kg	
Materials Cost	$250 million		$150 million	
Plant Life		15 years		15 years
Operation		300 days/year		300 days/year

8.0 Cost Savings by Using Microfiltration Pretreatment during SWRO (Sea Water Reverse Osmosis), Example 5.2

Pretreatment has been used to improve the performance and lower the overall cost of obtaining water using SWRO (sea water reverse osmosis) plants. Control of membrane fouling is agreed upon as a problem encountered during the operation of the SWRO plants. The conventional pretreatment method controls and minimizes the plugging potential of the feed water by coagulating, flocculating, and filtering out colloidal and suspended solids and by achievement of reduction in SDI (silt density index) of feed water. MF (microfiltration) pretreatment appears to be an attractive method. Turbidities of water can be lowered less than 0.1 NTU regardless of inflow turbidity level. UF pre-treatment results in the removal of TC (total coli) from the bacteria *Giardia* and *Cryptosporidium.* Viruses are also removed. The novel pretreatment strategy leads to reduction in capital cost, reduction in operating costs due to lower membrane replacement, less chemical consumption, elimination of cartridge filters, less downtime, less maintenance cost, less labor cost, etc. The MF unit is skid mounted and impurities larger than 200 nm are removed using this device. The machine consists of polypropylene filtration modules, circulation pump, associated valves, piping, and instrumentation and control systems.

The data needed to perform comparison of alternatives is given below in Table 5-10 and taken from [3]. The capital expenses such as treatment plants, pumps, etc. are financed over a 30-year period at 8% interest rate.

9.0 Bioethanol from Sugarcane Bagasse (Example 5.3)

In Brazil 387 million tons of sugarcane was produced in 2005/2006, and 104 million tons of bagasse came from the sugar mills. From a ton of sugarcane, 73 kg of fermentable sugars and 27 kg of dry bagasse can be produced. The composition of bagasse is as follows:

Cellulose 43%

Table 5-10 Economic Data for Evaluation of MF Pretreatment

	Conventional		Microfiltration	
Description	$ millions/year	$ (millions)	$ millions/year	$ (millions)
Plant		100		25
Pumps		1.5		1.5
Dosing Plant		0.10		0
Structural		6		6
Subtotal		80		30
Electricity	6		4	
Chemicals	2.3		0.75	
Filters	1.7			
Water Rate		12,500 m³/day		

Xylans 25%
Lignin 23%.

Hemicellulose is a polymer of xylose, and cellulose is a polymer of glucose. The sugarcane bagasse can be burned in boilers to generate electricity. Sugarcane bagasse can be converted to bioethanol and furfural by a dilute acid hydrolysis process. The acid hydrolysis process is a two-stage operation. In the first stage, hemicellulose is converted into sugar using dilute acid and steam. In the second stage, cellulose is converted to sugar by hydrolysis. Upon hydrolysis, the sugar can be processed in order to produce ethanol, furfural, and other products. Furfural can either be used alone or combined with phenol, acetone, or urea to make solid resins. Such resins are used to make fiberglass, aircraft components, and automotive brakes. Furfural can also be used as a hydrocarbon solvent. Coproduction of ethanol and furfural can make the process more profitable. The acid hydrolysis plant consists of the following equipment:

Pump and Heater;
Reactor to Produce Furfural and Glucose;
Purification and Separation.

After passing through the heater, the feedstock is treated with dilute sulfuric acid solution (0.5 wt%) at high temperature for a short time. Cellulose and pentose are converted to glucose and furfural, respectively. The hydrolyzed stream is then separated using a distillation column. The hydrolyzed material is then neutralized with lime. The upper stream is passed through a condenser, leading to the formation of furfural. The unreacted cellulosic residue and lignin from the stream can be burned to generate electricity or sold as a by-product. The total capital investment needed for the acid hydrolysis plant is about $8 million [4]. The furfural can be sold for $1.91/kg and ethanol can be sold for $1.37/kg. The bagasse suppliers must be paid at 18 cents per kg of feedstock. A dilute acid hydrolysis plant can operate at 10,000 kg/h of sugarcane bagasse. The utilities and labor costs were estimated and found to be $1.50 per kg of ethanol and $2/kg of furfural. The plant utilization factor is 85%. The yield of ethanol is 25% and that of furfural is 10% from the bagasse.

Which would be a better alternative: (i) start a dilute acid hydrolysis plant with an estimated life of 28 years; or (ii) generate electricity from bagasse using a power plant? The costs of the steam boiler and turbine are about $2 million each. The electricity can be sold at 12.0 cents per kWh. The calorific value of bagasse is 8.0 MJ/kg. The power plant thermal efficiency can be taken as 32%. The interest rate is 8%. For purposes of analysis, assume that the power plant life is equal to that of the acid hydrolysis plant, at 28 years. The operating expenses of the power plant are about 6 cents per kWh.

10.0 Sequestration by Dimethyl Carbonate Formation (Example 5.4)

Two routes for the chemical reuse of CO_2 (carbon dioxide) is considered. Interest in sequestration projects is increasing due to global warming concerns. Studies have shown that a 10% dimethyl carbonate (DMC) addition to diesel leads to 20% smoke reduction. Both plants operate at 10,800 h/year. CO_2 is available at no cost. Each ton of CO_2 sequestered leads to carbon credits of $21. Electric utilities cost 47 cents per kWh. Which is a better alternative at an interest rate of 4% and a plant life of 20 years?

Route A: Production from Ethylene Oxide: Ethylene oxide and CO_2 are allowed to react to form ethylene carbonate. Ethylene carbonate produced is reacted with methanol in a second PFR (plug flow reactor) leading to the production of DMC and ethylene glycol. The capital cost can be taken as $50 million; 70,000 tons/year of CO_2 are sequestered. The energy used in this process is 200 TJ/year. Revenue from the plant is $3500 per ton of CO_2 sequestered.

Route B: Production from Urea: Urea is produced by reacting ammonia and CO_2. DMC is produced by urea methanolysis. The capital cost for this route is given as $200 million; 50,000 tons/year of CO_2 are sequestered. The energy used in this process is 800 TJ/year. The revenue from the plant is $4000 per ton of CO_2 sequestered.

11.0 Life-Cycle Cost of Photocopier (Example 5.5)

The Xerox Work Center copier can handle up to 100,000 pages per month and has a copy speed of up to 45 pages per minute. It costs about $1000 and weighs 40 lbs. The toner cartridge costs about $65 per cartridge. It can print 1000 pages. This machine has a useful life of six years. Toshiba's e-STUDIO 455 can copy up to 45 pages per minute, and the base unit costs about $5,800. The toner yield is 15,000 pages and the cost is $90 each. The useful life of the e-STUDIO 455 is about 12 years. Which copier has the lower life-cycle cost: the Xerox Work Center or the Toshiba e-STUDIO? The interest rate is 6%. Assume that 1/2 million pages are copied every year.

12.0 Aviation Lighting—LEDs or Incandescent Bulbs? (Example 5.6)

Light-emitting diode works on the principle of electroluminescence, which is the release of photon energy from electron-hole recombinations within the device. The color of the light depends on the wavelength of the light corresponding to the energy released. LEDs have lower energy consumption and longer lives compared with incandescent lamps. Boeing wants you to calculate the life-cycle cost of LEDs and incandescent lamps for its new aircraft. They need 1000 lights at 80 W each. The incandescent lamps each have a 108-hr life and cost $1.16. The illumination received is 1500 lumens per bulb. The 250-W mercury LED lamp costs $20 per lamp and can last for 17,000 hours at an illumination of 32,000 lumens. Assume that the Boeing flight is in operation for 300 days a year. The cost of electricity is 12.5 cents per kWh. The interest rate is 10%.

Table 5-11 Cost and Revenue Information for Pharmaceutical Plant

	Plan A Manual Cartoning	Plan B Automatic Cartoning
Batches	72/quarter	195/year
Production	2 million tubes	2,599,936
Capital Cost (Equipment)	———	$900,000
Operating Cost	$437,631	$4,847,157
Revenue	$6,001,400	$9,835,500

13.0 Anti-Allergic Cream (Example 5.7)

A pharmaceutical plant is proposing to manufacture anti-allergic cream. The plant consists of six unit operations: (i) melting; (ii) blending; (iii) filling; (iv) cartoning; and (v) packaging both shrink wrapping and for shipment. Batches of emulsifying wax and foam stable are independently heated in a jacketed heater. Then emulsifier and ointment are added. Excipient 3 is dissolved in hot deionized water DI and then blended with the other ingredients. The active ingredient is finally added. Cooling procedures are instituted that last for 19 hours. The blended product is filled in tubes of 15 g each. The filling machine can fill 30 tubes per minute. Five sealed boxes per minute are prepared.

In a second method, a new multifunctional blending tank and automatic cartoning machine, with a line speed of 60 tubes per minute, are introduced. The cost is about $900,000. The data needed to evaluate the two alternatives are given in Table 5.3. The interest rate may be taken as 8%. A 20-year life of the modification can be assumed.

14.0 Refinancing for Steve Gandhi (Example 5.8)

Steve Gandhi purchased a home in New England in 1990 at a mortgage rate of 11% for 30 years. The price of the home was $170,000. In 2010 the mortgage rate fell to 4.5%. Steve went for refinancing. With closing costs of $2000, by how much did the monthly payment come down for Steve after the refinancing?

15.0 *Rent or Buy?*

Ms. Kay Smith is considering buying a home near Houston at a purchase price of $114,000. The federal government provides a tax credit of $7,500 for first-time buyers. The real estate home prices near the Houston area increase in value by 7% every year. Consider a five-year study period. Should Kay decide to rent an apartment, she has to pay $675 per month. The interest rate can be taken as 4%. The monthly mortgage payment on the new house, including principal and interest, real estate taxes, and mortgage insurance works out to be $1052.95. Is it better for Kay to rent an apartment or buy the house?

16.0 Software Developers

You are asked to review a business plan to develop software. The office building is purchased at $100,000. The computer equipment costs about $6000. Six software engineers are hired. Their salaries are about $50,000 each per year. The utilities and wires for the entire office building run about $6000 per year. The engineers develop a product that can be used by the customer along with the Internet. For a planning horizon of the next eight years, the number of software units, price of software units, and the revenues that can be expected are given in Table

Table 5-12 Software Unit Sales for Next 8 years

Software Sales

Year	Units	Price	Revenue
2011	500	$50	$25,000
2012	5000	$55	$275,000
2013	10000	$60	$600,000
2014	15000	$65	$975,000
2015	20000	$70	$1,400,000
2016	250000	$75	$18,750,000
2017	30000	$80	$2,400,000
2018	35000	$85	$2,975,000

5-12 below. At an interest rate of 4.0%, calculate the PW (present worth) of this software business. Is it better to invest the money in a mutual fund that gives an annualized return of 10%?

17.0 PEVs (Plug-in Electric Vehicles)

The 2011 Chevrolet Volt was unveiled recently by the CEO of General Motors Corp. It is a plug-in electric vehicle, or PEV. It has a better range. For up to the first 40 miles, the Volt is powered by electric energy stored in its onboard lithium-ion batteries, which are charged by connection to an electrical power outlet. The 16 kWh battery pack can be fully charged by connecting to a residential electrical outlet operated at 12–240 Volt AC. The cost of the vehicle is about $39,000. A $7,500 federal tax credit can be expected for purchasing a PEV. The fuel efficiency is 230 mpg of gasoline, plus 25 kWh per 100 miles. A 2010 Toyota Corolla costs about $21,880 and is an all-gasoline-fueled vehicle. It provides a fuel efficiency of 32 mpg. What is the break-even point in miles that must be driven by the owner before the Volt becomes comparable with the Corolla in total life-cycle cost? The useful life of a PEV is 10 years; that of the Corolla is also 10 years. The interest rate may be taken as 5%. The household electric utility charges 10.5c per kWh. The cost of gasoline at the pump is $4.50 per gallon.

18.0 Solar Thermal Power Plant

Solar thermal power plants are being constructed in two locations: Weberville, Texas, and South Chicago. The costs of building and operating a solar thermal power plant are as follows:

Fixed Costs (Capital Cost)

(i) Land;
(ii) Solar Photovoltaic Panels;
(iii) Steam Generators;
(iv) Other Equipment;
(v) Tax Credit Accrued.

Variable Costs

Table 5-13 Cost and Economic Data for Solar Power Plants

Item	Weberville, TX	South Chicago, IL
Power Plant Capacity	30 MW	10 MW
Land Used	300 acres	39 acres
# Photovoltaic Solar Panels	105,750	33,000
Per Acre Land Cost	$3000	$4000
Cost of Steam Turbine	$10.5 million	$3.5 million
Other Equipment	50% of Steam Turbine	50% of Steam Turbine
# Jobs	600	120
Tax Credit	15% of Capital Cost	15% of Capital Cost
Plant Life	25 years	25 years
i (%) Interest Rate	3.25%	3.25%

(i) Wages;
(ii) Operation & Management.

The cost and economic data for the two solar power plants in Texas and Illinois are given below in Table 5-13. The photovoltaic solar panels cost $808.64 each. The average salary per job in these power plants is $25,000 per year. The price of electricity can be set at about 15.3 cents/kWh. The power plants can be assumed to be operated at 66.67% capacity utilization factor. The operation and management expenses can be taken as 45% of the wages and salaries provided. Which plant is a better investment alternative?

19.0 Solar Thermal Power Plant

Solar thermal power plants are being constructed in two locations: (i) Weberville, Texas, and South Chicago. The cost and economic data for the two solar power plants in Texas and Illinois are given below in Table 5-14. The photovoltaic solar panels cost $808.64 each. The average salary per job in these power plants is $30,000 per year. The price of electricity can be set at about 12.5 cents/kWh. The power plants can be assumed to be operated at

Table 5-14 Cost and Economic Data for Solar Power Plants

Item	Weberville, TX	South Chicago, IL
Power Plant Capacity	30 MW	10 MW
Land Used	300 acres	39 acres
# Photovoltaic Solar Panels	105,750	33,000
Per Acre Land Cost	$3000	$4000
Cost of Steam Turbine	$10.5 million	$3.5 million
Other Equipment	40% of Steam Turbine	40% of Steam Turbine
# Jobs	600	120
Plant Life	25 years	25 years
i (%) Interest Rate	6.25%	6.25%

Table 5-15 Cost and Economic Data for Wind Power Plants

Item	1500 kW	1000 kW	600 kW
Power Plant Capacity	1500 kW	1000 kW	600 kW
Energy Production (MWh)	48,000	35,000	40,000
Renewable Energy Equipment (Wind Machine & Tower)	$26.89 million	$27.185 million	$27.785 million
Balance of Plant	$3.04 million	$3.368 million	$4.018 million
Miscellaneous Fixed Costs	$1.58 million	$1.61 million	$1.672 million
O & M, Operations & Maintenance Expenses	$0.9 million	$0.709 million	$0.77 million

60% capacity utilization factor. The operation and management expenses can be taken as 45% of the wages and salaries provided. Which plant is a better investment alternative ?

20.0 Wind Energy Conversion to Electric Power [9]

Wind energy can be tapped into for generating electric power. The profitability of these plants is higher when constructed at locations where the wind speed is higher and is prevalent for large portions of the year and when the capital cost is low. This kind of power plant uses a sustainable energy source and causes less pollution compared with the fossil fuel power plants. These power plants qualify for a tax credit at 15% of the cost of renewable energy equipment used, such as the wind machine and tower. Three different such power plants are considered for installation in Saudi Arabia. The cost and economic data are given below in Table 5-15. The plant lives are 15 years and the interest rate can be taken as 3%. The price of electricity can be set at 8.5 cents per kWh used. The development cost of $200,000 is the same for the three plants, with capacities of 1500 kW, 1000 kW, and 600 kW. Calculate the PW of each plant and rank the three projects according to their profitability.

21.0 Wind Energy Conversion to Electric Power [9]

Wind energy can be tapped into for generating electric power. The profitability of these plants is higher when constructed at locations where the wind speed is higher and is prevalent for large portions of the year and when the capital cost is low. This kind of power plant uses a sustainable energy source and causes less pollution compared with the fossil fuel power plants. These power plants qualify for a tax credit at 15% of the cost of renewable energy equipment used, such as the wind machine and tower. Three such power plants with the same capacity of 1500 kW are considered for installation at three locations in Saudi Arabia: (i) Al-Wajh; (ii) Yanbo; and (iii) Dhahran. The plant lives are 15 years and the interest rate can be taken as 3%. The cost and economic

Table 5-16 Cost and Economic Data for Wind Power Plants

Item	Al-Wajh	Yanbo	Dhahran
Power Plant Capacity	1500 kW	1500 kW	1500 kW
Energy Production (MWh)	48,000	83,000	70,000
Renewable Energy Equipment (Wind Machine & Tower)	$26.89 million	$26.89 million	$26.89 million
Balance of Plant	$3.04 million	$3.04 million	$3.04 million
Miscellaneous Fixed Costs	$1.58 million	$1.61 million	$1.61 million
O & M, Operations & Maintenance Expenses	$0.9 million	$0.9 million	$0.9 million

data are given below in Table 5-16. The price of electricity can be set at 8.5 cents per kWh used. The development cost of $200,000 is the same for the three plants at Al-Wajh, Yanbo, and Dhahran. The wind speeds at the three locations are as follows:

(i) Al-Wajh 4.1 m/s;
(ii) Yanbo 5.1 m/s;
(iii) Dhahran 4.72 m/s.

Calculate the PW of each plant and rank the three projects according to their profitability.

22.0 Printing Press

Mesopotamia Hardcopy Publishers purchased a new printing press at a cost of $1 million. After 14 years of use, the salvage value obtained by the printer is $100,000. The company uses it to run 120 books at 2000 copies each every year. Each book has an average of 500 pages. The per-page paper, ink, setting-up plate, and binding costs are 5 cents/page, 3 cents/page, and 1 cent/page, respectively. The average retail price of a book is $150 each. The authors receive 10% of the revenue from sales. The wholesale, warehousing, shipping to retail outlets, and display and sales at retailers all take up 45% of the revenues. There are 24 people who work for the press. These include the sponsoring editor, copyeditor, composition, acquisitions editor, proofreader, editorial supervisor, indexer, art director, project manager, production supervisor, lawyer, and other supporting staff. The average salary received by the team is $50,000. The marketing and advertisement budget is 3% of the revenues received.

Mesopotamia Kindle can get 300,000 readers to download the e-book version for a fee of $15 per e-book. The authors receive 10% of the revenue as royalties for their time and efforts. The publishing team is reduced in size to 12, at an average salary of $50,000 each. The advertisement and marketing fees are about 3% of the revenues. The eBay sites from which the books get downloaded receive 20% of the revenue.

Which is a better alternative: *Mesopotamia Hardcopy Publishers* or *Mesopotamia Kindle*?

23.0 Blow-Molding Press

Harappa Molding is considering the purchase of a new blow-molder. Five different molders are available to select from. The fixed and variable costs for the five mutually exclusive alternatives are provided in Table 5-17. The capacity of each machine is 175,000. The study period is six years. The price per unit produced is 47 cents. The interest rate is 6%. Rank the molders according to their profitability.

Table 5-17 Five Blow-Molding Machines

Item	Molder A	Molder B	Molder C	Molder D	Molder E
Purchase Price	$95,000	$15,000	$30,000	$40,000	$50,000
Useful Life (years)	6	6	6	6	6
Utilities (Annual)	$1,200	$2,400	$3,600	$4,800	$3,000
Wages	$15,000	$20,000	$30,000	$35,000	$40,000
Maintenance	$900	$2000	$1200	$1500	$1400
Property Tax, Insurance	$960	$990	$800	$700	$610

Table 5-18 Cost and Economic Data for Mohenjandaro Insurance

Item	Plan A (nonsmokers)	Plan B (smokers)
Period of Insurance	30 years	30 years
Premium Charged	\$2.05/month/\$1000 face amount	\$2.50/month/\$1000 face amount
Death Rate	8.2 per 1000	10.2
Number of Jobs Created	50	50
Average Salary of Each Job	\$25,000/year	\$25,000/year
Marketing Expenses	\$100/household/year	\$100/household/year
O & M Expenses	2% of Revenues	2% of Revenues
Interest Rate	3%	3%

24.0 Life Insurance

Mohenjandaro Insurance is considering two alternative plans for the town of Cypress, Texas. There are 15,207 households and a population of about 45,000. Further, 46% of the households have incomes above \$100,000, and 31% of the households have incomes between \$50,000–\$100,000. The percentage of households with incomes of less than \$50,000 is 23%. Each household takes out a life insurance policy of about twice their incomes, i.e., the face amount on the policies taken out by income group: (i) with greater than \$100,000, it is \$200,000; (ii) with incomes between \$50,000–\$100,000, it is \$150,000; and (iii) with incomes less than \$50,000, it is \$50,000. The cost and economic data for the two plans is given in Table 5-18. Which is a better alternative ?

25.0 Life Insurance

Mohenjandaro Insurance is considering two alternative plans for the town of Cypress, Texas: (i) Plan A, direct marketing; and (ii) Plan B, e-Insurance. With Plan A, insurance agents will be hired and sent to sell insurance products at the kitchen tables of the households. With Plan B, a website is created and the customers transact all business via the Internet. Computer purchase and website establishment costs about \$2 million. There are 15,207 households and a population of about 45,000. Additionally, 46% of the households have incomes above \$100,000, and 31% of households have incomes between \$50,000–\$100,000. Further, 23%

Table 5-19 Cost and Economic Data for Mohenjandaro Insurance

Item	Plan A (Direct Marketing)	Plan B (e-Insurance)
Capital Expenses	0	\$2 million
Period of Insurance	30 years	30 years
Premium Charged	\$2.05/month/\$1000 face amount	\$1.92/month/\$1000 face amount
Death Rate	8.0 per 1000	8.2
Number of Jobs Created	50	2
Average Salary of Each Job	\$25,000/year	\$25,000/year
Marketing Expenses	\$100/household/year	\$50/household/year
O & M Expenses	2% of Revenues	0.5% of Revenues
Interest Rate	3%	3%

Table 5-20 Cost and Economic Data for Bronze Oil Refinery

Item	Plan A	Plan B	Plan C
Fixed Costs (Equipment)	\$200,000	\$175,000	\$150,000
Annual Revenues	\$30,000	\$40,000	\$35,000
Annual Expenses	\$14,000	\$10,000	\$20,000
Salvage Value of Equipment	\$40,000	\$15,000	\$12,500

of households have incomes of less than \$50,000. Each household takes out a life insurance policy of about twice their incomes, i.e., the face amount on the policies taken out by the income group: (i) with greater than \$100,000, it is \$200,000; (ii) with incomes between \$50,000–\$100,000, it is \$150,000; and (iii) with incomes less than \$50,000, it is \$50,000. The cost and economic data for the two plans are given in Table 5-19. Which is a better alternative ?

26.0 Bronze Oil Refinery

Bronze Oil Refinery is considering modification to their plants to reduce emissions and score high marks with the EPA (Environmental Protection Agency) for protecting the environment. Three alternatives are considered. The additional fixed and variable costs are shown in Table 5-20. A study period of 12 years may be considered. The interest rate is 4%. Which alternative is selected ?

27.0 Improvements to Combined Cycle Power Plants

It has been found [10] that given the variation in outdoor air temperature through the year, cooling the inlet air temperature to the compressor of the gas turbine to 59°F can result in improved performance of the combined cycle power plant. In a 400 MW power plant, the improvements of introducing a lithium-bromide chiller, a heat exchanger, and other auxiliary equipment can result in an increase in power output of the gas turbine by 9.32%. The steam turbine output decreases by 3.42% due to the use of some steam by the chiller. The net combined cycle performance improvement is about 5.8%. The additional capital cost needed and the added benefit from additional revenues less the added expenses (ΔR-ΔE) is provided in Table 5-21 for six different combined cycle power plant capacities. Rank the modifications according to their profitability.

Table 5-21 Additional Equipment Costs and Additional Profit Generated

Combined Cycle Power Plant Capacity	Additional Capital Needed (Millions \$)	Added Benefit Accrued (ΔR - ΔE) (Millions \$)
100 MW	2.612	1.5
200 MW	4.35	4.0
300 MW	6.087	5.5
400 MW	7.824	9.0
500 MW	9.561	10.5
600 MW	11.298	13.0

Table 5-22 Cost and Economic Data for Four Different Types of Cooling Tower

Items	Wet Tower Forced Flow	Wet Tower Natural Flow	Dry Tower Forced Flow	Dry Tower Natural Flow
Fixed Costs (Equipment Purchase)	$2 million	$10 million	$4 million	$7 million
Utilities (Pumps & Fans)	$1.18/year	$1.10/year	$2.36	$1.8
Useful Life	40 years	40 years	40 years	40 years
Salvage Value	$200,000	$1 million	$450,000	$750,000

28.0 Four Different Cooling Tower Designs

Combined cycle power plants offer increased thermodynamic cycle efficiencies. By using this technology, the energy conversion efficiency from fossil fuels such as coal to electric power can be increased from 30% to greater than 50%. The gas turbine is used to tap into the energy from the gases formed from gasification of coal. This step is followed by combustion of the coal from the gasifier. Steam created in this step is bled down a steam turbine. Use of a gas turbine and a steam turbine is the attributable factor in the increase of cycle efficiency. The condenser water temperature would rise after prolonged used of the plant. Cooling towers can be used to decrease the temperature of the condensed water used in various operations in the power plant. Some of the water is evaporated in the cooling tower by contact with dry air. The humidity of the air will increase and the water temperature would decrease. Four different designs of cooling towers are possible. These are: (i) pumping air by forced flow into the wet tower; (ii) allowing air to rise naturally in the wet tower; (iii) pumping air by forced flow into the dry tower; and (iv) allowing air to rise naturally into the dry tower. The cost and economic data needed for evaluation of the four alternatives is provided in Table 5-22. Rank order the different alternatives according to their profitability. The interest rate is 5%.

29.0 Rechargeable Batteries for PEVs

Amsterdam Rechargeables is considering two plans for manufacturing lithium-ion rechargeable batteries used for many things, including electric and hybrid automobiles, motorcycles, wheelchairs, scooters, golf carts, power tools, electronics, and energy storage devices—to name but a few. Two kinds of batteries are manufactured: (i) Battery A has a useful life of seven years; (ii) Battery B has a useful life of nine years. The company provides solutions for sage, large-format battery packs and systems. Revenues expected are in the form of $60 million in contracts to be executed in the next seven years for Battery A, and $100 million in contracts to be executed over the next nine years for Battery B. The factory that would manufacture Battery A would create 30 jobs at an average salary of $30,000; the factory for Battery B would create 50 jobs. The operations and management expenses are 50% of the wages, salaries, and royalties paid. The material costs would run about $1 million for the manufacture of Battery A and $1.5 million for manufacturing Battery B. The capital cost of building either factory floor is estimated at $5 million. At an interest rate of 5%, which would be a better alternative: (i) manufacture Battery A; or (ii) manufacture Battery B?

30.0 Gold Extraction

Turin Gold Miners is a gold mining business that uses *heap leaching*. This process uses less capital investment, as it does not use any milling or other processing equipment. Gold ore is allowed to form in a heap. The heap is irrigated with dilute cyanide solution. The gold metal is leached out by percolation of the solution through the heap. The solution that contains the gold is called the pregnant solution. The pregnant solution drains and is

Table 5-23 Heap Leaching Process of Turin Gold Miners

Item	Quantity
Heap Size	500,000 tons/year
Asphalt Pad	$7.81 per ton of ore
Stacking Costs of Ore on Pad	$1.56 per ton of ore
Leaching Cost	$7.81 per ton of ore
Carbon Adsorption	$0.31 per ton of ore
Recoverable Gold in Ore	0.05 t oz per ton
Reactivation of Carbon	$0.31 per ton of ore
Labor Costs	$10 million/year
Study Period	8 years
i (%), Interest Rate	15%

stored in the storage pond. The pregnant solution is adsorbed using activated carbon. The carbon is deactivated and the gold recovered. The economic and cost data to evaluate the heap leaching process is shown in Table 5-23.

Frieberg Gold Miners is a gold mining business that uses *agitation leaching*. This process uses jaw crushers and ball mills in order to compact the ore into a small particle. Higher yields of gold can be expected using the agitation leaching process, as the mass transfer would be higher between the ore and solution used to extract the gold. The costs and economic data needed to evaluate the agitation leaching process of Frieberg Gold Miners are shown in Table 5-24.

Which business is more profitable, *Turin Gold Miners* or *Frieberg Gold Miners*?

Table 5-24 Agitation Leaching Process of Frieberg Gold Miners

Item	Quantity
Gold Ore Production Rate	41.5 ton per hour
Plant Utilization Factor	327 days/year
Raw Materials Cost	$6.52 million per year
Utilities Cost	$14.26 million per year
Labor Wages, Salary, Royalties	$20.24 million per year
Recoverable Gold	0.12 t oz per ton
Jaw Crusher	$2.7 million
Ball Mill	$21.1 million
Agitation Leaching Circuit (6 Tanks)	$7.5 million
Carbon Adsorbers	$8.7 million
Electrowinning Equipment	$4.2 million
Waste Treatment	$6.5 million
Study Period	8 years
i (%) Interest Rate	15%

31.0 Renovation of Macy's Department Store

Retail giant Macy's is considering adding more display counters at their Willowbrook Mall outfit near Houston. The additional area renovated is 625 sq. ft. The cost of the renovation runs about $200 per sq. ft. of shop floor space. Two additional employees are hired at an annual salary of $15,000 each. Additional revenue accrued is $160 per day. The utilization factor is 300 days in the year. The study period is 14 years and the interest rate is 5%. Compare this investment with running a mail-order catalog. Expenses for these catalogs are largely in the form of bulk mail. About 100 catalogs per day are sent at a cost of $1 to prepare the catalog and $1 to mail the catalog. The utilization factor is 300 days/year. About 2% of the recipients order with a revenue of $54 per order. The planning horizon is seven years at an interest rate of 5%.

Chapter 6.0

Depreciation and Replacement Analysis

Main Points

- Straight-Line Method
- Declining Balance Method
- Units of Production Method
- MACRS
- Property Class, Class Life
- Replacement Analysis
- EUAC

6.1 Overview

Depreciation can be used for accounting purposes. It can be used to establish an equivalent series of annual deductions to the value of an asset acquired as a single payment or transaction. Depreciation can also serve as a critical item in the determination of the ATCF (*After-Tax Cash Flow*). Estimation of the ATCF (after-tax cash flows) and *tax consequences* on decision analysis are described in detail in Chapter 7.0. Clever accountants can associate their depreciation calculations of assets to real-time deterioration of physical properties of the asset. For example, as soon as a new car rolls out of the dealership, it depreciates in value. Every year the book value of the car depreciates by a certain amount. The end of the useful life of the car occurs at, say, 6.67 years for an automobile with a 4-cylinder engine, or perhaps 10 years for an automobile with a 6-cylinder engine, or maybe 13.33 years for a car with an 8-cylinder engine.

Depreciation is a noncash cost. It is a deduction from before-tax income. The purpose of the use of depreciation is to establish the equivalence of the portion of the asset's value that is used in the production of income in a given year as annual deductions. A property or piece of equipment is said to be depreciable if the following criteria are met:

(i) it is used in business or used to bring in income;
(ii) it has a definite useful life greater than six months;
(iii) it is subject to wear and tear upon repeated use or deteriorates under natural causes;
(iv) it is not inventory, investment assets, in trade stock, etc.;
(v) it is physically tangible, such as a computer or intangible, such as IPR (intellectual property rights);
(vi) a depreciation schedule can be drawn up according to the equivalence establishment between the asset's value and annual deductions and/or the physical condition of the asset.

Cost Basis (Adjusted) is the amount that is used as a basis for further calculations. This is after the adjustments for allowable increases or decreases. For example, an addition of a second floor to a single-story house with a useful life greater than six months results in an increase in the initial cost basis. A loss by theft or hazard or casualty decreases the original value.

The amount paid to purchase an asset is called the *initial cost basis*. The sales tax and transportation costs of acquisition of the asset can be included in this basis. Any cost incurred that is needed to commission the asset can be included here. This is also referred to as *unadjusted cost basis*.

The *book value* of an asset is the current worth of the object as shown by the accountant of the enterprise. It is obtained from the initial cost basis after subtracting the depreciation deductions. The book value can also be looked at as the capital that remains in the asset that can be recovered during the useful life of the equipment, building, or object. The book value and market value of an item may be different from each other. The *market value* of an item is the amount the buyer is willing to pay for that item from the seller. The *salvage value* is the estimated market value of the item at the end of the study period. This can appear as a cash inflow in cash flow diagrams. The *useful life* of an equipment is the period over which the equipment is serviceable or functional.

The number of years over which an equipment or building is recovered is referred to as the *recovery period*. Usually, the useful life of the equipment is equal to the recovery period. Under a MACRS (modified accelerated cost recovery system), this period is the "property class" for the GDS (general depreciation system). It is the "class life" in the ADS (alternative depreciation system).

6.2 MACRS (Modified Accelerated Cost Recovery System)

The IRS (Internal Revenue Service) requires the use of MACRS (modified accelerated cost recovery system) for calculation of depreciation of assets [1]. All assets are categorized into classes. This ordains the period over which an asset's cost shall be recovered. MACRS was created with the TRA86, Tax Reform Act of 1986 (more discussion follows on TRA86 in Chapter 7.0). MACRS is applicable to tangible, depreciable property that was placed in service after December 31, 1986.

With the arrival of TRA86, ACRS was replaced with MACRS as the method for calculating depreciation in the United States. It is similar to ACRS. Before ACRS came about, most equipment purchases were depreciated by the method of straight line. This method allowed for the depreciation of an asset over its useful life. ACRS was in use between 1981–1986. It came about with the ERTA (Economic Recovery Tax Act) of 1981. Property classes were established in ERTA. Calculations were based on zero for salvage value. Shorter recovery periods were used to calculate annual depreciation. The result was an accelerated "write-off" of capital costs. The depreciation under ACRS was twice than that using the method of straight line.

MACRS differs from ACRS in two ways: (i) the number of property classes was expanded; and (ii) the semester convention was introduced to simplify the first and final years of the useful life of the item. MACRS allows for faster depreciation of capital assets. This can stimulate purchase of capital equipment driven by the lower after-tax present worth of the equipment. The tax deductible depreciation expense can be taken sooner. This results in an increase in the present worth of the capital equipment. The enterprise is allowed to retain more of its cash inflows or receipts earlier in the depreciation cycle. It is called a "front-loaded" tax benefit.

There are two systems under MACRS for calculating depreciation deductions. The main system is called the GDS (*General Depreciation System*) and the alternative system is called an *Alternative Depreciation System*. Generally, GDS is used unless the law specifically requires the use of ADS. Longer recovery periods can be realized using the ADS method. The method of straight line is used in ADS for depreciation. Tax-exempt property and capital equipment used overseas are examples of items whose depreciation has to be according to ADS. Items qualified under GDS can be depreciated using ADS by suitable election. Each system differs in the class life of the item. For example, office equipment (Table 6-1) is depreciated with a class life of seven years, whereas automobiles are depreciated with a class life of five years and industrial steam is depreciated over a class life of 15 years. The MACRS classes have a predetermined schedule, which is used to determine the fraction of the asset's cost that is depreciated each year (Tables 6-1–6.4).

- The 3-, 5-, 7-, and 10-year classes use 200% and the 15- and 20-year classes use 150% declining balance depreciation.
- All classes convert to straight-line depreciation in the optimal year, shown with an asterisk (*).
- A half-year depreciation is allowed in the first and last recovery years.
- If more than 40% of the year's MACRS property is placed in service in the last three months, then a mid-quarter convention must be used with depreciation tables that are not shown here.

The useful life is 39 years for nonresidential real property. Depreciation is straight line using the mid-month convention. Thus, a property placed in service in January would be allowed 11 1/2 months' depreciation for Recovery Year 1.

Table 6-1 MACRS "Property Class" and "Class Life"

IRS Asset Classes	Asset Description	ADS Class Life	GDS Class Life
00.11	Office furniture, fixtures, and equipment	10	7
00.12	Information systems: computers/peripherals	6	5
00.22	Automobiles, taxis	3	5
00.241	Light general-purpose trucks	4	5
00.25	Railroad cars and locomotives	15	7
00.40	Industrial steam and electric distribution	22	15
01.11	Cotton gin assets	10	7
01.21	Cattle, breeding or dairy	7	5
13.00	Offshore drilling assets	7.5	5
13.30	Petroleum refining assets	16	10
15.00	Construction assets	6	5
20.10	Manufacture of grain and grain mill products	17	10
20.20	Manufacture of yarn, thread, and woven fabric	11	7
24.10	Cutting of timber	6	5
32.20	Manufacture of cement	20	15
20.1	Manufacture of motor vehicles	12	7
48.10	Telephone distribution plant	24	15
48.2	Radio and television broadcasting equipment	6	5
49.12	Electric utility nuclear production plant	20	15
49.13	Electric utility steam production plant	28	20
49.23	Natural gas production plant	14	7
50.00	Municipal wastewater treatment plant	24	15
80.00	Theme and amusement park assets	12.5	7

Table 6.2 Property Class of Personal Properties

Property Class	Personal Property (all property except real estate)
3-year property	Special handling devices for food and beverage manufacture
	Special tools for the manufacture of finished plastic products, fabricated metal products, and motor vehicles
	Property with ADR class life of 4 years or less
5-year property	Information systems; computers/peripherals
	Aircraft (of non-air transport companies)
	Computers
	Petroleum drilling equipment
	Property with ADR class life of more than 4 years and less than 10 years
7-year property	All other property not assigned to another class
	Office furniture, fixtures, and equipment
	Property with ADR class life of more than 10 years and less than 16 years
10-year property	Assets used in petroleum refining and certain food products
	Vessels and water transportation equipment
	Property with ADR class life of 16 years or more and less than 20 years
15-year property	Telephone distribution plants
	Municipal sewage treatment plants
	Property with ADR class life of 20 years or more and less than 25 years
20-year property	Municipal sewers
	Property with ADR class life of 25 years or more
Property Class	**Real Property (real estate)**
27.5-year property	Residential rental property (does not include hotels and motels)
39-year property	Nonresidential real property

Example 6-1 Depreciation Charge of Offshore drilling Assets

Calculate the depreciated charge in tax year 3 of of-shore drilling equipment with an *unadjusted cost basis* of $100 millios.

The GDS class life of Offshore drilling assets from Table 6.1 can be seen as fiv5 years.

From Table 6.2 for tax year 3, the applicable percentage for five year life equipment is 19.2%.

Depreciation Charge = 0.192*$100 = $19.2 millios.

The information needed to calculate the depreciation deduction under MACRS are: (i) unadjusted cost basis; (ii) when the property was placed in service; (iii) property class and recovery period; (iv) method used for depreciation, GDS or ADS under MACRS; and (v) quarter, semester, or annual.

6.3 Methods of Depreciation

6.3.1 Method Of Straight Line

The method of *straight line* for calculation of depreciation is simple in construct. A uniform amount is deducted every year over the useful life of the capital equipment.

Table 6-3 MACRS Applicable Percentage for Property Class

Recovery Year	3-Year Property	5-Year Property	7-Year Property	10-Year Property	15-Year Property	20-Year Property
1	33.33	20.00	14.29	10.00	5.00	3.750
2	44.45	32.00	24.49	18.00	9.50	7.219
3	14.81 *	19.20	17.49	14.40	8.55	6.677
4	7.41	11.52 *	12.49	11.52	7.70	6.177
5		11.52	8.93 *	9.22	6.93	5.713
6		5.76	8.92	7.37	6.23	5.285
7			8.93	6.55 *	5.90 *	4.888
8			4.46	6.55	5.90	4.522
9				6.56	5.91	4.462 *
10				6.55	5.90	4.461
11				3.28	5.91	4.462
12					5.90	4.461
13					5.91	4.462
14					5.90	4.461
15					5.91	4.462
16					2.95	4.461
17						4.462
18						4.461
19						4.462
20						4.461
21						2.231

Table 6.4 MACRS Percentage for Real Property (real estate) Table

Recovery Year	Month 1	Month 2	Month 3	Month 4	Month 5	Month 6	Month 7	Month 8	Month 9	Month 10	Month 11	Month 12
1	2.461	2.247	2.033	1.819	1.605	1.391	1.177	0.963	0.749	0.535	0.321	0.107
2–39	2.564	2.564	2.564	2.564	2.564	2.564	2.564	2.564	2.564	2.564	2.564	2.564
40	0.107	0.321	0.535	0.749	0.963	1.177	1.391	1.605	1.819	2.033	2.247	2.461

$$d_j = \frac{B-S}{N} \tag{6.1}$$

Where d_j is the depreciation deduction in the jth year, B is the unadjusted cost basis, N is the useful life of the capital equipment, and S is the salvage value. Further, the book value BV_j at the end of year j can be seen to b

$$BV_j = B - d_j^* = B - \sum_{k=1}^{j} d_k \tag{6.2}$$

Wher, d_j^* is the cumulative deduction through year j. The cumulative deduction through year j can be seen to be

$$d_j^* = j * \left(\frac{B - S}{N}\right) \tag{6.3}$$

Example 6.2 Method of Straight Line for Depreciation of HRA Helical Ribbon Agitator)

The unadjusted cost basis of an HRA helical ribbonoagitatorr used in a continuous polymerization plant to manufacture ABS engineering thermoplastic is $10 millios. Determine the per-year depreciation deduction using the method of Straight Line. Tabulate the depreciation amounts and show the book value at the end of each year. The useful life of the HRA is 15 years. The salvage value of the HRA is $1.5 millios.

6.3.2 Method of Declining Balance

The method of declining balance is also called a *Matheson formula* or method of constant percentage. The annual depreciation deduction is calculated as a percentage of the book value of the capital equipment at the beginning

Table 6.5 Depreciation Deductions and Book Value at EOY

EOY, j	d_j	BV_j (millions)
0	0	$10.0000
1	$566,667	$9.4333
2	$566,667	$8.8667
3	$566,667	$8.3000
4	$566,667	$7.7333
5	$566,667	$7.1667
6	$566,667	$6.6000
7	$566,667	$6.0333
8	$566,667	$5.4667
9	$566,667	$4.9000
10	$566,667	$4.3333
11	$566,667	$3.7667
12	$566,667	$3.2000
13	$566,667	$2.6333
14	$566,667	$2.0667
15	$566,667	$1.5000

Table 6-6 Depreciation and Book Value by the Method of Declining Balance

Year, j	Depreciation	Book Value
0	0	B
1	B(f)	B(1-f)
2	Bf(1-f)	$B(1\text{-}f)^2$
3	$Bf(1\text{-}f)^2$	$B(1\text{-}f)^3$
....		
j	$Bf(1\text{-}f)^{j\text{-}1}$	$B(1\text{-}f)^j$

of the year. The depreciation is a constant fraction of the book value remaining after the prior deductions. This fraction f lies between the values of 0 and 1, i.e., 0 £ f £ 1.0.

$$d_j = B(1-f)^{j-1}(f) \tag{6.4}$$

The book value of the capital equipment at the end of year j can be seen to be as shown in Table 6-6. The cumulative deduction through year j, d_j^* can be seen to be

Table 6-7 Method of Declining Balance (i) f = 2.5/15

EOY, j	d_j	BV_j (millions)
0		$10.0000
1	$1,666,667	$8.3333
2	$1,388,889	$6.9444
3	$1,157,407	$5.7870
4	$964,506	$4.8225
5	$803,755	$4.0188
6	$669,796	$3.3490
7	$558,163	$2.7908
8	$465,136	$2.3257
9	$387,613	$1.9381
10	$323,011	$1.6151
11	$269,176	$1.3459
12	$224,313	$1.1216
13	$186,928	$0.9346
14	$155,773	$0.7789
15	$129,811	$0.6491

$$d_j^* = Bf + Bf(1-f) + Bf(1-f)^2 + \dots + Bf(1-f)^{j-1} \qquad (6.5)$$

Eq. (6.5) is a sum of a geometric series and can be seen to be

$$d_j^* = B(1-(1-f)^j) \qquad (6.6)$$

When f = 1/N, the depreciations by the method of declining balance is equal to that of the depreciation by the method of straight line.

Example 6.3 Method of Declining Balance Line for Depreciation of HRA (Helical Ribbon Agitator)

The unadjusted cost basis of an HRA (helical ribbon agitator) used in a continuous polymerization plant to manufacture ABS engineering thermoplastic is \$10 million. Determine the per-year depreciation deduction using the method of declining balance. Tabulate the depreciation amounts and show the book value at the end of each year. The useful life of the HRA is 15 years. The salvage value of the HRA is 0. The fraction f used in the calculations are

Table 6-8 Method of Declining Balance (ii) f = 2.0/15

EOY, j	d_j	BV_j (millions)
0		\$10.0000
1	\$1,333,333	\$8.6667
2	\$1,155,556	\$7.5111
3	\$1,001,481	\$6.5096
4	\$867,951	\$5.6417
5	\$752,224	\$4.8895
6	\$651,927	\$4.2375
7	\$565,004	\$3.6725
8	\$489,670	\$3.1829
9	\$424,381	\$2.7585
10	\$367,796	\$2.3907
11	\$318,757	\$2.0719
12	\$276,256	\$1.7957
13	\$239,422	\$1.5562
14	\$207,499	\$1.3487
15	\$179,832	\$1.1689

i. 2.5/N
ii. 2.0/N

6.3.2 Method of Units of Production

The methods of straight line and declining balance are based on time periods. This works well for capital equipment with a useful life of N years. An underlying assumption is that the capital equipment is used at a *uniform rate*. For example, Jack and Jill bought the same two new cars in the same year. Jack parked the car in his garage. Jill drove her car 25,000 miles per year. The depreciation amounts predicted by the methods of straight line and declining balance would yield the *same* deductions for Jack and Jill. A better method was needed to account for more usage by Jill. The method of units of production is developed with the basis of functional use rather than merely time. Thus, the depreciation per unit of production can be given as

$$UnitDepreciation = \frac{(B - S)}{\#units} \tag{6.7}$$

In the example of Jack and Jill, the depreciation will be based on *per mile* of car driven.

Example 6.4 Hexane Extraction of Rice-Bran Oil (Please see Example 4.11)

Rice-bran lipids can be extracted using hexane solvent from rice bran at a yield of about 26%. Rice is milled to produce the white long-grain rice sold in supermarkets. The outer layers of the rice kernel are removed. These layers include the hull, the germ, and the bran. The bran includes the testa, peripcarp, nucellus, and aleurone layer. Rice bran becomes rancid and must be discarded in landfills. Parboiled rice bran has higher lipid levels than unstabilized rice bran. Rice-bran oil consists largely of saponifiable compounds. Hexane costs about $1.15 per gallon. It is an excellent solvent for nonpolar lipids. Calculate the PW of a hexane extraction unit. The following information was obtained from the *Journal of the American Oil Chemists' Association* [2] and modified suitably for the PW analysis in Example 4.11. Use the method of declining balance to calculate the depreciable amount at a factor of 0.25.

Table 6-9 Cost Data for Hexane Extraction Plant for Rice-Bran Oil

Description	Hexane Extraction Unit
Capital Investment	$220,000
Manufacturing Cost	$5.18 /year/kg of rice bran
Materials Cost	$0.22/year/kg of rice bran
Labor Cost	$9.62/hr
Revenue from Rice-Bran Oil	$8.08/kg
Revenue from Rice Protein	$4.928/kg
Production Rate	30.96 gal rice-bran oil/day
Useful Life of Equipment	10 years
Operational Hours Per Year	8332 hrs
% Protein in Rice Bran	14.6%
Interest Rate, i	3.0%

Annual Labor Cost = 8332h*$9.62 = $80,154

Rice Bran Processed = 30.96*3.7854*365/0.26 = 164,525 kg/year

Annual Revenue = 30.96*3.7854*365*$8.08 = $345,634 (from rice-bran oil)

+ $4.928*164525*0.146 = $118,374 (4.29)

Annual Materials & Labor Cost = 164,525*(5.18+0.22) = $888,436 (4.30)

(P/A,3%,10) = 8.530203 (From Table A-7)

The depreciable amounts and book values at a depreciation factor of 0.25 are tabulated below in Table 6-10. The PW contribution from each of the depreciable amounts is also shown as a separate column at an interest rate of 3%.

PW = -$187,981.27 + (-888,436 + 345,634+ 118,374 – 80,154) 8.530203 +12,389 = -4.4798 millions.

Table 6-10 Depreciable Amounts of Capital Equipment and Contributions to PW

Hexane Oil Extraction

	f	0.25		
Capital Equipment Cost	$220,000			
k	d_k	BV_k	PW_k	(P/F,3%,k)
1	$55,000	$165,000	$53,398.07	0.970874
2	$41,250	$123,750	$38,882.09	0.942596
3	$30,938	$92,813	$28,312.21	0.915142
4	$23,203	$69,609	$20,615.67	0.888487
5	$17,402	$52,207	$15,011.42	0.862609
6	$13,052	$39,155	$10,930.64	0.837484
7	$9,789	$29,366	$7,740.89	0.790789
8	$7,342	$22,025	$5,795.54	0.789409
9	$5,506	$16,519	$4,221.90	0.766752
10	$4,130	$12,389	$3,072.85	0.744094
		PW	($187,981.27)	

The hexane extraction of rice-bran oil is not a profitable venture. However, the PW has increased by $44,401 when the depreciation charges are taken into account by the method of declining balance every year, as opposed to a one-time charge.

6.4 Replacement Analysis

Often the question arises as to whether to keep an asset that is owned at present *in service* or consider *immediate replacement* of it. There are good reasons for considering a replacement. These reasons can range from obsolescence as a result of the arrival of new technology, or physical deterioration, vandalism and theft, a change in needs of the organization, etc.The alternatives available are as follows:

(i) Keep the equipment in service;
(ii) Scrap the equipment without replacement;
(iii) Replace the equipment but store it as backup;
(iv) Retrofit the equipment and overhaul it;
(v) Scrap the equipment and replace it.

In order to better evaluate the economic merits of replacement items, the following jargon is introduced:

Useful Life: The time period of an asset kept in service is referred to as the useful life of the equipment.
Technoeconomic Life: The period of time in years that it takes for the minimum equivalent uniform annual cost (EUAC) of owning and working the equipment.
Ownership Life: This is the time that elapsed between the acquisition and final disposition of the equipment by the owner.
Physical Life: This is the time that elapsed between the original acquisition and final disposition over the entire life of the equipment.

Most studies on replacement analysis emphasize the *future* and not the past. Exceptions to this rule of thumb is when the tax consequences require deliberations of matters in the past. Only present and future cash flows are used during replacement analysis. Past decisions are relevant to a limited extent—only to the extent they affect the current situation. Sunk costs are an increasingly important factor. It is obtained as a difference between the book value of the equipment and the market value of the equipment.

In order to obtain the fair market value of a piece of equipment, an impartial *third party* is approached. The opportunity cost approach can also be used. The opportunity cost is the avenue foregone by choosing to hold on to an asset for more time. When a price hike is needed to meet the competition's bids, the realizable market value is increased to the level of the challenger. The defender thus has a price that is competitive with the challenger.

The EUAC (equivalent uniform annual cost) is minimized by the economic life of the challenger. The economic life of the defender is usually taken as one year. This basis allows for complete analysis between alternatives with different lives. As long as the marginal cost of the defender is less than the minimum EUAC of the challenger over its economic life, the defender may be retained for times greater than its economic life. Tax consequences ought to be considered during replacement analysis. Replacement of equipment often results in profit or loss from the transfer of depreciable property.

Example 6.5 Photocopier Before Tax

A leading law partner's office photocopier has a current market value of $5000. It can be in service for five more years. The salvage value after five years of the copier is zero. The operating and maintenance expenses are $1500 per year. The law partners can purchase an e-STUDIO with scanning capability for $15,000. After five years, the market value of the e-STUDIO is $7500. The operating and maintenance expenses are $800 per year. Should the law partners replace the old photocopier with the e-STUDIO for a study period of five years? Use a before-tax MARR of 10%.

Defender

$$PW(10\%) = -\$5,000 - \$1,500(P/A, 10\%, 5) \tag{4.31}$$

$$(P/A, 10\%, 5) = 3.7908 \text{ (From Appendix A)}$$

$$PW\ (10\%\ MARR) = -\$10,686.2 \tag{4.32}$$

Challenger

$$PW(10\%) = -\$15,000 + \$7,500 - \$800(P/A, 10\%, 5)$$

$$= -10,532.6 \tag{4.33}$$

PW of the challenger is greater than the PW of the defender. But the numbers are too close to call. They are within 1.4% of each other. At least 20% difference is needed to prefer one over the other.

The complete replacement analysis requires knowledge of the technoeconomic lives of the alternatives (min. EUAC). The EUAC of a new piece of equipment can be estimated should the fixed costs, maintenance and operational expenses, and year-by-year market values be known. In order to find the EUAC of the challenger, the total marginal cost of the challenger on an annual basis is needed. The minima of such values identifies the economic life. The PW can be estimated as

$$PW_j = C_F - BV_j(P/F, i\%, j) + \sum_{ki-1}^{j} E_k(P/F, i\%, k) \tag{4.34}$$

The total marginal cost is the equivalent worth at the end of year j. This is the increase in PW of the total cost from year j-1 to year j.

$$C_T^j = (PW_j - PW_{j-1})(F/P, i\%, j) \tag{4.35}$$

Combining Eq. (4.35) and Eq. (4.34)

$$C_T^j = SV_{j-1} - SV_j + iSV_{j-1} + E_j \tag{4.36}$$

The technoeconomic life of the e-STUDIO in Example 6.5 is estimated and shown in Table 6-11. The technoeconomic life of the defender in Example 6.5 is shown in Table 6-12. The following points may be noted during the estimate of EUAC of the defender:

Table 6-11 Technoeconomic Life of the E-Studio

	EOY 1	EOY 2	EOY 3	EOY 4	EOY 5
Market Value	$13,500	$12,000	$10,500	$9,000	$7,500
Operational & Maintenance Expenses	$800	$800	$800	$800	$800
Marginal Costs					
Recurring Expenses	$800	$800	$800	$800	$800
Depreciation	$1,500	$1,500	$1,500	$1,500	$1,500
Interest on Capital	$1,500	$1,350	$1,200	$1,050	$900
Total Cost	$3,800	$3,650	$3,500	$3,350	$3,200

Table 6-12 Technoeconomic Life of the Defender in Example 6.5

	EOY 1	EOY 2	EOY 3	EOY 4	EOY 5
Market Value	$4,000	$3,000	$2000	$1000	0
Operational & Maintenance Expenses	$1,500	$1,500	$1,500	$1,500	$1,500
Marginal Costs					
Recurring Expenses	$1,500	$1,500	$1,500	$1,500	$1,500
Depreciation	$1,000	$1,000	$1,000	$1,000	$1,000
Interest on Capital	$500	$400	$300	$200	$100
Total Cost	$3,000	$2,900	$2,800	$2,700	$2,600

(i) The time until the next major overhaul is the likely life resulting in minima in EUAC estimates.
(ii) The technoeconomic life can be taken as one year when the salvage value is zero and the recurring expenses are expected to increase.
(iii) The defender may be retained as long as its marginal cost is less than the minima of the best challenger.

When the defender is retained for times greater than when the total cost exceeds the minima in EUAC estimates for the challenger, the replacement becomes more imminent. Procrastination of replacement decisions can come about when the technology changes rapidly and solutions with better performance are offered. When the defender and challenger have different useful lives, the analysis centers around whether now is a good time for seeking replacement. As discussed in the previous chapter, comparison of apples and oranges is not appropriate. The repeatability and co-termination assumptions may be used in order to arrive at an appropriate study period.

Abandonment is retirement of the equipment or asset from service without replacement. Consider projects that have positive cash flows and a finite period of service. The question arises as to whether the project is profitable to pursue. Should it be profitable, what is the best year to abandon the project? What is the technoeconomic life of the equipment or asset? Both problem types, i.e., cost-dominated project or benefit-dominated project can be treated in this manner. The year the PW undergoes a maxima can be chosen as the year for abandonment.

Table 6-13 Microscopy Lab Services

	Depreciation	Book Value	
EOY	Depreciation	$80,000	Receipts
1	$32,000	$48,000	$43,000
2	$19,200	$28,800	$40,000
3	$11,520	$17,280	$35,000
4	$6,912	$10,368	$25,000
5	$4,147	$6,221	$15,000

Example 6.6 Best Year for Abandonment

Ms. Lisa Stone purchased a TEM, transmission electron microscope, for $80,000. The depreciation and book value for a five-year period is shown in Table 6-13. Each year the receipts from microscopy studies of premium samples are also shown in Table 6-13. At a MARR of 10%, when should Lisa abandon the TEM?

Keep for 1 year

PW = -80,000 + ($48,000 +$43,000)(P/F,10%,1)

= -80,000 + ($48,000 +$43,000)(0.90901)

= $2,719.91 (4.37)

Keep for 2 years

PW = -48,000 + ($40,000 +$28,800)(P/F,10%,2)

= -48,000 + ($40,000 +$28,800)(0.826446)

= $8,859.48 (4.38)

Keep for 3 years

PW = - $28,800 + ($35,000 +$17,280)(P/F,10%,3)

= -80,000 + ($48,000 +$43,000)(0.751315)

= $10,478.75 (4.39)

Keep for 4 years

PW = -17,280 + ($25,000 +$10,368)(P/F,10%,4)

= -80,000 + ($48,000 +$43,000)(0.683013)

= $6,876.80 (4.40)

Keep for 5 years

PW = -10,368 + ($15,000 +$6,221)(P/F,10%,5)

= -10,368 + ($15,000 +$6,221)(0.620921)

= $2,808.44 (4.41)

The PW is a maxima EOY 3. So the recommendation is to abandon the TEM at the end of year three.

Tax consequences can affect the decision for seeking replacement. Tax considerations during replacement analysis are paramount. Taxes ought to be considered not only for each year of operation of the equipment, but also in relation to the salvage value of the equipment. MS Excel spreadsheets can be used to study problems where the receipts and depreciation amounts change each and every year.

Eq. (4.13) upon taking into account the tax consequences can be written as follows:

$$PW_j = C_F - ((1-t)SV_j + tBV_j)(P/F,i\%,j) + \sum_{k=1}^{j}((1-t)E_k - td_k)(P/F,i\%,k) \tag{4.42}$$

The annual taxes and tax consequences on sale of equipment are included in Eq. (4.42). The total marginal cost for each year is then written as follows:

$$C_T^j = (1-t)(SV_{j-1} - SV_j + iSV_{j-1} + E_j) + i(t)(BV_{j-1}) \tag{4.43}$$

The salvage value of the equipment must be compared with the book value of the equipment. This is necessary to assess the tax ramifications. This can be included in the opportunity cost of retaining the defender. The net ATCF, when the defender is retained after taxes, is written as follows:

$$ATCF_j = -SV_j + t(SV_j - BV_j) \tag{4.44}$$

6.5 Summary

Estimation of ATCF (after-tax cash flows) and *tax consequences* on decision analysis are described in detail in Chapter 7.0. *Depreciation* can be used to establish an equivalent series of annual deductions to the value of an asset acquired as a single payment or transaction. *Cost basis (adjusted)* is the amount that is used as the basis for further calculations. The *book value* of an asset is the current worth of the object as shown by the accountant of the enterprise. The *useful life* of an equipment is the period over which the equipment is serviceable or functional.

The IRS (Internal Revenue Service) requires the use of MACRS (modified accelerated cost recovery system) for calculation of depreciation of assets [1]. There are two systems under MACRS for calculating depreciation deductions: The main system is called the GDS (*general depreciation system*) and the alternative system is called an *alternative depreciation system.* The MACRS classes have a predetermined schedule, which is used to determine the fraction of the asset's cost that is depreciated each year. (Tables 6-1–6-4). A worked example is shown in calculating the depreciation of offshore drilling equipment, a helical ribbon agitator, equipment for hexane extraction of rice-bran oil, etc.

Three different methods of calculating depreciation are discussed. These are: (i) method of straight line; (ii) method of declining balance; and (iii) method of units of production. A constant amount is deducted every year in the method of straight line. A constant percentage of the remaining balance is deducted every year in the method of declining balance. Deduction is based on units produced in the method of units of production rather than a time horizon or balance-based procedure.

Jargon needed for performing *replacement analysis* includes: useful life, technoeconomic life, ownership life, and physical life. EUAC is the equivalent uniform annual cost of equipment. The EUAC equivalent uniform annual cost is minimized by the economic life of the challenger. Tax consequences must be considered. A worked example on the photocopier is used to calculate the PW of the challenger and PW of the defender. The complete replacement analysis requires knowledge of the technoeconomic lives of the alternatives (min. EUAC). The EUAC of a new piece of equipment can be estimated, should the fixed costs, maintenance and operational expenses, and year-by-year market values be known. *Abandonment* is the retirement of the equipment or asset from service without replacement. The year the PW undergoes a maxima can be chosen as the year for abandonment.

The worked example on the TEM microscope is used to show how to calculate the year of abandonment. Exercises on a Versailles-type home, hydrogen from biomass, hybrid electric vehicle, olive oil business, short path distillation for paraffin wax fractionation, coffeehouse, propylene bag manufacture, steam boiler, sugar mill, HVAC, abandonment of a pretzel maker, automatic bagger, Keystone XL project, bioethanol from sugarcane bagasse, sequestration by dimethyl carbonate formation, and a baggage conveyor system at an airport are also developed.

6.6 References

[1] U.S. Department of the Treasury, Internal Revenue Service Publication 946, *How to Depreciate Property*. Washington, DC: U.S. Government Printing Office.

6.7 Exercises

1.0 Versailles—Largest Home for Sale in the United States (please see Exercise 13.0, Chapter 3.0)

David Siegel, a timeshare tycoon, started work on a 90,000-sq.-ft mansion in Windermere, Florida. The home has 23 bathrooms, 13 bedrooms, 10 kitchens, a 20-car garage with additional space for two limousines, three pools, a bowling alley, indoor roller ink, two-story movie theater, video arcade, fitness center, baseball fields, and two tennis courts. Mr. Siegel charges $75 million. The building can be finished upon carpeting, tiling, and interior wall construction for an additional $25 million. Calculate the depreciation amount using the method of straight line for a 100-year period. Assume that the salvage value of the home would be $2 million. Tabulate the depreciation amounts and show the book value at the end of each year.

2.0 Hydrogen from Biomass by Battelle/FERCO Low Pressure Process (please see Exercise 27.0, Chapter 3.0)

Hydrogen can be used as an alternative to fossil fuels. The Battelle/FERCO low pressure process involves two steps of gasification of the biomass followed by steam re-forming of the syngas produced. Water-gas shift reaction of syngas results in generation of hydrogen. The hydrogen is separated from the raw materials and by-products by the method of PSA, pressure swing adsorption. The McNeil Power Plant in Burlington, Vermont, is operated based on this process. The capital cost of the plant is about $53.8 million. Tabulate the depreciable amounts and book value of the plant: (a) by the method of straight line; and (b) by the method of declining balance, using a depreciation factor of 0.167. The useful life of the plant can be taken as 15 years.

3.0 Hybrid Electric Vehicle

A hybrid electric vehicle costs about $31,000. Calculate the depreciable amounts based on the unit of production method. The life of the automobile is 105,000 miles. Tabulate the results every 10,000 miles. The salvage value of the car is $2000.

4.0 Olive Oil Business (please see Exercise 13.0 in Chapter 4.0)

The capital equipment needed to manufacture olive oil is about $8,000. Calculate the depreciable amount by the method of straight line. The salvage value of the equipment is $100. The expected life of the plant is 16 years.

5.0 Short Path Distillation for Paraffin Wax Fractionation (please see Exercise 14.0 in Chapter 4.0)

Paraffin wax is present in crude oil reserves and can be produced using the Fischer-Tropsch process. Paraffin wax is widely used in applications such as treatment of paper and cardboard, printing inks, food, and the cosmetic and pharmaceutical industries. Prior to application, paraffin wax must be de-oiled and fractionated and tailored for the given situation. SPD (short path distillation) is used to recover low volatility components from liquid mixtures. It can operate at low pressures and can be used to fractionate waxes. Low pressure operation obviates high temperature operation, which would result in degradation of the wax. Krause and Nieuwoudt [Ref. 5 in Chapter 4.0] discuss an SPD process with four stages at a reflux ratio of 1.4. The capital cost is $17.1 million. Tabulate the depreciable amounts and book value of the plant: (a) by the method of straight line; and (b) by the method of declining balance, using a depreciation factor of 0.15. The useful life of the plant can be taken as 12 years.

6.0 Coffeehouse (please see Exercise 16.0 in Chapter 4.0)

Sam Bush started a 1,779-sq.-ft. coffeehouse at New Milford, Connecticut, 15 years ago. All types of coffees are served, including locally roasted blends, and 30 different tea selections are also available. Pastries and cookies are freshly baked on the premises. The coffeehouse serves breakfast and lunch only. An average of 250–300 customers per day stop in. The menu includes sandwiches, bagels, homemade muffins, cakes, bars, pies, puddings, and biscotti. During the day, soup, sandwiches, wraps, salads, and quiche are served. Wi-Fi was made available and entertainment with live music and other acts on most Friday nights are common. Mr. Bush had purchased the building for $160,000 in 1995. Tabulate the depreciable amounts and the book value of the coffeehouse building by the method of declining balance with a factor of 0.12.

7.0 Polypropylene Bag Manufacture (please see Exercise 21.0 in Chapter 4.0)

Polypropylene woven products such as fabrics and bags are used in packing agriculture products, military heavy-duty, the chemical industry, and regular commercial sandbags. A bag manufacturer works out of Houston and is a licensed USDA supplier. The customers include well-known companies such as ADM Milling, Cargill, Chevron Phillips, and JacintoPort International/Seaboard. It serves as a federal contractor that supplies polypropylene products to the USDA (United States Department of Agriculture,) the Defense Department, the U.S. Army, FEMA, and other federal, state, and local entities. A twin-screw extruder was purchased at a price of $5 million, with appropriate extrusion dies for bagging. Two freestanding buildings are used at a built area of 50,507 sq. ft. The cost of the building may be taken as $6.43 per sq. ft. The life of the extruder is about 21 years. The building can last 50 years. Tabulate the: (a) depreciable amounts and book value of the twin-screw extruder by the method of declining balance at a factor of 0.11; and (b) depreciable amounts and the book value of the buildings by the method of straight line. Assume that the salvage value for the buildings is negligible and can be taken as zero.

8.0 Steam Boiler (please see Exercise 23.0 in Chapter 4.0)

A steam boiler in a plant used for manufacturing activated carbon from bamboo costs about $1,033,338. The carbonization furnace has a purchase price of $1.3 million. The estimated life of the boiler and furnace is 10

Table 6-14 EOY Receipts and Costs

Year	Receipts Millions $	Cost Millions $
1	2.3	3.3
2	2.5	3.6
3	2	3.21
4	1.5	1.33
5	2	1.46
6	2.5	1.61
7	3	1.77
8	3.5	1.95
9	4	2.14

years. Tabulate the depreciable amounts and book value of the steam boiler and carbonization furnace by the method of declining balance for:

(i) $f = 2.5/N$
(ii) $f = 2/N$.

9.0 Annual Worth of a Sugar Mill

A business plan was presented to get a sugar mill installed in rural Texas (similar to the mill in Example 4.5). The cost of raw materials such as sugarcane and utility costs rise every year due to inflation. The revenue from the sale of sugar rises and falls in synchrony with the boom-and-bust cycles of the economy. The EOY (end of year) revenues and costs are shown in Table 6-14. The capital cost of the sugar mill, including land and all the necessary equipment, is estimated at $8 million. The depreciation time period can be taken to be the same as the study period of nine years. Calculate the depreciable amounts of the sugar mill equipment by the method of straight line. What is the AW of the sugar business at an interest rate of 5%?

10.0Annual Cost of an HVAC

Revisit Exercise 31.0 at the end of Chapter 4.0. Calculate the *annual cost* of the HVAC equipment in the residence of Sharron Stone. The useful life is estimated at 10 years. The novel high-efficiency gas furnace with add-on air conditioner cost is $15,183. Calculate the depreciable amounts by the method of straight line. The per annum energy costs remain at $900 and per annum maintenance costs at $60.

11.0 Best Year for Abandonment

Aunt Ethel purchased a pretzel maker for $18,880. The depreciation amounts for a five-year period by the method of declining balance and the receipts received from the sale of the pretzels are given below in Table 6-15. At a MARR of 10%, find the best year for abandonment of the pretzel maker.

Table 6-15 Pretzel Maker Service

EOY	Depreciation	$18,880	Receipts
1	$7,552	$11,328	$10,000
2	$4,531	$6,797	$8,000
3	$2,719	$4,078	$8,500
4	$1,631	$2,447	$6,500
5	$979	$1,468	$5,000

12.0 Automatic Bagger

A PP (polypropylene) bag manufacturer is considering replacing his plant operators and equipment with robots and automated handlers from Adept Technology. The wages and taxes for employing the workers are $7,500 per year. The salvage value of the equipment used with the operators is $4000. The automated equipment costs $10,000. After five years, the market value of the automated equipment is $3,500. The operating and maintenance expenses of the robots are $500 per year. Should the PP bag manufacturer replace the workers with robots? Consider a study period of five years. Use a before-tax MARR of 10%.

13.0 Keystone XL (please see Exercise 5.0 in Chapter 5.0)

A transcontinental pipeline known as Keystone XL is proposed that would ferry Canadian crude oil to Texas refineries. The Keystone XL runs from Alberta, Canada, through the states of Montana, South Dakota, Nebraska, Kansas, Oklahoma, and Texas, up to Port Arthur and Houston. The length of the 36" pipeline is about 2000 miles. The capacity of the pipeline in 900,000 BPD (barrels per day). The revenue from sales of one barrel of oil is about $75. Given a cost of $66.23 for a 72" stretch of the pipeline, calculate the capital cost to lay the entire pipeline. Include 10 pumps per mile at a cost of $5000 per pump. An estimated 3000 jobs are expected to be created at an average salary of $25,000 per annum. The overhead rate is $1 per $1 of wages. The land lease and taxes run about 30% of the revenue. For a pipeline life of 18 years, use the method of declining balance and calculate the depreciation amount and book value of the pipeline and pumps.

The factor used for calculation of depreciation amounts can be taken as 2.5/N, where N is the life of the pipeline. Calculate the PW of the project at an interest rate of 4.25%. The utility costs to operate the pumps are estimated at $25 million per year. What is the change in PW estimates when depreciation charges are taken into account, as opposed to a one-time charge? What are the tax consequences? What is the difference between PW using BTCF (before-tax cash flows) and ATCF (after-tax cash flows)?

14.0 Bioethanol from Sugarcane Bagasse (please see Example 5.3)

The sugarcane bagasse can be burned in boilers to generate electricity. Sugarcane bagasse can be converted to bioethanol and furfural by a dilute acid hydrolysis process. The acid hydrolysis process is a two-stage operation. In the first stage, hemicellulose is converted into sugar using dilute acid and steam. In the second stage, cellulose is converted to sugar by hydrolysis. Upon hydrolysis, the sugar can be processed in order to produce ethanol, furfural, and other products. Coproduction of ethanol and furfural can make the process more profitable. The acid hydrolysis plant consists of the following equipment:

Pump and Heater;

Reactor to Produce Furfural and Glucose;
Purification and Separation.

After passing through the heater, the feedstock is treated with dilute sulfuric acid solution (0.5 wt%) at high temperature for a short time. Cellulose and pentose are converted to glucose and furfural, respectively. The hydrolyzed stream is then separated using a distillation column. The hydrolyzed material is then neutralized with lime. The upper stream is passed through a condenser leading to the formation of furfural. The unreacted cellulosic residue and lignin from stream can be burned to generate electricity or sold as a by-product. The total capital investment needed for the acid hydrolysis plant is about $8 million. The furfural can be sold for $1.91/kg and the ethanol can be sold for $1.37/kg. The bagasse suppliers must be paid at 18 cents per kg of feedstock. A dilute acid hydrolysis plant can operate at 10,000 kg/h of sugarcane bagasse . The utilities and labor costs were estimated and found to be $1.50 per kg of ethanol and $2.0/kg of furfural. The plant utilization factor is 85%. The yield of ethanol is 25% and that of furfural is 10% from the bagasse.

Which would be a better alternative: (i) start a dilute acid hydrolysis plant with an estimated life of 28 years; or (ii) generate electricity from bagasse using a power plant? The cost of the steam boiler and turbine is about $2 million each. The electricity can be sold at 12.0 cents per kWh. The calorific value of bagasse is 8.0 MJ/kg. The power plant thermal efficiency can be taken as 32%. The interest rate is 8%. For purposes of analysis, assume that the power plant life is equal to that of the acid hydrolysis plant and is 28 years. The operating expenses of the power plant are about 6 cents per kWh.

Use the method of declining balance to obtain the depreciation amounts of the capital investments in the dilute acid hydrolysis plant and generation of electricity using power plant alternatives. The depreciation factor can be taken as 2.5/28, where 28 is the lives of the hydrolysis plant and steam power plants. Does the calculation of depreciation amounts affect the decision to select from the two alternatives?

15.0 Sequestration by Dimethyl Carbonate Formation (please see Example 5.4)

Two routes for the chemical reuse of CO_2 (carbon dioxide) are considered. Sequestration projects are creating increased interest due to concerns of global warming. Studies have shown that a 10% dimethyl carbonate (DMC) addition to diesel leads to 20% smoke reduction. Both plants operate at 10,800 h/year. CO_2 is available at no cost. Each ton of CO_2 sequestered leads to carbon credits of $21. Electric utilities cost 47 cents per kWh. Which is a better alternate at an interest rate of 4% and a plant life of 20 years?

Route A: Production from Ethylene Oxide: Ethylene oxide and CO_2 are allowed to react to form ethylene carbonate. Ethylene carbonate produced is reacted with methanol in a second PFR (plug flow reactor), leading to the production of DMC and ethylene glycol. The capital cost can be taken as $50 million; 70,000 tons/year of CO_2 are sequestered. The energy used in this process is 200 TJ/year. Revenue from the plant is $3500 per ton of CO_2 sequestered.

Route B: Production from Urea: Urea is produced by reacting ammonia and CO_2. DMC is produced by urea methanolysis. The capital cost for this route is given as $200 million; 50,000 tons/year of CO_2 are sequestered. The energy used in this process is 800 TJ/year. The revenue from the plant is $4000 per ton of CO_2 sequestered.

Use the method of declining balance to obtain the depreciation amounts of the capital investments in Routes A and B. The depreciation factor can be taken as 0.15. Does the calculation of depreciation amounts affect the decision to select from the two alternatives?

16.0 Baggage Conveyor System in Airport

The market value of the baggage conveyor system used by Indus Airlines is $80,000. From the property class as shown in Table 6-2, the conveyor system can be depreciated in five years. The salvage value is zero dollars at the end of five years. Indus Airlines is considering upgrading the conveyor system for an additional cost of $30,000. The annual expenses are expected to decrease from $2000 to $500 after the upgrade. There is an increase in revenue attributable to the baggage conveyor upgrade to the extent of $10,000 every year. The salvage value of the modified conveyor system after five years of use is $8,000. Should Indus Airlines go for the modification of the baggage conveyor system at the airport? The MARR is 10%.

Chapter 7.0

Taxes, Tariffs, and Duties

Learning Objectives

- Income Tax
- State and City Taxes
- Sales Tax
- Custom Duties
- Tariffs
- ATCF, BTCF
- Tax Consequences on PW, AW, FW, IRR, and ERR Methods
- Tax Reform under Presidents Reagan, Clinton, Bush, and Obama

7.1 Overview

From time immemorial, taxes have been collected by monarchs and kings from their subjects. According to Benjamin Franklin, "Nothing in the world is certain but death and taxes!" Ratified on February 13, 1913, the 16th Amendment to the Constitution of the United States under the presidency of William Taft, states:

> *The Congress shall have the power to lay and collect taxes on incomes, from whatever source derived, without apportionment among the several states, and without regard to any census or enumeration.*

The 16th Amendment allowed for direct taxation by the federal government based on incomes of individuals, business entities, and other organizations. The Civil War was funded by revenue raised by authority from the *Revenue Act of 1861*. The Internal Revenue Service (IRS) is the implementing government agency for tax collection. The *Internal Revenue Code of 1986* is the main text of the statutory law governing income tax, payroll taxes, gift taxes, estate taxes, and excise duties.

Income taxes can have a significant effect on the estimated cash flows in a project. Income taxes can be a cash outflow. This can be used during evaluation of profitability of projects. The cash flows discussed in Chapter 4.0 and Chapter 5.0 are *BTCF* (before-tax cash flow). The Tax Reform Act of 1986 (TRA 86) provided a general procedure for calculation of *ATCF* (after-tax cash flow). Salient changes haven been made to TRA 86 in the *Omnibus Budget Reconciliation Act of 1993* (OBRA 93) and *Taxpayer Relief Act of 1997*.

7.2 Tax Reform

Under the presidency of Ronald Reagan, Congress passed the *Tax Reform Act of 1986* (TRA 86) [1]. The income tax code was simplified, the tax base was expanded, and many a tax shelter was eliminated. Every taxpayer saw a decrease in tax bills. The number of tax deductions and number of tax brackets was reduced. The top income tax rate was decreased from 50% to 28%. The lowest income tax rate was increased from 11% to 15%. The upper income level of the lowest tax rate was increased from $5,720 per year to $29,750 per year. Additionally, 15 levels of tax brackets were reduced to four levels of tax brackets. Capital gains were taxed at the same rate as ordinary income. Interest on credit card debt was no longer deductible.

Incentives were provided for owner-occupied housing compared to rental housing by increasing the home mortgage interest deduction. The IRA (individual retirement account) deduction was restricted. Depreciation deductions were curtailed. The act required people claiming children as dependents on their tax returns to obtain and list a social security number for each child claimed as proof of the child's existence.

The *Omnibus Budget Reconciliation Act of 1993* (OBRA 93) [2] was passed by Congress and signed by President Bill Clinton. The top rate was increased again. A 36%, 39.6% rate for individuals in the top 1.2% of wage earners was created. Corporations were taxed at 35%. Medicare taxes were not capped. Fuel tax for vehicles was increased by 4.3 cents per gallon. The taxable portion of social security benefits was expanded. Limits on itemized deductions were indefinitely extended. Earned income tax credit was introduced.

The *Taxpayer Relief Act of 1997* [3] came about under the presidency of Bill Clinton. Several federal taxes were cut back. Top capital gains rates fell from 28% to 20%. The 15% tax bracket was lowered to 10%. Starting in 1998, a $400 tax credit for each child under the age of 17 was introduced. This was increased to $500 in 1999. This incentive was phased out for high-income families. Profits from the sale of a personal residence of up to $500,000 for married couples filing jointly and $250,000 for singles were declared *tax exempt*. Estate tax exemption was increased from $600,000 to $1 million gradually by the year 2006. Small businesses and farms owned by families can claim tax exemptions of $1.3 million. The $10,000 annual gift tax exclusion was adjusted for inflation starting from the year 1999. Tax relief was provided for retirement accounts and college savings plans. Credits were given for lifelong learning.

President George W. Bush administered federal tax cuts between 2001 and 2003 for all taxpayers. The lowest income tax rate was brought down from 15% to 10%. The 27% was changed to 25%, the 30% was changed to 28%, and the 35% rate was brought down to 33%. The top rate was changed from 39.6% to 35%. Tax credit for having children went from $500 to $1000. The marriage penalty was reduced. Tax cuts will expire in 2011 unless Congress enacts legislation. The Bush administration tax policy has led to income inequality. The gap is formed between the top 1% and the bottom 99%. Education and skill sets were attributed as causative factors. However, noted economists like P. Krugman pointed out the inequality between the top and the bottom cannot be explained by education alone. Wages of highly educated earners have fallen far behind those of the wealthiest top echelons. The U.S. national debt rose from 2001 to 2008. This was attributable to lower tax receipts. From a budget *surplus* the debt went to $400 billion in *deficit*.

President Barack Obama has introduced stimulus bills. These are intended to bring the nation out of the "great recession." The CBO (congressional budget office) reported that in 2009, the budget deficit increased by $1.9 trillion during fiscal year (FY) 2009, vs. a $1 trillion increase in FY 2008. This was because of a decline in tax receipts due to the recession, tax cuts, bailout efforts, additional spending, increase in spending of Medicare, Medicaid, unemployment insurance, social security, defense, and war expenses in Afghanistan and Iraq. The federal debt is about $12.7 trillion as of March 2010. This is about 80% of the GDP. The federal debt is expected to double between 2008 and 2015. It may become 100% of the GDP. Fifteen cents on every tax dollar in 2008 go toward payment of interest on debt. The exchange value of the dollar is expected to fall. The *Economic Stimulus Act of 2008* [4] provides tax rebates to stimulate the economy. Tax credits, extended unemployment benefits, and monies for infrastructure programs were introduced. The 2010 budget proposal of President Obama has health care, clean energy, education, and infrastructure as priorities. The national debt is proposed to be increased every year between 2010–2019 by $900 billion each year. Tax cuts are removed for the wealthiest top echelon and marginal rates returned to President Clinton levels.

7.3 Types of Taxes

The following different types of taxes have been selected by leaders and politicians:

(i) **Income Tax**: This is collected by the IRS as a function of gross income less allowable deductions. Income-based taxes can also be collected by state governments and local governments of cities.
(ii) **Property Tax:** This is assessed based on the value of the property owned, such as land, buildings, jewelry, etc. These taxes are levied by local governments, such as municipalities or counties.
(iii) **Sales Tax:** Sales tax can be levied by state or local governments. The amount of sales tax is a certain percentage of the dollar value of transactions of goods and services. This can be added to the cost of items acquired.
(iv) **Excise Taxes:** Nonessentials, when transacted, incur a duty called excise tax. This can be collected by the federal government. Part of it is borne by the manufacturer and some of it is passed along to the customer making the purchase.
(v) **Luxury Tax:** A good example of a luxury tax is the one levied in a five-star hotel such as a Hilton in a big city. This is in addition to the hotel charges incurred. The amount of luxury tax is a certain percentage of the bill.
(vi) **Tariffs:** The federal line subscription charge due to a telephone company (such as AT&T) for providing landline telephone services is a good example of a tariff.

7.4 Tax Consequencs of Evaluation of a Single Project

The MARR (minimum acceptable rate of return) discussed in earlier chapters is based on before-tax calculations. The MARR after tax can be estimated as

$$MARR(after - tax) = MARR(before - tax) * (1 - TaxRate) \tag{7.1}$$

The value of money calculated by the interest rate, i (%), needs to be modified for tax. The cost of capital is a weighted average

$$C_{WACC} = i'(1 - t_r)\gamma + (1 - \gamma)i \tag{7.2}$$

Where C_{WACC} is the weighted average cost of capital, i' (%) is the interest rate before taxation, ⊠ is the fraction of the capital that is borrowed, and i (%) is the interest rate after taxation. Interest on borrowed capital is tax deductible.

Business enterprises usually distinguish between *gross income* and *net income*. Gross income is the revenues less the expenses before tax. Net income is the profit made after payment of taxes.

The federal corporate income tax rate structure in 2010 is shown in Table 7-1.

Table 7-1 Corporate Federal Income Tax Rates (2010)

Taxable Income Range	*Tax Rate*
\$0–\$50,000	15%
\$50,000–\$75,000	25% (R > \$50,000) +\$7,500
\$75,000–\$100,000	34%(R > \$75,000) +\$13,750
\$100,000–\$335,000	39%(R > \$100,000) +\$22,250
\$335,000–\$10 million	34%(R > \$335,000) +\$113,900
\$10 million–\$15 million	35%(R > \$10 million) +\$3.4 million
\$15 million–\$18.33 million	38%(R > \$15 million) +\$5.15 million
\$18.33 million and up	35% (flat rate)

A flat rate of 35% is levied for incomes of more than \$18.33 million. The state tax rates are usually lower than that of the federal income tax and range about 6–12%. There are two kinds of tax consequences for the sale of an asset:

(i) Depreciation Recapture: When the sale value is greater than the book value of the asset;
(ii) Capital Loss: When the sale value is lower than the book value of the asset.

The cash flow diagram can be modified to reflect the tax consequences. The term ATCF is introduced. This is called after-tax cash flow. This is different from the BTCF, which is the before-tax cash flow. As can be recalled from Chapters 4.0 and 5.0, the income each year of the enterprise is revenues, R_k less the expenses, E_k incurred each year, and the depreciation of capital equipment for that year d_k. Thus,

$$BTCF_k = R_k - E_k - d_k \tag{7.3}$$

Let the tax consequence in the kth year be denoted by T_k. Then the $ATCF_k$ for the kth year can be written as

$$ATCF_k = BTCF_k \pm T_k \tag{7.4}$$

It can be seen that T_k can be calculated from Table 7-1 as

$$T_k = -t_r\,(R_k - E_k - d_k) \tag{7.5}$$

Where t_r is the tax rate. Combining Eqs. (7.3-7.5)

$$ATCF_k = R_k - E_k - d_k - t_r\,(R_k - E_k - d_k)$$

$$= (1 - t_r)(R_k - E_k) + t_r d_k \tag{7.5}$$

The $ATCF_k$ as given by Eq. (7.5) has two components: (i) a component that represents the *net income* accrued in the kth year. This is gross income $(R_k - E_k)$ less the tax paid to the government, $t_r(R_k - E_k)$. The second component reflects a tax savings attributable to depreciation, $+t_r d_k$.

Table 7-2 EOY Receipts and Costs

Year	Receipts Millions $	Cost Millions $
1	2.3	1.00
2	2.5	1.10
3	2	1.21
4	1.5	1.33
5	2	1.46
6	2.5	1.61
7	3	1.77
8	3.5	1.95
9	4	2.14
10	3.5	2.36
11	3	2.59

Example 7.1 Present Worth of a Sugar Mill After Tax Consequences

A business plan (Example 4.5) was presented that would get a sugar mill installed in rural Texas. The costs of raw materials such as sugar cane and utility costs rise every year due to inflation. The revenue from the sale of sugar rises and falls in synchrony with the boom-and-bust cycles of the economy. The EOY (end of year) revenues and costs are shown in Table 7-2.

The capital cost of the sugar mill, including land and all the necessary equipment, is estimated at $8 million. What is the PW of the sugar business at an interest rate of 3%, after taking into account the tax consequences? The tax rate given in Table 7-1 can be considered.

Another table was created in an MS Excel spreadsheet. The results are shown in Table 7-3. The $BTCF_k$ (before-tax cash flow) was calculated by subtracting the costs from the revenue column. It can be seen from the column under Profit (Before Tax) in Table 7-3 that the profits for the 11 years are greater than $335,000 and less than $10 million. So the tax rate can be seen from Table 7-1 as

$$T_k = \$113{,}900 + 0.34(Pr_k - \$335{,}000) \quad (7.6)$$

This was calculated and shown as a separate column T_k in Table 7-3. The profit after tax is calculated by subtracting the tax consequence column from the profit (before tax) column. The after-tax profit is shown as a separate column in Table 7-3. Since the profits vary from year to year, the (P/F, 3%,k) multiplier is used for each year in order to calculate the time value of money; k is varied from 1 to 11. The contribution to the PW for each kth year is calculated at $PW_k = \text{Profit}/(1+i)^k$ and shown as a separate column PW_k in Table 7-3. This column is summed up and the PW of the project is calculated taking into account the initial $8 million of capital investment.

It can be seen that PW has gone from positive (+$1.451 million) to negative territory (-$1.76 million). It is not profitable to start the sugar mill under the current tax rate.

The cash flow diagram after taking into account the tax consequences is shown in Figure 7.1.

Table 7-3 PW Analysis of Sugar Mill after Tax Consequences (All Quantities in Millions $)

		Before Tax			After Tax	
Year	Receipts	Cost	Profit	T_k	Profit	PW_k
1	$2.30	$1.00	$1.30	$0.44	$0.86	0.83301
2	$2.50	$1.10	$1.40	$0.48	$0.92	0.870959
3	$2.00	$1.21	$0.79	$0.27	$0.52	0.477155
4	$1.50	$1.33	$0.17	$0.06	$0.11	0.099102
5	$2.00	$1.46	$0.54	$0.18	$0.35	0.3051
6	$2.50	$1.61	$0.89	$0.30	$0.59	0.491656
7	$3.00	$1.77	$1.23	$0.42	$0.81	0.65923
8	$3.50	$1.95	$1.55	$0.53	$1.02	0.808234
9	$4.00	$2.14	$1.86	$0.63	$1.23	0.939038
10	$3.50	$2.36	$1.14	$0.39	$0.75	0.560864
11	$3.00	$2.59	$0.41	$0.14	$0.27	0.193703
	PW					-1.76195

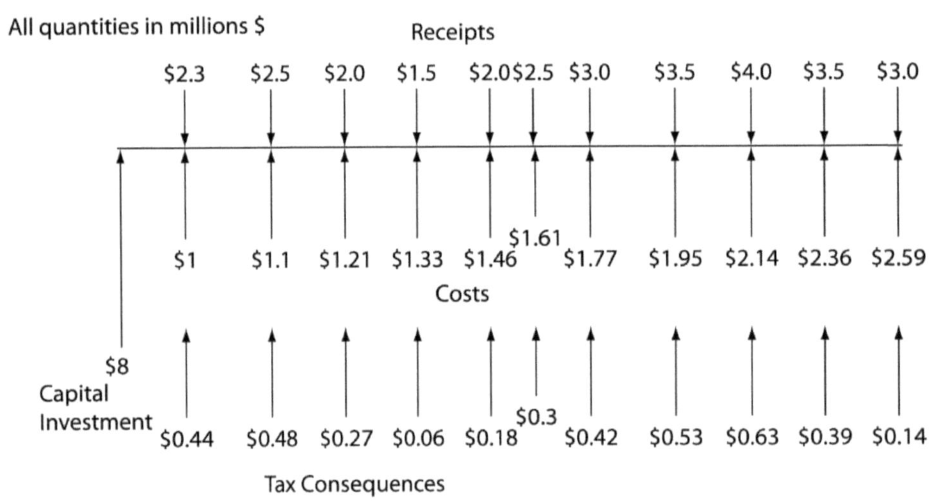

Figure 7.1 Cash Flow Diagram for Sugar Mill in a Boom-and-Bust Economy with Tax Consequences

Example 7.2 PW of ABS Plant Taking into Account Inflation and Tax Consequences

The inflation rates for the past 10 years, 1999–2009, are given below in Table 7-4. This table was prepared using the information provided by the Bureau of Labor Statistics (Example 4.8).

In 1999 dollars, calculate the PW (present worth) of an ABS (acrylonitrile butadiene styrene) engineering thermoplastic continuous polymerization plant. The capital cost of a new plant in 1999 dollars was 80 million. The selling price of ABS is $4 per pound. The raw materials cost rises every year because of inflation (Table 7-5). The price in year 1998 was $2.8 per pound of ABS sold. The process cost also goes up with inflation due to the increase in utility costs and wages to workers. The process cost can be taken as 30 cents per pound of ABS produced in 1998.

Table 7-4 Inflation Rates for 1999–2009

	(%)
Year	Inflation
1999	2.19
2000	3.38
2001	2.83
2002	1.59
2003	2.27
2004	2.68
2005	3.39
2006	3.24
2007	2.85
2008	3.85
2009	-0.34

Table 7-5 Effect of Inflation on Monomer Prices in an ABS Engineering Thermoplastic Plant

				(%)	Cost	Cost	Revenue
			Year	Inflation	Materials	Process	Millions $
			1999	2.19	2.861	0.3066	297.84
Product Rate	10000	lb/hr	2000	3.38	2.958	0.3169	297.84
ABS Price	4	$/lb	2001	2.83	3.042	0.3259	297.84
Materials	2.8	$/lb	2002	1.59	3.090	0.3311	297.84
Process Cost	0.3	$/lb	2003	2.27	3.160	0.3386	297.84
			2004	2.68	3.245	0.3477	297.84
Production	7E+07	lbs	2005	3.39	3.355	0.3595	297.84
	74.46	million lb	2006	3.24	3.464	0.3711	297.84
i	11	%	2007	2.85	3.562	0.3817	297.84
			2008	3.85	3.700	0.3964	297.84
			2009	-0.34	3.687	0.3950	297.84

The production rate from the two CSTR and falling strand devolatilizer plant is 10,000 lb/hr. Around 85% of the time the plant can be expected to run. The selling price of ABS remains flat during the 10-year period. An interest rate of 11% may be assumed. Consider the tax consequences. The corporate tax rate given in Table 7-1 may be used.

The inflation rates given in Table 7-4 were used to calculate the materials cost and process cost. This is shown in the column in Table 7-5 under Cost–Materials and Cost–Process. Each row was $(1+f_i)$ times the previous row,

Table 7-5 PW of ABS Engineering Thermoplastic Plant after Accounting for Inflation and Tax Consequences

								Before Tax	**After Tax**	
			Year	(%) Inflation	Cost Materials	Cost Process	Revenue Millions $	Profit Millions $	Profit	PW Million $
			1999	2.19	2.861	0.3066	297.84	61.95891	40.27329	$40.27
Product Rate	10000	lb/hr	2000	3.38	2.958	0.3169	297.84	53.98613	35.09098	$31.61
ABS Price	4	$/lb	2001	2.83	3.042	0.3259	297.84	47.08507	30.60529	$27.57
Materials	2.8	$/lb	2002	1.59	3.090	0.3311	297.84	43.09806	28.01374	$25.24
Process Cost	0.3	$/lb	2003	2.27	3.160	0.3386	297.84	37.31542	24.25502	$21.85
			2004	2.68	3.245	0.3477	297.84	30.33336	19.71668	$17.76
Production	7E+07	lbs	2005	3.39	3.355	0.3595	297.84	21.26489	13.82218	$12.45
	74.46	million lb	2006	3.24	3.464	0.3711	297.84	12.30385	4.20635	$3.79
i	11	%	2007	2.85	3.562	0.3817	297.84	4.16607	1.41646	$1.28
			2008	3.85	3.700	0.3964	297.84	-7.14037	-7.14037	($6.43)
			2009	-0.34	3.687	0.3950	297.84	-6.10344	-6.10344	($5.50)
Capital Cost of Plant										($80)
								Total		$89.90

where f_i is the inflation rate. Inflation rate was calculated by dividing the values provided under the column (%) inflation by 100. The revenue was calculated at a flat price of $4 per lb. of ABS multiplied with the quantity of ABS produced, i.e., 74.46 million lbs. This was arrived at from the production rate of 10,000 lb/hr multiplied with the operating time of the plant 24*365*0.85, where 0.85 is the utilization factor. The inflation effects on the materials and process costs resulted in loss in years 2008 and 2009. In other years there was a profit. The profit was obtained by subtracting the total expenses of materials and process from the revenue from sales of ABS. After-tax profit was calculated using the tax rates given in Table 7-1.

The PW contribution of each cell in the profit column was calculated using the single payment compound amount factor of $\frac{Pr_k}{(1+i)^{Year-1999}}$ where k is varied from 0 to 10 and Pr_k was the profit earned in each year. All the PW contributions from 1999 to 2009 were added, using the SUM command in an MS Excel spreadsheet on a desktop computer. The capital cost of $80 million was also subtracted as a one-time charge. No salvage value was attributed in 2009. The PW of the ABS plant in 1999 dollars was seen to be $89.90 million after taking into account the tax consequences. This has decreased from a PW of $157.07 million for the same plant before tax consequences. The results are shown in Table 7-5.

Example 7.3 Profitability of Liquefaction Plants

The conversion of natural gas to liquid (GTL) fuel using the Fischer-Tropsch process was first developed in 1923. Syngas ($CO + H_2$) was converted into synthetic fuels. At a Society of Petroleum Engineers symposium, a novel method of evaluating the economics of GTL plants was presented (Example 4.15). The capital expenses (CAPEX) are pegged to the production of one barrel of hydrocarbon liquid per day (BLPD). Annual operational expenses (OPEX) are expressed as a certain percentage of the CAPEX. It is assumed that the overall thermal efficiency of GTL plants is 60% and the plant operates 330 days per annum. Consider one instance of CAPEX of $40,000/ BLPD and OPEX of 7% of CAPEX. The plant is considered to be in existence for eight years. The price of crude oil is $37.65/bbl. Calculate the IRR for the project after taking into account the tax consequences. The tax rate given in Table 7-1 can be used.

Basis of Production: 1 Bbl a Day of liquid fuel/oil

Annual Revenue = $37.65*330* 1 = $12,424.5

Capital Expenses = $40,000

Annual Expenses = 0.07*$40,000 = $2800

PW = -$40,000 + $12,424.5*(P/A,i%,8) – 2800*(P/A,i%,8)

The PW for different interest rates was calculated using an MS Excel Spreadsheet on a desktop computer. The P/A values for the interest rates used in the simulation were read from the annuity tables given in Appendix A. The tax rate can be seen from Table 7-1 to be 15%. The values are given in Table 7-6 below. The PW as a function of interest rate is plotted in Figure 7.2 The IRR can be read from Figure 7.2 as 11.3%. Should the MARR be less than the IRR, the project is considered *profitable*.

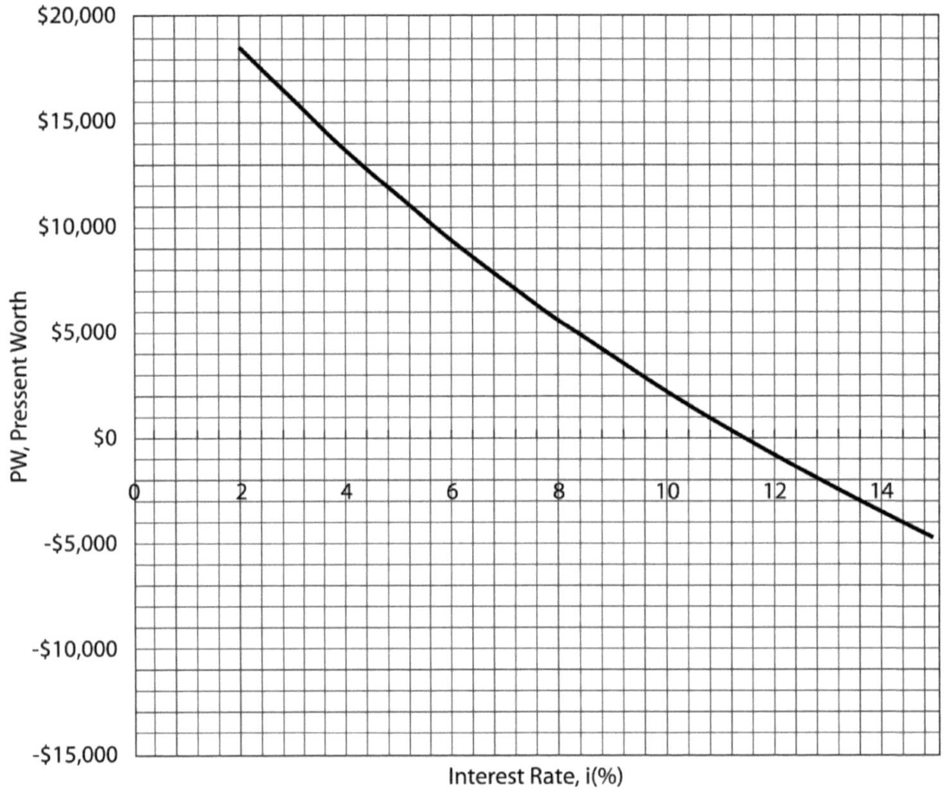

Figure 7-2 IRR Calculations for GTL Plant after Tax Consequences

Table 7-6 IRR Analysis for GTL Plant at 1 Bbl per Day with Tax Consequences

N	8		CAPEX	-$40,000
P/A	i	PW	Revenue	$12,424.50
7.325481	2	$18,484.80	OPEX	-$2,800
6.732745	4	$13,635.73	Tax	$1,443.68
6.2098	6	$9,357.61		
5.7466	8	$5,568.25		
5.3349	10	$2,200.21		
4.9676	12	-$804.61		
4.4873	15	-$4,733.86		

7.5 Summary

Enacted in 1913, the 16th Amendment allows for direct taxation by the federal government based on the incomes of individuals, business entities, and other organizations. Income taxes can have a significant effect on the estimated cash flows in a project. Income taxes can be a cash outflow. BTCF is before-tax cash flow and ATCF is after-tax cash flow. The Tax Reform Act of 1986 (TRA 86) provided a general procedure for calculation of ATCF (after-tax cash flow). Salient changes haven been made to TRA 86 in the Omnibus Budget Reconciliation Act of 1993 (OBRA 93) and Taxpayer Relief Act of 1997.

The different types of taxes are income tax, property tax, sales tax, excise tax, luxury tax, and tariffs. The tax consequences can be reflected in the MARR calculation by calculation of an after-tax MARR. The cost of capital can be expressed as an weighted average of amounts before taxation and after taxation. The $ATCF_k$ includes the tax rate, t_r as shown in Eq. (7.5). This includes the depreciation in addition to expenses and revenue. Worked examples on a sugar mill, a manufacturing plant for ABS engineering thermoplastic, effects of inflation, and tax consequences on the profitability of liquefaction plants are shown. Exercises are developed on tax consequences on an outpatient drug treatment center, gas station and convenience store, public Internet, video chat, and printing services, olive oil business, short path distillation for paraffin wax fractionation, frozen yogurt parlor, coffeehouse, car rental, turnaround business, onshore oil well, custom foam fabricator, and propylene bag manufacturer.

7.6 References

[1] Tax Reform Act of 1986 (TRA) (Pub.L. 99–514, 100 Stat. 2085, enacted October 22, 1986)
[2] Pub.L. 103–66, 107 Stat. 312, enacted August 10, 1993
[3] Pub.L. 105–34, Taxpayer Relief Act of 1997

7.7 Exercises

1.0 Outpatient Drug Treatment Center

A successful outpatient addiction treatment center with methadone maintenance and intensive counseling was established in 2002. Addiction disease is an epidemic. The treatment center has 14 employees, who find working in the center emotionally rewarding. The asking price of the business is $3.5 million. The net profit generated per year is around $650,000. At an interest rate of 8%, what would be the future worth of the business in 10 years from now if the treatment center were purchased today? The tax rate given in Table 7-1 can be used.

2.0 Gas Station and Convenience Store

A lucrative group of businesses includes a gas station, convenience store, tunnel car wash, and dog wash, as well as the land and improvements. An average of 2 million gallons of gasoline are pumped every year at the gas station. Over 700 transactions per day can be expected at the convenience store at an average transaction of $30. In 2009, 75,000 cars were washed at the conveyorized soft cloth car wash. The system can wash over 120 cars per hour. The average cost of gasoline per gallon in 2009 was $3.50. What is the present worth of the business after bearing the tax consequences? The group of businesses was purchased at $3.59 million. The convenience store complex is expected to be in use for 10 years, and the interest rate can be taken as 8%. Each car wash fetched an average of $5 per wash. Expenses are about $40,000 per day.

3.0 Public Internet, Video Chat, and Printing Services

The company offers public Internet, video chat, and printing services in Houston. It requires 750 sq. ft. of office space. It has 100 high-traffic locations in the city. The business also licenses its services to locations in New York City, San Francisco, Los Angeles, and Las Vegas. The service is ordered by quick-service restaurants and independent food and beverage purveyors. The company's proprietary software and systems enable it to deliver a reliable, quality service to

Table 7-7 Expenses and Revenue from Olive Oil Business

#	Expenses	Revenue
1	$400	$2000
2	$410	$2100
3	$420	$2200
4	$431	$2500
5	$420	$2400
6	$433	$2100
7	$446	$2000
8	$460	$2000

its customers, with minimal employee resources and overhead. The company's services are managed and supported by three full-time employees. End-user demand for the company's services is primarily driven by demand for printing maps, tickets, and other tourist- related information and by the growing use (both by tourists and full-time residents) of social media such as Facebook and other Web 2.0 services. This company was purchased for $1.4 million dollars. It is expected to be in use for 12 years. The annual revenue is about $1.95 million, and expenses run about $1.45 million per year. What is the AW of the business at an interest rate of 3% upon taking into account the tax consequences?

4.0 Olive Oil Business

Andrew Cuomo has convinced you to invest in his olive oil business. This requires $8000 for the initial investment. The revenue and expenses expected every year are as follows:

You can sell your share of the business after eight years for $10,000. What is the profitability of the project at a MARR of 13% upon facing the tax consequences?

5.0 Short Path Distillation for Paraffin Wax Fractionation

Paraffin wax is present in crude oil reserves and can be produced using the Fischer-Tropsch process. Paraffin wax is widely used in applications such as treatment of paper and cardboard, printing inks, and the food, cosmetic, and pharmaceutical industries. Prior to application, paraffin wax has to be de-oiled and fractionated and tailored for the given situation. SPD (short path distillation) is used to recover low volatility components from liquid mixtures. It can operate at low pressures and can be used to fractionate waxes. Low pressure operation obviates high temperature operation, which would result in degradation of the wax. Krause and Nieuwoudt ([5] in Chapter 4.0) discuss an SPD process with four stages, at a reflux ratio of 1.4. The capital cost is $17.1 million and the energy cost is $10.8/ton of wax. Calculate the IRR for a pay period of eight years, after taking into account the tax consequences. The capacity of the plant is 100,000 tons/year. The price of paraffin wax is $50/ton.

6.0 Frozen Yogurt Parlor

Jack Smith started a self-service frozen yogurt parlor in Sacramento. Five yogurt machines were purchased at $20,000 each. Up to nine flavors are available for customers to select from. Customers serve their own yogurt and toppings, and then Jack weighs them and collects the money. Around 48 customers can be seated in the 1200-sq.-ft. outfit. The three-year lease expires in 2013. The number of transactions per day is about 150 at

Table 7-8 Cement Factory—Loss

EOY	Expenses	Revenues
1	$10,000	$8,000
2	$9,000	$6,000
3	$10,000	$9,000

Table 7-9 Cash Flows in the Restructured Cement Factory

EOY	Expenses	Revenues
4	$6,000	$9,500
5	$5,500	$10,000
6	$5,000	$10,500
7	$4,500	$11,000
8	$4,000	$11,500

about $5 per transaction. Assume that the parlor is open for about 300 days in the year. Seven employees work for the parlor at an average salary of $20,000. What is the payback period at an interest rate of 8%? The utility and material costs are lumped into $1.50 per transaction. Take into account the tax consequences.

7.0 Coffee house

Sam Bush started a 2,280-sq.-ft. coffeehouse in New Milford, Connecticut, 15 years ago. All types of coffees are served, including locally roasted blends; 30 different tea selections are also available. Pastries and cookies are freshly baked on the premises. The coffeehouse serves breakfast and lunch only. An average of 250–300 customers per day stop in. The menu includes sandwiches, bagels, homemade muffins, cakes, bars, pies, puddings, and biscotti. During the day, soup, sandwiches, wraps, salads, and quiche are served. Wi-Fi is available, and entertainment with live music and other acts on most Friday nights is common. The revenues were about $328,000 per year. The costs were around $248,600 per year. Mr. Bush had purchased the building at $160,000 in 1995. At an interest rate of 5%, what is the 2010 worth of the coffeehouse upon accounting for tax consequences?

8.0 Libra Rental

Robert Byrd purchased six cars at a total cost of $120,000 to start Libra Rental. He charged $30/car/day for renting. The annual maintenance charges were about $150 per car per month. Calculate the IRR for the project for a period of six years. The car rental utilization rate is about 70%. The salvage value of the cars are $1800 per car at the end of the six-year period. Take into account the tax consequences.

9.0 Turnaround

A cement factory held a loss for a three-year period. The EOY (end of year) cash flows were as follows:

The capital expenses to start the cement factory were $30,000. A Harvard MBA graduate was hired to turn around the company's fortunes. He ordered a new kiln at an additional expense of $10,000. This led to a lower cost of production. A marketing program was introduced that boosted sales. The next five-year cash flows are as follows:

At 8% interest rate, what is the change in the PW of the cement factory before the restructuring in year 1 and after the restructuring in year 4? Take into account the tax consequences.

10.0 Onshore Oil Well

The southern and central Great Plains and the southwestern regions of our nation are dotted by onshore wells. With the recent oil spill disaster in an offshore well (BP America, 2010) interest in onshore wells is on the rise. Onshore wells are less expensive than offshore wells, which must be operated in the depths of the oceans and seas. The capital cost of an onshore well is about $1.1 million. The life of an oil well consists of the planning, drilling, completion, production, and abandonment phases. A well is created by drilling a hole 5–36" in diameter into the earth with a drilling rig that rotates a drill string with a bit attached. As the hole is drilled, sections of steel pipe, slightly smaller in diameter than the borehole, are placed in the hole. Cement may be placed outside the casing and the borehole. Texas Oil Field is asking $145,000 to purchase their onshore oil business. Eight BOPD (barrels per day of crude oil) can be produced. The price of crude oil per barrel is $80. The utility costs and labor wages can be lumped into $10 per barrel of crude oil produced. For the life of the oil well, estimated at 15 years at an interest rate of 6%, is it worth the asking price of the business? Take into account the tax consequences.

11.0 Custom Foam Fabricator

Evaluate the future worth of a custom foam fabricator in Houston after bearing the tax consequences. The service offers custom packaging, architectural columns and crown molding, monuments, signs, and theatrical scenery. Coatings and stucco supplies are also sold. Automated equipment and skilled employees are used. Builders, contractors, sign-up companies, stucco distributors, churches, and schools are their customers. The outfit is housed on 1.5 acres in two metal shop buildings with an area of 12,575 sq. ft. The average annual expenses are estimated at $673,000, and annual revenues are calculated at approximately $750,000. A period of 21 years can be assumed at 5% interest rate.

12.0 Polypropylene Bag Manufacture

Polypropylene woven products such as fabrics and bags are used in packing agriculture products, military heavy-duty, chemical industry, and regular commercial sandbags. A bag manufacturer works out of Houston and is a licensed USDA supplier. The customers include well-known companies such as ADM Milling, Cargill, Chevron Phillips, and JacintoPort International/Seaboard. The company serves as a federal contractor that supplies polypropylene products to the USDA (United States Department of Agriculture), Defense Department, U.S. Army, FEMA, and other federal, state, and local entities. A twin-screw extruder was purchased at a price of $5 million, with appropriate extrusion dies for bagging. The unit is housed on 10 acres of land. The land price is about $7000 per acre in Texas. Two freestanding buildings are used at a built area of 50,507 sq. ft. The cost of the building may be taken as $6.43 per sq. ft. Assuming an operation of 250 days in the year at a production rate of 10,000 lbs. per hour, calculate the AW (annual worth) of the business. The life of the extruder is about 21 years. The interest rate is about 6%. The price of finished polypropylene bag is about 7.67 cents per pound. The utility and labor costs can be lumped into 1 cent per pound of finished polypropylene products. Take into account the tax consequences.

Chapter 8.0

Public Sector Initiatives and Benefit-To-Cost Ratio

Main Topics Discussed in This Chapter

- Examples of Public Sector Projects
- Costs, Benefits, and Disbenefits
- B/C Ratio by PW
- B/C Ratio by AW
- B/C Ratio by FW
- B/C Ration by CW

8.1 Introduction

The evaluation methods of a single project and methods for selection of alternates discussed in earlier chapters are largely for the private sector and/or for-profit organizations. *Public sector* alternatives are different from private sector alternatives. Public sector projects are usually owned by the government, which provides for the good of its citizens. Public sector projects involve a lot of scrutiny and care of officials of government or international agencies such as the World Bank. The methods discussed for private sector enterprises may not be applicable for public sector projects. Public sector projects are built for the common good of millions of citizens. This is usually undertaken by the monarch or the federal government, and by state and local governments as well. *Au contraire* private sector projects, such as the *Chevy Volt* of General Motors Corp., are for the profit of the shareholders of the corporation. The characteristics of public sector projects are the large size of investment, lofty ideals carried in the vision, and undertaken for the common good. The project durations are longer for public sector projects. The public sector does not have a profit objective. There are cash flow diagrams with costs, benefits, disbenefits, etc. Private sector projects have the ulterior motive of profit. Cash flow diagrams with costs, revenues, and taxes are available. Examples of public sector initiatives include the nation's economic infrastructure such as airports, canals, dams, dikes, pipelines, railroads, interstate highways, tunnels, and artificial harbors.

Some specific examples of public sector projects in the history of mankind are as follows:

8.1.1 Marshall Plan

The Marshall Plan was implemented in 1947 and dispensed $13 billion in assistance. This economic plan was used to reconstruct western Europe after World War II The project duration was four years.

8.1.2 Taj Mahal

One of the wonders of the world, the mogul emperor Shah Jahan, Akbar's grandson, built this monument as a mausoleum for his wife, the begum Mumtaj Mahal. She died in childbirth. The construction cost of the tomb was 32 million rupees. The period of construction was 20 years. The building is entirely constructed of imported white marble. To this day, the Taj Mahal is a renowned tourist attraction.

8.1.3 Great Wall of China

Considered by some as the mightiest work of mankind, this wall stretches 5,500 miles and was maintained from the 5th century B.C. through the 16th century B.C. The wall was built during the Ming Dynasty. Stones and rammed earth were used for its construction.

8.1.4 Great Pyramid of Giza

The construction of the Great Pyramid of Giza took 20 years to complete. About 200,000 workers participated. The accuracy achieved on the pyramid was 0.05%. For about 3,800 years, this was the tallest man-made construction in the world. The Egyptian pharaoh Khufu built this as a tomb for himself and his family. The pyramid is composed of 2.5 million limestone blocks, each weighing about 36 tons.

8.1.5 Eiffel Tower

The Eiffel Tower has been visited by 200 million people since its completion in 1889 to commemorate the centennial of the French Revolution. It is the most-visited paid monument in the world. Before the construction of the Chrysler Building in New York City in 1930, this was the world's tallest construction. It is a feat of engineering.

8.1.6 Suez Canal

The Suez Canal provides the *critical* connection between the Mediterranean Sea and the Red Sea. The canal allows for water transportation between Europe and Asia. If this canal were shut down for some reason, the ships would have to take a lengthy detour around Africa. The Suez Canal is a little over 100 miles in length. The Cold War between the United States and the erstwhile USSR led to the Suez Crisis in 1956. An event such as this one clearly sets apart projects such as these from those intended to make a profit for privately owned enterprises. So many nations are involved, so many treaties are signed, and so many "peacekeeping" forces are in place that such a project cannot be listed as a private sector project. As it is for the good of the word traders at large and offers a shorter path between East and West, this can be considered a public sector project. L. B Pearson was awarded the Nobel Peace Prize for averting World War III arising from the Suez Crisis in 1956. About 7.5% of the world sea trade is carried out via the Suez canal.

8.1.7 Hoover Dam

President Franklin D. Roosevelt dedicated the Hoover Dam to the nation in 1935. The dam, located in Nevada, produces hydroelectric power. Commissioned 75 years ago, the public sector project to this day serves as an example that renewable energy projects stem more from government than from private entrepreneurs. After the dark days of the Great Depression, this public sector project lifted the nation's morale.

8.1.8 Apollo Space Program

The first humans landed on the moon by this project. To gain supremacy in the "space race" with the Soviet Union, President John F. Kennedy shared his vision in an address to Congress in 1961 "... I believe that this nation should commit itself to achieving the goal, before this decade is out, of landing a man on the Moon and returning him back safely to the earth. No single space project in this period will be more impressive to mankind, or more important for the long-range exploration of space; and none will be so difficult or expensive to accomplish." He further went on to say "We choose to go the Moon in this decade and do the other things, not because they are easy, but because they are hard." This project improved the world's pride. The greedy for-profit approach of some private sector companies would not have come up with such a project. This can be considered an excellent public sector project.

8.1.9 NASA Mars Science Laboratory Mission

A large mobile laboratory, the NASA rover *Curiosity* will land on the planet Mars. The duration of the study is planned at 23 months. Dozens of samples drilled from rocks or scooped ground will be analyzed. The *Curiosity* will carry the most advanced payload scientific gear ever used on a Martian surface. The focus of the investigations is on whether favorable conditions for microbial life existed or does exist!. The launch is slated for December 18, 2011, and landing is expected around August 2012. The rover's electrical power will be supplied by U.S. Department of Energy radioisotope power generator. Electricity is generated from heat by the radioactive decay of plutonium 238. A suite of instruments named Sample Analysis at Mars will be used to analyze samples of materials collected and delivered by the rover's arm. The suite of instruments includes a gas chromatograph, mass spectrometer, and tunable laser spectrometer capable of measuring isotope ratios. Isotope ratios can be used for better understanding the history of the Martian atmosphere and water. An X-ray diffraction and fluorescence instrument called CheMin will be used to examine samples gathered by the rover's robotic arm. Quantitation of minerals in rocks and soil and measurement of bulk composition will be the objects of the study. The Mars Hand Lens Imager will be used to obtain close-up photographs of rocks, soil, and ice (if present), with spatial resolution smaller than the width of a human hair.

8.1.10 Interstate Highways

This is the largest public works project in history. These are the interstate highways that allow for driving long distances on the road for vacation or business. The system has a total length of 46,876 miles. About 70% of the construction and maintenance costs of highways are collected through user fees and tolls. The rest come from fuel taxes and other taxes levied by the government.

After landslide electoral victories of Republican presidents, the image of the public sector project is poor in the United States. Lists of public sector projects include hospitals, clinics, parks and recreational sites, water, electricity, gas, sewer, sanitation, utilities, schools, convention centers, sports arenas, transportation highways, bridges, waterways, police and fire protection, food stamps and public assistance welfare programs, codes and standards, etc.

The government usually assigns the tasks in a public sector project to contractors. The contractors who work on these projects take on the work under a lump-sum fixed price or cost reimbursement basis. Sometimes the public and private form a public-private partnership. The *BOT* (build-operate-transfer) arrangement may require the contractor to be completely or partially responsible for the construction, operation, and maintenance activities for the time of the project duration. After the project duration, the government becomes the owner. The title of ownership is thus transferred to the government.

8.2 B-C-D Method

The ratio of benefit to cost can be used in selecting public sector projects. The *disbenefits* are not considered in private sector projects, but can be considered during the evaluation of public sector projects. Public sector projects have

(i) Costs: These are expenses incurred by the government during the procurement, construction, and execution phases of the public sector project.
(ii) Benefits: The advantages availed by the citizens include income, savings, comfort of commute, etc.
(iii) Disbenefits: Expected unwanted consequences to the owners.

Disbenefits can cause public controversy and agitation or even picketing. Benefits to one group of taxpayers are disbenefits to another group of taxpayers. For example, a project to expand a four-lane highway into a six-lane highway may decrease congestion and decrease the commute time. This project offers advantages to the citizens who commute using that highway. Another section of citizens receives the disbenefits of higher prices at the gasoline pump due to the fuel tax levied to garner revenue for the project. A public sector project to light a section of highway with laser lighting in order to decrease the life-cycle costs may draw praise from the citizens driving through the highway. The same project incurs criticism from other taxpayers who do not drive on that highway but who still have to pay higher taxes for the highway lighting.

The finances to commission and operate a public sector project are drawn from

(i) Taxes;
(ii) User Fees;
(iii) Tolls;
(iv) Bonds;
(v) Loans;
(vi) Gifts from Charitable Trusts.

Usually, the interest rates for public sector projects are lower than for the cash flows in private sector projects. This is because a number of these public sector projects are tax exempt. Municipalities are allowed to float tax-exempt bonds for private investors as well. The loans are *subsidized* by the government. Tax credits are provided that result in a lower interest rate.

The selection criteria for projects in the private sector are solely based on the MARR (minimum acceptable rate of return). The public sector projects are screened and selected based on several criteria, such as economic and noneconomic parameters, special interests, political philosophy, etc. Public sector projects are discussed in town hall meetings.

The *Flood Control Act of 1936* was signed into law by President Franklin D. Roosevelt. Civil engineering projects such as dams, dikes, levees, and other flood control measures can be undertaken by the U.S. Army Corps of Engineers with authority. The act was established to protect people and property on about 100 million acres. The *economic benefits* had to exceed the *costs*. Local interests had to meet the ABC requirements for local projects. Under the authority of this act, 375 major reservoirs have been built. These reservoirs have saved billions of dollars in property damage and protected millions of people from tension, anxiety, injury, and disabilities. Rivaled only by the highway system, these are significant landmarks of technical skills and the human spirit. The B/C (benefit-to-cost ratio) was defined for evaluation of public sector projects based on the Flood Control Act of 1936.

$$\frac{B}{C} = \frac{PW(benefits)}{PW(cost)} \tag{8.1}$$

Or Eq. (8.1) may be defined in terms of AW (annualized worth), FW (future worth), or CW (capitalized worth):

$$\frac{B}{C} = \frac{FW(benefits)}{FW(\cos t)} \tag{8.2}$$

or

$$\frac{B}{C} = \frac{AW(benefits)}{AW(\cos t)} \tag{8.3}$$

or

$$\frac{B}{C} = \frac{CW(benefits)}{CW(\cos t)} \tag{8.4}$$

The costs are indicated by a *plus sign* and not negative, as discussed in the evaluation of single projects in earlier chapters. *Disbenefits* can be subtracted from the *benefits* in the numerator. The B/C ratio is always positive. When the B/C ratio is ^{3} 1, the project can be considered acceptable. When the B/C ratio is < 1, the project is considered unacceptable.

The disbenefits may be subtracted from the benefits as follows:

$$\frac{B}{C} = \frac{PW(benefits) - PW(disbenefits)}{PW(\cos t)} \tag{8.5}$$

Or Eq. (8.5) may be defined in terms of AW (annualized worth), FW (future worth), or CW (capitalized worth):

$$\frac{B}{C} = \frac{FW(benefits) - FW(disbenefits)}{FW(\cos t)} \tag{8.6}$$

Or

$$\frac{B}{C} = \frac{AW(benefits) - AW(disbenefits)}{AW(\cos t)} \tag{8.7}$$

Or

$$\frac{B}{C} = \frac{CW(benefits) - CW(disbenefits)}{CW(\cos t)} \tag{8.8}$$

There is some discussion in the literature on whether to add the disbenefits to the costs in the denominator! A modified B/C ratio may be defined as

$$\frac{B}{C} = \frac{PW(benefits) - PW(disbenefits) - PW(O\&M \exp enses)}{investment} \tag{8.9}$$

Or Eq. (8.9) may be defined in terms of AW (annualized worth), FW (future worth), or CW (capitalized worth):

$$\frac{B}{C} = \frac{FW(benefits) - FW(disbenefits) - FW(O\&M\ expenses)}{investment} \tag{8.10}$$

$$\frac{B}{C} = \frac{AW(benefits) - AW(disbenefits) - AW(O\&M\ expenses)}{investment} \tag{8.11}$$

$$\frac{B}{C} = \frac{CW(benefits) - CW(disbenefits) - CW(O\&M\ expenses)}{investment} \tag{8.12}$$

Example 8.1 Firefighting in Yellowstone National Park in 1988

Fire broke out in Yellowstone National Park in the states of Wyoming, Montana, and Idaho in 1988. There was discussion in the news as to whether to fight the fires. The costs for this firefighting project were about $120 million. At a prime interest rate of 3.0%, calculate the B/C ratio based on AW (annualized worth). The revenues from wolf watchers alone is about $8.5 million per year. Allow for the payback period up to the year 2010.

AW (Benefits) = $8.5 million (8.13)

AW (Costs) = (A/P, i%, N) = (A/120, 3.25%, 22)*120 (8.14)

From annuity tables (Appendix A), (A/P, 3%, 22) = 0.062747 = 7.53 million

From Eq. (8.3) B/C = 8.5/7.53 = 1.12 (8.15)

As the B/C ratio is greater than 1, the firefighting efforts can be selected.

Example 8.2 Replacement for the World Trade Center (WTC)

One proposal to replace the World Trade Center (WTC) suggested that the mayor of New York City build another high-rise to replace the WTC, which was destroyed by terrorists in September 2001. In a typical week, 50,000 people are expected to work in these towers. Additionally, 200,000 visitors are expected to go the top floor to obtain a glimpse of York City from the 110th floor. The cost of constructing the building is estimated at $10 billion. Assume a net profit of collecting rent from the occupants is $250 per person per week and a visitor fee of $10. The funds are obtained by the mayor selling New York City tax-exempt bonds. The interest rate is 2%. The project horizon is 20 years. Is this a favorable public sector project?

The PW-based B/C ratio can be used. Eq. (8.1) can be used to evaluate the B/C ratio. No disbenefits are considered in this analysis.

Rental Fee collected per year = $250*50{,}000*52/10^6$ = $ 650 million (8.16)

Visitor Fee collected per year = $200{,}000*10*52/10^6$ = $104 million (8.17)

(P/A, 2%, 20) = 16.35143 (from Appendix A, 2% annuity Tables) (8.18)

PW (Benefits) = 16.35143*(650+104) = 12.329 billions. (8.19)

From Eq. (8.1), B/C = 12.329/10 = 1.2329 (8.20)

It can be seen from Eq. (8.20) that the B/C ratio is greater than 1. This is an *acceptable* public sector project.

8.3 Summary

Public sector alternates are different from private sector alternates. Public sector projects are usually owned by the government and are operated for the good of its citizens. The evaluation methods of a single project and methods for selection of alternatives discussed in earlier chapters are largely for the private sector and/or for-profit organizations. In this chapter, the B/C ratio method is introduced to evaluate public sector projects. Benefit-to-cost ratios may be calculated based on the PW, FW, AW, and CW of the benefits, and the PW, FW, AW, and CW of the costs incurred. In addition to benefits and costs, another item—disbenefits—is introduced. Ten examples of successful public sector projects are discussed. Worked examples and exercises on firefighting in Yellowstone National Park, a replacement for the WTC, solar thermal power plants from photovoltaic and SD (Stirling dish) technology, windmills, Keystone pipeline projects, and expansion of federal highways using high-performance nanostructured concrete are discussed.

8.4 References

http://en.wikipedia.org

8.5 Exercises

1.0 Classify whether the following projects are private sector or public sector in nature:

- A solar power plant (with a government tax credit given) is built by Edison Electric Co.
- Hoover Dam is commissioned by the federal government.
- The WTC is replaced with a mosque by private individuals.
- The WTC is replaced by the mayor of New York City.
- The Suez Canal is owned by the Suez Co.
- The Suez Canal is nationalized and owned by the government of Egypt.

2.0 Expansion of Federal Highways from Eight Lanes to 16 Lanes

There is a proposal to expand I-45 from eight lanes into 16 lanes for a stretch of 30 miles in the vicinity of Houston, Texas. It would cost the city of Houston $50 million. The costs incurred are from the use of *ultrahigh-performance nanostructured concrete.* This is expected to be in service for 100 years. The commuters will see a decrease in commute time of 30 minutes per trip due to the lack of congestion. This can result in a cost savings of $1 million per year. The disbenefits to the land owners near the highway can be estimated at $75,000 per year. The mayor is expected to raise the monies by selling tax-exempt municipal bonds. The interest rate is about 1%. Is this an acceptable public sector project?

3.0 Keystone XL

A transcontinental pipeline known as Keystone XL is proposed that would ferry Canadian crude oil to Texas refineries. The Keystone XL runs from Alberta, Canada, through the states of Montana, South Dakota, Nebraska, Kansas, Oklahoma, and Texas up to Port Arthur and Houston. The length of the 36" pipeline is about 2000 miles. The capacity of the pipeline in 900,000 BPD (barrels per day). The revenue from the sale of one barrel of oil is about $75. Given a cost of $66.23 for a 72" stretch of the pipeline, calculate the capital cost to lay the entire pipeline. Include 10 pumps per mile at a cost of $5000 per pump. An estimated 3000 jobs are expected to be created at an average salary of $25,000 per annum. The overhead rate is $1 per $1 of wages. The land lease and taxes run about 30% of the revenue. For a pipeline life of 30 years, calculate the B/C ratio using PW of benefits and PW of costs of the public sector project. The interest rate can be assumed to be 2%. The utility costs to operate the pumps are estimated at $25 million per year. Is this an acceptable public sector project ?

4.0 SD (Stirling Dish) Solar Power Plant

Upon graduation, you are hired by the federal government's DOE, Department of Energy. You are given the task of selecting between two different plans to generate electricity using Stirling dish technology. There is increased interest in recent years to use solar energy to generate electricity. The Stirling engine is environmentally clean with zero emissions. Solar-to-electric conversion efficiencies in the range of 30% can be realized using SD (Stirling dish) solar electric generating systems ([8], Chapter 5.0). Individual units range in capacity between 5–25 kW. Solar power plants become attractive from an economic standpoint when the land cost is low and government incentives are high for generation of electricity in a pollution-free manner. Each unit is comprised of a solar concentrator and a power conversion unit is located at the focus of the parabolic dish. It consists of a cavity receiver and a Stirling heat engine, with an electric generator or alternator. The concentrator reflects and concentrates solar radiation and delivers to the receiver. The light is absorbed by the receiver, and heat is transferred to a working fluid such as helium and hydrogen. Alternate compression and expansion of the working fluid in a piston arrangement leads to generation of electricity. Parabolic dish concentrators can be used to achieve temperatures greater than 1500°C. A 5 kW unit would require a 5.5 m diameter dish and a 25 kW unit would require a 10 m diameter dish; 25% of the cost of the SD systems is the cost of the concentrators. The cost and economic data for the two plans, A and B, are given below in Table 8-1. The PW method of analysis is recommended to arrive at the B/C ratios of the two plans.

5.0 Solar Thermal Power Plant

The federal government's Department of Energy is considering construction of solar thermal power plants in Weberville, Texas, and South Chicago. The costs of building and operating a solar thermal power plant are as follows:

Fixed Costs (Capital Cost)

(i) Land;
(ii) Solar Photovoltaic Panels;

Table 8-1 Cost and Economic Data for Plans A and B for Stirling Dish Solar Power Plant

	Plan A	Plan B
Capacity	50 MW	50 MW
# SD Units	10,000	2000
Annual Solar Radiation (kWh/m^2)	1.728	1.728
Annual Electricity Generated	7 GWh	7 GWh
Life of Solar Power Plant	30 years	30 years
Interest rate (i)	10%	10%
Sale Price of Electricity	7.3c/kWh	7.3c/kWh
Equipment Costs	$22.4 per unit	$324.45 per unit
Transport Costs	$3.36 per unit	$48.65 per unit
Land Cost	$19,000	$19,000
Earthworks	$22,000	$99,600
Other Costs	$7.46 per unit	$10.8 per unit
Operation & Management Expense	$10,122	$10,122

(iii) Steam Generators;
(iv) Other Equipment;
(v) Tax Credit Accrued.

Variable Costs

(i) Wages;
(ii) Operation & Management.

The cost and economic data for the two solar power plants in Texas and Illinois are given below in Table 8-2. The photovoltaic solar panels cost $808.64 each. The average salary per job in these power plants is $25,000 per year. The price of electricity can be set at about 15.3 cents/kWh. The power plants can be assumed to be operated

Table 8-2 Cost and Economic Data for Solar Power Plants

Item	**Weberville, TX**	**South Chicago, IL**
Power Plant Capacity	30 MW	10 MW
Land Used	300 acres	39 acres
# Photovoltaic Solar Panels	105,750	33,000
Per Acre Land Cost	$3000	$4000
Cost of Steam Turbine	$10.5 million	$3.5 million
Other Equipment	50% of Steam Turbine	50% of Steam Turbine
# Jobs	600	120
Plant Life	40 years	40 years
i (%) Interest Rate	2.0%	2.0%

Table 8-3 Cost and Economic Data for Solar Power Plants

Item	Weberville, TX	**South Chicago, IL**
Power Plant Capacity	30 MW	10 MW
Land Used	300 acres	39 acres
# Photovoltaic Solar Panels	105,750	33,000
Per Acre Land Cost	$3000	$4000
Cost of Steam Turbine	$10.5 million	$3.5 million
Other Equipment	40% of Steam Turbine	40% of Steam Turbine
# Jobs	600	120
Plant Life	40 years	40 years
i (%) Interest Rate	2.0%	2.0 %

at 66.67% capacity utilization factor. The operation and management expenses can be taken as 45% of the wages and salaries provided. Which plant has a higher B/C ratio based on the PW of benefits and the PW of costs?

6.0 Solar Thermal Power Plant

The federal government's Department of Energy is considering constructing solar thermal power plants at two locations: (i) Weberville, Texas; and (ii) South Chicago. The cost and economic data for these two solar power plants are given below in Table 8-3. The photovoltaic solar panels cost $808.64 each. The average salary per job in these power plants is $30,000 per year. The price of electricity can be set at about 12.5 cents/kWh. The power plants can be assumed to be operated at 60% capacity utilization factor. The operation and management expenses can be taken as 45% of the wages and salaries provided. Which plant has a better B/C ratio? Use Eq. (8.1) based on the PW of benefits and the PW of costs.

7.0 Wind Energy Conversion to Electric Power (Ref. [9] in Chapter 5.0)

Wind energy can be tapped into for generating electric power. The acceptability of wind energy plants is higher when constructed at locations where the wind speed is higher and is prevalent for a large portion of the year and when the capital cost is low. This kind of power plant uses a sustainable energy source and causes less pollution compared with fossil fuel power plants. These power plants qualify for a tax credit at 15% of the cost of renewable energy equipment used, such as the wind machine and tower. Three different such power plants are considered for installation in Saudi Arabia by that country's government. The plant lives are 15 years and the interest rate can be taken as 2%. The price of electricity can be set at 8.5 cents per kWh used. The development cost of $200,000 is the same for the three plants, with capacities of 1500 kW, 1000 kW, and 600 kW. Calculate the B/C ratio based on the PW of benefits and the PW of costs for each plant and rank the three projects according to their acceptability. The cost and economic data of the three plants are given below in Table 8-4.

8.0 Wind Energy Conversion to Electric Power (Ref. [9] in Chapter 5.0)

Wind energy can be tapped into for generating electric power. The acceptability of these plants is higher when constructed at locations where the wind speed is higher and the wind is prevalent for a large portion of the year, and when the capital cost is low. This kind of power plant uses sustainable energy source and causes

Table 8-4 Cost and Economic Data for Wind Power Plants

Item	1500 kW	1000 kW	600 kW
Power Plant Capacity	1500 kW	1000 kW	600 kW
Energy Production (MWh)	48,000	35,000	40,000
Renewable Energy Equipment (Wind Machine & Tower)	$26.89 million	$27.185 million	$27.785 million
Balance of Plant	$3.04 million	$3.368 million	$4.018 million
Miscellaneous Fixed Costs	$1.58 million	$1.61 million	$1.672 million
O & M, Operation & Maintenance Expenses	$0.9 million	$0.709 million	$0.77 million

less pollution compared with fossil fuel power plants. These power plants qualify for a tax credit at 15% of the cost of renewable energy equipment used, such as the wind machine and tower. Three such power plants with the same capacity of 1500 kW are considered for installation at three locations in Saudi Arabia by their government: (i) Al-Wajh; (ii) Yanbo; and (iii) Dhahran. The plant lives are 15 years and the interest rate can be taken as 1%. The price of electricity can be set at 8.5 cents per kWh used. The development cost of $200,000 is the same for the three plants at Al-Wajh, Yanbo, and Dhahran. The wind speeds at the three locations are as follows:

(i) Al-Wajh 4.1 m/s;
(ii) Yanbo 5.1 m/s;
(iii) Dhahran 4.72 m/s.

Calculate the B/C ratio based on the AW of benefits and the AW of costs for each plant and rank the three projects according to their acceptability. The cost and economic data for the three plant locations are given below in Table 8-5.

Table 8-5 Cost and Economic Data for Wind Power Plants

Item	Al-Wajh	Yanbo	Dhahran
Power Plant Capacity	1500 kW	1500 kW	1500 kW
Energy Production (MWh)	48,000	83,000	70,000
Renewable Energy Equipment (Wind Machine & Tower)	$26.89 million	$26.89 million	$26.89 million
Balance of Plant	$3.04 million	$3.04 million	$3.04 million
Miscellaneous Fixed Costs	$1.58 million	$1.61 million	$1.61 million
O & M, Operation & Maintenance Expenses	$0.9 million	$0.9 million	$0.9 million

Chapter 9.0

Break-Even Analysis and Spider Plots

Main Topics Discussed in This Chapter

- Perform Break-Even Analysis
- Calculate Break-Even Interest Rate
- Calculate Payback Period
- Construct Spider Plots
- Interpret Sensitivity Analysis
- What Is a "Decision Reversal?"

9.1 Overview

In Chapter 5.0, decisions were made based upon comparison of alternatives. The alternatives were compared using one of the five methods described in Chapter 4.0: (i) PW (present worth); (ii) FW (future worth); (iii) AW (annual worth); (iv) IRR (internal rate of return); and (v) ERR (external rate of return). It can be seen from the worked examples and exercises that the dollar-and-cents number arrived at as the worth can differ with variation in the data provided for calculation of costs and revenue. An EW (equivalent worth) can refer to PW, FW, or AW. When two alternatives, A and B, are compared with each other, the EW_A, equivalent worth of Project A is a function of several factors. Consider one factor x.

$$EWA = f(x) \tag{9.1}$$

The EWB, equivalent worth of project B is also a function of the same factor x. At the break-even point

$$EWA = EWB \tag{9.2}$$

The factors can be several. These can be

(i) Capital Expenses;
(ii) Annual Revenue;
(iii) Annual Cost;Interest Rate;
(iv) Rate of Return;

(v) Salvage Value;
(vi) Useful Life, N;
(vii) Capacity Utilization.

Each of these eight factors can be varied one at a time by 10% increments and 10% decrements. The EW (equivalent worth) can be calculated and plotted as a function of the increments and decrements for each of the eight factors. Such a plot is called a *spider plot*. The purpose of a spider plot is to bring out the sensitivity of the factors to the decision or estimate made of the project's worthiness.

Example 9.1 Break-Even Analysis for the PEV Chevy Volt

The CEO of General Motors Corp. recently unveiled the Chevrolet Volt, a plug-in electric vehicle (PEV). It has a better range. For up to the first 40 miles, the Volt is powered by electric energy stored in its onboard lithium-ion batteries, which are charged by connection to an electrical power outlet. The 16 kWh battery pack can be fully charged by connecting to a residential electrical outlet operated at 12–240 Volt AC. The cost of the vehicle is about $41,000. A $7,500 federal tax credit can be expected for purchase of the PEV. The fuel efficiency is 230 mpg of gasoline plus 25 kWh per 100 miles. A 2010 Toyota Corolla costs about $18,880 and is a standard gasoline-powered vehicle. It provides a fuel efficiency of 32 mpg. What is the break-even point in miles that must be driven by the owner before the Volt becomes comparable with the Corolla in a total life-cycle cost? The useful lives of both vehicles may be taken as seven years. The interest rate may be taken as 7%. The household electric utility charges 12.5c per kWh. The cost of gasoline at the pump is $4.75 per gallon.

Let the number of miles driven per year by passenger = X miles/year (9.3)

$$\text{Annual Fuel Expenses for Volt} = \frac{0.125*25X}{100} + \frac{4.75X}{230} = 0.051902X \quad (9.4)$$

$$(P/A,7\%,7) = 0.5(4.7665+5.9713) = 5.3689 \quad (9.5)$$

$$PW_{volt} = -\$41{,}000+\$7{,}500 -5.3689*0.051902X = -33{,}500 -0.27866X \quad (9.6)$$

$$PWcorolla = -18{,}880-5.3689*4.75X/32 = -18{,}880-0.796946X \quad (9.7)$$

At the break-even point

$$PWvolt = PWcorolla \quad (9.8)$$

Combining Eq. (10.6) and Eq. (10.7), it can be seen that X is

$$X = \frac{33{,}500 - 18{,}880}{(0.796946 - 0.27866)} = 28{,}208.2 miles \quad (9.9)$$

Example 9.2 Spider Plot for Life-Cycle Cost of Chevy Volt

Construct the spider plot for the PEV Chevy Volt as discussed in Example 9.1. Assume that the passenger drives 30,000 miles every year.

$$PWvolt = -33{,}500 -0.27866X = -\$41{,}859.7 \quad (9.10)$$

The information needed to construct a spider plot was calculated using an MS Excel spreadsheet on a desktop computer and shown in Table 9-1.

Table 9-1 Simulation Results for Spider Plot of Life-Cycle Cost of PEV Chevy Volt

Spider Plot

% Change	MSRP	PW	Miles/Year	Tax Credit	$4.75 Gas Price	Interest Rate Interest Rate	P/A	PW
-40%	24,600	-$25,460	-$38,516	-$44,860	-$40,529	4.20%	5.957943	-$42,777
-30%	28,700	-$29,560	-$39,352	-$44,110	-$40,862	4.90%	5.807402	-$42,542
-20%	32,800	-$33,660	-$40,188	-$43,360	-$41,194	5.60%	5.662627	-$42,317
-10%	36,900	-$37,760	-$41,024	-$42,610	-$41,527	6.30%	5.523344	-$42,100
0%	41,000	-$41,860	-$41,860	-$41,860	-$41,860	7.00%	5.3689	-$41,860
10%	45,100	-$45,960	-$42,696	-$41,110	-$42,192	7.70%	5.260219	-$41,690
20%	49,200	-$50,060	-$43,532	-$40,360	-$42,525	8.40%	5.135899	-$41,497
30%	53,300	-$54,160	-$44,368	-$39,610	-$42,858	9.10%	5.016109	-$41,310
40%	57,400	-$58,260	-$45,204	-$38,860	-$43,190	9.80%	4.900643	-$41,131

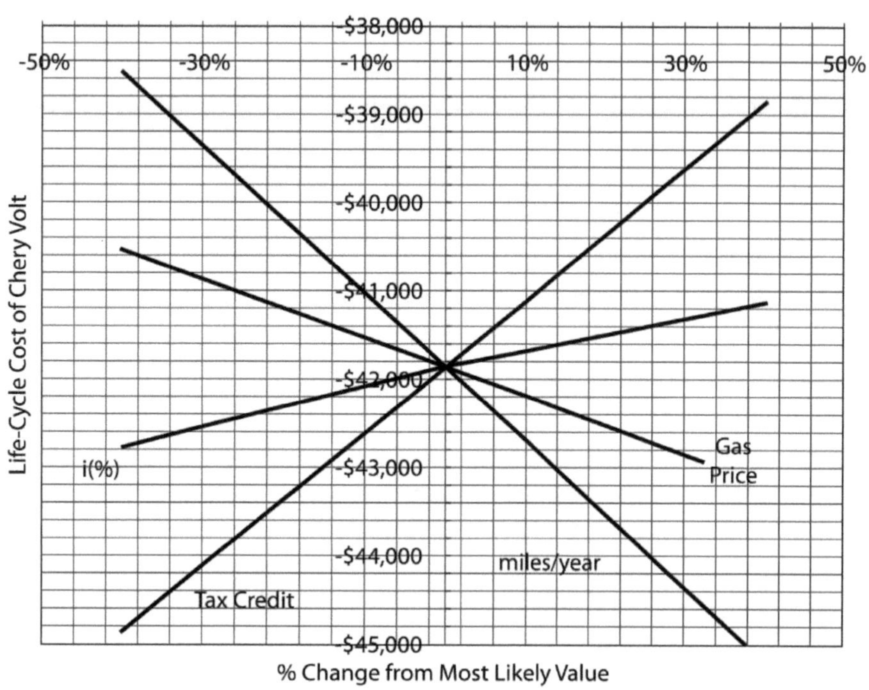

Figure 9.1 Spider Plot of Life-Cycle Cost of 2011 Chevy Volt

Table 9-2 Software Unit Sales for Next 8 Years

Software Sales

Year	Units	Price	Revenue
2011	500	$50	$25,000
2012	5000	$55	$275,000
2013	10000	$60	$600,000
2014	15000	$65	$975,000
2015	20000	$70	$1,400,000
2016	250000	$75	$18,750,000
2017	30000	$80	$2,400,000
2018	35000	$85	$2,975,000

The effect of percentage change in likely values of the miles driven per year by the commuter, tax credit given by the federal government for the purchase of the PEV, gas price, and interest rate are shown in Figure 9.1.

9.2 Exercises

1.0 Software Developers

You are asked to review a business plan to develop software. The office building is purchased at $100,000. The computer equipment costs about $6000. Six software engineers are hired. Their salaries are about $50,000 each per year. The utilities and wires for the entire office building run about $6000 per year. The developers come up with a product that can be used by the customer along with the Internet. For a planning horizon of the next eight years, the number of software units, price of software units, and the revenues that can be expected are given in Table 9-2 below. At an interest rate of 4%, calculate the PW (present worth) of this software business. Construct a spider plot showing the effects of: (i) annual revenue less the expenses; (ii) capital equipment; (iii) interest rate; and (iv) planning horizon.

2.0 Rent or Buy

Ms. Kay Smith is considering buying a home near Houston at a purchase price of $114,000. The federal government provides a tax credit for first-time buyers at $7,500. The real estate home prices near the Houston area increase by 7% in value every year. Consider a five-year study period. Should Kay decide to rent an apartment, she will pay $675 per month. The interest rate can be taken as 4%. The monthly mortgage payment on the new house, including principal and interest, real estate taxes, and mortgage insurance works out to be $1052.95. Is it better for Kay to rent an apartment or buy the house? Construct a spider plot showing the effects of: (i) purchase price of the house; (ii) annual mortgage payments; (iii) annual rent expenses; and (iv) real estate home price increase factor.

3.0 Spider Plot for Gas Station and Convenience Store

Construct the spider plot for Exercise 9.0 at the end of Chapter 4.0. Show the effects of: (i) annual amount of gasoline pumped; (ii) number of cars washed every year; (iii) number of transactions per day at the convenience store; (iv) interest rate; (v) expenses per day; (vi) car wash price; and (vii) average transactions per day. A lucrative group of businesses includes a gas station, convenience store, tunnel car wash, and dog wash, as well as the land and improvements. An average of 2 million gallons of gasoline are pumped every year at the gas station. Over 700 transactions per day can be expected at the convenience store at an average transaction of $30. In 2009, 75,000 cars were washed at the conveyorized soft cloth car wash. The system can wash over 120 cars per hour. The average cost of gasoline per gallon in 2009 was $3.50. What is the present worth of the business? The group of businesses was purchased for $3.59 million. The convenience store complex is expected to be in use for 10 years and the interest rate can be taken as 8%. Each car wash fetched an average of $5 per wash. Expenses are about $40,000 per day.

4.0 Spider Plot for Frozen Yogurt Parlor

Construct the spider plot for Exercise 15.0 at the end of Chapter 4.0. Show the effects of: (i) number of transactions per day; (ii) interest rate; (iii) purchase price of yogurt machines; and (iv) utility and materials costs. Jack Smith started a self-serve frozen yogurt parlor in Sacramento. Five yogurt machines were purchased at $20,000 each. Up to nine flavors are available for customers to select from. Customers serve their own yogurt and toppings, then Jack weighs the yogurt and collects the money. Around 48 customers can be seated in the 1200-sq.-ft. outfit. The three-year lease expires in 2013. The number of transactions per day is about 150 at about $5 per transaction. Assume that the parlor is open for about 300 days in the year. Seven employees work for Jack at an average salary of $20,000. What is the payback period at an interest rate of 8%? The utility and material costs are lumped into $1.50 per transaction

5.0 Spider Plot for Energy-Efficient Windows

Construct a spider plot for Exercise 6.0 at the end of Chapter 4.0. Show the effects of: (i) life of the windows; (ii) interest rate; (iii) price of each window; and (iv) tax credit from the federal government.

Window World can install vinyl replacement windows in your home. These double-hung, premium white windows are expected to be more energy efficient and can result in savings on energy utility bills. The federal government gives a tax credit of $1500. Each window is priced at $189. The number of windows to be installed can be taken as 14. What should the monthly savings in energy be to justify this purchase? The interest rate is 6% and the life of the windows may be taken as 20 years.

6.0 Spider Plot for Outpatient Drug Treatment Center

Construct a spider plot for Exercise 8.0 at the end of Chapter 4.0. Show the effects of: (i) net profit generated per year; (ii) interest rate; (iii) asking price of business; and (iv) planning horizon. A successful outpatient addiction treatment center with methadone maintenance and intensive counseling was established in 2002. Addiction disease is epidemic. The center has 14 employees, who find their work emotionally rewarding. The asking price of the business is $3.5 million dollars. The net profit generated per year is around $650,000. At an interest rate of 8%, what would be the future worth of the business in 10 years if the treatment center were purchased today?

7.0 Spider Plot for Public Internet, Video Chat, and Printing Services

Construct a spider plot for Exercise 10.0 at the end of Chapter 4.0. Show the effects of:

> (i) net profit generated per year; (ii) interest rate; (iii) asking price of business; and (iv) useful life.
> The company offers public Internet, video chat, and printing services in Houston. It requires 750 sq.

ft. of office space. It has 100 high-traffic locations in the city. The company also licenses its services to locations in New York City, San Francisco, Los Angeles, and Las Vegas. The service is ordered by quick-service restaurants and independent food and beverage purveyors. The company's proprietary software and systems enable it to deliver a reliable, quality service to its customers, with minimal employee resources and overhead. The company's services are managed and supported by three full-time employees. End-user demand for the company's services is primarily driven by demand for printing maps, tickets, and other tourist-related information and by the growing use (both by tourists and full-time residents) of social media such as Facebook and other Web 2.0 services. This service was purchased for $1.4 million. It is expected to be in use for 12 years. The annual revenue is about $1.95 million and expenses run about $1.45 million per year. What is the AW of the business at an interest rate of 3%?

8.0 Spider Plot for Short Path Distillation for Paraffin Wax Fractionation

Construct a spider plot for Exercise 14.0 at the end of Chapter 4.0. Show the effects of:

(i) capital cost; (ii) energy cost; (iii) pay period; (iv) price of paraffin wax; (v) capacity of plant; and (vi) interest rate. Paraffin wax is present in crude oil reserves and can be produced using the Fischer-Tropsch process. This wax is widely used in applications such as treatment of paper and cardboard, printing inks, and the food, cosmetic, and pharmaceutical industries. Prior to application, paraffin wax has to be de-oiled and fractionated and tailored for the given situation. SPD (short path distillation) is used to recover low volatility components from liquid mixtures. It can operate at low pressures and can be used to fractionate waxes. Low pressure operation obviates high temperature operation, which would result in degradation of the wax. Krause and Nieuwoudt [5] discuss an SPD process with four stages at a reflux ratio of 1.4. The capital cost is $17.1 million and the energy cost is $10.8/ton of wax. Calculate the PW of the business for a pay period of eight years. The interest rate is 7%. The capacity of the plant is 100,000 tons/year. The price of paraffin wax is $50/ton.

9.0 Spider Plot for Coffeehouse

Construct a spider plot for Exercise 16.0 at the end of Chapter 4.0. Show the effects of:

(i) annual revenue; (ii) annual cost; (iii) purchase price of the building; and (iv) planning horizon. Sam Bush started a 2,280-sq.-ft. coffeehouse in New Milford, Connecticut, 15 years ago. All types of coffees are served, including locally roasted blends; 30 different tea selections are also available. Pastries and cookies are freshly baked on the premises. The coffeehouse serves breakfast and lunch only. An average of 250–300 customers per day stop in. The menu includes sandwiches, bagels, homemade muffins, cakes, bars, pies, puddings, and biscotti. During the day, soup, sandwiches, wraps, salads, and quiche are served. Wi-Fi is available, and entertainment with live music and other acts on most Friday nights is common. The revenues are about $328,000 per year. The costs are around $248,600 per year. Mr. Bush purchased the building for $160,000 in 1995. At an interest rate of 5%, what is the 2010 worth of the coffeehouse?

10.0 Spider Plot for Libra Rental

Construct a spider plot for Exercise 17.0 at the end of Chapter 4.0. Show the effects of:

(i) car rental utilization rate; (ii) salvage value; (iii) purchase price of cars; (iv) car rental charge; (v) annual maintenance costs; and (vi) useful life. Robert Byrd purchased six cars at a total cost of $120,000 to start Libra Rental. He charged $30/car/day for renting a car. The annual maintenance charges were about $150 per car per month. Calculate the PW for the project for a period of six years at an interest rate of 7%. The car rental utilization rate is about 70%. The salvage value of the cars is $1800 per car at the end of the six-year period.

11.0 Spider Plot for Onshore Oil Well

Construct a spider plot for Exercise 19.0 at the end of Chapter 4.0. Show the effects of:

(i) capital cost of the oil well; (ii) price of crude oil; (iii) utility costs and wages; (iv) production rate of oil; (v) planning horizon; and (vi) interest rate. The southern and central Great Plains and the southwestern regions of our nation are dotted by onshore wells. With the recent oil spill disaster in an offshore well (BP America, 2010), interest in onshore wells is on the rise. Onshore wells are less expensive than offshore wells, which must be operated in the depths of the oceans and seas. The capital cost of an onshore well is about $1.1 million. The life of an oil well consists of the planning, drilling, completion, production, and abandonment phases. A well is created by drilling a hole 5–36" in diameter into the earth with a drilling rig that rotates a drill string with a bit attached. As the hole is drilled, sections of steel pipe, slightly smaller in diameter than the borehole, are placed in the hole. Cement may be placed outside the casing and the borehole. Eight BOPD (barrels per day of crude oil) can be produced. The price of crude oil per barrel is $80. The utility costs and labor wages can be lumped into $10 per barrel of crude oil produced. For the life of the oil well estimated at 15 years at an interest rate of 6%, calculate the PW of the business.

12.0 Spider Plot for Custom Foam Fabricator

Construct a spider plot for Exercise 20.0 at the end of Chapter 4.0. Show the effects of:

(i) annual profit; (ii) interest rate; (iii) planning horizon; and (iv) purchase price of the outfit. Evaluate the future worth of a custom foam fabricator in Houston. The service offers custom packaging, architectural columns and crown molding, monuments, signs, and theatrical scenery. Coatings and stucco supplies are also sold. Automated equipment and skilled employees are used. Builders, contractors, sign-up companies, stucco distributors, churches, and schools are their customers. The outfit is housed on 1.5 acres in two metal shop buildings with an area of 12,575 sq. ft. The purchase price of the outfit is at $100 per sq. ft. The average annual expenses are estimated at $673,000 and annual revenues are calculated at approximately $750,000. A period of 21 years can be assumed at 5% interest rate.

13.0 Spider Plot for Polypropylene Bag Manufacture

Construct a spider plot for Exercise 21.0 at the end of Chapter 4.0. Show the effects of:

(i) purchase price of a twin-screw extruder; (ii) land price per acre in Texas; (iii) construction cost of buildings; (iv) production rate; (v) useful life of the extruder; (vi) price of the polypropylene bag; and (vii) utility and labor costs. Polypropylene woven products, such as fabrics and bags, are used in packing agriculture products, military heavy-duty, chemical industry, and regular commercial sandbags. A bag manufacturer works out of Houston and is a licensed USDA supplier. The customers include well-known companies such as ADM Milling, Cargill, Chevron Phillips, and JacintoPort International/Seaboard. It serves as a federal contractor that supplies polypropylene products to the USDA (United States Department of Agriculture), Department of Defense, the U.S. Army, FEMA, and other federal, state, and local entities. A twin-screw extruder was purchased at a price of $5 million, with appropriate extrusion dies for bagging. The unit is housed on 10 acres of land. The land price is about $7000 per acre in Texas. Two freestanding buildings are used at a built area of 50,507 sq. ft. The cost of the building may be taken as $6.43 per sq. ft. Assuming an operation of 250 days in the year at a production rate of 10,000 lbs. per hour, calculate the AW of the business. The life of the extruder is about 21 years. The interest rate is about 6%. The price of a finished polypropylene bag is about 7.67 cents per pound. The utility and labor costs can be lumped into 1 cent per pound of finished polypropylene products.

14.0 Spider Plot for Manufacture of Activated Carbon from Bamboo

Construct a spider plot for Exercise 23.0 at the end of Chapter 4.0. Show the effects of:

(i) annual revenue; (ii) annual cost; (iii) capital expenses; (iv) capacity utilization; and (v) useful life of the manufacturing plant. Bamboo is a tropical plant common in China, Thailand, and Vietnam. Bamboo is available from construction projects as scaffolding waste. A range of carbon chars and activated carbons can be prepared from bamboo waste. The bamboo cane can be carbonized/charred in a furnace at high temperature under anaerobic conditions in order to produce carbon chars. In order to increase the *profitability*, the plant is integrated with a thermal electric generating boiler plant. The process consists of reacting bamboo with KOH (potassium hydroxide) in a CSTR. The alkali treatment results in char formation. The activated carbon is made in a carbonization furnace at $700^{\circ C.}$ The KOH is recovered by washing the solid effluent from the furnace with cold water and the KOH is recycled back to the CSTR. The volatile generated is converted to water and CO_2 in a combustion chamber. The heat liberated in this step is used to generate steam using heat exchanger tube bundles. The steam is used to turn turbines and electricity is generated. This can result in revenues that may improve the profitability of the project. Further, by piggybacking onto an existing power plant, the gas clean-up technology (such as the use of scrubber and stacks) is tapped into rather than building these devices twice over. This does result in cost savings in capital expenses. Calculate the IRR for the integrated plant. The data provided in Table 9-3 is from Keith et al. [see Chapter 4.0], suitably modified for analysis here. The life of the plant is estimated at 10 years.

15.0 Spider Plot for Meglumine Antimonate Drug by Supercritical Extraction

Construct a spider plot for Exercise 24.0 at the end of Chapter 4.0. Show the effects of:

(i) price of the drug; (ii) pre-processing cost; (iii) capital expenses; (iv) interest rate; and (v) yield of alkaloid.

The price of the meglumine antimonite drug is roughly $2,000 $kg^{-1.}$ According to the World Health Organization (WHO), leishmaniasis is an endemic health problem in 88 countries. The disease threatens 350 million men, women, and children. It is a parasitic disease transmitted to humans by sandflies. It has a wide

Table 9-3 Integrated Plant to Manufacture Activated Carbon from Bamboo

Item	$ Amount	Quantity
Mixer, Dryer, Washing Unit	$30,000	
Carbonization Furnace	$1.3 million	
Combustor, Cyclone	$114,500	
Steam Boiler	$1,033,338	
Scrubber and Flue Gas Processing	$50,000	
Materials and Utility Cost	$200/hr	
Fixed Operating Cost	$3,450/day	
General Expenses	$1,800/day	
Price of Activated Carbon	$1.93/kg	
Product Rate		800 lbs/hour
Days of Operation		250 days/year
Electricity Generated	300kW	
Price of Electricity	12.5 cents/kWh	
Other Capital Expenses	$6.0 million	

range of clinical symptoms: (i) cutaneous; (ii) mucocutaneous; and (iii) visceral. Cutaneous forms of the disease produce skin ulcers on the exposed parts of the body such as the face, arms, and legs.

The disease can produce a large number of lesions—sometimes up to 200—causing severe disability and leaving the patient permanently disfigured. This stigma can be fodder for serious social prejudice. In mucocutaneous forms of leishmaniasis, lesions can lead to partial or total destruction of the mucous membranes of the nose, mouth and throat cavities, and surrounding tissues. Some disabling and degrading forms of leishmaniasis can result in victims becoming outcasts from society. Visceral leishmaniasis is characterized by irregular bouts of fever, substantial weight loss, swelling of the spleen and liver, and anemia. If left untreated, the fatality rate in developing countries can be as high as 100% within two years.

The alkaloids extracted from *Tabernaemontana catharinensis* showed in vitro antileishmanial activity. *T. catharinensis* is a native tree in the southern part of Brazil. These trees have been studied for their biological properties: antitumoral, anti-inflammatory, analgesic, anticancer, antioxidant, and antimycobacterial, trypanocidal, and antileishmanial activities. Since the yields of indole alkaloids obtained by the low-pressure organic solvent extraction are very low and the organic solvent consumption in the conventional process is very high, supercritical extraction can be an advantageous process.

Two supercritical extraction columns cost about $2 million. The tree branches from which the alkaloids are extracted cost $83 per ton. A pre-processing cost of communition and drying is $30 per ton. The other relevant information needed to perform an IRR are given below in Table 9-4. Calculate the AW of the business, should the capital expenses be recovered over a 20-year period at an interest rate of 8%.

16.0 Spider Plot for Hydrogen as Alternative Fuel

Construct a spider plot for Exercise 26.0 at the end of Chapter 4.0. Show the effects of:

(i) plant capacity utilization; (ii) raw materials cost; (iii) selling price of hydrogen; (iv) interest rate; (v) capital expenses; and (vi) useful life of the plant. As discussed in Example 4.1, hydrogen is seriously considered as an alternative fuel in the transportation sector. In one process, the biomass is pyrolyzed

Table 9-4 Cost Information for Supercritical Extraction Process for Alkaloid

Price of Drug	$2,000	per kg		
2 Supercritical Extractors	$2,000,000			
T. catharinensis Tree Branches	$83	per ton		
Pre-processing Cost	$30	per ton		
CO_2	$150	per ton	2%	loss
Ethanol	$221	per ton	10%	loss
Labor Cost	$3.00	per hour		
Days of Operation		330	per year	
Utilities	$828,536/year	5280	batches	
Fractionator & Others	$35,000			Product(kg)
Product		1.29	kg/batch	6811.2
Alkaloids		44.70%		3044.61
Fractionating Cost	$440.31		per kg	Alkaloid(kg)
Yield	0.80%			
Raw Materials	851400	kg/year		

and then steam re-formed to yield hydrogen. The biomass is dried and then converted to an oil by very quick exposure to heated particles in a fluidized bed. The char and gases produced are combusted to supply heat to the reactor. The product oils are cooled and condensed. Bio-oil is then shipped by truck from the plant location(s) to the hydrogen production facility. By shipping the bio-oil, which has a higher energy density than the biomass, transportation costs are reduced. On arrival, the bio-oil is fractionated using water extraction into carbohydrate fraction and lignin fractions. The carbohydrate fraction is steam re-formed, and the hydrogen that is formed is separated using PSA (pressure swing adsorption). Consider a plant that produces 75,790 kg/day of hydrogen by the pyrolysis process. The biomass feed rate is about 1806 Mg/day. Capital investment fixed costs are $79.4 million. The selling price of hydrogen is $10/GJ. The storage and transportation cost of hydrogen by railroad is $0.94/GJ. The calorific value of hydrogen is 142 MJ/kg. At a MARR of 15%, calculate the PW of the project. The plant has operated for five years. The biomass feedstock cost was $16.5/Mg. The plant operated at 85% time during the year. The cost of utility and wages of laborers can be lumped into 15c/kg of hydrogen produced.

17.0 Spider Plot for University Apartments

Construct a spider plot for Exercise 28.0 at the end of Chapter 4.0. Show the effects of:

(i) occupancy rate; (ii) rental fees; (iii) annual costs; (iv) interest rate; (v) capital expenses; and (vi) salvage value. A group of university alumni and professors invests $20 million to build 200 new apartments for students near a state university, as discussed in Example 4.4. The money is borrowed at a rate of 7.25%, calculated on a yearly basis. The period of the loan is for 30 years. The variable expenses, including maintenance and operation, run the group $3500 per apartment per year. The rental fees collected are about $12,000 per apartment per year. The occupancy rate is about 70%. What is the present worth of the enterprise, should the salvage value of the apartments be $4 million at the end of 30 years?

18.0 Spider Plot for Municipal Garbage Collection Truck

Construct a spider plot for Exercise 32.0 at the end of Chapter 4.0. Show the effects of:

(i) number of households served; (ii) gasoline cost; (iii) life of the truck; (iv) interest rate; and (v) cost of the truck. The cost of the truck used for collecting garbage from residences is about $41,450. The truck can be used to serve 1000 households, as discussed in Example 4.10. A weekly charge per household of $5 can be collected. The gasoline cost runs $150 per month. The labor costs for two drivers are $3200 per month. A one-time tax credit of $5000 from the federal government for recycling is given. Is it profitable to run the garbage business at a MARR of 15%? The life of the truck is expected to be six years.

19.0 Spider Plot for Hexane Extraction of Rice-Bran Oil (see Example 4.11)

Construct a spider plot for Exercise 33.0 at the end of Chapter 4.0. Show the effects of:

(i) operational hours per year; (ii) raw materials cost; (iii) useful life of equipment; (iv) interest rate; (v) capital expenses; and (vi) hexane price. Rice-bran lipids can be extracted using hexane solvent from rice bran at a yield of about 26%. Rice is milled to produce the white long-grain rice sold in supermarkets. The outer layers of the rice kernel are removed. Rice bran becomes rancid and must be discarded in landfills. Parboiled rice bran has higher lipid levels than unstabilized rice bran. Rice-bran oil consists largely of saponifiable compounds. Hexane costs about $1.15 per gallon. It is an excellent solvent for nonpolar lipids. Calculate the PW of a hexane extraction unit. The following information in Table 9-5 is provided for purposes of analysis:

Table 9-5 Cost Data for Hexane Extraction Plant for Rice-Bran Oil

Description	Hexane Extraction Unit
Capital Investment	$250,000
Manufacturing Cost	$5.18 /year/kg of rice bran
Materials Cost	$0.22/year/kg of rice bran
Labor Cost	$12.00/hr
Revenue from Rice-Bran Oil	$8.08/kg
Revenue from Rice Protein	$4.928/kg
Production Rate	25.96 gal rice-bran oil/day
Useful Life of Equipment	8 years
Operational Hours Per Year	7332 hrs
% Protein in Rice Bran	14.6%
Interest Rate, i	8.0%

20.0 Spider Plot for Biodiesel Plant in Taiwan (see Example 4.12)

Construct a spider plot for Exercise 34.0 at the end of Chapter 4.0. Show the effects of:

(i) raw materials cost; (iii) annual revenues; (iv) interest rate; (v) capital expenses; and (vi) useful life of the manufacturing plant.

Biodiesel is produced by transesterification reactions. The alkali catalyst used was sodium hydroxide (NaOH). Biodiesel is an attractive fuel due to its environmental benefits. It is prepared from renewable energy resources such as vegetable oil. Using the information provided in Table 9-6, calculate the PW of the biodiesel plant. The plant is expected to last for 15 years. The interest rate for equivalence calculations can be taken as 8%. The primary costs in these plants are the raw material costs.

Table 9-6 Cost and Revenue Data for Biodiesel Production in Taiwan

Biodiesel Production in Taiwan

#	Description	Cost	Quantity	
1	Transesterification Reactor	$300,000		
2	Neutralization Reactor	$25,000		
3	Washing Column	$115,000		
4	FAME Distillation Column	$175,000		
5	Heat Exchangers	$4,000		
6	Pumps	$50,000		
7	Separator, Vacuum Systems	$50,000		
	Production Rate		800,000	kg/year
	Materials			
8	Soybean Oil Feedstock	$6,000,000		
9	Methanol	$200,000		
10	Catalyst and Solvent	$350,000		
	Labor Cost	$550,000		
	Utilities	$100,000		
	Overhead	$400,000		
	Revenue From Biodiesel	$7,000,000		

Appendix A

Discrete Compounding—Interest and Annuity Tables, Table A-1 to Table A-23

APPENDIX A

DISCRETE COMPOUNDING – INTEREST AND ANNUITY TABLES

Discrete Compounding			i	1/8%			Table	A-1
	Single	**Payment**	**Uniform**	**Series**			**Gradient**	**Series**
	Compound Amount Factor	Present Amount Factor	Compound Amount Factor	Present Worth Factor	Sinking Fund Factor	Capital Recovery Factor	Gradient Present Worth Factor	Gradient Uniform Series Factor
N	F/P	P/F	F/A	P/A	A/F	A/P	P/G	A/G
1	1.001250	0.998752	1.000000	0.998752	1.000000	1.001250	0.000000	0.000000
2	1.002502	0.997505	2.001250	1.996256	0.499688	0.500938	0.997505	0.499688
3	1.003755	0.996259	3.003752	2.992516	0.332917	0.334167	2.990023	0.999167
4	1.005009	0.995016	4.007506	3.987531	0.249532	0.250782	5.975070	1.498438
5	1.006266	0.993773	5.012516	4.981305	0.199501	0.200751	9.950164	1.997502
6	1.007523	0.992533	6.018781	5.973837	0.166147	0.167397	14.912827	2.496356
8	1.010044	0.990056	8.035088	7.955187	0.124454	0.125704	27.790981	3.493442
10	1.012571	0.987586	10.056438	9.931592	0.099439	0.100689	44.589810	4.489694
12	1.015104	0.985121	12.082845	11.903066	0.082762	0.084012	65.289669	5.485114
14	1.017643	0.982663	14.114321	13.869620	0.070850	0.072100	89.870983	6.479700
16	1.020189	0.980211	16.150879	15.831267	0.061916	0.063166	118.314253	7.473454
18	1.022741	0.977765	18.192531	17.788020	0.054968	0.056218	150.600053	8.466375
20	1.025299	0.975325	20.239291	19.739889	0.049409	0.050659	186.709028	9.458464
22	1.027864	0.972891	22.291171	21.686888	0.044861	0.046111	226.621897	10.449720
24	1.030435	0.970464	24.348183	23.629028	0.041071	0.042321	270.319452	11.440142
26	1.033013	0.968042	26.410342	25.566323	0.037864	0.039114	317.782556	12.429733
28	1.035597	0.965627	28.477659	27.498783	0.035115	0.036365	368.992144	13.418490
30	1.038188	0.963217	30.550148	29.426421	0.032733	0.033983	423.929225	14.406415
36	1.045998	0.956024	36.798772	35.180522	0.027175	0.028425	610.916556	17.365193
40	1.051238	0.951259	40.990618	38.992699	0.024396	0.025646	753.867237	19.333548
44	1.056504	0.946518	45.203462	42.785875	0.022122	0.023372	911.278094	21.298574
48	1.061797	0.941800	49.437409	46.560143	0.020228	0.021478	1083.001425	23.260268
52	1.067116	0.937106	53.692566	50.315599	0.018625	0.019875	1268.890640	25.218633
56	1.072461	0.932435	57.969039	54.052337	0.017251	0.018501	1468.800256	27.173668
60	1.077834	0.927787	62.266935	57.770449	0.016060	0.017310	1682.585888	29.125373
66	1.085943	0.920859	68.754180	63.312897	0.014545	0.015795	2028.968705	32.046689
72	1.094113	0.913983	75.290231	68.813958	0.013282	0.014532	2405.771346	34.960514
84	1.110638	0.900384	88.510226	79.693153	0.011298	0.012548	3248.746985	40.765698
96	1.127412	0.886987	101.929890	90.410478	0.009811	0.011061	4207.788030	46.540933
108	1.144440	0.873790	115.552239	100.968341	0.008654	0.009904	5279.254029	52.286231
∞				800.000000		0.001250		

Discrete Compounding			i	1/4%			Table	A-2
	Single	**Payment**	**Uniform**	**Series**			**Gradient**	**Series**
	Compound Amount Factor	Present Amount Factor	Compound Amount Factor	Present Worth Factor	Sinking Fund Factor	Capital Recovery Factor	Gradient Present Worth Factor	Gradient Uniform Series Factor
N	F/P	P/F	F/A	P/A	A/F	A/P	P/G	A/G
1	1.002500	0.997506	1.000000	0.997506	1.000000	1.002500	0.000000	0.000000
2	1.005006	0.995019	2.002500	1.992525	0.499376	0.501876	0.995019	0.499376
3	1.007519	0.992537	3.007506	2.985062	0.332501	0.335001	2.980093	0.998335
4	1.010038	0.990062	4.015025	3.975124	0.249064	0.251564	5.950280	1.496879
5	1.012563	0.987593	5.025063	4.962718	0.199002	0.201502	9.900653	1.995006
6	1.015094	0.985130	6.037625	5.947848	0.165628	0.168128	14.826305	2.492717
8	1.020176	0.980223	8.070351	7.910745	0.123910	0.126410	27.583909	3.486891
10	1.025283	0.975340	10.113253	9.863864	0.098880	0.101380	44.184201	4.479401
12	1.030416	0.970482	12.166383	11.807254	0.082194	0.084694	64.588583	5.470246
14	1.035574	0.965648	14.229791	13.740963	0.070275	0.072775	88.758742	6.459427
16	1.040759	0.960837	16.303529	15.665040	0.061336	0.063836	116.656656	7.446943
18	1.045969	0.956051	18.387648	17.579533	0.054384	0.056884	148.244586	8.432795
20	1.051206	0.951289	20.482201	19.484488	0.048823	0.051323	183.485079	9.416982
22	1.056468	0.946550	22.587240	21.379955	0.044273	0.046773	222.340961	10.399506
24	1.061757	0.941835	24.702818	23.265980	0.040481	0.042981	264.775340	11.380365
26	1.067072	0.937143	26.828986	25.142609	0.037273	0.039773	310.751599	12.359560
28	1.072414	0.932475	28.965799	27.009891	0.034523	0.037023	360.233399	13.337092
30	1.077783	0.927830	31.113309	28.867871	0.032141	0.034641	413.184675	14.312960
36	1.094051	0.914034	37.620560	34.386465	0.026581	0.029081	592.498783	17.230581
40	1.105033	0.904950	42.013204	38.019863	0.023802	0.026302	728.739878	19.167346
44	1.116125	0.895957	46.449939	41.617154	0.021529	0.024029	878.016195	21.097459
48	1.127328	0.887053	50.931208	45.178695	0.019634	0.022134	1040.055196	23.020922
52	1.138644	0.878238	55.457459	48.704842	0.018032	0.020532	1214.588473	24.937736
56	1.150073	0.869510	60.029141	52.195947	0.016659	0.019159	1401.351692	26.847903
60	1.161617	0.860869	64.646713	55.652358	0.015469	0.017969	1600.084536	28.751424
66	1.179150	0.848068	71.660119	60.772676	0.013955	0.016455	1920.067161	31.594251
72	1.196948	0.835458	78.779387	65.816858	0.012694	0.015194	2265.556855	34.422136
84	1.233355	0.810797	93.341920	75.681321	0.010713	0.013213	3029.759228	40.033118
96	1.270868	0.786863	108.347387	85.254603	0.009230	0.011730	3886.283161	45.584438
108	1.309523	0.763637	123.809259	94.545300	0.008077	0.010577	4829.012470	51.076177
∞				400.000000		0.002500		

Discrete Compounding			i	1/2%			Table	A-3
	Single	**Payment**	**Uniform**	**Series**			**Gradient**	**Series**
	Compound Amount Factor	Present Amount Factor	Compound Amount Factor	Present Worth Factor	Sinking Fund Factor	Capital Recovery Factor	Gradient Present Worth Factor	Gradient Uniform Series Factor
N	F/P	P/F	F/A	P/A	A/F	A/P	P/G	A/G
1	1.005000	0.995025	1.000000	0.995025	1.000000	1.005000	0.000000	0.000000
2	1.010025	0.990075	2.005000	1.985099	0.498753	0.503753	0.990075	0.498753
3	1.015075	0.985149	3.015025	2.970248	0.331672	0.336672	2.960372	0.996675
4	1.020151	0.980248	4.030100	3.950496	0.248133	0.253133	5.901115	1.493766
5	1.025251	0.975371	5.050251	4.925866	0.198010	0.203010	9.802597	1.990025
6	1.030378	0.970518	6.075502	5.896384	0.164595	0.169595	14.655188	2.485453
8	1.040707	0.960885	8.141409	7.822959	0.122829	0.127829	27.175522	3.473816
10	1.051140	0.951348	10.228026	9.730412	0.097771	0.102771	43.386491	4.458855
12	1.061678	0.941905	12.335562	11.618932	0.081066	0.086066	63.213598	5.440569
14	1.072321	0.932556	14.464226	13.488708	0.069136	0.074136	86.583463	6.418959
16	1.083071	0.923300	16.614230	15.339925	0.060189	0.065189	113.423805	7.394026
18	1.093929	0.914136	18.785788	17.172768	0.053232	0.058232	143.663429	8.365770
20	1.104896	0.905063	20.979115	18.987419	0.047666	0.052666	177.232212	9.334192
22	1.115972	0.896080	23.194431	20.784059	0.043114	0.048114	214.061088	10.299292
24	1.127160	0.887186	25.431955	22.562866	0.039321	0.044321	254.082034	11.261071
26	1.138460	0.878380	27.691911	24.324018	0.036112	0.041112	297.228055	12.219530
28	1.149873	0.869662	29.974522	26.067689	0.033362	0.038362	343.433173	13.174669
30	1.161400	0.861030	32.280017	27.794054	0.030979	0.035979	392.632412	14.126490
36	1.196681	0.835645	39.336105	32.871016	0.025422	0.030422	557.559832	16.962050
40	1.220794	0.819139	44.158847	36.172228	0.022646	0.027646	681.334687	18.835851
44	1.245394	0.802959	49.078770	39.408232	0.020375	0.025375	815.608700	20.696404
48	1.270489	0.787098	54.097832	42.580318	0.018485	0.023485	959.918810	22.543721
52	1.296090	0.771551	59.218031	45.689747	0.016887	0.021887	1113.816153	24.377814
56	1.322207	0.756311	64.441404	48.737757	0.015518	0.020518	1276.865682	26.198696
60	1.348850	0.741372	69.770031	51.725561	0.014333	0.019333	1448.645795	28.006382
66	1.389825	0.719515	77.964972	56.096976	0.012826	0.017826	1721.795671	30.693199
72	1.432044	0.698302	86.408856	60.339514	0.011573	0.016573	2012.347790	33.350414
84	1.520370	0.657735	104.073927	68.453042	0.009609	0.014609	2640.664052	38.576285
96	1.614143	0.619524	122.828542	76.095218	0.008141	0.013141	3324.184603	43.684540
108	1.713699	0.583533	142.739900	83.293424	0.007006	0.012006	4054.374734	48.675808
∞				200.000000		0.005000		

Discrete Compounding			i	3/4%			Table	A-4
	Single	**Payment**	**Uniform**	**Series**			**Gradient**	**Series**
	Compound Amount Factor	Present Amount Factor	Compound Amount Factor	Present Worth Factor	Sinking Fund Factor	Capital Recovery Factor	Gradient Present Worth Factor	Gradient Uniform Series Factor
N	F/P	P/F	F/A	P/A	A/F	A/P	P/G	A/G
1	1.007500	0.992556	1.000000	0.992556	1.000000	1.007500	0.000000	0.000000
2	1.015056	0.985167	2.007500	1.977723	0.498132	0.505632	0.985167	0.498132
3	1.022669	0.977833	3.022556	2.955556	0.330846	0.338346	2.940834	0.995019
4	1.030339	0.970554	4.045225	3.926110	0.247205	0.254705	5.852496	1.490660
5	1.038067	0.963329	5.075565	4.889440	0.197022	0.204522	9.705813	1.985056
6	1.045852	0.956158	6.113631	5.845598	0.163569	0.171069	14.486603	2.478207
8	1.061599	0.941975	8.213180	7.736613	0.121756	0.129256	26.774672	3.460774
10	1.077583	0.928003	10.344339	9.599580	0.096671	0.104171	42.606406	4.438362
12	1.093807	0.914238	12.507586	11.434913	0.079951	0.087451	61.873975	5.410971
14	1.110276	0.900677	14.703404	13.243022	0.068011	0.075511	84.471969	6.378602
16	1.126992	0.887318	16.932282	15.024313	0.059059	0.066559	110.297350	7.341258
18	1.143960	0.874156	19.194718	16.779181	0.052098	0.059598	139.249401	8.298939
20	1.161184	0.861190	21.491219	18.508020	0.046531	0.054031	171.229686	9.251648
22	1.178667	0.848416	23.822296	20.211215	0.041977	0.049477	206.142000	10.199387
24	1.196414	0.835831	26.188471	21.889146	0.038185	0.045685	243.892326	11.142158
26	1.214427	0.823434	28.590271	23.542189	0.034977	0.042477	284.388789	12.079964
28	1.232712	0.811220	31.028233	25.170713	0.032229	0.039729	327.541619	13.012807
30	1.251272	0.799187	33.502902	26.775080	0.029848	0.037348	373.263101	13.940690
36	1.308645	0.764149	41.152716	31.446805	0.024300	0.031800	524.992356	16.694617
40	1.348349	0.741648	46.446482	34.446938	0.021530	0.029030	637.469330	18.505834
44	1.389256	0.719810	51.900856	37.358730	0.019268	0.026768	758.281493	20.297304
48	1.431405	0.698614	57.520711	40.184782	0.017385	0.024885	886.840449	22.069062
52	1.474833	0.678043	63.311068	42.927618	0.015795	0.023295	1022.585224	23.821150
56	1.519578	0.658077	69.277100	45.589689	0.014435	0.021935	1164.981167	25.553611
60	1.565681	0.638700	75.424137	48.173374	0.013258	0.020758	1313.518881	27.266492
66	1.637471	0.610698	84.996134	51.906955	0.011765	0.019265	1546.786356	29.799212
72	1.712553	0.583924	95.007028	55.476849	0.010526	0.018026	1791.246287	32.288177
84	1.873202	0.533845	116.426928	62.153965	0.008589	0.016089	2308.128298	37.135657
96	2.048921	0.488062	139.856164	68.258439	0.007150	0.014650	2853.935242	41.810731
108	2.241124	0.446205	165.483223	73.839382	0.006043	0.013543	3419.904093	46.315449
∞				133.333333		0.007500		

Discrete Compounding			i	1%			Table	A-5
	Single	**Payment**	**Uniform**	**Series**			**Gradient**	**Series**
	Compound Amount Factor	Present Amount Factor	Compound Amount Factor	Present Worth Factor	Sinking Fund Factor	Capital Recovery Factor	Gradient Present Worth Factor	Gradient Uniform Series Factor
N	F/P	P/F	F/A	P/A	A/F	A/P	P/G	A/G
1	1.010000	0.990099	1.000000	0.990099	1.000000	1.010000	0.000000	0.000000
2	1.020100	0.980296	2.010000	1.970395	0.497512	0.507512	0.980296	0.497512
3	1.030301	0.970590	3.030100	2.940985	0.330022	0.340022	2.921476	0.993367
4	1.040604	0.960980	4.060401	3.901966	0.246281	0.256281	5.804417	1.487562
5	1.051010	0.951466	5.101005	4.853431	0.196040	0.206040	9.610280	1.980100
6	1.061520	0.942045	6.152015	5.795476	0.162548	0.172548	14.320506	2.470980
8	1.082857	0.923483	8.285671	7.651678	0.120690	0.130690	26.381197	3.447766
10	1.104622	0.905287	10.462213	9.471305	0.095582	0.105582	41.843498	4.417923
12	1.126825	0.887449	12.682503	11.255077	0.078849	0.088849	60.568677	5.381454
14	1.149474	0.869963	14.947421	13.003703	0.066901	0.076901	82.422147	6.338360
16	1.172579	0.852821	17.257864	14.717874	0.057945	0.067945	107.273358	7.288645
18	1.196147	0.836017	19.614748	16.398269	0.050982	0.060982	134.995693	8.232314
20	1.220190	0.819544	22.019004	18.045553	0.045415	0.055415	165.466356	9.169370
22	1.244716	0.803396	24.471586	19.660379	0.040864	0.050864	198.566280	10.099819
24	1.269735	0.787566	26.973465	21.243387	0.037073	0.047073	234.180020	11.023667
26	1.295256	0.772048	29.525631	22.795204	0.033869	0.043869	272.195662	11.940918
28	1.321291	0.756836	32.129097	24.316443	0.031124	0.041124	312.504724	12.851580
30	1.347849	0.741923	34.784892	25.807708	0.028748	0.038748	355.002069	13.755660
36	1.430769	0.698925	43.076878	30.107505	0.023214	0.033214	494.620685	16.428485
40	1.488864	0.671653	48.886373	32.834686	0.020456	0.030456	596.856056	18.177608
44	1.549318	0.645445	54.931757	35.455454	0.018204	0.028204	705.585308	19.900614
48	1.612226	0.620260	61.222608	37.973959	0.016334	0.026334	820.146005	21.597590
52	1.677689	0.596058	67.768892	40.394194	0.014756	0.024756	939.917523	23.268629
56	1.745810	0.572800	74.580982	42.719992	0.013408	0.023408	1064.318789	24.913834
60	1.816697	0.550450	81.669670	44.955038	0.012244	0.022244	1192.806145	26.533314
66	1.928460	0.518548	92.846015	48.145156	0.010771	0.020771	1392.095930	28.914558
72	2.047099	0.488496	104.709931	51.150391	0.009550	0.019550	1597.867334	31.238614
84	2.306723	0.433515	130.672274	56.648453	0.007653	0.017653	2023.315308	35.717045
96	2.599273	0.384723	159.927293	61.527703	0.006253	0.016253	2459.429786	39.972722
108	2.928926	0.341422	192.892579	65.857790	0.005184	0.015184	2898.420284	44.010288
∞				100.000000		0.010000		

Discrete Compounding			i	2%			Table	A-6
	Single	**Payment**	**Uniform**	**Series**			**Gradient**	**Series**
	Compound Amount Factor	Present Amount Factor	Compound Amount Factor	Present Worth Factor	Sinking Fund Factor	Capital Recovery Factor	Gradient Present Worth Factor	Gradient Uniform Series Factor
N	F/P	P/F	F/A	P/A	A/F	A/P	P/G	A/G
1	1.020000	0.980392	1.000000	0.980392	1.000000	1.020000	0.000000	0.000000
2	1.040400	0.961169	2.020000	1.941561	0.495050	0.515050	0.961169	0.495050
3	1.061208	0.942322	3.060400	2.883883	0.326755	0.346755	2.845813	0.986799
4	1.082432	0.923845	4.121608	3.807729	0.242624	0.262624	5.617350	1.475249
5	1.104081	0.905731	5.204040	4.713460	0.192158	0.212158	9.240273	1.960401
6	1.126162	0.887971	6.308121	5.601431	0.158526	0.178526	13.680130	2.442256
8	1.171659	0.853490	8.582969	7.325481	0.116510	0.136510	24.877924	3.396080
10	1.218994	0.820348	10.949721	8.982585	0.091327	0.111327	38.955100	4.336736
12	1.268242	0.788493	13.412090	10.575341	0.074560	0.094560	55.671156	5.264242
14	1.319479	0.757875	15.973938	12.106249	0.062602	0.082602	74.799921	6.178621
16	1.372786	0.728446	18.639285	13.577709	0.053650	0.073650	96.128815	7.079899
18	1.428246	0.700159	21.412312	14.992031	0.046702	0.066702	119.458125	7.968108
20	1.485947	0.672971	24.297370	16.351433	0.041157	0.061157	144.600334	8.843282
22	1.545980	0.646839	27.298984	17.658048	0.036631	0.056631	171.379470	9.705459
24	1.608437	0.621721	30.421862	18.913926	0.032871	0.052871	199.630495	10.554683
26	1.673418	0.597579	33.670906	20.121036	0.029699	0.049699	229.198718	11.391000
28	1.741024	0.574375	37.051210	21.281272	0.026990	0.046990	259.939244	12.214460
30	1.811362	0.552071	40.568079	22.396456	0.024650	0.044650	291.716444	13.025117
36	2.039887	0.490223	51.994367	25.488842	0.019233	0.039233	392.040453	15.380865
40	2.208040	0.452890	60.401983	27.355479	0.016556	0.036556	461.993132	16.888504
44	2.390053	0.418401	69.502657	29.079963	0.014388	0.034388	533.516529	18.346534
48	2.587070	0.386538	79.353519	30.673120	0.012602	0.032602	605.965718	19.755595
52	2.800328	0.357101	90.016409	32.144950	0.011109	0.031109	678.784892	21.116377
56	3.031165	0.329906	101.558264	33.504694	0.009847	0.029847	751.497527	22.429619
60	3.281031	0.304782	114.051539	34.760887	0.008768	0.028768	823.697534	23.696103
66	3.694974	0.270638	134.748679	36.468103	0.007421	0.027421	930.300004	25.509964
72	4.161140	0.240319	158.057019	37.984063	0.006327	0.026327	1034.055703	27.223409
84	5.277332	0.189490	213.866607	40.525516	0.004676	0.024676	1230.419116	30.361591
96	6.692933	0.149411	284.646659	42.529434	0.003513	0.023513	1409.297343	33.136988
108	8.488258	0.117810	374.412879	44.109510	0.002671	0.022671	1569.302514	35.577419
∞				50.000000		0.020000		

Discrete Compounding			i	3%			Table	A-7
	Single	Payment	Uniform	Series			Gradient	Series
	Compound Amount Factor	Present Amount Factor	Compound Amount Factor	Present Worth Factor	Sinking Fund Factor	Capital Recovery Factor	Gradient Present Worth Factor	Gradient Uniform Series Factor
N	F/P	P/F	F/A	P/A	A/F	A/P	P/G	A/G
1	1.030000	0.970874	1.000000	0.970874	1.000000	1.030000	0.000000	0.000000
2	1.060900	0.942596	2.030000	1.913470	0.492611	0.522611	0.942596	0.492611
3	1.092727	0.915142	3.090900	2.828611	0.323530	0.353530	2.772879	0.980297
4	1.125509	0.888487	4.183627	3.717098	0.239027	0.269027	5.438340	1.463061
5	1.159274	0.862609	5.309136	4.579707	0.188355	0.218355	8.888776	1.940905
6	1.194052	0.837484	6.468410	5.417191	0.154598	0.184598	13.076197	2.413833
8	1.266770	0.789409	8.892336	7.019692	0.112456	0.142456	23.480611	3.344963
10	1.343916	0.744094	11.463879	8.530203	0.087231	0.117231	36.308790	4.256498
12	1.425761	0.701380	14.192030	9.954004	0.070462	0.100462	51.248181	5.148499
14	1.512590	0.661118	17.086324	11.296073	0.058526	0.088526	68.014129	6.021042
16	1.604706	0.623167	20.156881	12.561102	0.049611	0.079611	86.347700	6.874214
18	1.702433	0.587395	23.414435	13.753513	0.042709	0.072709	106.013671	7.708116
20	1.806111	0.553676	26.870374	14.877475	0.037216	0.067216	126.798659	8.522862
22	1.916103	0.521893	30.536780	15.936917	0.032747	0.062747	148.509387	9.318577
24	2.032794	0.491934	34.426470	16.935542	0.029047	0.059047	170.971082	10.095401
26	2.156591	0.463695	38.553042	17.876842	0.025938	0.055938	194.025984	10.853482
28	2.287928	0.437077	42.930923	18.764108	0.023293	0.053293	217.531971	11.592982
30	2.427262	0.411987	47.575416	19.600441	0.021019	0.051019	241.361285	12.314074
36	2.898278	0.345032	63.275944	21.832252	0.015804	0.045804	313.702840	14.368780
40	3.262038	0.306557	75.401260	23.114772	0.013262	0.043262	361.749945	15.650163
44	3.671452	0.272372	89.048409	24.254274	0.011230	0.041230	408.997183	16.862891
48	4.132252	0.241999	104.408396	25.266707	0.009578	0.039578	455.025473	18.008895
52	4.650886	0.215013	121.696197	26.166240	0.008217	0.038217	499.519146	19.090215
56	5.234613	0.191036	141.153768	26.965464	0.007084	0.037084	542.248093	20.108985
60	5.891603	0.169733	163.053437	27.675564	0.006133	0.036133	583.052609	21.067416
66	7.034882	0.142149	201.162741	28.595040	0.004971	0.034971	640.440671	22.396914
72	8.400017	0.119047	246.667242	29.365088	0.004054	0.034054	693.122552	23.603626
84	11.976416	0.083497	365.880536	30.550086	0.002733	0.032733	784.543373	25.680562
96	17.075506	0.058563	535.850186	31.381219	0.001866	0.031866	858.637702	27.361515
108	24.345588	0.041075	778.186267	31.964160	0.001285	0.031285	917.601260	28.707192
∞				33.333333		0.030000		

Discrete Compounding			**i**	**4%**			**Table**	**A-8**
	Single	**Payment**	**Uniform**	**Series**			**Gradient**	**Series**
	Compound Amount Factor	Present Amount Factor	Compound Amount Factor	Present Worth Factor	Sinking Fund Factor	Capital Recovery Factor	Gradient Present Worth Factor	Gradient Uniform Series Factor
N	F/P	P/F	F/A	P/A	A/F	A/P	P/G	A/G
1	1.040000	0.961538	1.000000	0.961538	1.000000	1.040000	0.000000	0.000000
2	1.081600	0.924556	2.040000	1.886095	0.490196	0.530196	0.924556	0.490196
3	1.124864	0.888996	3.121600	2.775091	0.320349	0.360349	2.702549	0.973860
4	1.169859	0.854804	4.246464	3.629895	0.235490	0.275490	5.266962	1.450995
5	1.216653	0.821927	5.416323	4.451822	0.184627	0.224627	8.554670	1.921611
6	1.265319	0.790315	6.632975	5.242137	0.150762	0.190762	12.506243	2.385715
8	1.368569	0.730690	9.214226	6.732745	0.108528	0.148528	22.180581	3.294434
10	1.480244	0.675564	12.006107	8.110896	0.083291	0.123291	33.881352	4.177264
12	1.601032	0.624597	15.025805	9.385074	0.066552	0.106552	47.247729	5.034348
14	1.731676	0.577475	18.291911	10.563123	0.054669	0.094669	61.961794	5.865859
16	1.872981	0.533908	21.824531	11.652296	0.045820	0.085820	77.744120	6.672000
18	2.025817	0.493628	25.645413	12.659297	0.038993	0.078993	94.349770	7.453002
20	2.191123	0.456387	29.778079	13.590326	0.033582	0.073582	111.564686	8.209125
22	2.369919	0.421955	34.247970	14.451115	0.029199	0.069199	129.202421	8.940654
24	2.563304	0.390121	39.082604	15.246963	0.025587	0.065587	147.101194	9.647901
26	2.772470	0.360689	44.311745	15.982769	0.022567	0.062567	165.121228	10.331203
28	2.998703	0.333477	49.967583	16.663063	0.020013	0.060013	183.142351	10.990917
30	3.243398	0.308319	56.084938	17.292033	0.017830	0.057830	201.061832	11.627426
36	4.103933	0.243669	77.598314	18.908282	0.012887	0.052887	253.405199	13.401810
40	4.801021	0.208289	95.025516	19.792774	0.010523	0.050523	286.530302	14.476511
44	5.616515	0.178046	115.412877	20.548841	0.008665	0.048665	317.870049	15.469001
48	6.570528	0.152195	139.263206	21.195131	0.007181	0.047181	347.244554	16.383223
52	7.686589	0.130097	167.164718	21.747582	0.005982	0.045982	374.563809	17.223239
56	8.992222	0.111207	199.805540	22.219819	0.005005	0.045005	399.805372	17.993187
60	10.519627	0.095060	237.990685	22.623490	0.004202	0.044202	422.996648	18.697232
66	13.310685	0.075128	307.767116	23.121810	0.003249	0.043249	454.084674	19.638803
72	16.842262	0.059374	396.056560	23.515639	0.002525	0.042525	481.016968	20.455195
84	26.965005	0.037085	649.125119	24.072872	0.001541	0.041541	523.943092	21.764876
96	43.171841	0.023163	1054.30	24.420919	0.000949	0.040949	554.931180	22.723600
108	69.119509	0.014468	1702.99	24.638308	0.000587	0.040587	576.894913	23.414551
∞				25.000000		0.040000		

Discrete Compounding			i	5%			Table	A-9
	Single	**Payment**	**Uniform**	**Series**			**Gradient**	**Series**
	Compound Amount Factor	Present Amount Factor	Compound Amount Factor	Present Worth Factor	Sinking Fund Factor	Capital Recovery Factor	Gradient Present Worth Factor	Gradient Uniform Series Factor
N	F/P	P/F	F/A	P/A	A/F	A/P	P/G	A/G
1	1.050000	0.952381	1.0000	0.9524	1.000000	1.050000	0.000000	0.000000
2	1.102500	0.907029	2.0500	1.8594	0.487805	0.537805	0.907029	0.487805
3	1.157625	0.863838	3.1525	2.7232	0.317209	0.367209	2.6347	0.967486
4	1.215506	0.822702	4.3101	3.5460	0.232012	0.282012	5.1028	1.439053
5	1.276282	0.783526	5.5256	4.3295	0.180975	0.230975	8.2369	1.902520
6	1.340096	0.746215	6.8019	5.0757	0.147017	0.197017	11.9680	2.357904
8	1.477455	0.676839	9.5491	6.4632	0.104722	0.154722	20.9700	3.244510
10	1.628895	0.613913	12.5779	7.7217	0.079505	0.129505	31.6520	4.099085
12	1.795856	0.556837	15.9171	8.8633	0.062825	0.112825	43.6241	4.921902
14	1.979932	0.505068	19.5986	9.8986	0.051024	0.101024	56.5538	5.713289
16	2.182875	0.458112	23.6575	10.8378	0.042270	0.092270	70.1597	6.473629
18	2.406619	0.415521	28.1324	11.6896	0.035546	0.085546	84.2043	7.203360
20	2.653298	0.376889	33.0660	12.4622	0.030243	0.080243	98.4884	7.902965
22	2.925261	0.341850	38.5052	13.1630	0.025971	0.075971	112.8461	8.572976
24	3.225100	0.310068	44.5020	13.7986	0.022471	0.072471	127.1402	9.213968
26	3.555673	0.281241	51.1135	14.3752	0.019564	0.069564	141.2585	9.826553
28	3.920129	0.255094	58.4026	14.8981	0.017123	0.067123	155.1101	10.411383
30	4.321942	0.231377	66.4388	15.3725	0.015051	0.065051	168.6226	10.969139
36	5.791816	0.172657	95.8363	16.5469	0.010434	0.060434	206.6237	12.487191
40	7.039989	0.142046	120.80	17.1591	0.008278	0.058278	229.5452	13.377471
44	8.557150	0.116861	151.14	17.6628	0.006616	0.056616	250.4175	14.177699
48	10.401270	0.096142	188.03	18.0772	0.005318	0.055318	269.2467	14.894307
52	12.642808	0.079096	232.86	18.4181	0.004294	0.054294	286.1013	15.533724
56	15.367412	0.065073	287.35	18.6985	0.003480	0.053480	301.0894	16.102291
60	18.679186	0.053536	353.58	18.9293	0.002828	0.052828	314.3432	16.606179
66	25.031896	0.039949	480.64	19.2010	0.002081	0.052081	331.2877	17.253650
72	33.545134	0.029811	650.90	19.4038	0.001536	0.051536	345.1485	17.787688
84	60.242241	0.016600	1184.84	19.6680	0.000844	0.050844	365.4727	18.582093
96	108.186410	0.009243	2143.73	19.8151	0.000466	0.050466	378.5555	19.104364
108	194.287249	0.005147	3865.74	19.8971	0.000259	0.050259	386.8236	19.441246
∞				20.0000		0.050000		

Discrete Compounding			i	6%			Table	A-10
	Single	**Payment**	**Uniform**	**Series**			**Gradient**	**Series**
	Compound Amount Factor	Present Amount Factor	Compound Amount Factor	Present Worth Factor	Sinking Fund Factor	Capital Recovery Factor	Gradient Present Worth Factor	Gradient Uniform Series Factor
N	F/P	P/F	F/A	P/A	A/F	A/P	P/G	A/G
1	1.060000	0.943396	1.0000	0.9434	1.000000	1.060000	0.000000	0.000000
2	1.123600	0.889996	2.0600	1.8334	0.485437	0.545437	0.889996	0.485437
3	1.191016	0.839619	3.1836	2.6730	0.314110	0.374110	2.5692	0.961176
4	1.262477	0.792094	4.3746	3.4651	0.228591	0.288591	4.9455	1.427234
5	1.338226	0.747258	5.6371	4.2124	0.177396	0.237396	7.9345	1.883633
6	1.418519	0.704961	6.9753	4.9173	0.143363	0.203363	11.4594	2.330404
8	1.593848	0.627412	9.8975	6.2098	0.101036	0.161036	19.8416	3.195208
10	1.790848	0.558395	13.1808	7.3601	0.075868	0.135868	29.6023	4.022007
12	2.012196	0.496969	16.8699	8.3838	0.059277	0.119277	40.3369	4.811261
14	2.260904	0.442301	21.0151	9.2950	0.047585	0.107585	51.7128	5.563521
16	2.540352	0.393646	25.6725	10.1059	0.038952	0.098952	63.4592	6.279428
18	2.854339	0.350344	30.9057	10.8276	0.032357	0.092357	75.3569	6.959705
20	3.207135	0.311805	36.7856	11.4699	0.027185	0.087185	87.2304	7.605148
22	3.603537	0.277505	43.3923	12.0416	0.023046	0.083046	98.9412	8.216625
24	4.048935	0.246979	50.8156	12.5504	0.019679	0.079679	110.3812	8.795065
26	4.549383	0.219810	59.1564	13.0032	0.016904	0.076904	121.4684	9.341450
28	5.111687	0.195630	68.5281	13.4062	0.014593	0.074593	132.1420	9.856809
30	5.743491	0.174110	79.0582	13.7648	0.012649	0.072649	142.3588	10.342211
36	8.147252	0.122741	119.1209	14.6210	0.008395	0.068395	170.0387	11.629766
40	10.285718	0.097222	154.76	15.0463	0.006462	0.066462	185.9568	12.358976
44	12.985482	0.077009	199.76	15.3832	0.005006	0.065006	199.9130	12.995559
48	16.393872	0.060998	256.56	15.6500	0.003898	0.063898	212.0351	13.548543
52	20.696885	0.048316	328.28	15.8614	0.003046	0.063046	222.4823	14.026655
56	26.129341	0.038271	418.82	16.0288	0.002388	0.062388	231.4272	14.438196
60	32.987691	0.030314	533.13	16.1614	0.001876	0.061876	239.0428	14.790945
66	46.793670	0.021370	763.23	16.3105	0.001310	0.061310	248.3341	15.225419
72	66.377715	0.015065	1089.63	16.4156	0.000918	0.060918	255.5146	15.565374
84	133.565004	0.007487	2209.42	16.5419	0.000453	0.060453	265.2163	16.033015
96	268.759030	0.003721	4462.65	16.6047	0.000224	0.060224	270.7909	16.308135
108	540.795972	0.001849	8996.60	16.6358	0.000111	0.060111	273.9357	16.466591
∞				16.6667		0.060000		

Discrete Compounding			i	7%			Table	A-11
	Single	**Payment**	**Uniform**	**Series**			**Gradient**	**Series**
	Compound Amount Factor	Present Amount Factor	Compound Amount Factor	Present Worth Factor	Sinking Fund Factor	Capital Recovery Factor	Gradient Present Worth Factor	Gradient Uniform Series Factor
N	F/P	P/F	F/A	P/A	A/F	A/P	P/G	A/G
1	1.07	0.934579	1.0000	0.9346	1.000000	1.070000	0.000000	0.000000
2	1.14	0.873439	2.0700	1.8080	0.483092	0.553092	0.873439	0.483092
3	1.23	0.816298	3.2149	2.6243	0.311052	0.381052	2.5060	0.954929
4	1.31	0.762895	4.4399	3.3872	0.225228	0.295228	4.7947	1.415536
5	1.40	0.712986	5.7507	4.1002	0.173891	0.243891	7.6467	1.864950
6	1.50	0.666342	7.1533	4.7665	0.139796	0.209796	10.9784	2.303217
8	1.72	0.582009	10.2598	5.9713	0.097468	0.167468	18.7889	3.146541
10	1.97	0.508349	13.8164	7.0236	0.072378	0.142378	27.7156	3.946071
12	2.25	0.444012	17.8885	7.9427	0.055902	0.125902	37.3506	4.702516
14	2.58	0.387817	22.5505	8.7455	0.044345	0.114345	47.3718	5.416727
16	2.95	0.338735	27.8881	9.4466	0.035858	0.105858	57.5271	6.089681
18	3.38	0.295864	33.9990	10.0591	0.029413	0.099413	67.6219	6.722474
20	3.87	0.258419	40.9955	10.5940	0.024393	0.094393	77.5091	7.316307
22	4.43	0.225713	49.0057	11.0612	0.020406	0.090406	87.0793	7.872471
24	5.07	0.197147	58.1767	11.4693	0.017189	0.087189	96.2545	8.392336
26	5.81	0.172195	68.6765	11.8258	0.014561	0.084561	104.9814	8.877332
28	6.65	0.150402	80.6977	12.1371	0.012392	0.082392	113.2264	9.328943
30	7.61	0.131367	94.4608	12.4090	0.010586	0.080586	120.9718	9.748684
36	11.42	0.087535	148.9135	13.0352	0.006715	0.076715	141.1990	10.832126
40	14.97	0.066780	199.64	13.3317	0.005009	0.075009	152.2928	11.423349
44	19.63	0.050946	266.12	13.5579	0.003758	0.073758	161.6609	11.923737
48	25.73	0.038867	353.27	13.7305	0.002831	0.072831	169.4981	12.344666
52	33.73	0.029651	467.50	13.8621	0.002139	0.072139	176.0037	12.696732
56	44.21	0.022621	617.24	13.9626	0.001620	0.071620	181.3685	12.989630
60	57.95	0.017257	813.52	14.0392	0.001229	0.071229	185.7677	13.232092
66	86.96	0.011499	1228.03	14.1214	0.000814	0.070814	190.8927	13.517933
72	130.51	0.007662	1850.09	14.1763	0.000541	0.070541	194.6365	13.729757
84	293.93	0.003402	4184.65	14.2371	0.000239	0.070239	199.3046	13.998952
96	661.98	0.001511	9442.52	14.2641	0.000106	0.070106	201.7016	14.140475
108	1490.90	small	21284.26	14.2761	small	0.070047	202.9099	14.213226
∞				14.2857		0.070000		

Discrete Compounding		i	8%			Table	A-12
	Single	**Payment**	**Uniform**	**Series**			**Gradient**	**Series**
	Compound Amount Factor	Present Amount Factor	Compound Amount Factor	Present Worth Factor	Sinking Fund Factor	Capital Recovery Factor	Gradient Present Worth Factor	Gradient Uniform Series Factor
N	F/P	P/F	F/A	P/A	A/F	A/P	P/G	A/G
1	1.08	0.925926	1.0000	0.9259	1.000000	1.080000	0.000000	0.000000
2	1.17	0.857339	2.0800	1.7833	0.480769	0.560769	0.857339	0.480769
3	1.26	0.793832	3.2464	2.5771	0.308034	0.388034	2.4450	0.948743
4	1.36	0.735030	4.5061	3.3121	0.221921	0.301921	4.6501	1.403960
5	1.47	0.680583	5.8666	3.9927	0.170456	0.250456	7.3724	1.846472
6	1.59	0.630170	7.3359	4.6229	0.136315	0.216315	10.5233	2.276346
8	1.85	0.540269	10.6366	5.7466	0.094015	0.174015	17.8061	3.098524
10	2.16	0.463193	14.4866	6.7101	0.069029	0.149029	25.9768	3.871314
12	2.52	0.397114	18.9771	7.5361	0.052695	0.132695	34.6339	4.595747
14	2.94	0.340461	24.2149	8.2442	0.041297	0.121297	43.4723	5.273051
16	3.43	0.291890	30.3243	8.8514	0.032977	0.112977	52.2640	5.904626
18	4.00	0.250249	37.4502	9.3719	0.026702	0.106702	60.8426	6.492028
20	4.66	0.214548	45.7620	9.8181	0.021852	0.101852	69.0898	7.036948
22	5.44	0.183941	55.4568	10.2007	0.018032	0.098032	76.9257	7.541181
24	6.34	0.157699	66.7648	10.5288	0.014978	0.094978	84.2997	8.006612
26	7.40	0.135202	79.9544	10.8100	0.012507	0.092507	91.1842	8.435184
28	8.63	0.115914	95.3388	11.0511	0.010489	0.090489	97.5687	8.828883
30	10.06	0.099377	113.2832	11.2578	0.008827	0.088827	103.4558	9.189712
36	15.97	0.062625	187.1021	11.7172	0.005345	0.085345	118.2839	10.094897
40	21.72	0.046031	259.06	11.9246	0.003860	0.083860	126.0422	10.569919
44	29.56	0.033834	356.95	12.0771	0.002802	0.082802	132.3547	10.959166
48	40.21	0.024869	490.13	12.1891	0.002040	0.082040	137.4428	11.275840
52	54.71	0.018280	671.33	12.2715	0.001490	0.081490	141.5121	11.531766
56	74.43	0.013436	917.84	12.3321	0.001090	0.081090	144.7454	11.737337
60	101.26	0.009876	1253.21	12.3766	0.000798	0.080798	147.3000	11.901538
66	160.68	0.006223	1996.03	12.4222	0.000501	0.080501	150.1432	12.086679
72	254.98	0.003922	3174.78	12.4510	0.000315	0.080315	152.1076	12.216516
84	642.09	0.001557	8013.62	12.4805	0.000125	0.080125	154.3714	12.368973
96	1616.89	0.000618	20198.63	12.4923	small	0.080050	155.4112	12.440590
108	4071.60	0.000246	50882.56	12.4969	small	0.080020	155.8801	12.473468
∞				12.5000		0.080000		

Discrete Compounding			**i**	**8%**			**Table**	**A-12**
	Single	**Payment**	**Uniform**	**Series**			**Gradient**	**Series**
	Compound Amount Factor	Present Amount Factor	Compound Amount Factor	Present Worth Factor	Sinking Fund Factor	Capital Recovery Factor	Gradient Present Worth Factor	Gradient Uniform Series Factor
N	F/P	P/F	F/A	P/A	A/F	A/P	P/G	A/G
1	1.08	0.925926	1.0000	0.9259	1.000000	1.080000	0.000000	0.000000
2	1.17	0.857339	2.0800	1.7833	0.480769	0.560769	0.857339	0.480769
3	1.26	0.793832	3.2464	2.5771	0.308034	0.388034	2.4450	0.948743
4	1.36	0.735030	4.5061	3.3121	0.221921	0.301921	4.6501	1.403960
5	1.47	0.680583	5.8666	3.9927	0.170456	0.250456	7.3724	1.846472
6	1.59	0.630170	7.3359	4.6229	0.136315	0.216315	10.5233	2.276346
8	1.85	0.540269	10.6366	5.7466	0.094015	0.174015	17.8061	3.098524
10	2.16	0.463193	14.4866	6.7101	0.069029	0.149029	25.9768	3.871314
12	2.52	0.397114	18.9771	7.5361	0.052695	0.132695	34.6339	4.595747
14	2.94	0.340461	24.2149	8.2442	0.041297	0.121297	43.4723	5.273051
16	3.43	0.291890	30.3243	8.8514	0.032977	0.112977	52.2640	5.904626
18	4.00	0.250249	37.4502	9.3719	0.026702	0.106702	60.8426	6.492028
20	4.66	0.214548	45.7620	9.8181	0.021852	0.101852	69.0898	7.036948
22	5.44	0.183941	55.4568	10.2007	0.018032	0.098032	76.9257	7.541181
24	6.34	0.157699	66.7648	10.5288	0.014978	0.094978	84.2997	8.006612
26	7.40	0.135202	79.9544	10.8100	0.012507	0.092507	91.1842	8.435184
28	8.63	0.115914	95.3388	11.0511	0.010489	0.090489	97.5687	8.828883
30	10.06	0.099377	113.2832	11.2578	0.008827	0.088827	103.4558	9.189712
36	15.97	0.062625	187.1021	11.7172	0.005345	0.085345	118.2839	10.094897
40	21.72	0.046031	259.06	11.9246	0.003860	0.083860	126.0422	10.569919
44	29.56	0.033834	356.95	12.0771	0.002802	0.082802	132.3547	10.959166
48	40.21	0.024869	490.13	12.1891	0.002040	0.082040	137.4428	11.275840
52	54.71	0.018280	671.33	12.2715	0.001490	0.081490	141.5121	11.531766
56	74.43	0.013436	917.84	12.3321	0.001090	0.081090	144.7454	11.737337
60	101.26	0.009876	1253.21	12.3766	0.000798	0.080798	147.3000	11.901538
66	160.68	0.006223	1996.03	12.4222	0.000501	0.080501	150.1432	12.086679
72	254.98	0.003922	3174.78	12.4510	0.000315	0.080315	152.1076	12.216516
84	642.09	0.001557	8013.62	12.4805	0.000125	0.080125	154.3714	12.368973
96	1616.89	0.000618	20198.63	12.4923	small	0.080050	155.4112	12.440590
108	4071.60	0.000246	50882.56	12.4969	small	0.080020	155.8801	12.473468
∞				12.5000		0.080000		

Discrete Compounding			i	10%			Table	A-14
	Single	**Payment**	**Uniform**	**Series**			**Gradient**	**Series**
	Compound Amount Factor	Present Amount Factor	Compound Amount Factor	Present Worth Factor	Sinking Fund Factor	Capital Recovery Factor	Gradient Present Worth Factor	Gradient Uniform Series Factor
N	F/P	P/F	F/A	P/A	A/F	A/P	P/G	A/G
1	1.10	0.909091	1.0000	0.9091	1.000000	1.100000	0.000000	0.000000
2	1.21	0.826446	2.1000	1.7355	0.476190	0.576190	0.826446	0.476190
3	1.33	0.751315	3.3100	2.4869	0.302115	0.402115	2.3291	0.936556
4	1.46	0.683013	4.6410	3.1699	0.215471	0.315471	4.3781	1.381168
5	1.61	0.620921	6.1051	3.7908	0.163797	0.263797	6.8618	1.810126
6	1.77	0.564474	7.7156	4.3553	0.129607	0.229607	9.6842	2.223557
8	2.14	0.466507	11.4359	5.3349	0.087444	0.187444	16.0287	3.004479
10	2.59	0.385543	15.9374	6.1446	0.062745	0.162745	22.8913	3.725461
12	3.14	0.318631	21.3843	6.8137	0.046763	0.146763	29.9012	4.388402
14	3.80	0.263331	27.9750	7.3667	0.035746	0.135746	36.8005	4.995529
16	4.59	0.217629	35.9497	7.8237	0.027817	0.127817	43.4164	5.549341
18	5.56	0.179859	45.5992	8.2014	0.021930	0.121930	49.6395	6.052560
20	6.73	0.148644	57.2750	8.5136	0.017460	0.117460	55.4069	6.508075
22	8.14	0.122846	71.4027	8.7715	0.014005	0.114005	60.6893	6.918886
24	9.85	0.101526	88.4973	8.9847	0.011300	0.111300	65.4813	7.288054
26	11.92	0.083905	109.1818	9.1609	0.009159	0.109159	69.7940	7.618650
28	14.42	0.069343	134.2099	9.3066	0.007451	0.107451	73.6495	7.913716
30	17.45	0.057309	164.4940	9.4269	0.006079	0.106079	77.0766	8.176226
36	30.91	0.032349	299.1268	9.6765	0.003343	0.103343	85.1194	8.796497
40	45.26	0.022095	442.59	9.7791	0.002259	0.102259	88.9525	9.096234
44	66.26	0.015091	652.64	9.8491	0.001532	0.101532	91.8508	9.325816
48	97.02	0.010307	960.17	9.8969	0.001041	0.101041	94.0217	9.500090
52	142.04	0.007040	1410.43	9.9296	0.000709	0.100709	95.6351	9.631318
56	207.97	0.004809	2069.65	9.9519	0.000483	0.100483	96.8264	9.729423
60	304.48	0.003284	3034.82	9.9672	0.000330	0.100330	97.7010	9.802294
66	539.41	0.001854	5384.08	9.9815	0.000186	0.100186	98.5910	9.877416
72	955.59	0.001046	9545.94	9.9895	0.000105	0.100105	99.1419	9.924575
84	2999.06	0.000333	29980.63	9.9967	small	0.100033	99.6866	9.971982
96	9412.34	0.000106	94113.44	9.9989	small	0.100011	99.8874	9.989800
108	29539.97	small	295389.66	9.9997	small	0.100003	99.9601	9.996344
∞				10.0000		0.100000		

Discrete Compounding			i	11%			Table	A-15
	Single	**Payment**	**Uniform**	**Series**			**Gradient**	**Series**
	Compound Amount Factor	Present Amount Factor	Compound Amount Factor	Present Worth Factor	Sinking Fund Factor	Capital Recovery Factor	Gradient Present Worth Factor	Gradient Uniform Series Factor
N	F/P	P/F	F/A	P/A	A/F	A/P	P/G	A/G
1	1.11	0.900901	1.0000	0.9009	1.000000	1.110000	0.000000	0.000000
2	1.23	0.811622	2.1100	1.7125	0.473934	0.583934	0.811622	0.473934
3	1.37	0.731191	3.3421	2.4437	0.299213	0.409213	2.2740	0.930553
4	1.52	0.658731	4.7097	3.1024	0.212326	0.322326	4.2502	1.369951
5	1.69	0.593451	6.2278	3.6959	0.160570	0.270570	6.6240	1.792259
6	1.87	0.534641	7.9129	4.2305	0.126377	0.236377	9.2972	2.197642
8	2.30	0.433926	11.8594	5.1461	0.084321	0.194321	15.2246	2.958469
10	2.84	0.352184	16.7220	5.8892	0.059801	0.169801	21.5217	3.654416
12	3.50	0.285841	22.7132	6.4924	0.044027	0.154027	27.8388	4.287932
14	4.31	0.231995	30.0949	6.9819	0.033228	0.143228	33.9449	4.861865
16	5.31	0.188292	39.1899	7.3792	0.025517	0.135517	39.6953	5.379382
18	6.54	0.152822	50.3959	7.7016	0.019843	0.129843	45.0074	5.843894
20	8.06	0.124034	64.2028	7.9633	0.015576	0.125576	49.8423	6.258975
22	9.93	0.100669	81.2143	8.1757	0.012313	0.122313	54.1912	6.628289
24	12.24	0.081705	102.1742	8.3481	0.009787	0.119787	58.0656	6.955518
26	15.08	0.066314	127.9988	8.4881	0.007813	0.117813	61.4900	7.244300
28	18.58	0.053822	159.8173	8.6016	0.006257	0.116257	64.4965	7.498181
30	22.89	0.043683	199.0209	8.6938	0.005025	0.115025	67.1210	7.720564
36	42.82	0.023355	380.1644	8.8786	0.002630	0.112630	73.0712	8.230038
40	65.00	0.015384	581.83	8.9511	0.001719	0.111719	75.7789	8.465918
44	98.68	0.010134	887.96	8.9988	0.001126	0.111126	77.7534	8.640440
48	149.80	0.006676	1352.70	9.0302	0.000739	0.110739	79.1799	8.768322
52	227.40	0.004397	2058.20	9.0509	0.000486	0.110486	80.2024	8.861229
56	345.21	0.002897	3129.21	9.0646	0.000320	0.110320	80.9305	8.928219
60	524.06	0.001908	4755.07	9.0736	0.000210	0.110210	81.4461	8.976199
66	980.20	0.001020	8901.86	9.0816	0.000112	0.110112	81.9482	9.023507
72	1833.39	0.000545	16658.08	9.0860	small	0.110060	82.2425	9.051616
84	6414.02	0.000156	58300.17	9.0895	small	0.110017	82.5127	9.077811
96	22439.13	small	203982.98	9.0905	small	0.110005	82.6021	9.086631
108	78502.18	small	713647.08	9.0908	small	0.110001	82.6311	9.089533
∞				9.0909		0.110000		

Discrete Compounding			i	12%			Table	A-16
	Single	Payment	Uniform	Series			Gradient	Series
	Compound Amount Factor	Present Amount Factor	Compound Amount Factor	Present Worth Factor	Sinking Fund Factor	Capital Recovery Factor	Gradient Present Worth Factor	Gradient Uniform Series Factor
N	F/P	P/F	F/A	P/A	A/F	A/P	P/G	A/G
1	1.12	0.892857	1.0000	0.8929	1.000000	1.120000	0.000000	0.000000
2	1.25	0.797194	2.1200	1.6901	0.471698	0.591698	0.797194	0.471698
3	1.40	0.711780	3.3744	2.4018	0.296349	0.416349	2.2208	0.924609
4	1.57	0.635518	4.7793	3.0373	0.209234	0.329234	4.1273	1.358852
5	1.76	0.567427	6.3528	3.6048	0.157410	0.277410	6.3970	1.774595
6	1.97	0.506631	8.1152	4.1114	0.123226	0.243226	8.9302	2.172047
8	2.48	0.403883	12.2997	4.9676	0.081303	0.201303	14.4714	2.913144
10	3.11	0.321973	17.5487	5.6502	0.056984	0.176984	20.2541	3.584653
12	3.90	0.256675	24.1331	6.1944	0.041437	0.161437	25.9523	4.189653
14	4.89	0.204620	32.3926	6.6282	0.030871	0.150871	31.3624	4.731688
16	6.13	0.163122	42.7533	6.9740	0.023390	0.143390	36.3670	5.214664
18	7.69	0.130040	55.7497	7.2497	0.017937	0.137937	40.9080	5.642737
20	9.65	0.103667	72.0524	7.4694	0.013879	0.133879	44.9676	6.020203
22	12.10	0.082643	92.5026	7.6446	0.010811	0.130811	48.5543	6.351407
24	15.18	0.065882	118.1552	7.7843	0.008463	0.128463	51.6929	6.640645
26	19.04	0.052521	150.3339	7.8957	0.006652	0.126652	54.4177	6.892097
28	23.88	0.041869	190.6989	7.9844	0.005244	0.125244	56.7674	7.109764
30	29.96	0.033378	241.3327	8.0552	0.004144	0.124144	58.7821	7.297419
36	59.14	0.016910	484.4631	8.1924	0.002064	0.122064	63.1970	7.714091
40	93.05	0.010747	767.09	8.2438	0.001304	0.121304	65.1159	7.898791
44	146.42	0.006830	1211.81	8.2764	0.000825	0.120825	66.4659	8.030756
48	230.39	0.004340	1911.59	8.2972	0.000523	0.120523	67.4068	8.124083
52	362.52	0.002758	3012.70	8.3103	0.000332	0.120332	68.0576	8.189498
56	570.44	0.001753	4745.33	8.3187	0.000211	0.120211	68.5046	8.234991
60	897.60	0.001114	7471.64	8.3240	0.000134	0.120134	68.8100	8.266414
66	1771.70	0.000564	14755.81	8.3286	small	0.120068	69.0948	8.296060
72	3497.02	0.000286	29133.47	8.3310	small	0.120034	69.2530	8.312738
84	13624.29	small	113527.42	8.3327	small	0.120009	69.3880	8.327167
96	53079.91	small	442324.25	8.3332	small	0.120002	69.4281	8.331525
108	206798.05	small	1723308.79	8.3333	small	0.120001	69.4398	8.332811
∞				8.3333		0.120000		

Discrete Compounding			i	13%			Table	A-17
	Single	**Payment**	**Uniform**	**Series**			**Gradient**	**Series**
	Compound Amount Factor	Present Amount Factor	Compound Amount Factor	Present Worth Factor	Sinking Fund Factor	Capital Recovery Factor	Gradient Present Worth Factor	Gradient Uniform Series Factor
N	F/P	P/F	F/A	P/A	A/F	A/P	P/G	A/G
1	1.13	0.884956	1.0000	0.8850	1.000000	1.130000	0.000000	0.000000
2	1.28	0.783147	2.1300	1.6681	0.469484	0.599484	0.783147	0.469484
3	1.44	0.693050	3.4069	2.3612	0.293522	0.423522	2.1692	0.918724
4	1.63	0.613319	4.8498	2.9745	0.206194	0.336194	4.0092	1.347871
5	1.84	0.542760	6.4803	3.5172	0.154315	0.284315	6.1802	1.757133
6	2.08	0.480319	8.3227	3.9975	0.120153	0.250153	8.5818	2.146774
8	2.66	0.376160	12.7573	4.7988	0.078387	0.208387	13.7653	2.868510
10	3.39	0.294588	18.4197	5.4262	0.054290	0.184290	19.0797	3.516188
12	4.33	0.230706	25.6502	5.9176	0.038986	0.168986	24.2244	4.093592
14	5.53	0.180677	34.8827	6.3025	0.028667	0.158667	29.0232	4.605039
16	7.07	0.141496	46.6717	6.6039	0.021426	0.151426	33.3841	5.055231
18	9.02	0.110812	61.7251	6.8399	0.016201	0.146201	37.2714	5.449112
20	11.52	0.086782	80.9468	7.0248	0.012354	0.142354	40.6854	5.791725
22	14.71	0.067963	105.4910	7.1695	0.009479	0.139479	43.6486	6.088088
24	18.79	0.053225	136.8315	7.2829	0.007308	0.137308	46.1960	6.343090
26	23.99	0.041683	176.8501	7.3717	0.005655	0.135655	48.3685	6.561406
28	30.63	0.032644	227.9499	7.4412	0.004387	0.134387	50.2090	6.747431
30	39.12	0.025565	293.1992	7.4957	0.003411	0.133411	51.7592	6.905235
36	81.44	0.012279	618.7493	7.5979	0.001616	0.131616	55.0446	7.244755
40	132.78	0.007531	1013.70	7.6344	0.000986	0.130986	56.4087	7.388775
44	216.50	0.004619	1657.67	7.6568	0.000603	0.130603	57.3349	7.488128
48	352.99	0.002833	2707.63	7.6705	0.000369	0.130369	57.9580	7.555941
52	575.54	0.001737	4419.57	7.6789	0.000226	0.130226	58.3738	7.601801
56	938.41	0.001066	7210.85	7.6841	0.000139	0.130139	58.6495	7.632569
60	1530.05	0.000654	11761.95	7.6873	small	0.130085	58.8313	7.653068
66	3185.50	0.000314	24496.13	7.6899	small	0.130041	58.9936	7.671582
72	6632.05	0.000151	51008.09	7.6911	small	0.130020	59.0792	7.681450
84	28746.78	small	221121.41	7.6920	small	0.130005	59.1471	7.689386
96	124603.60	small	958481.50	7.6922	small	0.130001	59.1652	7.691537
108	540097.16	small	4154585.87	7.6923	small	0.130000	59.1699	7.692108
∞				7.6923		0.130000		

Discrete Compounding		i	15%			Table	A-18
	Single	**Payment**	**Uniform**	**Series**			**Gradient**	**Series**
	Compound Amount Factor	Present Amount Factor	Compound Amount Factor	Present Worth Factor	Sinking Fund Factor	Capital Recovery Factor	Gradient Present Worth Factor	Gradient Uniform Series Factor
N	F/P	P/F	F/A	P/A	A/F	A/P	P/G	A/G
1	1.15	0.869565	1.0000	0.8696	1.000000	1.150000	0.000000	0.000000
2	1.32	0.756144	2.1500	1.6257	0.465116	0.615116	0.756144	0.465116
3	1.52	0.657516	3.4725	2.2832	0.287977	0.437977	2.0712	0.907127
4	1.75	0.571753	4.9934	2.8550	0.200265	0.350265	3.7864	1.326257
5	2.01	0.497177	6.7424	3.3522	0.148316	0.298316	5.7751	1.722815
6	2.31	0.432328	8.7537	3.7845	0.114237	0.264237	7.9368	2.097190
8	3.06	0.326902	13.7268	4.4873	0.072850	0.222850	12.4807	2.781329
10	4.05	0.247185	20.3037	5.0188	0.049252	0.199252	16.9795	3.383196
12	5.35	0.186907	29.0017	5.4206	0.034481	0.184481	21.1849	3.908205
14	7.08	0.141329	40.5047	5.7245	0.024688	0.174688	24.9725	4.362408
16	9.36	0.106865	55.7175	5.9542	0.017948	0.167948	28.2960	4.752246
18	12.38	0.080805	75.8364	6.1280	0.013186	0.163186	31.1565	5.084312
20	16.37	0.061100	102.4436	6.2593	0.009761	0.159761	33.5822	5.365137
22	21.64	0.046201	137.6316	6.3587	0.007266	0.157266	35.6150	5.601020
24	28.63	0.034934	184.1678	6.4338	0.005430	0.155430	37.3023	5.797894
26	37.86	0.026415	245.7120	6.4906	0.004070	0.154070	38.6918	5.961234
28	50.07	0.019974	327.1041	6.5335	0.003057	0.153057	39.8283	6.096002
30	66.21	0.015103	434.7451	6.5660	0.002300	0.152300	40.7526	6.206627
36	153.15	0.006529	1014.3457	6.6231	0.000986	0.150986	42.5872	6.430061
40	267.86	0.003733	1779.09	6.6418	0.000562	0.150562	43.2830	6.516777
44	468.50	0.002134	3116.63	6.6524	0.000321	0.150321	43.7235	6.572548
48	819.40	0.001220	5456.00	6.6585	0.000183	0.150183	43.9997	6.608016
52	1433.14	0.000698	9547.58	6.6620	0.000105	0.150105	44.1715	6.630357
56	2506.57	0.000399	16703.77	6.6640	small	0.150060	44.2778	6.644316
60	4384.00	0.000228	29219.99	6.6651	small	0.150034	44.3431	6.652977
66	10140.46	0.000099	67596.37	6.6660	small	0.150015	44.3967	6.660157
72	23455	small	156363.27	6.6664	small	0.150006	44.4221	6.663597
84	125493	small	836611.58	6.6666	small	0.150001	44.4396	6.665997
96	671418	small	4476110.18	6.6667	small	0.150000	44.4434	6.666524
108	3592252	small	23948338	6.6667	small	0.150000	44.4442	6.666637
∞				6.6667		0.150000		

Discrete Compounding			i	17%			Table	A-19
	Single	**Payment**	**Uniform**	**Series**			**Gradient**	**Series**
	Compound Amount Factor	Present Amount Factor	Compound Amount Factor	Present Worth Factor	Sinking Fund Factor	Capital Recovery Factor	Gradient Present Worth Factor	Gradient Uniform Series Factor
N	F/P	P/F	F/A	P/A	A/F	A/P	P/G	A/G
1	1.17	0.854701	1.0000	0.8547	1.000000	1.170000	0.000000	0.000000
2	1.37	0.730514	2.1700	1.5852	0.460829	0.630829	0.730514	0.460829
3	1.60	0.624371	3.5389	2.2096	0.282574	0.452574	1.9793	0.895759
4	1.87	0.533650	5.1405	2.7432	0.194533	0.364533	3.5802	1.305103
5	2.19	0.456111	7.0144	3.1993	0.142564	0.312564	5.4046	1.689298
6	2.57	0.389839	9.2068	3.5892	0.108615	0.278615	7.3538	2.048889
8	3.51	0.284782	14.7733	4.2072	0.067690	0.237690	11.3465	2.696946
10	4.81	0.208037	22.3931	4.6586	0.044657	0.214657	15.1661	3.255494
12	6.58	0.151974	32.8239	4.9884	0.030466	0.200466	18.6159	3.731841
14	9.01	0.111019	47.1027	5.2293	0.021230	0.191230	21.6178	4.133982
16	12.33	0.081101	66.6488	5.4053	0.015004	0.185004	24.1628	4.470211
18	16.88	0.059245	93.4056	5.5339	0.010706	0.180706	26.2790	4.748777
20	23.11	0.043280	130.0329	5.6278	0.007690	0.177690	28.0128	4.977605
22	31.63	0.031616	180.1721	5.6964	0.005550	0.175550	29.4166	5.164085
24	43.30	0.023096	248.8076	5.7465	0.004019	0.174019	30.5423	5.314941
26	59.27	0.016872	342.7627	5.7831	0.002917	0.172917	31.4378	5.436152
28	81.13	0.012325	471.3778	5.8099	0.002121	0.172121	32.1456	5.532939
30	111.06	0.009004	647.4391	5.8294	0.001545	0.171545	32.7016	5.609786
36	284.90	0.003510	1669.9945	5.8617	0.000599	0.170599	33.7373	5.755547
40	533.87	0.001873	3134.52	5.8713	0.000319	0.170319	34.0965	5.807288
44	1000.41	0.001000	5878.88	5.8765	0.000170	0.170170	34.3088	5.838327
48	1874.66	0.000533	11021.50	5.8792	small	0.170091	34.4330	5.856735
52	3512.89	0.000285	20658.19	5.8807	small	0.170048	34.5052	5.867546
56	6582.76	0.000152	38716	5.8815	small	0.170026	34.5468	5.873845
60	12335.36	small	72555	5.8819	small	0.170014	34.5707	5.877488
66	31642.21	small	186125	5.8822	small	0.170005	34.5887	5.880267
72	81167	small	477450	5.8823	small	0.170002	34.5964	5.881466
84	534087	small	3141685	5.8823	small	0.170000	34.6011	5.882196
96	3514332	small	20672532	5.8824	small	0.170000	34.6019	5.882326
108	23124538	small	136026689	5.8824	small	0.170000	34.6020	5.882348
∞				5.8824		0.170000		

Discrete Compounding			i	**19%**			**Table**	**A-20**
	Single	**Payment**	**Uniform**	**Series**			**Gradient**	**Series**
	Compound Amount Factor	Present Amount Factor	Compound Amount Factor	Present Worth Factor	Sinking Fund Factor	Capital Recovery Factor	Gradient Present Worth Factor	Gradient Uniform Series Factor
N	F/P	P/F	F/A	P/A	A/F	A/P	P/G	A/G
1	1.19	0.840336	1.0000	0.8403	1.000000	1.190000	0.000000	0.000000
2	1.42	0.706165	2.1900	1.5465	0.456621	0.646621	0.706165	0.456621
3	1.69	0.593416	3.6061	2.1399	0.277308	0.467308	1.8930	0.884612
4	2.01	0.498669	5.2913	2.6386	0.188991	0.378991	3.3890	1.284401
5	2.39	0.419049	7.2966	3.0576	0.137050	0.327050	5.0652	1.656575
6	2.84	0.352142	9.6830	3.4098	0.103274	0.293274	6.8259	2.001864
8	4.02	0.248671	15.9020	3.9544	0.062885	0.252885	10.3421	2.615366
10	5.69	0.175602	24.7089	4.3389	0.040471	0.230471	13.5943	3.133089
12	8.06	0.124004	37.1802	4.6105	0.026896	0.216896	16.4340	3.564462
14	11.42	0.087567	54.8409	4.8023	0.018235	0.208235	18.8228	3.919559
16	16.17	0.061837	79.8502	4.9377	0.012523	0.202523	20.7806	4.208552
18	22.90	0.043667	115.2659	5.0333	0.008676	0.198676	22.3543	4.441260
20	32.43	0.030836	165.4180	5.1009	0.006045	0.196045	23.6007	4.626812
22	45.92	0.021775	236.4385	5.1486	0.004229	0.194229	24.5763	4.773434
24	65.03	0.015377	337.0105	5.1822	0.002967	0.192967	25.3325	4.888345
26	92.09	0.010859	479.4306	5.2060	0.002086	0.192086	25.9141	4.977732
28	130.41	0.007668	681.1116	5.2228	0.001468	0.191468	26.3584	5.046793
30	184.68	0.005415	966.7122	5.2347	0.001034	0.191034	26.6958	5.099826
36	524.43	0.001907	2754.9143	5.2531	0.000363	0.190363	27.2867	5.194381
40	1051.67	0.000951	5529.83	5.2582	0.000181	0.190181	27.4743	5.225087
44	2108.95	0.000474	11094.47	5.2607	small	0.190090	27.5779	5.242285
48	4229.16	0.000236	22253.48	5.2619	small	0.190045	27.6345	5.251805
52	8480.90	0.000118	44631.06	5.2625	small	0.190022	27.6653	5.257026
56	17007.08	small	89506	5.2628	small	0.190011	27.6819	5.259865
60	34104.97	small	179495	5.2630	small	0.190006	27.6908	5.261399
66	96849.96	small	509731	5.2631	small	0.190002	27.6970	5.262476
72	275031	small	1447525	5.2631	small	0.190001	27.6994	5.262896
84	2217914	small	11673228	5.2632	small	0.190000	27.7006	5.263120
96	17885797	small	94135768	5.2632	small	0.190000	27.7008	5.263153
108	144235389	small	759133621	5.2632	small	0.190000	27.7008	5.263157
∞				5.2632		0.190000		

Discrete Compounding		i	21%			Table	A-21
	Single	**Payment**	**Uniform**	**Series**			**Gradient**	**Series**
	Compound Amount Factor	Present Amount Factor	Compound Amount Factor	Present Worth Factor	Sinking Fund Factor	Capital Recovery Factor	Gradient Present Worth Factor	Gradient Uniform Series Factor
N	F/P	P/F	F/A	P/A	A/F	A/P	P/G	A/G
1	1.21	0.826446	1.0000	0.8264	1.000000	1.210000	0.000000	0.000000
2	1.46	0.683013	2.2100	1.5095	0.452489	0.662489	0.683013	0.452489
3	1.77	0.564474	3.6741	2.0739	0.272175	0.482175	1.8120	0.873683
4	2.14	0.466507	5.4457	2.5404	0.183632	0.393632	3.2115	1.264144
5	2.59	0.385543	7.5892	2.9260	0.131765	0.341765	4.7537	1.624635
6	3.14	0.318631	10.1830	3.2446	0.098203	0.308203	6.3468	1.956106
8	4.59	0.217629	17.1189	3.7256	0.058415	0.268415	9.4502	2.536575
10	6.73	0.148644	27.2738	4.0541	0.036665	0.246665	12.2269	3.015942
12	9.85	0.101526	42.1416	4.2784	0.023730	0.233730	14.5721	3.405932
14	14.42	0.069343	63.9095	4.4317	0.015647	0.225647	16.4804	3.718763
16	21.11	0.047362	95.7799	4.5364	0.010441	0.220441	17.9932	3.966430
18	30.91	0.032349	142.4413	4.6079	0.007020	0.217020	19.1694	4.160153
20	45.26	0.022095	210.7584	4.6567	0.004745	0.214745	20.0704	4.310022
22	66.26	0.015091	310.7813	4.6900	0.003218	0.213218	20.7526	4.424813
24	97.02	0.010307	457.2249	4.7128	0.002187	0.212187	21.2640	4.511950
26	142.04	0.007040	671.6330	4.7284	0.001489	0.211489	21.6445	4.577564
28	207.97	0.004809	985.5479	4.7390	0.001015	0.211015	21.9256	4.626616
30	304.48	0.003284	1445.1507	4.7463	0.000692	0.210692	22.1321	4.663052
36	955.59	0.001046	4545.6848	4.7569	0.000220	0.210220	22.4726	4.724192
40	2048.40	0.000488	9749.52	4.7596	0.000103	0.210103	22.5717	4.742368
44	4390.93	0.000228	20904.42	4.7608	small	0.210048	22.6229	4.751882
48	9412.34	0.000106	44815.92	4.7614	small	0.210022	22.6490	4.756805
52	20176.19	small	96072.35	4.7617	small	0.210010	22.6623	4.759327
56	43249.46	small	205945	4.7618	small	0.210005	22.6690	4.760610
60	92709.07	small	441467	4.7619	small	0.210002	22.6724	4.761258
66	290960.77	small	1385523	4.7619	small	0.210001	22.6746	4.761678
72	913160	small	4348374	4.7619	small	0.210000	22.6753	4.761826
84	8994377	small	42830364	4.7619	small	0.210000	22.6757	4.761895
96	88592213	small	421867676	4.7619	small	0.210000	22.6757	4.761904
108	872609615	small	4155283878	4.7619	small	0.210000	22.6757	4.761905
∞				4.7619		0.210000		

Discrete Compounding			i	25%			Table	A-22
	Single	**Payment**	**Uniform**	**Series**			**Gradient**	**Series**
	Compound Amount Factor	Present Amount Factor	Compound Amount Factor	Present Worth Factor	Sinking Fund Factor	Capital Recovery Factor	Gradient Present Worth Factor	Gradient Uniform Series Factor
N	F/P	P/F	F/A	P/A	A/F	A/P	P/G	A/G
1	1.25	0.800000	1.0000	0.8000	1.000000	1.250000	0.000000	0.000000
2	1.56	0.640000	2.2500	1.4400	0.444444	0.694444	0.640000	0.444444
3	1.95	0.512000	3.8125	1.9520	0.262295	0.512295	1.6640	0.852459
4	2.44	0.409600	5.7656	2.3616	0.173442	0.423442	2.8928	1.224932
5	3.05	0.327680	8.2070	2.6893	0.121847	0.371847	4.2035	1.563065
6	3.81	0.262144	11.2588	2.9514	0.088819	0.338819	5.5142	1.868332
8	5.96	0.167772	19.8419	3.3289	0.050399	0.300399	7.9469	2.387248
10	9.31	0.107374	33.2529	3.5705	0.030073	0.280073	9.9870	2.797098
12	14.55	0.068719	54.2077	3.7251	0.018448	0.268448	11.6020	3.114516
14	22.74	0.043980	86.9495	3.8241	0.011501	0.261501	12.8334	3.355948
16	35.53	0.028147	138.1085	3.8874	0.007241	0.257241	13.7482	3.536596
18	55.51	0.018014	218.0446	3.9279	0.004586	0.254586	14.4147	3.669792
20	86.74	0.011529	342.9447	3.9539	0.002916	0.252916	14.8932	3.766726
22	135.53	0.007379	538.1011	3.9705	0.001858	0.251858	15.2326	3.836462
24	211.76	0.004722	843.0329	3.9811	0.001186	0.251186	15.4711	3.886125
26	330.87	0.003022	1319.4890	3.9879	0.000758	0.250758	15.6373	3.921182
28	516.99	0.001934	2063.9515	3.9923	0.000485	0.250485	15.7524	3.945735
30	807.79	0.001238	3227.1743	3.9950	0.000310	0.250310	15.8316	3.962816
36	3081.49	0.000325	12321.9516	3.9987	0.000081	0.250081	15.9481	3.988314
40	7523.16	0.000133	30088.66	3.9995	small	0.250033	15.9766	3.994682
44	18367.10	small	73464.40	3.9998	small	0.250014	15.9895	3.997604
48	44841.55	small	179362.20	3.9999	small	0.250006	15.9954	3.998930
52	109476.44	small	437901.77	4.0000	small	0.250002	15.9980	3.999525
56	267276.47	small	1069102	4.0000	small	0.250001	15.9991	3.999790
60	652530.45	small	2610118	4.0000	small	0.250000	15.9996	3.999908
66	2489206.11	small	9956820	4.0000	small	0.250000	15.9999	3.999973
72	9495568	small	37982267	4.0000	small	0.250000	16.0000	3.999992
84	138178697	small	552714784	4.0000	small	0.250000	16.0000	3.999999
96	2010764683	small	8043058730	4.0000	small	0.250000	16.0000	4.000000
∞				4.0000		0.250000		

Discrete Compounding			i	30%			Table	A-23
	Single	**Payment**	**Uniform**	**Series**			**Gradient**	**Series**
	Compound Amount Factor	Present Amount Factor	Compound Amount Factor	Present Worth Factor	Sinking Fund Factor	Capital Recovery Factor	Gradient Present Worth Factor	Gradient Uniform Series Factor
N	F/P	P/F	F/A	P/A	A/F	A/P	P/G	A/G
1	1.30	0.769231	1.0000	0.7692	1.000000	1.300000	0.000000	0.000000
2	1.69	0.591716	2.3000	1.3609	0.434783	0.734783	0.591716	0.434783
3	2.20	0.455166	3.9900	1.8161	0.250627	0.550627	1.5020	0.827068
4	2.86	0.350128	6.1870	2.1662	0.161629	0.461629	2.5524	1.178277
5	3.71	0.269329	9.0431	2.4356	0.110582	0.410582	3.6297	1.490308
6	4.83	0.207176	12.7560	2.6427	0.078394	0.378394	4.6656	1.765447
8	8.16	0.122589	23.8577	2.9247	0.041915	0.341915	6.4800	2.215595
10	13.79	0.072538	42.6195	3.0915	0.023463	0.323463	7.8872	2.551219
12	23.30	0.042922	74.3270	3.1903	0.013454	0.313454	8.9173	2.795171
14	39.37	0.025398	127.9125	3.2487	0.007818	0.307818	9.6437	2.968501
16	66.54	0.015028	218.4722	3.2832	0.004577	0.304577	10.1426	3.089214
18	112.46	0.008892	371.5180	3.3037	0.002692	0.302692	10.4788	3.171834
20	190.05	0.005262	630.1655	3.3158	0.001587	0.301587	10.7019	3.227541
22	321.18	0.003113	1067.2796	3.3230	0.000937	0.300937	10.8482	3.264623
24	542.80	0.001842	1806.0026	3.3272	0.000554	0.300554	10.9433	3.289037
26	917.33	0.001090	3054.4443	3.3297	0.000327	0.300327	11.0045	3.304959
28	1550.29	small	5164.3109	3.3312	0.000194	0.300194	11.0437	3.315261
30	2620.00	small	8729.9855	3.3321	0.000115	0.300115	11.0687	3.321879
36	12646.22	small	42150.7285	3.3331	small	0.300024	11.1007	3.330486
40	36118.86	small	120392.88	3.3332	small	0.300008	11.1071	3.332226
44	103159.09	small	343860.30	3.3333	small	0.300003	11.1096	3.332907
60	6864377.17	small	22881254	3.3333	small	0.300000	11.1111	3.333325
∞				3.3333		0.300000		

Appendix B

Continuous Compounding—Interest and Annuity Tables, Table B-1 to B-25

APPENDIX B

CONTINUOUS COMPOUNDING – INTEREST AND ANNUITY TABLES

Continuous Compounding			**i**	**1/16%**	**Table**	**B-1**
	Single Payment	Uniform	Series	Uniform	Series	
	Compound Amount Factor	Present Amount Factor	Compound Amount Factor	Present Worth Factor	Sinking Fund Factor	Capital Recovery Factor
N	F/P	P/F	F/A	P/A	A/F	A/P
1	1.000625	0.999375	1.000000	0.999375	1.000000	1.000625
2	1.001251	0.998751	2.000625	1.998126	0.499844	0.500469
3	1.001877	0.998127	3.001876	2.996253	0.333125	0.333750
4	1.002503	0.997503	4.003753	3.993756	0.249766	0.250391
5	1.003130	0.996880	5.006256	4.990636	0.199750	0.200375
6	1.003757	0.996257	6.009386	5.986893	0.166406	0.167032
8	1.005013	0.995012	8.017527	7.977540	0.124727	0.125352
10	1.006270	0.993769	10.028181	9.965700	0.099719	0.100344
12	1.007528	0.992528	12.041349	11.951377	0.083047	0.083672
14	1.008788	0.991288	14.057035	13.934573	0.071139	0.071764
16	1.010050	0.990050	16.075243	15.915291	0.062207	0.062833
18	1.011314	0.988813	18.095975	17.893536	0.055261	0.055886
20	1.012578	0.987578	20.119234	19.869309	0.049704	0.050329
22	1.013845	0.986344	22.145024	21.842614	0.045157	0.045782
24	1.015113	0.985112	24.173348	23.813453	0.041368	0.041993
26	1.016383	0.983881	26.204208	25.781831	0.038162	0.038787
28	1.017654	0.982652	28.237609	27.747750	0.035414	0.036039
30	1.018927	0.981425	30.273554	29.711213	0.033032	0.033657
36	1.022755	0.977751	36.396678	35.586897	0.027475	0.028100
40	1.025315	0.975310	40.491537	39.491797	0.024697	0.025322
44	1.027882	0.972875	44.596645	43.386947	0.022423	0.023048
48	1.030455	0.970446	48.712029	47.272371	0.020529	0.021154
52	1.033034	0.968022	52.837714	51.148093	0.018926	0.019551
56	1.035620	0.965605	56.973726	55.014138	0.017552	0.018177
60	1.038212	0.963194	61.120091	58.870531	0.016361	0.016986
66	1.042113	0.959589	67.359108	64.637072	0.014846	0.015471
72	1.046028	0.955997	73.621564	70.382030	0.013583	0.014208
84	1.053903	0.948854	86.217151	81.807516	0.011599	0.012224
96	1.061837	0.941765	98.907559	93.147632	0.010110	0.010736
108	1.069830	0.934728	111.693504	104.403014	0.008953	0.009578
∞				1599.500052		0.000625

Continuous Compounding			i	1/12%	Table	B-2
	Single Payment	Uniform	Series	Uniform	Series	
	Compound Amount Factor	Present Amount Factor	Compound Amount Factor	Present Worth Factor	Sinking Fund Factor	Capital Recovery Factor
N	F/P	P/F	F/A	P/A	A/F	A/P
1	1.000834	0.999167	1.000000	0.999167	1.000000	1.000834
2	1.001668	0.998335	2.000834	1.997502	0.499792	0.500625
3	1.002503	0.997503	3.002502	2.995005	0.333056	0.333889
4	1.003339	0.996672	4.005005	3.991677	0.249688	0.250521
5	1.004175	0.995842	5.008344	4.987519	0.199667	0.200500
6	1.005013	0.995012	6.012519	5.982532	0.166320	0.167153
8	1.006689	0.993356	8.023382	7.970071	0.124636	0.125469
10	1.008368	0.991701	10.037599	9.954300	0.099625	0.100459
12	1.010050	0.990050	12.055176	11.935225	0.082952	0.083786
14	1.011735	0.988401	14.076119	13.912851	0.071042	0.071876
16	1.013423	0.986755	16.100432	15.887184	0.062110	0.062944
18	1.015113	0.985112	18.128122	17.858229	0.055163	0.055997
20	1.016806	0.983471	20.159194	19.825992	0.049605	0.050439
22	1.018502	0.981834	22.193655	21.790478	0.045058	0.045892
24	1.020201	0.980199	24.231509	23.751693	0.041269	0.042102
26	1.021903	0.978566	26.272762	25.709641	0.038062	0.038896
28	1.023608	0.976937	28.317420	27.664329	0.035314	0.036148
30	1.025315	0.975310	30.365489	29.615762	0.032932	0.033766
36	1.030455	0.970446	36.530216	35.450585	0.027375	0.028208
40	1.033895	0.967216	40.657191	39.324290	0.024596	0.025430
44	1.037347	0.963997	44.797946	43.185104	0.022322	0.023156
48	1.040811	0.960789	48.952526	47.033070	0.020428	0.021262
52	1.044286	0.957592	53.120979	50.868232	0.018825	0.019659
56	1.047773	0.954405	57.303349	54.690630	0.017451	0.018285
60	1.051271	0.951229	61.499684	58.500309	0.016260	0.017094
66	1.056541	0.946485	67.820471	64.191069	0.014745	0.015578
72	1.061837	0.941765	74.172942	69.853446	0.013482	0.014316
84	1.072508	0.932394	86.973568	81.093618	0.011498	0.012331
96	1.083287	0.923116	99.902843	92.221948	0.010010	0.010843
108	1.094174	0.913931	112.962060	103.239549	0.008853	0.009686
∞				1199.500069		0.000834

Continuous Compounding		i		1/8 %	Table	B-3
	Single Payment	Uniform	Series	Uniform	Series	
	Compound Amount Factor	Present Amount Factor	Compound Amount Factor	Present Worth Factor	Sinking Fund Factor	Capital Recovery Factor
N	F/P	P/F	F/A	P/A	A/F	A/P
1	1.001251	0.998751	1.000000	0.998751	1.000000	1.001251
2	1.002503	0.997503	2.001251	1.996254	0.499688	0.500938
3	1.003757	0.996257	3.003754	2.992511	0.332917	0.334168
4	1.005013	0.995012	4.007511	3.987523	0.249531	0.250782
5	1.006270	0.993769	5.012523	4.981293	0.199500	0.200751
6	1.007528	0.992528	6.018793	5.973821	0.166146	0.167397
8	1.010050	0.990050	8.035110	7.955159	0.124454	0.125705
10	1.012578	0.987578	10.056473	9.931550	0.099438	0.100689
12	1.015113	0.985112	12.082897	11.903006	0.082762	0.084012
14	1.017654	0.982652	14.114393	13.869539	0.070850	0.072100
16	1.020201	0.980199	16.150973	15.831163	0.061916	0.063167
18	1.022755	0.977751	18.192652	17.787888	0.054967	0.056218
20	1.025315	0.975310	20.239441	19.739728	0.049408	0.050659
22	1.027882	0.972875	22.291354	21.686694	0.044860	0.046111
24	1.030455	0.970446	24.348403	23.628799	0.041070	0.042321
26	1.033034	0.968022	26.410601	25.566055	0.037864	0.039114
28	1.035620	0.965605	28.477961	27.498473	0.035115	0.036366
30	1.038212	0.963194	30.550496	29.426067	0.032733	0.033983
36	1.046028	0.955997	36.799279	35.180018	0.027174	0.028425
40	1.051271	0.951229	40.991247	38.992080	0.024395	0.025646
44	1.056541	0.946485	45.204227	42.785130	0.022122	0.023373
48	1.061837	0.941765	49.438325	46.559261	0.020227	0.021478
52	1.067159	0.937067	53.693647	50.314570	0.018624	0.019875
56	1.072508	0.932394	57.970298	54.051148	0.017250	0.018501
60	1.077884	0.927743	62.268387	57.769090	0.016060	0.017310
66	1.085999	0.920811	68.755948	63.311264	0.014544	0.015795
72	1.094174	0.913931	75.292350	68.812026	0.013282	0.014532
84	1.110711	0.900325	88.513145	79.690555	0.011298	0.012549
96	1.127497	0.886920	101.933746	90.407123	0.009810	0.011061
108	1.144537	0.873716	115.557174	100.964142	0.008654	0.009905
∞				799.500104		0.001251

Continuous Compounding		i		1/4%	Table	B-4
	Single Payment	Uniform	Series	Uniform	Series	
	Compound Amount Factor	Present Amount Factor	Compound Amount Factor	Present Worth Factor	Sinking Fund Factor	Capital Recovery Factor
N	F/P	P/F	F/A	P/A	A/F	A/P
1	1.002503	0.997503	1.000000	0.997503	1.000000	1.002503
2	1.005013	0.995012	2.002503	1.992516	0.499375	0.501878
3	1.007528	0.992528	3.007516	2.985044	0.332500	0.335003
4	1.010050	0.990050	4.015044	3.975093	0.249063	0.251566
5	1.012578	0.987578	5.025094	4.962671	0.199001	0.201504
6	1.015113	0.985112	6.037672	5.947783	0.165627	0.168130
8	1.020201	0.980199	8.070440	7.910634	0.123909	0.126412
10	1.025315	0.975310	10.113396	9.863695	0.098879	0.101382
12	1.030455	0.970446	12.166593	11.807016	0.082192	0.084695
14	1.035620	0.965605	14.230081	13.740643	0.070274	0.072777
16	1.040811	0.960789	16.303913	15.664627	0.061335	0.063838
18	1.046028	0.955997	18.388140	17.579015	0.054383	0.056886
20	1.051271	0.951229	20.482814	19.483855	0.048821	0.051325
22	1.056541	0.946485	22.587987	21.379195	0.044271	0.046774
24	1.061837	0.941765	24.703713	23.265081	0.040480	0.042983
26	1.067159	0.937067	26.830044	25.141561	0.037272	0.039775
28	1.072508	0.932394	28.967034	27.008683	0.034522	0.037025
30	1.077884	0.927743	31.114735	28.866492	0.032139	0.034642
36	1.094174	0.913931	37.622646	34.384509	0.026580	0.029083
40	1.105171	0.904837	42.015804	38.017471	0.023801	0.026304
44	1.116278	0.895834	46.453113	41.614285	0.021527	0.024030
48	1.127497	0.886920	50.935019	45.175309	0.019633	0.022136
52	1.138828	0.878095	55.461968	48.700901	0.018030	0.020534
56	1.150274	0.869358	60.034414	52.191412	0.016657	0.019160
60	1.161834	0.860708	64.652814	55.647192	0.015467	0.017970
66	1.179393	0.847894	71.667588	60.766497	0.013953	0.016456
72	1.197217	0.835270	78.788378	65.809585	0.012692	0.015195
84	1.233678	0.810584	93.354434	75.671633	0.010712	0.013215
96	1.271249	0.786628	108.364092	85.242214	0.009228	0.011731
108	1.309964	0.763379	123.830863	94.529941	0.008076	0.010579
∞				399.500208		0.002503

Continuous Compounding		i		1/2%	Table	B-5
	Single Payment	Uniform	Series	Uniform	Series	
	Compound Amount Factor	Present Amount Factor	Compound Amount Factor	Present Worth Factor	Sinking Fund Factor	Capital Recovery Factor
N	F/P	P/F	F/A	P/A	A/F	A/P
1	1.005013	0.995012	1.000000	0.995012	1.000000	1.005013
2	1.010050	0.990050	2.005013	1.985062	0.498750	0.503763
3	1.015113	0.985112	3.015063	2.970174	0.331668	0.336681
4	1.020201	0.980199	4.030176	3.950373	0.248128	0.253141
5	1.025315	0.975310	5.050377	4.925683	0.198005	0.203018
6	1.030455	0.970446	6.075692	5.896128	0.164590	0.169603
8	1.040811	0.960789	8.141766	7.822523	0.122823	0.127836
10	1.051271	0.951229	10.228605	9.729750	0.097765	0.102778
12	1.061837	0.941765	12.336417	11.618000	0.081061	0.086073
14	1.072508	0.932394	14.465412	13.487461	0.069130	0.074143
16	1.083287	0.923116	16.615805	15.338321	0.060184	0.065196
18	1.094174	0.913931	18.787809	17.170764	0.053226	0.058239
20	1.105171	0.904837	20.981642	18.984975	0.047661	0.052673
22	1.116278	0.895834	23.197524	20.781133	0.043108	0.048121
24	1.127497	0.886920	25.435675	22.559420	0.039315	0.044327
26	1.138828	0.878095	27.696320	24.320012	0.036106	0.041118
28	1.150274	0.869358	29.979685	26.063086	0.033356	0.038368
30	1.161834	0.860708	32.285999	27.788817	0.030973	0.035986
36	1.197217	0.835270	39.344946	32.863661	0.025416	0.030429
40	1.221403	0.818731	44.169943	36.163290	0.022640	0.027652
44	1.246077	0.802519	49.092410	39.397582	0.020370	0.025382
48	1.271249	0.786628	54.114319	42.567831	0.018479	0.023492
52	1.296930	0.771052	59.237676	45.675304	0.016881	0.021894
56	1.323130	0.755784	64.464532	48.721245	0.015512	0.020525
60	1.349859	0.740818	69.796978	51.706873	0.014327	0.019340
66	1.390968	0.718924	77.998305	56.074832	0.012821	0.017833
72	1.433329	0.697676	86.449399	60.313699	0.011567	0.016580
84	1.521962	0.657047	104.131548	68.419302	0.009603	0.014616
96	1.616074	0.618783	122.907100	76.052872	0.008136	0.013149
108	1.716007	0.582748	142.843667	83.241898	0.007001	0.012013
∞				199.500417		0.005013

Continuous Compounding			i	3/4%	Table	B-6
	Single Payment	Uniform	Series	Uniform	Series	
	Compound Amount Factor	Present Amount Factor	Compound Amount Factor	Present Worth Factor	Sinking Fund Factor	Capital Recovery Factor
N	F/P	P/F	F/A	P/A	A/F	A/P
1	1.007528	0.992528	1.000000	0.992528	1.000000	1.007528
2	1.015113	0.985112	2.007528	1.977640	0.498125	0.505653
3	1.022755	0.977751	3.022641	2.955391	0.330836	0.338365
4	1.030455	0.970446	4.045396	3.925837	0.247195	0.254723
5	1.038212	0.963194	5.075851	4.889031	0.197011	0.204540
6	1.046028	0.955997	6.114063	5.845029	0.163557	0.171086
8	1.061837	0.941765	8.213993	7.735648	0.121743	0.129272
10	1.077884	0.927743	10.345660	9.598119	0.096659	0.104187
12	1.094174	0.913931	12.509543	11.432861	0.079939	0.087467
14	1.110711	0.900325	14.706129	13.240288	0.067999	0.075527
16	1.127497	0.886920	16.935911	15.020806	0.059046	0.066574
18	1.144537	0.873716	19.199393	16.774815	0.052085	0.059613
20	1.161834	0.860708	21.497083	18.502711	0.046518	0.054046
22	1.179393	0.847894	23.829498	20.204881	0.041965	0.049493
24	1.197217	0.835270	26.197163	21.881710	0.038172	0.045700
26	1.215311	0.822835	28.600611	23.533574	0.034964	0.042492
28	1.233678	0.810584	31.040382	25.160844	0.032216	0.039744
30	1.252323	0.798516	33.517025	26.763888	0.029836	0.037364
36	1.309964	0.763379	41.173805	31.431238	0.024287	0.031815
40	1.349859	0.740818	46.473130	34.428142	0.021518	0.029046
44	1.390968	0.718924	51.933844	37.336473	0.019255	0.026783
48	1.433329	0.697676	57.560861	40.158850	0.017373	0.024901
52	1.476981	0.677057	63.359247	42.897814	0.015783	0.023311
56	1.521962	0.657047	69.334220	45.555828	0.014423	0.021951
60	1.568312	0.637628	75.491157	48.135287	0.013247	0.020775
66	1.640498	0.609571	85.079916	51.862242	0.011754	0.019282
72	1.716007	0.582748	95.110026	55.425201	0.010514	0.018042
84	1.877611	0.532592	116.576487	62.087681	0.008578	0.016106
96	2.054433	0.486752	140.064537	68.176729	0.007140	0.014668
108	2.247908	0.444858	165.764558	73.741701	0.006033	0.013561
∞				132.833958		0.007528

Continuous Compounding			**i**	**1%**	**Table**	**B-7**
Single Payment			Uniform	Series	Uniform	Series
	Compound Amount Factor	Present Amount Factor	Compound Amount Factor	Present Worth Factor	Sinking Fund Factor	Capital Recovery Factor
N	F/P	P/F	F/A	P/A	A/F	A/P
1	1.010050	0.990050	1.000000	0.990050	1.000000	1.010050
2	1.020201	0.980199	2.010050	1.970249	0.497500	0.507550
3	1.030455	0.970446	3.030252	2.940694	0.330006	0.340056
4	1.040811	0.960789	4.060706	3.901483	0.246263	0.256313
5	1.051271	0.951229	5.101517	4.852713	0.196020	0.206070
6	1.061837	0.941765	6.152788	5.794477	0.162528	0.172578
8	1.083287	0.923116	8.287133	7.649988	0.120669	0.130719
10	1.105171	0.904837	10.464594	9.468756	0.095560	0.105610
12	1.127497	0.886920	12.686043	11.251511	0.078827	0.088877
14	1.150274	0.869358	14.952368	12.998964	0.066879	0.076929
16	1.173511	0.852144	17.264476	14.711816	0.057922	0.067973
18	1.197217	0.835270	19.623292	16.390751	0.050960	0.061010
20	1.221403	0.818731	22.029759	18.036441	0.045393	0.055443
22	1.246077	0.802519	24.484840	19.649544	0.040842	0.050892
24	1.271249	0.786628	26.989516	21.230706	0.037051	0.047102
26	1.296930	0.771052	29.544791	22.780558	0.033847	0.043897
28	1.323130	0.755784	32.151686	24.299721	0.031103	0.041153
30	1.349859	0.740818	34.811243	25.788803	0.028726	0.038777
36	1.433329	0.697676	43.116638	30.081457	0.023193	0.033243
40	1.491825	0.670320	48.936967	32.803430	0.020434	0.030485
44	1.552707	0.644036	54.994829	35.418673	0.018184	0.028234
48	1.616074	0.618783	61.299916	37.931370	0.016313	0.026363
52	1.682028	0.594521	67.862320	40.345543	0.014736	0.024786
56	1.750673	0.571209	74.692539	42.665055	0.013388	0.023438
60	1.822119	0.548812	81.801506	44.893618	0.012225	0.022275
66	1.934792	0.516851	93.012616	48.073695	0.010751	0.020801
72	2.054433	0.486752	104.916983	51.068578	0.009531	0.019582
84	2.316367	0.431711	130.979611	56.545276	0.007635	0.017685
96	2.611696	0.382893	160.365142	61.402672	0.006236	0.016286
108	2.944680	0.339596	193.497236	65.710796	0.005168	0.015218
∞				99.500833		0.010050

Continuous Compounding		i		2%	Table	B-8
	Single Payment	Uniform	Series	Uniform	Series	
	Compound Amount Factor	Present Amount Factor	Compound Amount Factor	Present Worth Factor	Sinking Fund Factor	Capital Recovery Factor
N	F/P	P/F	F/A	P/A	A/F	A/P
1	1.020201	0.980199	1.000000	0.980199	1.000000	1.020201
2	1.040811	0.960789	2.020201	1.940988	0.495000	0.515202
3	1.061837	0.941765	3.061012	2.882753	0.326689	0.346891
4	1.083287	0.923116	4.122849	3.805869	0.242551	0.262752
5	1.105171	0.904837	5.206136	4.710706	0.192081	0.212282
6	1.127497	0.886920	6.311307	5.597627	0.158446	0.178647
8	1.173511	0.852144	8.589077	7.319129	0.116427	0.136628
10	1.221403	0.818731	10.959806	8.973130	0.091242	0.111444
12	1.271249	0.786628	13.427285	10.562276	0.074475	0.094677
14	1.323130	0.755784	15.995464	12.089112	0.062518	0.082719
16	1.377128	0.726149	18.668453	13.556079	0.053566	0.073768
18	1.433329	0.697676	21.450528	14.965526	0.046619	0.066820
20	1.491825	0.670320	24.346142	16.319707	0.041074	0.061276
22	1.552707	0.644036	27.359928	17.620790	0.036550	0.056751
24	1.616074	0.618783	30.496710	18.870857	0.032790	0.052992
26	1.682028	0.594521	33.761505	20.071909	0.029620	0.049821
28	1.750673	0.571209	37.159540	21.225866	0.026911	0.047112
30	1.822119	0.548812	40.696251	22.334576	0.024572	0.044774
36	2.054433	0.486752	52.196201	25.406619	0.019158	0.039360
40	2.225541	0.449329	60.666319	27.259134	0.016484	0.036685
44	2.410900	0.414783	69.841887	28.969221	0.014318	0.034519
48	2.611696	0.382893	79.781662	30.547831	0.012534	0.032736
52	2.829217	0.353455	90.549291	32.005071	0.011044	0.031245
56	3.064854	0.326280	102.213724	33.350273	0.009783	0.029985
60	3.320117	0.301194	114.849655	34.592051	0.008707	0.028908
66	3.743421	0.267135	135.803931	36.278024	0.007364	0.027565
72	4.220696	0.236928	159.429811	37.773348	0.006272	0.026474
84	5.365556	0.186374	216.102296	40.275844	0.004627	0.024829
96	6.820958	0.146607	288.147146	42.244378	0.003470	0.023672
108	8.671138	0.115325	379.734099	43.792881	0.002633	0.022835
∞				49.501667		0.020201

Continuous Compounding		i	3%	**Table**	**B-9**	
	Single Payment	Uniform	Series	Uniform	Series	
	Compound Amount Factor	Present Amount Factor	Compound Amount Factor	Present Worth Factor	Sinking Fund Factor	Capital Recovery Factor
N	F/P	P/F	F/A	P/A	A/F	A/P
1	1.030455	0.970446	1.000000	0.970446	1.000000	1.030455
2	1.061837	0.941765	2.030455	1.912210	0.492501	0.522955
3	1.094174	0.913931	3.092291	2.826141	0.323385	0.353839
4	1.127497	0.886920	4.186465	3.713062	0.238865	0.269320
5	1.161834	0.860708	5.313962	4.573770	0.188183	0.218638
6	1.197217	0.835270	6.475796	5.409040	0.154421	0.184876
8	1.271249	0.786628	8.906692	7.006252	0.112275	0.142730
10	1.349859	0.740818	11.487905	8.510450	0.087048	0.117503
12	1.433329	0.697676	14.228732	9.927050	0.070280	0.100735
14	1.521962	0.657047	17.139043	11.261153	0.058346	0.088801
16	1.616074	0.618783	20.229316	12.517565	0.049433	0.079888
18	1.716007	0.582748	23.510682	13.700809	0.042534	0.072988
20	1.822119	0.548812	26.994956	14.815146	0.037044	0.067498
22	1.934792	0.516851	30.694685	15.864589	0.032579	0.063033
24	2.054433	0.486752	34.623193	16.852917	0.028882	0.059337
26	2.181472	0.458406	38.794626	17.783690	0.025777	0.056231
28	2.316367	0.431711	43.224007	18.660259	0.023135	0.053590
30	2.459603	0.406570	47.927284	19.485780	0.020865	0.051319
36	2.944680	0.339596	63.855174	21.684931	0.015660	0.046115
40	3.320117	0.301194	76.182973	22.945870	0.013126	0.043581
44	3.743421	0.267135	90.082527	24.064223	0.011101	0.041555
48	4.220696	0.236928	105.754231	25.056113	0.009456	0.039910
52	4.758821	0.210136	123.424028	25.935840	0.008102	0.038557
56	5.365556	0.186374	143.346668	26.716088	0.006976	0.037431
60	6.049647	0.165299	165.809382	27.408107	0.006031	0.036486
66	7.242743	0.138069	204.985668	28.302215	0.004878	0.035333
72	8.671138	0.115325	251.888197	29.049037	0.003970	0.034425
84	12.428597	0.080460	375.267495	30.193875	0.002665	0.033119
96	17.814273	0.056135	552.110671	30.992602	0.001811	0.032266
108	25.533722	0.039164	805.585197	31.549854	0.001241	0.031696
∞				32.835833		0.030455

Continuous Compounding			**i**	**4%**	**Table**	**B-10**
	Single Payment	Uniform	Series	Uniform	Series	
	Compound Amount Factor	Present Amount Factor	Compound Amount Factor	Present Worth Factor	Sinking Fund Factor	Capital Recovery Factor
N	F/P	P/F	F/A	P/A	A/F	A/P
1	1.040811	0.960789	1.000000	0.960789	1.000000	1.040811
2	1.083287	0.923116	2.040811	1.883906	0.490001	0.530812
3	1.127497	0.886920	3.124098	2.770826	0.320092	0.360903
4	1.173511	0.852144	4.251595	3.622970	0.235206	0.276017
5	1.221403	0.818731	5.425106	4.441701	0.184328	0.225139
6	1.271249	0.786628	6.646508	5.228329	0.150455	0.191266
8	1.377128	0.726149	9.240887	6.710261	0.108215	0.149025
10	1.491825	0.670320	12.051344	8.078258	0.082978	0.123789
12	1.616074	0.618783	15.095876	9.341078	0.066243	0.107054
14	1.750673	0.571209	18.393978	10.506807	0.054366	0.095176
16	1.896481	0.527292	21.966770	11.582911	0.045523	0.086334
18	2.054433	0.486752	25.837128	12.576281	0.038704	0.079515
20	2.225541	0.449329	30.029838	13.493276	0.033300	0.074111
22	2.410900	0.414783	34.571746	14.339769	0.028925	0.069736
24	2.611696	0.382893	39.491936	15.121181	0.025322	0.066132
26	2.829217	0.353455	44.821914	15.842515	0.022311	0.063121
28	3.064854	0.326280	50.595811	16.508391	0.019764	0.060575
30	3.320117	0.301194	56.850598	17.123071	0.017590	0.058401
36	4.220696	0.236928	78.917783	18.697813	0.012671	0.053482
40	4.953032	0.201897	96.862471	19.556196	0.010324	0.051135
44	5.812437	0.172045	117.920757	20.287661	0.008480	0.049291
48	6.820958	0.146607	142.632885	20.910974	0.007011	0.047822
52	8.004469	0.124930	171.632836	21.442127	0.005826	0.046637
56	9.393331	0.106459	205.664594	21.894745	0.004862	0.045673
60	11.023176	0.090718	245.601231	22.280441	0.004072	0.044882
∞				24.503333		0.040811

Continuous Compounding		i		5%	Table	B-11
	Single Payment	Uniform	Series	Uniform	Series	
	Compound Amount Factor	Present Amount Factor	Compound Amount Factor	Present Worth Factor	Sinking Fund Factor	Capital Recovery Factor
N	F/P	P/F	F/A	P/A	A/F	A/P
1	1.051271	0.951229	1.000000	0.951229	1.000000	1.051271
2	1.105171	0.904837	2.051271	1.856067	0.487503	0.538774
3	1.161834	0.860708	3.156442	2.716775	0.316812	0.368084
4	1.221403	0.818731	4.318276	3.535506	0.231574	0.282845
5	1.284025	0.778801	5.539679	4.314306	0.180516	0.231787
6	1.349859	0.740818	6.823704	5.055125	0.146548	0.197819
8	1.491825	0.670320	9.592631	6.430133	0.104247	0.155518
10	1.648721	0.606531	12.652768	7.674292	0.079034	0.130305
12	1.822119	0.548812	16.034742	8.800053	0.062365	0.113636
14	2.013753	0.496585	19.772402	9.818684	0.050576	0.101847
16	2.225541	0.449329	23.903154	10.740380	0.041835	0.093107
18	2.459603	0.406570	28.468342	11.574364	0.035127	0.086398
20	2.718282	0.367879	33.513655	12.328985	0.029839	0.081110
22	3.004166	0.332871	39.089588	13.011793	0.025582	0.076853
24	3.320117	0.301194	45.251947	13.629624	0.022098	0.073370
26	3.669297	0.272532	52.062407	14.188661	0.019208	0.070479
28	4.055200	0.246597	59.589129	14.694498	0.016782	0.068053
30	4.481689	0.223130	67.907443	15.152199	0.014726	0.065997
36	6.049647	0.165299	98.489165	16.280149	0.010153	0.061424
40	7.389056	0.135335	124.613214	16.864565	0.008025	0.059296
44	9.025013	0.110803	156.521199	17.343043	0.006389	0.057660
48	11.023176	0.090718	195.493701	17.734788	0.005115	0.056386
52	13.463738	0.074274	243.094822	18.055522	0.004114	0.055385
56	16.444647	0.060810	301.234962	18.318117	0.003320	0.054591
60	20.085537	0.049787	372.247490	18.533111	0.002686	0.053957
∞				19.504166		0.051271

Continuous Compounding		i	6%	Table	B-12
	Single Payment	Uniform	Series	Uniform	Series	
	Compound Amount Factor	Present Amount Factor	Compound Amount Factor	Present Worth Factor	Sinking Fund Factor	Capital Recovery Factor
N	F/P	P/F	F/A	P/A	A/F	A/P
1	1.061837	0.941765	1.000000	0.941765	1.000000	1.061837
2	1.127497	0.886920	2.061837	1.828685	0.485004	0.546841
3	1.197217	0.835270	3.189333	2.663955	0.313545	0.375382
4	1.271249	0.786628	4.386551	3.450583	0.227970	0.289806
5	1.349859	0.740818	5.657800	4.191401	0.176747	0.238584
6	1.433329	0.697676	7.007659	4.889078	0.142701	0.204538
8	1.616074	0.618783	9.962950	6.164908	0.100372	0.162208
10	1.822119	0.548812	13.295031	7.296468	0.075216	0.137053
12	2.054433	0.486752	17.051942	8.300071	0.058644	0.120481
14	2.316367	0.431711	21.287848	9.190188	0.046975	0.108812
16	2.611696	0.382893	26.063818	9.979650	0.038367	0.100204
18	2.944680	0.339596	31.448709	10.679841	0.031798	0.093634
20	3.320117	0.301194	37.520157	11.300854	0.026652	0.088489
22	3.743421	0.267135	44.365695	11.851643	0.022540	0.084376
24	4.220696	0.236928	52.084018	12.340150	0.019200	0.081036
26	4.758821	0.210136	60.786403	12.773416	0.016451	0.078288
28	5.365556	0.186374	70.598315	13.157689	0.014165	0.076001
30	6.049647	0.165299	81.661214	13.498508	0.012246	0.074082
36	8.671138	0.115325	124.055079	14.306667	0.008061	0.069897
40	11.023176	0.090718	162.091464	14.704606	0.006169	0.068006
44	14.013204	0.071361	210.445187	15.017636	0.004752	0.066588
48	17.814273	0.056135	271.914816	15.263874	0.003678	0.065514
52	22.646380	0.044157	350.058030	15.457571	0.002857	0.064693
56	28.789191	0.034735	449.397523	15.609939	0.002225	0.064062
60	36.598234	0.027324	575.682771	15.729796	0.001737	0.063574
∞				16.171666		0.061837

Continuous Compounding			**i**	**7%**	**Table**	**B-13**
	Single Payment	Uniform	Series	Uniform	Series	
	Compound Amount Factor	Present Amount Factor	Compound Amount Factor	Present Worth Factor	Sinking Fund Factor	Capital Recovery Factor
N	F/P	P/F	F/A	P/A	A/F	A/P
1	1.072508	0.932394	1.000000	0.932394	1.000000	1.072508
2	1.150274	0.869358	2.072508	1.801752	0.482507	0.555015
3	1.233678	0.810584	3.222782	2.612336	0.310291	0.382799
4	1.323130	0.755784	4.456460	3.368120	0.224393	0.296902
5	1.419068	0.704688	5.779590	4.072808	0.173023	0.245531
6	1.521962	0.657047	7.198657	4.729855	0.138915	0.211423
8	1.750673	0.571209	10.352935	5.913690	0.096591	0.169099
10	2.013753	0.496585	13.981218	6.942868	0.071525	0.144033
12	2.316367	0.431711	18.154737	7.837591	0.055082	0.127590
14	2.664456	0.375311	22.955427	8.615426	0.043563	0.116071
16	3.064854	0.326280	28.477534	9.291644	0.035115	0.107624
18	3.525421	0.283654	34.829469	9.879519	0.028711	0.101219
20	4.055200	0.246597	42.135934	10.390593	0.023733	0.096241
22	4.664590	0.214381	50.540369	10.834900	0.019786	0.092294
24	5.365556	0.186374	60.207771	11.221162	0.016609	0.089117
26	6.171858	0.162026	71.327930	11.556961	0.014020	0.086528
28	7.099327	0.140858	84.119157	11.848892	0.011888	0.084396
30	8.166170	0.122456	98.832570	12.102684	0.010118	0.082626
36	12.428597	0.080460	157.618030	12.681885	0.006344	0.078853
40	16.444647	0.060810	213.005574	12.952882	0.004695	0.077203
44	21.758402	0.045959	286.290485	13.157698	0.003493	0.076001
48	28.789191	0.034735	383.255936	13.312494	0.002609	0.075117
52	38.091837	0.026252	511.553815	13.429487	0.001955	0.074463
56	50.400445	0.019841	681.308563	13.517908	0.001468	0.073976
60	66.686331	0.014996	905.916131	13.584735	0.001104	0.073612
∞				13.791547		0.072508

Continuous Compounding		i		8%	Table	B-14
	Single Payment	Uniform	Series	Uniform	Series	
	Compound Amount Factor	Present Amount Factor	Compound Amount Factor	Present Worth Factor	Sinking Fund Factor	Capital Recovery Factor
N	F/P	P/F	F/A	P/A	A/F	A/P
1	1.083287	0.923116	1.000000	0.923116	1.000000	1.083287
2	1.173511	0.852144	2.083287	1.775260	0.480011	0.563298
3	1.271249	0.786628	3.256798	2.561888	0.307050	0.390337
4	1.377128	0.726149	4.528047	3.288037	0.220846	0.304133
5	1.491825	0.670320	5.905175	3.958357	0.169343	0.252630
6	1.616074	0.618783	7.397000	4.577140	0.135190	0.218477
8	1.896481	0.527292	10.763746	5.675642	0.092904	0.176192
10	2.225541	0.449329	14.714661	6.611723	0.067959	0.151247
12	2.611696	0.382893	19.351101	7.409399	0.051677	0.134964
14	3.064854	0.326280	24.792015	8.089133	0.040336	0.123623
16	3.596640	0.278037	31.176986	8.668365	0.032075	0.115362
18	4.220696	0.236928	38.669819	9.161954	0.025860	0.109147
20	4.953032	0.201897	47.462740	9.582562	0.021069	0.104356
22	5.812437	0.172045	57.781328	9.940981	0.017307	0.100594
24	6.820958	0.146607	69.890304	10.246405	0.014308	0.097595
26	8.004469	0.124930	84.100318	10.506671	0.011891	0.095178
28	9.393331	0.106459	100.775925	10.728454	0.009923	0.093210
30	11.023176	0.090718	120.344931	10.917446	0.008309	0.091597
36	17.814273	0.056135	201.883361	11.332675	0.004953	0.088240
40	24.532530	0.040762	282.547229	11.517248	0.003539	0.086826
44	33.784428	0.029599	393.631681	11.651275	0.002540	0.085828
48	46.525474	0.021494	546.609164	11.748599	0.001829	0.085117
52	64.071523	0.015608	757.278703	11.819271	0.001321	0.084608
56	88.234673	0.011333	1047.397575	11.870589	0.000955	0.084242
60	121.510418	0.008230	1446.928327	11.907854	0.000691	0.083978
∞				12.006666		0.083287

Continuous Compounding		i	**9%**	**Table**	**B-15**	
	Single Payment	Uniform	Series	Uniform	Series	
	Compound Amount Factor	Present Amount Factor	Compound Amount Factor	Present Worth Factor	Sinking Fund Factor	Capital Recovery Factor
N	F/P	P/F	F/A	P/A	A/F	A/P
1	1.094174	0.913931	1.000000	0.913931	1.000000	1.094174
2	1.197217	0.835270	2.094174	1.749201	0.477515	0.571689
3	1.309964	0.763379	3.291392	2.512581	0.303823	0.397997
4	1.433329	0.697676	4.601356	3.210257	0.217327	0.311502
5	1.568312	0.637628	6.034686	3.847885	0.165709	0.259883
6	1.716007	0.582748	7.602998	4.430634	0.131527	0.225701
8	2.054433	0.486752	11.196615	5.449978	0.089313	0.183487
10	2.459603	0.406570	15.498956	6.301405	0.064520	0.158695
12	2.944680	0.339596	20.649794	7.012578	0.048427	0.142601
14	3.525421	0.283654	26.816466	7.606599	0.037291	0.131465
16	4.220696	0.236928	34.199313	8.102767	0.029240	0.123415
18	5.053090	0.197899	43.038186	8.517201	0.023235	0.117409
20	6.049647	0.165299	53.620238	8.863366	0.018650	0.112824
22	7.242743	0.138069	66.289254	9.152507	0.015085	0.109260
24	8.671138	0.115325	81.456820	9.394018	0.012276	0.106451
26	10.381237	0.096328	99.615693	9.595744	0.010039	0.104213
28	12.428597	0.080460	121.355812	9.764241	0.008240	0.102415
30	14.879732	0.067206	147.383459	9.904981	0.006785	0.100959
36	25.533722	0.039164	260.514026	10.202744	0.003839	0.098013
40	36.598234	0.027324	378.003772	10.328470	0.002645	0.096820
44	52.457326	0.019063	546.405281	10.416186	0.001830	0.096004
48	75.188628	0.013300	787.780118	10.477384	0.001269	0.095444
52	107.770073	0.009279	1133.749771	10.520080	0.000882	0.095056
56	154.470015	0.006474	1629.638251	10.549868	0.000614	0.094788
60	221.406416	0.004517	2340.409797	10.570650	0.000427	0.094602
∞				10.618610		0.094174

Continuous Compounding		i		10%	Table	B-16
	Single Payment	Uniform	Series	Uniform	Series	
	Compound Amount Factor	Present Amount Factor	Compound Amount Factor	Present Worth Factor	Sinking Fund Factor	Capital Recovery Factor
N	F/P	P/F	F/A	P/A	A/F	A/P
1	1.105171	0.904837	1.000000	0.904837	1.000000	1.105171
2	1.221403	0.818731	2.105171	1.723568	0.475021	0.580192
3	1.349859	0.740818	3.326574	2.464386	0.300610	0.405781
4	1.491825	0.670320	4.676432	3.134706	0.213838	0.319009
5	1.648721	0.606531	6.168257	3.741237	0.162120	0.267291
6	1.822119	0.548812	7.816978	4.290049	0.127927	0.233098
8	2.225541	0.449329	11.652850	5.235963	0.085816	0.190987
10	2.718282	0.367879	16.337994	6.010412	0.061207	0.166378
12	3.320117	0.301194	22.060442	6.644477	0.045330	0.150501
14	4.055200	0.246597	29.049855	7.163606	0.034424	0.139594
16	4.953032	0.201897	37.586744	7.588633	0.026605	0.131776
18	6.049647	0.165299	48.013724	7.936615	0.020827	0.125998
20	7.389056	0.135335	60.749266	8.221519	0.016461	0.121632
22	9.025013	0.110803	76.304492	8.454779	0.013105	0.118276
24	11.023176	0.090718	95.303688	8.645756	0.010493	0.115664
26	13.463738	0.074274	118.509359	8.802114	0.008438	0.113609
28	16.444647	0.060810	146.852828	8.930130	0.006810	0.111980
30	20.085537	0.049787	181.471620	9.034940	0.005511	0.110681
36	36.598234	0.027324	338.479830	9.248529	0.002954	0.108125
40	54.598150	0.018316	509.629002	9.334181	0.001962	0.107133
44	81.450869	0.012277	764.953565	9.391595	0.001307	0.106478
48	121.510418	0.008230	1145.853053	9.430081	0.000873	0.106044
52	181.272242	0.005517	1714.088316	9.455879	0.000583	0.105754
56	270.426407	0.003698	2561.795716	9.473171	0.000390	0.105561
60	403.428793	0.002479	3826.426553	9.484763	0.000261	0.105432
∞				9.508332		0.105171

Continuous Compounding		i		11%	Table	B-17
	Single Payment	Uniform	Series	Uniform	Series	
	Compound Amount Factor	Present Amount Factor	Compound Amount Factor	Present Worth Factor	Sinking Fund Factor	Capital Recovery Factor
N	F/P	P/F	F/A	P/A	A/F	A/P
1	1.116278	0.895834	1.000000	0.895834	1.000000	1.116278
2	1.246077	0.802519	2.116278	1.698353	0.472528	0.588806
3	1.390968	0.718924	3.362355	2.417277	0.297411	0.413689
4	1.552707	0.644036	4.753323	3.061313	0.210379	0.326657
5	1.733253	0.576950	6.306030	3.638263	0.158578	0.274856
6	1.934792	0.516851	8.039283	4.155114	0.124389	0.240667
8	2.410900	0.414783	12.133842	5.032910	0.082414	0.198692
10	3.004166	0.332871	17.235976	5.737358	0.058018	0.174296
12	3.743421	0.267135	23.593627	6.302691	0.042384	0.158662
14	4.664590	0.214381	31.515747	6.756381	0.031730	0.148008
16	5.812437	0.172045	41.387317	7.120475	0.024162	0.140440
18	7.242743	0.138069	53.688051	7.412668	0.018626	0.134904
20	9.025013	0.110803	69.015709	7.647159	0.014489	0.130768
22	11.245859	0.088922	88.115147	7.835341	0.011349	0.127627
24	14.013204	0.071361	111.914513	7.986362	0.008935	0.125213
26	17.461527	0.057269	141.570348	8.107558	0.007064	0.123342
28	21.758402	0.045959	178.523795	8.204821	0.005601	0.121880
30	27.112639	0.036883	224.570625	8.282876	0.004453	0.120731
36	52.457326	0.019063	442.536806	8.436130	0.002260	0.118538
40	81.450869	0.012277	691.883417	8.494488	0.001445	0.117723
44	126.469352	0.007907	1079.045698	8.532073	0.000927	0.117205
48	196.369875	0.005092	1680.195368	8.556279	0.000595	0.116873
52	304.904923	0.003280	2613.604799	8.571868	0.000383	0.116661
56	473.428075	0.002112	4062.916361	8.581908	0.000246	0.116524
60	735.095189	0.001360	6313.272884	8.588375	0.000158	0.116436
∞				8.600074		0.116278

Continuous Compounding		i		12%	Table	B-18
	Single Payment	Uniform	Series	Uniform	Series	
	Compound Amount Factor	Present Amount Factor	Compound Amount Factor	Present Worth Factor	Sinking Fund Factor	Capital Recovery Factor
N	F/P	P/F	F/A	P/A	A/F	A/P
1	1.127497	0.886920	1.000000	0.886920	1.000000	1.127497
2	1.271249	0.786628	2.127497	1.673548	0.470036	0.597533
3	1.433329	0.697676	3.398746	2.371225	0.294226	0.421723
4	1.616074	0.618783	4.832075	2.990008	0.206950	0.334447
5	1.822119	0.548812	6.448150	3.538820	0.155083	0.282580
6	2.054433	0.486752	8.270269	4.025572	0.120915	0.248412
8	2.611696	0.382893	12.641069	4.840175	0.079107	0.206604
10	3.320117	0.301194	18.197445	5.480965	0.054953	0.182450
12	4.220696	0.236928	25.260983	5.985028	0.039587	0.167084
14	5.365556	0.186374	34.240500	6.381538	0.029205	0.156702
16	6.820958	0.146607	45.655704	6.693444	0.021903	0.149400
18	8.671138	0.115325	60.167271	6.938798	0.016620	0.144117
20	11.023176	0.090718	78.615089	7.131800	0.012720	0.140217
22	14.013204	0.071361	102.066862	7.283621	0.009797	0.137294
24	17.814273	0.056135	131.879909	7.403047	0.007583	0.135080
26	22.646380	0.044157	169.779719	7.496992	0.005890	0.133387
28	28.789191	0.034735	217.959820	7.570891	0.004588	0.132085
30	36.598234	0.027324	279.208733	7.629022	0.003582	0.131078
36	75.188628	0.013300	581.885963	7.739016	0.001719	0.129215
40	121.510418	0.008230	945.203086	7.778782	0.001058	0.128555
44	196.369875	0.005092	1532.350587	7.803389	0.000653	0.128149
48	317.348329	0.003151	2481.224634	7.818616	0.000403	0.127900
52	512.858511	0.001950	4014.675693	7.828038	0.000249	0.127746
56	828.817511	0.001207	6492.846696	7.833868	0.000154	0.127651
60	1339.430764	0.000747	10497.755418	7.837475	0.000095	0.127592
∞				7.843331		0.127497

Continuous Compounding			**i**	**13%**	**Table**	**B-19**
	Single Payment	Uniform	Series	Uniform	Series	
	Compound Amount Factor	Present Amount Factor	Compound Amount Factor	Present Worth Factor	Sinking Fund Factor	Capital Recovery Factor
N	F/P	P/F	F/A	P/A	A/F	A/P
1	1.13883	0.878095	1.00000	0.878095	1.000000	1.138828
2	1.29693	0.771052	2.13883	1.64915	0.467546	0.606374
3	1.47698	0.677057	3.43576	2.32620	0.291057	0.429885
4	1.68203	0.594521	4.91274	2.92072	0.203552	0.342381
5	1.91554	0.522046	6.59477	3.44277	0.151635	0.290464
6	2.18147	0.458406	8.51031	3.90118	0.117505	0.256333
8	2.82922	0.353455	13.1761	4.65716	0.075895	0.214723
10	3.66930	0.272532	19.2273	5.24005	0.052009	0.190838
12	4.75882	0.210136	27.0753	5.68950	0.036934	0.175762
14	6.17186	0.162026	37.2536	6.03604	0.026843	0.165671
16	8.00447	0.124930	50.4542	6.30325	0.019820	0.158648
18	10.3812	0.096328	67.5743	6.50928	0.014799	0.153627
20	13.4637	0.074274	89.7780	6.66814	0.011139	0.149967
22	17.4615	0.057269	118.575	6.79062	0.008434	0.147262
24	22.6464	0.044157	155.922	6.88507	0.006413	0.145242
26	29.3708	0.034047	204.359	6.95789	0.004893	0.143722
28	38.0918	0.026252	267.178	7.01404	0.003743	0.142571
30	49.4024	0.020242	348.650	7.05733	0.002868	0.141697
36	107.8	0.009279	769.080	7.13630	0.001300	0.140129
40	181.3	0.005517	1298.526	7.16340	0.000770	0.139598
44	304.9	0.003280	2189.069	7.17951	0.000457	0.139285
48	512.9	0.001950	3686.987	7.18909	0.000271	0.139100
52	862.6	0.001159	6206.528	7.19479	0.000161	0.138990
56	1451.0	0.000689	10444.464	7.19817	small	0.138924
60	2440.6	0.000410	17572.790	7.20019	small	0.138885
∞				7.20314		0.138828

Continuous Compounding		i		15%	Table	B-20
	Single Payment	Uniform	Series	Uniform	Series	
	Compound Amount Factor	Present Amount Factor	Compound Amount Factor	Present Worth Factor	Sinking Fund Factor	Capital Recovery Factor
N	F/P	P/F	F/A	P/A	A/F	A/P
1	1.16183	0.860708	1.00000	0.860708	1.000000	1.161834
2	1.34986	0.740818	2.16183	1.60153	0.462570	0.624404
3	1.56831	0.637628	3.51169	2.23915	0.284763	0.446597
4	1.82212	0.548812	5.08001	2.78797	0.196850	0.358684
5	2.11700	0.472367	6.90212	3.26033	0.144883	0.306717
6	2.45960	0.406570	9.01912	3.66690	0.110876	0.272710
8	3.32012	0.301194	14.3364	4.31803	0.069753	0.231587
10	4.48169	0.223130	21.5139	4.80040	0.046482	0.208316
12	6.04965	0.165299	31.2026	5.15775	0.032049	0.193883
14	8.16617	0.122456	44.2809	5.42248	0.022583	0.184417
16	11.02318	0.090718	61.9348	5.61860	0.016146	0.177980
18	14.8797	0.067206	85.7651	5.76389	0.011660	0.173494
20	20.0855	0.049787	117.9326	5.87152	0.008479	0.170314
22	27.1126	0.036883	161.354	5.95125	0.006198	0.168032
24	36.5982	0.027324	219.967	6.01032	0.004546	0.166380
26	49.4024	0.020242	299.087	6.05408	0.003344	0.165178
28	66.6863	0.014996	405.886	6.08650	0.002464	0.164298
30	90.0171	0.011109	550.051	6.11052	0.001818	0.163652
36	221.4	0.004517	1361.927	6.15125	0.000734	0.162568
40	403.4	0.002479	2486.673	6.16385	0.000402	0.162236
44	735.1	0.001360	4536.093	6.17076	0.000220	0.162055
48	1339.4	0.000747	8270.380	6.17455	0.000121	0.161955
52	2440.6	0.000410	15074.696	6.17663	small	0.161901
56	4447.1	0.000225	27472.967	6.17777	small	0.161871
60	8103.1	0.000123	50064.089	6.17840	small	0.161854
∞				6.17916		0.161834

Continuous Compounding			i	17%	Table	B-21
	Single Payment	Uniform	Series	Uniform	Series	
	Compound Amount Factor	Present Amount Factor	Compound Amount Factor	Present Worth Factor	Sinking Fund Factor	Capital Recovery Factor
N	F/P	P/F	F/A	P/A	A/F	A/P
1	1.18530	0.843665	1.00000	0.843665	1.000000	1.185305
2	1.40495	0.711770	2.18530	1.55544	0.457602	0.642907
3	1.66529	0.600496	3.59025	2.15593	0.278532	0.463837
4	1.97388	0.506617	5.25554	2.66255	0.190275	0.375580
5	2.33965	0.427415	7.22942	3.08996	0.138324	0.323629
6	2.77319	0.360595	9.56907	3.45056	0.104503	0.289808
8	3.89619	0.256661	15.6293	4.01144	0.063982	0.249287
10	5.47395	0.182684	24.1437	4.41066	0.041419	0.226723
12	7.69061	0.130029	36.1060	4.69481	0.027696	0.213001
14	10.80490	0.092551	52.9123	4.89706	0.018899	0.204204
16	15.18032	0.065875	76.5243	5.04102	0.013068	0.198373
18	21.3276	0.046888	109.6979	5.14348	0.009116	0.194421
20	29.9641	0.033373	156.3051	5.21641	0.006398	0.191703
22	42.0980	0.023754	221.786	5.26832	0.004509	0.189814
24	59.1455	0.016907	313.783	5.30527	0.003187	0.188492
26	83.0963	0.012034	443.034	5.33157	0.002257	0.187562
28	116.7459	0.008566	624.624	5.35029	0.001601	0.186906
30	164.0219	0.006097	879.750	5.36361	0.001137	0.186442
36	454.9	0.002198	2449.287	5.38465	0.000408	0.185713
40	897.8	0.001114	4839.848	5.39050	0.000207	0.185511
44	1772.2	0.000564	9558.523	5.39347	0.000105	0.185409
48	3498.2	0.000286	18872.612	5.39497	small	0.185358
52	6905.0	0.000145	37257.485	5.39573	small	0.185332
56	13629.6	0.000073	73546.975	5.39612	small	0.185318
60	26903.2	0.000037	145177.991	5.39631	small	0.185312
∞				5.39651		0.185305

Continuous Compounding		i		19%	Table	B-22
	Single Payment	Uniform	Series	Uniform	Series	
	Compound Amount Factor	Present Amount Factor	Compound Amount Factor	Present Worth Factor	Sinking Fund Factor	Capital Recovery Factor
N	F/P	P/F	F/A	P/A	A/F	A/P
1	1.20925	0.826959	1.00000	0.826959	1.000000	1.209250
2	1.46228	0.683861	2.20925	1.51082	0.452642	0.661892
3	1.76827	0.565525	3.67153	2.07635	0.272366	0.481615
4	2.13828	0.467666	5.43980	2.54401	0.183830	0.393080
5	2.58571	0.386741	7.57808	2.93075	0.131960	0.341209
6	3.12677	0.319819	10.16379	3.25057	0.098389	0.307638
8	4.57223	0.218712	17.0716	3.73376	0.058577	0.267826
10	6.68589	0.149569	27.1728	4.06420	0.036802	0.246051
12	9.77668	0.102284	41.9436	4.29017	0.023842	0.233091
14	14.29629	0.069948	63.5427	4.44470	0.015737	0.224987
16	20.90524	0.047835	95.1268	4.55038	0.010512	0.219762
18	30.5694	0.032712	141.312	4.62265	0.007077	0.216326
20	44.7012	0.022371	208.847	4.67207	0.004788	0.214038
22	65.3659	0.015299	307.603	4.70587	0.003251	0.212501
24	95.5835	0.010462	452.013	4.72898	0.002212	0.211462
26	139.770	0.007155	663.180	4.74479	0.001508	0.210757
28	204.384	0.004893	971.968	4.75560	0.001029	0.210278
30	298.867	0.003346	1423.50	4.76299	0.000702	0.209952
36	934.5	0.001070	4461.13	4.77387	0.000224	0.209474
40	1998.2	0.000500	9544.56	4.77659	0.000105	0.209354
44	4272.7	0.000234	20414.4	4.77786	small	0.209299
48	9136.2	0.000109	43657.0	4.77846	small	0.209273
52	19535.7	small	93356.1	4.77874	small	0.209260
56	41772.8	small	199626.5	4.77887	small	0.209255
60	89321.7	small	426862.1	4.77893	small	0.209252
∞				4.77898		0.209250

Continuous Compounding			**i**	**21%**	**Table**	**B-23**
	Single Payment	Uniform	Series	Uniform	Series	
	Compound Amount Factor	Present Amount Factor	Compound Amount Factor	Present Worth Factor	Sinking Fund Factor	Capital Recovery Factor
N	F/P	P/F	F/A	P/A	A/F	A/P
1	1.23368	0.810584	1.00000	0.810584	1.000000	1.233678
2	1.52196	0.657047	2.23368	1.46763	0.447692	0.681370
3	1.87761	0.532592	3.75564	2.00022	0.266266	0.499944
4	2.31637	0.431711	5.63325	2.43193	0.177517	0.411195
5	2.85765	0.349938	7.94962	2.78187	0.125792	0.359470
6	3.52542	0.283654	10.80727	3.06553	0.092530	0.326208
8	5.36556	0.186374	18.6819	3.48182	0.053528	0.287206
10	8.16617	0.122456	30.6668	3.75535	0.032609	0.266287
12	12.42860	0.080460	48.9074	3.93507	0.020447	0.254125
14	18.91585	0.052866	76.6689	4.05316	0.013043	0.246721
16	28.78919	0.034735	118.9208	4.13075	0.008409	0.242087
18	43.8160	0.022823	183.227	4.18172	0.005458	0.239136
20	66.6863	0.014996	281.098	4.21522	0.003557	0.237236
22	101.4940	0.009853	430.053	4.23723	0.002325	0.236003
24	154.4700	0.006474	656.758	4.25169	0.001523	0.235201
26	235.097	0.004254	1001.795	4.26119	0.000998	0.234676
28	357.809	0.002795	1526.927	4.26743	0.000655	0.234333
30	544.572	0.001836	2326.16	4.27153	0.000430	0.234108
36	1919.8	0.000521	8211.49	4.27716	0.000122	0.233800
40	4447.1	0.000225	19026.46	4.27843	small	0.233731
44	10301.0	0.000097	44077.9	4.27898	small	0.233701
48	23861.0	small	102106.2	4.27921	small	0.233688
52	55270.8	small	236521.1	4.27931	small	0.233682
56	128027.5	small	547875.4	4.27936	small	0.233680
60	296558.6	small	1269086.0	4.27938	small	0.233679
∞				4.27939		0.233678

Continuous Compounding		i		25%	Table	B-24
	Single Payment	Uniform	Series	Uniform	Series	
	Compound Amount Factor	Present Amount Factor	Compound Amount Factor	Present Worth Factor	Sinking Fund Factor	Capital Recovery Factor
N	F/P	P/F	F/A	P/A	A/F	A/P
1	1.28403	0.778801	1.00000	0.778801	1.000000	1.284025
2	1.64872	0.606531	2.28403	1.38533	0.437823	0.721849
3	2.11700	0.472367	3.93275	1.85770	0.254275	0.538301
4	2.71828	0.367879	6.04975	2.22558	0.165296	0.449322
5	3.49034	0.286505	8.76803	2.51208	0.114051	0.398076
6	4.48169	0.223130	12.25837	2.73521	0.081577	0.365602
8	7.38906	0.135335	22.4947	3.04432	0.044455	0.328480
10	12.18249	0.082085	39.3715	3.23181	0.025399	0.309425
12	20.08554	0.049787	67.1966	3.34552	0.014882	0.298907
14	33.11545	0.030197	113.0725	3.41449	0.008844	0.292869
16	54.59815	0.018316	188.7090	3.45633	0.005299	0.289325
18	90.0171	0.011109	313.413	3.48170	0.003191	0.287216
20	148.4132	0.006738	519.014	3.49709	0.001927	0.285952
22	244.6919	0.004087	857.993	3.50642	0.001166	0.285191
24	403.4288	0.002479	1416.876	3.51208	0.000706	0.284731
26	665.142	0.001503	2338.318	3.51552	0.000428	0.284453
28	1096.633	0.000912	3857.518	3.51760	0.000259	0.284285
30	1808.042	0.000553	6362.26	3.51886	0.000157	0.284183
36	8103.1	0.000123	28525.91	3.52038	small	0.284060
40	22026.5	0.000045	77547.52	3.52065	small	0.284038
44	59874.1	0.000017	210802	3.52075	small	0.284030
48	162755	small	573025	3.52079	small	0.284027
52	442413	small	1557651	3.52080	small	0.284026
56	1202604	small	4234140	3.52081	small	0.284026
60	3269017	small	11509591	3.52081	small	0.284026
∞				3.52081		0.284025

Continuous Compounding			i	30%	Table	B-25
	Single Payment	Uniform	Series	Uniform	Series	
	Compound Amount Factor	Present Amount Factor	Compound Amount Factor	Present Worth Factor	Sinking Fund Factor	Capital Recovery Factor
N	F/P	P/F	F/A	P/A	A/F	A/P
1	1.34986	0.740818	1.00000	0.740818	1.000000	1.349859
2	1.82212	0.548812	2.34986	1.28963	0.425557	0.775416
3	2.45960	0.406570	4.17198	1.69620	0.239694	0.589553
4	3.32012	0.301194	6.63158	1.99739	0.150794	0.500652
5	4.48169	0.223130	9.95170	2.22052	0.100485	0.450344
6	6.04965	0.165299	14.43339	2.38582	0.069284	0.419143
8	11.02318	0.090718	28.6492	2.59900	0.034905	0.384764
10	20.08554	0.049787	54.5521	2.71599	0.018331	0.368190
12	36.59823	0.027324	101.7503	2.78020	0.009828	0.359687
14	66.68633	0.014996	187.7510	2.81543	0.005326	0.355185
16	121.51042	0.008230	344.4544	2.83477	0.002903	0.352762
18	221.4064	0.004517	629.987	2.84539	0.001587	0.351446
20	403.4288	0.002479	1150.261	2.85121	0.000869	0.350728
22	735.0952	0.001360	2098.261	2.85441	0.000477	0.350335
24	1339.4308	0.000747	3825.631	2.85616	0.000261	0.350120
26	2440.602	0.000410	6973.104	2.85712	0.000143	0.350002
28	4447.067	0.000225	12708.174	2.85765	small	0.349937
30	8103.084	0.000123	23158.15	2.85794	small	0.349902
36	49020.8	small	140113.10	2.85824	small	0.349866
40	162755	small	465198.50	2.85828	small	0.349861
44	540365	small	1544520	2.85829	small	0.349859
48	1794075	small	5127994	2.85829	small	0.349859
52	5956538	small	17025545	2.85830	small	0.349859
56	19776403	small	56526808	2.85830	small	0.349859
60	65659969	small	187675619	2.85830	small	0.349859
∞				2.85830		0.349859

9 781609 278267

Printed by Libri Plureos GmbH in Hamburg,
Germany